AL-MAʾMŪN, THE INQUISITION, AND THE QUEST FOR CALIPHAL AUTHORITY

RESOURCES IN ARABIC AND ISLAMIC STUDIES

series editors

Joseph E. Lowry
Devin J. Stewart
Shawkat M. Toorawa

Number 4
Al-Maʾmūn, the Inquisition, and the Quest for Caliphal Authority

AL-MAʾMŪN, THE INQUISITION, AND THE QUEST FOR CALIPHAL AUTHORITY

John Abdallah Nawas

Atlanta, Georgia
2015

AL-MAʾMŪN, THE INQUISITION, AND THE QUEST FOR CALIPHAL AUTHORITY

ISBN: 978-1-937040-55-0

Library of Congress Control Number: 2015954890

Cover image: "Caliph Maʾmun and His Soldiers Being Greeted by a Man with a Tray of Fruit." Illustration from the Khamsa of Atai (d. 1044/1624). Walters MS 666 (1133/1721). Source: Wikimedia Commons/Walters Art Museum.

Printed in the United States of America on acid-free paper.

For Monique

CONTENTS

Series Editors' Preface ix

Foreword xi

Author's Preface xiv

Acknowledgments xv

CHAPTER 1: INTRODUCTION 1

1.1. Aim of This Study 1
1.2. Previous Explanations of al-Maʾmūn's Motives 2
1.3. The Approach of This Study 3
1.4. Sources 5
1.5. The Caliphates 5
1.6. The Sunnites and the Shiʿites 11
1.7. The Muʿtazilites 14
1.8. The Doctrine of the Createdness of the Qur'an 16
1.9. The *Miḥna* 16

CHAPTER 2: ʿABDALLĀH AL-MAʾMŪN: HIS LIFE AND REIGN 21

2.1. Early Life 21
2.2. The Civil War 23
2.3. Al-Maʾmūn's Reign 24

CHAPTER 3: THE MUʿTAZILISM, THE SHIʿISM, AND THE ʿALID HYPOTHESES 31

3.1. The Muʿtazilism Hypothesis 31
3.2. The Shiʿism Hypothesis 37
3.3. The ʿAlid Hypothesis 41

CHAPTER 4: THE CALIPHAL AUTHORITY HYPOTHESIS 51

4.1. Modern Scholars' Formulations of This Hypothesis 51
4.2. The Argument of This Study 54

4.3. Al-Maʾmūn's Vision of the Caliphate 56
4.4. The *Miḥna* Letters 59
4.5. The Timing of the *Miḥna* 65
4.6. The Strategic Value of the Doctrine of the Createdness of the Qur'an 67
4.7. Interrogated Individuals 69

CHAPTER 5: CONCLUSION 77

Appendix 1: Chronological Information, by Genre, on the Compilers of the Sources Used 83

Appendix 2: Information on Those Interrogated 95

Appendix 3: Timetable of Key Events during al-Maʾmūn's Reign 107

Bibliography 109

Index 125

William Patton, *Aḥmed ibn Ḥanbal and the Miḥna* (1897) [131]

SERIES EDITORS' PREFACE

The "inquisition" (Ar. *miḥna*) unleashed by the seventh Abbasid caliph, ʿAbdallāh al-Maʾmūn (r. 813–833), has long attracted the attention of modern scholars of the intellectual, political, and religious history of the early Abbasid era. Because this event—which began in 833 and stretched through the reigns of two of al-Maʾmūn's successors—appears at a convergence of prominent currents in systematic theology, rationalist thought, theocratic politics, and nascent trends in Shiism and Sunnism, historians have seen it as the key to a wide array of puzzles and problems in early Islamic history. In this incisive study, Professor John Nawas of the University of Leuven (KU Leuven), Belgium, subjects the various proposed explanations of these events to a sober and searching analysis and, in the process, presents a new interpretation of al-Maʾmūn's political and religious policies, contextualized against the background of early Abbasid intellectual and social history.

One of the very first analyses of the politico-religious policies of al-Maʾmūn was undertaken by W.M. Patton, in his 1897 study *Aḥmed ibn Ḥanbal and the Miḥna*, which focused especially on the hero of proto-Sunni resistance to al-Maʾmūn's policies, Aḥmad ibn Ḥanbal (d. 855). Patton's work still has much that is useful for moderns scholarship, but it has one additional, enormous benefit for those who work on this material—it contains most of the relevant passages from the relevant Arabic primary sources in Arabic. Included here at the end of the volume, it is once again being made available to modern researchers as a companion to Professor Nawas's study.

Although *Al-Maʾmūn, the Inquisition, and the Quest for Caliphal Authority* deals with subject matter that has traditionally been the preserve of specialists working with medieval Arabic sources, this volume aims, for the first time, to make the problematics of these events and materials available to a wider readership. We are thus very pleased indeed to be able to publish this volume as part of our series, Resources in Arabic and Islamic Studies. We are also extremely gratified that the eminent historian Michael Cook, Class of 1943 Professor of Near Eastern Studies at Princeton University, has provided a Foreword to this important work.

Joseph E. Lowry
Devin J. Stewart
Shawkat M. Toorawa

FOREWORD

Michael A. Cook

No caliph between the accession of Abū Bakr and the Mongol destruction of Baghdad did as many surprising things as al-Maʾmūn. They range from the unique to the downright odd. He was the only caliph ever to rule from Khurāsān and the only one to visit Egypt. No other ʿAbbāsid (let alone Umayyad) caliph appointed an ʿAlid as his heir—and stranger still, an ʿAlid who must have been two decades his senior. No other caliph adopted the doctrine of the created Qurʾan, or any other theological doctrine, as a litmus test of orthodoxy to be imposed by institutionalized persecution; his immediate successors merely continued what he had begun. By any standards al-Maʾmūn was an idiosyncratic caliph, and sometimes a bizarre one.

This does not mean that the unusual things he did were a kind of behavioural gibberish. They were not the ravings of a lunatic who had slipped his cultural moorings. Attempting to rule the caliphate from a center as eccentric as Khurāsān may not have been a particularly good idea; but Khurāsān was undoubtedly a province that mattered, for reasons at once historical, economic, political, and military, and it was the region with which al-Maʾmūn was best connected. His visit to Egypt goes against the grain of Near Eastern geopolitics in the early centuries of Islam, in which the country was relegated to a somewhat marginal role; but Egypt mattered economically, it boasted interesting sites for a caliphal tourist, and it was in the throes of an obstinate rebellion. Appointing an ʿAlid heir who was unlikely to outlive him looks like a very bad idea, and probably was—it could be relied on to alienate a lot of people who mattered without securing a viable alternative basis for the power of the caliphate. But it went well with al-Maʾmūn's consistent partiality for ʿAlī and his descendants, a partiality that has always been widely shared in Islam, and it may also have made some sense in terms of eschatological beliefs that were current at the time. Adopting as official dogma an unpopular elite doctrine may not have been politic, but the created Qurʾan was no brainchild of al-Maʾmūn's: it was one of the few issues on which the dialectical theologians of the day—the *ahl al-kalām*—were in agreement. Imposing this doctrine by heavy-handed state action, to the point that it was rumored that it would be taught to children in primary schools, made little political sense: it meant picking a fight with a part of the population that was otherwise not particularly likely to rebel, and at a time when rebellions were epidemic in the caliphate. But the idea of "examining" people to verify that they were believers is grounded in the Qurʾan: "O believers, when believing women come to you as emigrants, test them.... Then, if you know them to be believers, return them not to the unbelievers" (Q 60:10). The verb here translated as "test" (*imtaḥana*) was likewise used by al-Maʾmūn, and derives from the same root that gives us the standard term for his "inquisition" (*miḥna*).

However, showing that all of al-Maʾmūn's unusual actions must have made some kind of sense to contemporaries, and indeed to posterity, does not add up to explaining why he chose to behave in those particular ways. The world of the possible contains innumerable things that humans could intelligibly do, many things that at some level they would like to do, and far fewer that they actually do. In the case of al-Maʾmūn it is hard not to come away with the sense that a particular personality was in play. Here was someone intelligent, educated, imaginative, and creative; someone who had a way of coming up with bright but bad ideas, getting hooked on them, and persisting with them till disaster or death forced a change of course. (Indeed al-Maʾmūn's relatively early death looms large in all this: he never had the opportunity to grow old and wise.) And of course we know nothing about the intimate processes whereby he came up with his ideas and got hooked on them. The implication of this line of thought, were we to pursue it further, would be that while we can say some worthwhile things by way of setting out necessary conditions for al-Maʾmūn's more unusual actions, identifying sufficient conditions is beyond our reach and likely to remain so. This, of course, would be a rather defeatist conclusion. The fact is that al-Maʾmūn is a puzzle, and confronted with an interesting and historically significant puzzle it seems a pity to give up on it.

At the time when John Nawas sent me a copy of his dissertation, Ibn Ḥanbal was an everpresent figure in my daily life. I was engaged in writing a study of "commanding right and forbidding wrong" in which he stood at the center of a key chapter. This meant that I was at least tangentially interested in the inquisitorial procedure initiated by al-Maʾmūn, since one of its most celebrated victims was to be Ibn Ḥanbal. It was in this context two things immediately caught my eye about the dissertation.

The first was that Nawas did not simply push a line of his own while ignoring or dismissing other views. Instead he set up a systematic taxonomy of the rather chaotic landscape of the secondary scholarship, identifying a limited number of hypotheses in terms of which the various trends in the field could be reduced to order. He then took the reader through these hypotheses one by one, even-handedly showing what evidence supported them and what evidence counted against them, and judging them accordingly on the basis of the full range of primary sources. It was hard not to agree with his rejection of the Muʿtazilite hypothesis, the idea that al-Maʾmūn's links to the Muʿtazilites—and more broadly the *ahl al-kalām*—could explain his decision to impose the doctrine of the created Qurʾan. These links were clearly a necessary condition for the decision, and as such an indispensable part of any explanation, but they were far from being sufficient. The same was true of the related but distinct Shīʿite and ʿAlid hypotheses; they did not identify even a necessary condition, except to the extent that we may see al-Maʾmūn's Shīʿite or ʿAlid sympathies as linked to his strong conception of caliphal authority—and as Nawas points out, his thinking on this issue does not seem to have been very different from that of his predecessors.

The second thing that caught my eye was that the view favored by Nawas—namely the caliphal authority hypothesis—was more comprehensive and held more water than its rivals. This view presents al-Maʾmūn's inquisition as a quintessential example of authority dramatization. It is indeed eminently plausible that a ruler with his strong sense of occupying a God-given office would have felt intensely frustrated and grossly disrespected by the level of disarray that prevailed in his domains, and would accordingly feel a strong urge to dramatize his authority. Of course as Nawas points out, this hypothesis still leaves several questions unanswered, for example the timing of the inquisition—why did al-Maʾmūn put up with the cacophony of the traditionists and their associates for two decades, only to launch his campaign against them near the end of his reign? But if the puzzle can be solved at all, Nawas has made a major contribution to its solution.

Author's Preface

In 1993, during a typically august and traditional European ceremony, I publicly defended a dissertation entitled "Al-Maʾmūn: Miḥna and Caliphate," which I had written at the Katholieke Universiteit Nijmegen (later renamed Radboud Universiteit Nijmegen) in the Netherlands. Perhaps the grandiosity of this very formal, old-fashioned and somewhat outmoded ceremony instilled in me the diffidence that dissuaded me from publishing the dissertation immediately, though it was always in the back of my mind. I did soon after notice that it was being regularly used and cited, but, convinced though I was that I had to find time to sit down and do the necessary work to get the manuscript into book form, the years rolled by. Two decades on, I was unexpectedly invited to have it included in the series Resources in Arabic and Islamic Studies (RAIS). I considered this honor an exceptional opportunity to finalize the manuscript in the manner I had always envisioned, then as now, namely to address it not only to Arabists and Islamicists but also to a broader readership. I have accordingly revised the text and changed the chapter structure. I have also updated the notes by including secondary literature that has appeared since 1993 in cases where the new material makes a direct contribution to the topic: these are indicated by an asterisk (*) in both the notes and the Bibliography. For a comprehensive annotated listing of the existing literature, see my historiographical essay on the *miḥna* published in Oxford Bibliographies Online (Nawas 2014), which is regularly updated.

Acknowledgments

I am grateful to the editors of this series, Joseph E. Lowry, Devin J. Stewart, and Shawkat M. Toorawa, for inviting me to publish in Resources in Arabic and Islamic Studies (RAIS) and for their editorial guidance. I especially want to thank the gifted copyeditor they engaged. Michael Cook did me the honor of writing the foreword; it is not only his help to others but also his dedication to Islamic Studies that inspires us all.

I was fortunate to have had the benefit of receiving help when I was writing the dissertation. The people to whom I owe thanks are many. I would like explicitly to acknowledge my debt to several scholars on whose time and expertise I had no claim whatsoever but who, nonetheless, graciously responded to my queries in ways that no novice has a right to expect: Edmund Bosworth, Mayke de Jong, Carol Hillenbrand, Etan Kohlberg, Wilferd Madelung, Harald Motzki, Jan Peters, Peter Rietbergen, Dominique Sourdel, Arjo Vanderjagt, Geert-Jan van Gelder and W.M. Watt. I am also most grateful to Gual Juynboll, whose extended discussions with me taught me much and which I still cherish deeply. His passing is a loss I feel every day. Kees Versteegh helped me wade through a number of thorny Arabic grammatical constructions, which he thought funny as they were the very examples "his" grammarians would use to explain the Arabic language. Needless to say, any shortcomings are mine alone.

A special word of thanks goes to Jerry Atlas and Debby Tanzer for a friendship that has spanned decades: *al-ṣadīq ʿind al-ḍīq* (a friend in need is a friend indeed), as the Arabic proverb goes; and, as the Yiddish proverb goes, what soap is to the body, laughter is to the soul. I thank both your souls for giving Monique and me so much moral support and for making us laugh so much together.

I am blessed again to be able to thank my parents, who are approaching 90 but whose persevering and tenacious spirits are stronger than ever. My mother-in-law Diny Bernards-Hendriks leads us in longevity and wisdom, acquired as she raised and fed five children almost on her own; her oldest, my much lamented brother-in-law, Frans Bernards, passed away in 2009 and is missed for his unconventional intellectual curiosity, which only made us more curious than we already were. My sister Carmen and my brother Mike, together with their spouses, Paulus and Anne (and my nieces and nephews, Sander, Lisa, Tom, Max, and Lydia) deserve separate mention here for their support.

I am happy to be able to thank my own PhD students for the intellectual journeys that they shared and continue to share with me: Stijn Aerts, Ahmed Azzouz, Thijs Delva, Talat Shinnawe, and Jessika Soors. I also thank them for our research group "History of the Fundamentals of Islam" at the KU Leuven and the Institute for Advanced Arabic and Islamic Studies, Antwerp, Belgium, which provides an extremely stimulating intellectual climate.

Finally, I thank Cambridge University Press for permission to use material drawn from my "A Reexamination of Three Current Explanations for al Maʾmun's Introduction of the Mihna," *International Journal of Middle East Studies* 26 (1994): 615–29.

CHAPTER 1
INTRODUCTION

1.1. Aim of This Study

ʿAbdallāh al-Maʾmūn, like his father the caliph Hārūn al-Rashīd (r. 170–193/786–809), presided over what some have called the "golden age" of Islam. But one event within the career of al-Maʾmūn stands in sharp contrast with the image of a "golden age." After having declared in 212/827 as religious doctrine that the Qur'an was created, al-Maʾmūn issued a decree instituting the *miḥna*, a sort of "inquisition" expressly directed at enforcing the doctrine of the createdness of the Qur'an. The date of its issuance is Rabīʿ I, 218/ March-April, 833, the year the caliph died.

The state's use of force in implementing a religious doctrine was a novelty in Islam. While al-Maʾmūn was not the first to consider "heretical" those views which contradicted his own, the *miḥna* that he initiated was nonetheless "the first systematic inquisition into heresy and the earliest formal attempt to stamp it out" (Hitti 1970, 430).[1] It runs counter to the tradition, spirit and indeed the letter of the Islamic religion as it had been understood until that time.[2] Not only did al-Maʾmūn—allegedly a deeply religious man—violate the prescriptions of Islam by his innovation, but the issuance of the *miḥna*

1. Long before al-Maʾmūn, the Umayyad caliph Hishām ibn ʿAbd al-Malik (r. 105–125/724–743) had Ghaylān al-Dimashqī killed for speaking of "free will," which Hishām considered heresy (on this episode cf. Van Ess [1970] as well as his article on "*qadariyya*" in *EI2*). Al-Maʾmūn's great-grandfather, al-Mahdī (r. 158–169/775–785), and grandfather, al-Hādī (169–170/785–786), had also crucified a number of men for what they considered heresy. On heresy in Islam in general see Lewis (1953). *See the wide-ranging two-volume work on heresiographical literature, *Der Eine und Das Andere: Beobachtungen an islamischen Häresiographischen Texten* (Van Ess 2011).

2. Cf. Qur'anic verse 2:256: "*Lā ikrāh^{a} fī al-dīn ...*," meaning "no compulsion in religion." *The understanding of this verse changed over time; Crone (2009) discusses the various interpretations across Islamic sects and centuries ending with the modern period; add to Crone's bibliography Paret 1969.

decree is also incompatible with the freedom of thought which he is believed to have championed. The intolerance which the *miḥna* symbolizes contrasts sharply indeed with the portrayal of the caliph as tolerant, a picture that emerges from his encouragement of religious debates between Muslim scholars and their counterparts from other faiths, monotheists and polytheists alike. One may assume, then, that al-Maʾmūn must have had compelling reasons for issuing his decree. Fathoming these motives is the aim of this study.

1.2. Previous Explanations of al-Maʾmūn's Motives

Scholars have proposed numerous explanations for al-Maʾmūn's declaration that the Qur'an was created and his issuance of the *miḥna* decree, yet no one explanation has gained general acceptance. While the range of these explanations is very wide, they can be categorized into two broad groups: those which focus in a fragmentary way on the personal qualities of al-Maʾmūn and those which view his actions as integrated within the complex network of circumstances and events surrounding him.

The fragmentary explanations are essentially descriptions of al-Maʾmūn's character or his conduct. Muir (1891, 506), for example, proposes that al-Maʾmūn was a "cruel" man; likewise, Patton (1897, 6–7) sees the caliph as a "spiritual and physical tyrant" and reads into his actions "religious intolerance." Huddāra (1985, 260), much impressed by the caliph's "deep religiosity," takes the view that it was "for the sake of faith and God" that al-Maʾmūn spoke of the doctrine and ordered the *miḥna*. Zaydān (1902–6) and Hitti (1968), adding nuance to the views of Muir and Weil (1848) before them, take the position that al-Maʾmūn was a "free thinker" who, however, carried this notion to the extreme of denying the exercise of free thought to anyone who dared to disagree with him. Similarly, Rifāʿī (1927, 1:398) concludes that the two events in question reflect a "tragic policy" of a "free thinker" who was also "eccentric."

Of course, it is reasonable to presume that the caliph's personality did play a role in shaping his decisions. However, labels are poor explanations at best. Character descriptions are also problematic in that they tend to assume that the caliph was acting in isolation from the world around him, immune to its forces.

The explanations which fall into the integrating group are more credible, because they do greater justice to the complex network of circumstances, events, and persons surrounding the declaration of the doctrine of the createdness of the Qur'an and the introduction of the *miḥna*. The scholars proposing these explanations include Amīn (1933–36), Cahen (1968), Crone and Hinds (1986), Gabrieli (1929), Hinds (*EI2*, s.v. "*miḥna*"), Lapidus (1975), Nagel (1975), Sourdel (1962), ʿUmar (1977) and Watt (1950, 1963, 1973). Given their different disciplines, their theories display understandable differences in content and emphasis. Quite often, issues which are central to one interpretation are merely peripheral to another. They differ, too, in the degree to which they are willing to "enter the mind" of the caliph to tell us how he might have thought and felt.

Most scholars see the caliph as *homo politicus*. His tactics are variously described as mild and benevolent (Gabrieli 1929) or Machiavellian (al-Dūrī 1945). Lapidus (1975) sees al-Maʾmūn as calculating, while others[3] envision him more as struggling to steady the ship of state by what seems like one desperate maneuver after another. Nagel (1975) and Crone and Hinds (1986) view al-Maʾmūn's vision of caliphal authority and his determination to stamp out opposition to its exercise as the key elements in the proclamation of the createdness of the Qur'an and the issuance of the *miḥna* decree.

These views are shared by Gabrieli (1929), Sourdel (1962) and ʿUmar (1977). For Sourdel and ʿUmar in particular, the caliph's actions betray a deliberate attempt to forge for himself and for the caliphate a power base and authority which his ʿAbbāsid predecessors had never been able to secure fully. A major cause of this failure was the incessant and wide-spread upheavals among resentful Shiʿites who had helped the ʿAbbāsids wrest the caliphate from the Umayyads, only to be rewarded with repeated suppressions. Zaydān (1902–6) and Gabrieli (1929) similarly believe that al-Maʾmūn was intent on repaying the ʿAlids and their partisans the debt owed to them by al-Saffāḥ and al-Manṣūr.

In explaining the *miḥna* and the complex circumstances which the caliph was confronting, scholars have also had much to say about the development of *fiqh* (jurisprudence) at the time (Crone and Hinds 1986), the growing authority of the *ʿulamāʾ* (Hodgson 1974 and Lapidus 1975) and the role of the Muʿtazilites (Amīn 1933–36 and Laoust 1965). Within the broad spectrum of these discussions, three hypotheses are promising as explanatory frameworks, which focus, respectively, (1) on al-Maʾmūn's affinities with the Muʿtazilites; (2) on his affinities with Shiʿism and the ʿAlids; and (3) on his conception of the caliphate and the domain of its authority. It is, however, rare indeed to find a scholar who endorses one explanation only. The evaluation of these hypotheses is taken up in detail below.

1.3. The Approach of This Study

This study seeks to evaluate the hypotheses concerning al-Maʾmūn's motives in the secondary works discussed above. Its specific aim can be stated in the form of two parallel questions. (1) What factor or factors motivated al-Maʾmūn to declare the view that the Qur'an was created? (2) What factor or factors motivated him to issue the *miḥna* decree six years later?

As is evident from these questions, this study departs from the approach of previous studies by construing al-Maʾmūn's declaration of the doctrine of the createdness of the Qur'an as an issue separate from that of the declaration of the *miḥna*. Given that scholars have treated the public declaration that the Qur'an was created and the institution of the

3. Primarily Sourdel 1962 and Watt 1973.

miḥna as two events among many in al-Maʾmūn's caliphate, and given also that the *miḥna* was enacted to enforce the earlier decree, it is understandable that the earlier declaration has come to be subsumed under the more dramatic *miḥna* decree. However, there is reported to have been a time lapse of six years between the two events. We cannot assume that the al-Maʾmūn of 212/827—then enjoying a period of relative repose—was the same as the al-Maʾmūn of 218/833. As I will discuss in chapter two, in 218/833 the caliph was in Tarsus, preparing to engage the Byzantine Empire in battle. Shortly before, he had put down an insurrection in Egypt, one that was of such seriousness as to require his personal supervision. It is therefore reasonable to assume that the circumstances and forces prevailing in 212/827 were not the same six years later. Hence, in collecting and analyzing relevant information from the primary sources, I have treated the caliph's declaration that the Qur'an was created and his *miḥna* decree as separate events.

Furthermore, the main concern of scholars in the works discussed above has been to understand the overall policies of al-Maʾmūn and to place his reign within the context of the ʿAbbāsid caliphate. This aim, which differs from mine, made it necessary for them to address all of the caliph's important actions and decisions, of which the decree and the *miḥna* are only two. An approach which focuses on the broader context has its merits, but it tends to push otherwise pivotal moments to the sideline, and occasionally into insignificance. Al-Dūrī (1945), for instance, makes no mention whatsoever of the *miḥna* in his chapter on al-Maʾmūn's caliphate, and he writes of the createdness of the Qur'an only in passing. In the present study, however, I have placed both issues in the foreground, along with the circumstances, events, and persons immediately surrounding them. With the exception of two studies by Patton (1897) and Abusaq (1971), this perspective represents a reversal in the manner in which the two issues have until now been treated.

Patton's study focuses on the *miḥna*, permitting him to bring into sharp relief the most salient features of the Ḥanbalite school of law and the role of its eponym, Aḥmad ibn Ḥanbal.[4] Similarly, by construing the *miḥna* as a pivot upon which other events rotated, Abusaq was able to account for the evolution of numerous theological factions and orientations. Beyond this agreement on the centrality of the *miḥna*, I part company with both Patton and Abusaq. Their perspective was theological, and their primary interest lay in the consequences of the *miḥna*. My interest lies in al-Maʾmūn's motivations, and my questions revolve around why the declaration was made and the *miḥna* introduced.[5]

---

4. *See on Ibn Ḥanbal: Hurvitz 2001a, 2001b, 2002a and 2002b; cf. Cooperson 2001; the views of Ibn Ḥanbal regarding the Qur'an have been studied by Melchert 2004.

5. *I have nevertheless included Patton 1897 as an appendix because, though dated and out of print, it has been central to all discussions of the *miḥna* since it was published.

1.4. Sources

In explaining scholars' disagreements concerning al-Maʾmūn's motivations, subjectivity naturally plays an important role; however, it is unlikely to be the sole basis for these variations. A scholar's selection of sources is probably a contributory factor and one that warrants special attention. In preparation for this study, I therefore compiled a "master list" of all the major primary sources on al-Maʾmūn and the two issues under discussion. I then checked this list against the primary sources which Rifāʿī (1927), Gabrieli (1929), Amīn (1933–6), Nagel (1975), Sourdel (1962) and Watt (1973) consulted. As a result, the range of primary sources used in this investigation is wider than that of previous studies. They include universal and local histories, biographical dictionaries, genealogical works, *adab* works, theoretical works, and other texts. The time spanned is the period from the *miḥna* itself (our earliest chronicler, Ibn Saʿd, died in 230/845, twelve years after the introduction of the *miḥna* and was himself one of the first to be interrogated) to Ibn al-ʿImād's (d. 1089/1679) *Shadharāt al-dhahab*, some eight centuries later. Appendix 1 summarizes what is known about the intellectual orientation and partisan inclination of the historians and chroniclers whose works were used in this study, which is sometimes disappointingly little.

The primary sources have been examined in the order suggested by their authors' death dates. The rationale for this procedure goes beyond the economy which an orderly process is likely to yield. We need to know al-Maʾmūn from every possible perspective, including that of time. While we may never have a definitive answer about this man and his motives in declaring the createdness of the Qur'an or ordering the *miḥna*, it is important to try to capture the "images" which successive generations of chroniclers have projected of him. With this in mind, each source mentioning al-Maʾmūn or his reign has been scrutinized for any reference to the doctrine of the createdness of the Qur'an or the *miḥna* and for whatever material can throw light on his motives. The three hypotheses described above have served as frameworks for gathering the information, and data in favor of or against each proposition noted. The results of this inquiry are the subject of chapters three and four. Before proceeding to this analysis, however, we will turn our attention in the remainder of this chapter to the broader historical context and then, in chapter two, to the career of al-Maʾmūn.

1.5. The Caliphates

The word "caliph" comes from the Arabic *khalīfa*, meaning "successor" or "deputy."[6] It refers to the office held by those men who succeeded the prophet Muḥammad (570–632

6. For various interpretations of "caliph" and related titles, see Goldziher 1897, Abel 1957, Lewis 1968, Paret 1970 and 1974, Balog 1977, Hassuri 1982, Crone and Hinds 1986, and al-Qadi 1988. *See Nawas

CE) in his capacity as spiritual and political leader of the Islamic *umma* (Community) and the territories occupied or subjugated by Muslim forces.[7] Of relevance to this study are (a) the first four caliphs; (b) the Umayyad Caliphate, beginning with Muʿāwiya (r. 41–60/661–680) and ending with Marwān II (r. 127–132/744–750); and (c) the ʿAbbāsid Caliphate, from Abū al-ʿAbbās (al-Saffāḥ) (r. 132–136/749–754) through al-Mutawakkil (r. 232–247/847–861).[8]

1.5.1. The First Four Caliphs

The first four successors to Muḥammad—Abū Bakr, ʿUmar, ʿUthmān and ʿAlī—are known within the Islamic tradition as the Rightly-Guided Caliphs (*al-khulafāʾ al-rāshidūn*). Abū Bakr (r. 11–13/632–634) is believed to have been the first to use the title of *khalīfat rasūl Allāh* or "successor to the messenger of God." Like Muḥammad, he belonged to the Meccan tribe of Quraysh. He was also the father of ʿĀʾisha, a wife of the Prophet. After Muḥammad's death, he was chosen as his successor by notables of the Muslim Community. Before the choice could be sealed by a pledge of allegiance (*bayʿa*), it had to be ratified.[9] However, Muḥammad's son-in-law ʿAlī ibn Abī Ṭālib also claimed the right to succeed Muḥammad on the grounds that Muḥammad had designated him as his successor. On the basis of this claim he withheld his consent for several months after Abū Bakr's ratification. The mature Shiʿite tradition would later identify the failure to recognize ʿAlī as the first caliph as a major cause leading to the division between the Sunnites and the Shiʿites, as we will discuss further below. Abū Bakr's brief caliphate was primarily occupied with the *ridda* (secession, apostasy) wars, from which he emerged victorious.[10] Abū Bakr, who died of an illness, was the only one of the first four caliphs who was not assassinated.

Abū Bakr was succeeded by ʿUmar ibn al- Khaṭṭāb (r. 13–23/634–644). ʿUmar, too, was a member of the Quraysh tribe and the father of one of Muḥammad's wives, Ḥafṣa. The second caliph was more effective in expanding the boundaries of the early Islamic state and organizing its affairs than any of the other early caliphs. This success was due in part to ʿUmar's relatively long tenure, longer than the reigns of Abū Bakr and ʿAlī

1993a and 1993b.

7. The traditional Islamic view is that Muhammad's successors inherited only his political authority. This view is followed by most orientalists, amongst whom Nagel (1975), who speaks of three "*Ersatzinstitutionen*," i.e., the Qur'an, the *Sunna* (Prophetic Practice) and the imāmate, which alternated in filling the vacuum. Crone and Hinds (1986), however, argue that the caliphs were both political and religious leaders until the early ʿAbbāsid period.

8. The ʿAbbāsid Caliphate lasted till 945/1538.

9. The bonds of loyalty in medieval Islamic society are examined by Mottahedeh (1980). Authority in the early Community is analyzed within a Weberian framework by Dabashi (1989). *See Marsham 2009.

10. *Ridda* refers to Abū Bakr's battles against the renegade Arab tribes in the peninsula. *See Shoufani 1973/Shūfānī 1995, and Ibrahim 1994.

combined, and in greater measure to his abilities as a leader. In addition to the title of *khalīfa*, ʿUmar reportedly adopted the title "*amīr al-muʾminīn*" (Commander of the Faithful), a formal designation which later became as standard as the title "caliph." ʿUmar was assassinated by a slave of the governor of al-Baṣra, reportedly in anger over a tax which ʿUmar refused to repeal.

ʿUthmān ibn ʿAffān (r. 23–35/644–656) was almost sixty when he was chosen as the third caliph. A member of the Banū Umayya branch of the Quraysh, ʿUthmān was a son-in-law of the Prophet, having married his daughter Ruqayya. He was regarded as a weak leader who favored his kinsmen, the Umayyads, a perception that limited his ability to govern. Continuing the momentum of ʿUmar's expansion, ʿUthmān's forces made some additions to Muslim territory. ʿUthmān met his death in Medina at the hands of a group from Egypt[11] who had become disaffected by ʿUthmān's misrule; they were led by the son of the first caliph, Abū Bakr.

The fourth caliph, ʿAlī ibn Abī Ṭālib (r. 35–40/656–661), born ca. 600 CE, was more closely connected to the Prophet than any of his predecessors. ʿAlī was a paternal first cousin of Muḥammad; embraced Islam when he was still a youth; was raised by Muḥammad and educated under his supervision; and was given Muḥammad's only surviving child, his daughter Fāṭima, in marriage. ʿAlī's initial bid to succeed his father-in-law had failed a generation earlier, and his subsequent accession did not occur without bitter opposition that pitted Meccan elites and the favorite wife of the Prophet, ʿĀʾisha, against ʿAlī, in part because of his perceived failure to punish those responsible for the assassination of ʿUthmān. This rift is one of the root causes of the lasting Shiʿite-Sunnite divide.

After defeating ʿĀʾisha and the Meccan elites at the Battle of the Camel in 36/656, ʿAlī faced another challenge to his designation as caliph, this time from Muʿāwiya ibn Abī Sufyān,[12] an Umayyad relative of ʿUthmān whose governorship of Syria ʿUmar had confirmed. Muʿāwiya and his supporters accused ʿAlī of being directly responsible for ʿUthmān's assassination. While the battle between ʿAlī and Muʿāwiya at Ṣiffin in 36–37/657 ended in an agreement to seek arbitration, the undercurrent of dissension and antagonism from multiple factions never abated. As a result of incessant disturbances, ʿAlī was finally assassinated with a poisoned dagger in al-Kūfa, the Iraqi garrison city (*miṣr*) he had made his capital.

1.5.2. The Umayyad Caliphate

Although ʿAlī's son al-Ḥasan initially claimed the caliphate after his father's assassination, he soon negotiated a settlement with his rival Muʿāwiya (r. 41–60/661–680), who

11. For a detailed analysis of ʿUthmān's assassination and the parties involved, see Hinds 1972a.
12. For the particulars of this struggle, see Petersen 1959, 1963 and Hinds 1972b.

was proclaimed caliph in Jerusalem. The dynasty was named for Muʿāwiya's great-grandfather Umayya of the tribe of Quraysh, and Damascus became its capital, from which seat the majority of Umayyad caliphs ruled.[13] Muʿāwiya's choice of Damascus was a logical one, because he had strong military support there and had allied himself through marriage with the dominant tribe of the region, the Banū Kalb.

Muʿāwiya was confronted by many of the same challenges which faced his predecessors, including the rapid expansion of Muslim territory and incessant friction among the Arab tribes. The first of these did not present any insurmountable problems.[14] The tide and momentum were on Muʿāwiya's side, as can be seen from the fact that his armies were to reach the Atlantic Ocean only one year after his death. Tribal frictions and rivalries,[15] on the other hand, were to prove far more intractable, although Muʿāwiya was able to maintain the unity of the Muslim Community.

Muʿāwiya's rise to power was a deep humiliation to those who held that the progeny of ʿAlī ibn Abī Ṭālib (the ʿAlids) were the rightful successors to the Prophet. The ʿAbbāsids, another wing of the Banū Hāshim clan and cousins to the ʿAlids, were also at odds with Muʿāwiya. Despite this opposition, Muʿāwiya was largely successful in pacifying tribal disputes. He succeeded in forging alliances, however fragile, through marriages, gifts and appointments but also through his skillful negotiation of relationships and his willingness to overlook slights.

Muʿāwiya was the first caliph to designate his son as heir, an action which he justified on the grounds that the traditional Arab method of electing a leader was neither practicable nor predictable for an empire so vast and complex. He required that notables swear allegiance to his son and heir, Yazīd I. With heredity now a basis for accession to the caliphate, the tradition of consensual choice had come to an end.[16]

Umayyad rule in Damascus lasted some ninety years. After Muʿāwiya's own twenty-year reign, thirteen subsequent caliphs ruled over the course of the remaining seventy years. Besides the dynasty's founder, notable Umayyad caliphs include ʿAbd al-Malik (r. 65–86/685–705),[17] who introduced Arabic as the official administrative language of the empire and standardized the coinage system, and ʿUmar ibn ʿAbd al-ʿAzīz (r. 99–101/717–720), who was known for being deeply religious, ascetic and humane and whose sense of justice reportedly matched only that of his namesake, the second caliph, ʿUmar. Probably as a consequence of this reputation, ʿUmar ibn ʿAbd al-ʿAzīz's grave was the only

13. For a general history of the Umayyad caliphate, see Hawting 1987. *See now Hawting 2000, second edition.

14. Donner (1981) provides an elaborate analysis of the early expansion of Islam.

15. On these rivalries, see Hinds 1971. *See Madelung 1997.

16. For a history of the succession to the caliphate until the early ʿAbbāsid period, see Chejne 1960 and Kennedy 1980.

17. *On ʿAbd al-Malik, see Robinson 2007.

Umayyad tomb not desecrated by the ʿAbbāsids after they came to power. Later Islamic sources typically portray the Umayyads as secular Arab kings, a portrayal likely shaped by the fact that surviving sources on the Umayyads were written under the regime that toppled them from power.

1.5.3. The Founding of the ʿAbbāsid Caliphate

At the turn of the second/eighth century, the ʿAlids' supporters undertook a propaganda campaign focused on Khurasan that involved denouncing the injustices of the Umayyads and the coming of a savior (*al-mahdī*) from the house of the Prophet. The Khurasanians were a receptive audience for such a message, in part because the region had experienced significant conversion to Islam among the local non-Arab populace, which perceived itself as excluded and exploited by the Arab-centric Umayyads. The ʿAlids were not the only branch of the Quraysh tribe hoping to win the support of Khurasanian military strength, however. The ʿAbbāsids were just as eager as the ʿAlids to see an end to Umayyad rule. Like Muḥammad himself, both the ʿAbbāsids and the ʿAlids belonged to the Banū Hāshim branch of the Quraysh tribe, and they were envious of the power of the Umayyad branch of Quraysh both before and after the appearance of Islam. This power was the more unjust, they felt, because of the Umayyads' initial hostility to Islam.

A freedman from al-Kūfa named Abū Muslim led the ʿAbbāsid *daʿwa*, or mission, in Khurasan,[18] where he succeeded in gaining both local Khurasanian and ʿAlid support by making vague promises of a caliph who would be *al-riḍā min āl Muḥammad* (the chosen one from the family of Muḥammad), without specifying exactly what branch of the Prophet's family he would come from.[19] The ʿAbbāsids, ʿAlids, and Khurasanians thus found themselves united in opposition to a common enemy, the Umayyads.[20] In 129/746–747, Abū Muslim began a military uprising in Khurasan against the Umayyads. However, the ʿAlids and their partisans were growing restive and wanted more than just implicit recognition that they were the rightful successors to the Prophet. The leading ʿAbbāsids, Abū al-ʿAbbās (later al-Saffāḥ) and his brother Abū Jaʿfar (later al-Manṣūr), like their propagandists, made an effort to win over ʿAlid support by allaying Shiʿite concerns that the post-Umayyad caliphate would be monopolized by the ʿAbbāsids. However, the resulting Shiʿite optimism turned out to be misplaced. On 28 November 749/12 Rabi II 132, Abū

18. *For more on revolts in Iran, see Crone 2012.

19. More information on Abū Muslim can be found in Frye 1947 and *Encyclopaedia Iranica*, s.n. "Abū Moslem K̲orāsānī" (G.H. Yūsofī). *See *EI3* s.n. "Abū Muslim" (Agha).

20. On the composition of the anti-Umayyad forces and in particular the connection between the ʿAlids and ʿAbbāsids, see Cahen 1963, Nagel 1972, Omar 1975, Sharon 1983, and Elad 1986. *See also Daniel 1996, Elad 2000, Agha 2003, Marín-Guzmán 1990. On the ʿAbbāsid support in the province of Khurasan, see Shacklady 1986, Blankinship 1988. *See also Amabe 1995, Elad 2000 and 2010.

al-ʿAbbās was declared caliph in al-Kūfa and took the regnal name of al-Saffāḥ. One year later Marwān II was pursued into Syria where the final blow to Umayyad rule was dealt.[21]

During his brief reign, the first ʿAbbāsid caliph al-Saffāḥ (r. 132–136/749–754) directed his efforts toward consolidating power and neutralizing his opponents.[22] He established a pattern of administration that was to endure after him by entrusting different regions of the empire to his relatives. Khurasan he placed under the governorship of Abū Muslim, whose support had been indispensable for securing the caliphate. However, the ʿAbbāsids became distrustful of Abū Muslim's popularity among the Khurasanians and his independent power base, especially in light of their own struggles to establish legitimacy. When the opportunity arose, the second ʿAbbāsid caliph Abū Jaʿfar al-Manṣūr (r. 136–158/754–775)[23] summoned Abū Muslim to his court and executed the unsuspecting governor. Some Khurasanians rebelled in response, but al-Manṣūr was able to quell them without much difficulty. The ʿAlids and emerging Shiʿites, however, continued to rebel for decades and never ceased to press their claims to the caliphate, despite suppressions which were quite brutal at times.

In 145/762 al-Manṣūr founded a capital for the new ʿAbbāsid Caliphate at Baghdad, which would soon become not only the military and fiscal center of the caliphate, but also a major cultural, religious and scholarly center. Al-Manṣūr also established the centralized bureaucracy which, under the caliph al-Mahdī (r. 158–169/775–785), would come to be controlled by the Barmakid family. While al-Mahdī largely continued the policies of al-Manṣūr, he also appears to have emphasized the religious nature of the caliphate in addition to its political power, likely as part of an effort to reconcile with the ʿAlids. This policy of reconciliation with the ʿAlids and emerging Shiʿites was reversed during the brief reign of al-Hādī (r. 169–170/785–786), who also faced a number of revolts. Although the rule of his successor, Hārūn al-Rashīd (r. 170–193/786–809), has been perceived as a "golden age" due to the cultural achievements of that period as well as al-Rashīd's military exploits against the Byzantines, his reign, too, was challenged by revolts and increasing unrest. The succession to Hārūn al-Rashīd and the reign of his son al-Maʾmūn are the subject of the next chapter.

In name, the ʿAbbāsid caliphate lasted five centuries. Its effective power, however, was as brief as Umayyad rule. The ʿAbbāsid caliphate began to show clear signs of weakness soon after the caliphates of al-Rashīd and al-Maʾmūn. It then entered a long pe-

21. Marwān was one of numerous Umayyad notables killed in 132/749–750, the year which marks the beginning of the dynastic ʿAbbāsid caliphate. One of the Umayyads lucky to escape death was ʿAbd al-Raḥmān I; he managed to flee to Africa and thence to Spain where he founded the Umayyad dynasty of Cordoba a few years later. *See Abū Ḥabīb 1995.

22. An account of changes in the style of government from the late Umayyads to the early ʿAbbāsids is given by Biddle 1972. The development of early ʿAbbāsid administration has been charted by Nicol 1979.

23. For more information on al-Manṣūr's reign, see Dietrich 1952.

riod of almost continuous decline (the reign of al-Muʿtaḍid [r. 279–289/892–902] was one exception), which has sometimes been blamed on the so-called "Persianization of the ʿAbbāsid caliphate" or on the influence of the Turks.

1.6. Sunnites and Shiʿites

Muslims today form two major sects, the Sunnites and the Shiʿites. Sunnite and Shiʿite identities only crystallized toward the end of the third/ninth century, however, and it is inaccurate to retroject such clear-cut divisions onto an earlier period of history, as we will see below.[24]

1.6.1. The Sunnites

The Sunnites, who have historically comprised a large majority of the Muslim Community, derive their name from the Arabic phrase "*ahl al-sunna wa-l-jamāʿa*," or the people of the *sunna* and community." The word *sunna* ("path") refers to the path of the Prophet, an important source of doctrine for Sunnite Muslims.[25] The *Sunna* has been preserved for posterity by the *muḥaddithūn* or *ahl al-ḥadīth*, "traditionists," who collect and pass down reports about the statements, conduct and practices of the Prophet.[26] The Sunnites are also people of the "community" because they accept the authority of the political majority of the Community (*jamāʿa*) and the history of the Muslim Community as it evolved, in contrast with the Shiʿite claim that the Community has been in error since the failure to accept ʿAlī as Muḥammad's successor.

Sunnites deny that Muḥammad designated ʿAlī as his successor. They hold that the caliphate is an elective office whose occupant does not have to be a member of the family of the Prophet Muḥammad. Inasmuch as the first four caliphs were elected to the office, Sunnites accept their legitimacy. All Muslims recognize the Qur'an and Sunna as authoritative sources of doctrine and practice, but the Sunnites and Shiʿites recognize different collections of hadiths (Prophetic reports) as canonical. Most Sunnite jurists engaged in

24. Cf. Watt 1985, 56 ff.

25. For more information on the complexity of the semantic development of the word *sunna*, see *Dictionary of the Middle Ages*, s.v. "*sunna*" (Juynboll). *See also *EI2*, s.v. "*sunna*" (Juynboll).

26. There is a tendency especially among non-Arab writers to equate the traditionists with "conservatives," which is only partially accurate. This association has come about in part because the English word "tradition" has a connotation of past-orientedness and conservatism, and in part because traditionists were in fact concerned with preserving the past (see Hodgson 1974, 65–66). Equally misleading is the term *ahl al-sunna* (Juynboll 1987) which is sometimes used as a synonym for "traditionists." To avoid confusion, I shall only use "traditionists" or its Arabic equivalents, "*muḥaddithūn*" and "*ahl al-ḥadīth*" to refer to the activity of Hadith collection or transmission.

expounding God's law would further come to view *ijmāʿ* (consensus)[27] and *qiyās* (legal analogy)[28] as sources of law in addition to the Qur'an and Sunna. By accepting consensus as a source of the law, the Sunnites may be understood to invest ultimate interpretive authority in the community of jurists.

Collectively, the four sources of Qur'an, Sunna, consensus, and legal analogy are understood by the mature Sunnite tradition to constitute the *uṣūl al-fiqh*, or the roots of jurisprudence. Over time, jurists came to recognize four major Sunnite schools of law: Ḥanafite, Mālikite, Shāfiʿite and Ḥanbalite. The Ḥanbalites can be regarded as the most rigorous in preserving the external, pre-interpretive meanings of texts. Leaders and proponents of these four schools of law assiduously cultivated the various branches of Islamic theology and jurisprudence and trained thousands of *ʿulamāʾ* (learned men) in centers at Baghdad, Damascus, Kairouan, and Cordoba, among other places.

1.6.2. The Shiʿites

The Shiʿites are distinguished from the Sunnites by their adherence to a distinctive body of religious doctrine and ritual and their belief that the leader of the Community must be a member of the family of the Prophet. The Arabic term "*Shīʿa*" is an abbreviation of "*shīʿat ʿAlī*," or the "partisans of ʿAlī," a term which first appeared during ʿAlī's caliphate to distinguish his supporters from the "*shīʿat ʿUthmān*," the partisans of the assassinated third caliph.

The terms "ʿAlid" and "Ṭālibid," in contrast, refer to the descendants of ʿAlī ibn Abī Ṭālib and his father Abū Ṭālib, respectively. The vast majority of Shiʿites believe that an ʿAlid should lead the Community; they disagree concerning whether precedence should be given to descendants of ʿAlī's son al-Ḥasan (the Ḥasanids), to descendants of his son al-Ḥusayn (the Ḥusaynids), or to descendants of some other branch of the family. It is possible to have ʿAlid sympathies without being a Shiʿite, since Shiʿism implies adherence to a body of religious doctrine in addition to a political claim about who is entitled to lead the Community.[29] While proponents of ʿAlī and the ʿAlids participated in the earliest debates over succession to Muḥammad, Shiʿite identity emerged only gradually, crystallizing in the late third/ninth century.

---

27. For more information on this technical term, see *EI2*, s.v. "*idjmāʿ*" (Bernand). *See Calder 1983 and Hallaq 1986 and 1997.

28. On *qiyās*, see *EI2*, s.v. "*ḳiyās. In law.*" (Bernand). *See Hallaq 1997, Hasan 2007, and Shehaby 1982.

29. Shiʿism as a political theory and a view on the past struggle between ʿAlī and his opponents (*tashayyuʿ*) emerged early indeed; in fact, the seed for it was sown in the dissent which emerged immediately upon the Prophet's death (described above) and which served to transform the word *shīʿa* as "partisanship" (in favor of ʿAlī) into Shiʿism. As time went by, the political aspects of Shiʿism assumed less significance than its religious doctrine. A more specific definition of *tashayyuʿ* is found in Juynboll 1983, 48–49. *On political theory in Islam, see Black 2001 and Crone 2004.

After ʿAlī's assassination in 40/661 his supporters declared him a *shahīd* (martyr), and the town of Najaf in present-day Iraq in which he was interred became a holy shrine. ʿAlī's supporters further declared his elder son al-Ḥasan as his successor, leading to the confrontation with Muʿāwiya mentioned above. After al-Ḥasan abdicated and recognized the caliphate of Muʿāwiya, he retired to Medina, where he died around the year 49/669–670. Claiming that al-Ḥasan was poisoned at the instigation of Muʿāwiya or his men, ʿAlid supporters proclaimed him a martyr as well.

ʿAlī's son al-Ḥusayn met a similar fate. When Yazīd I assumed the caliphate in 60/680 upon the death of his father Muʿāwiya, al-Ḥusayn refused to acknowledge him. Instead, he renounced his political quietism and answered the invitation of his supporters in al-Kūfa to claim his right to the imāmate. Vastly outnumbered by the Umayyad forces, al-Ḥusayn was killed on 10 Muḥarram 61/10 October 680 at Karbalāʾ near al-Kūfa, where he was later buried. The emerging Shiʿites declared al-Ḥusayn a martyr and Karbalāʾ a holy shrine. Shiʿites continue to this day to commemorate al-Ḥusayn's death by observing the first ten days of the month of Muḥarram as "days of lamentation."

The Shiʿite tradition thus considers ʿAlī, al-Ḥasan and al-Ḥusayn to have been the first three *imāms*, or "true caliphs." The caliphs recognized by the Sunnites—at least from Muʿāwiya onward—are, accordingly, considered by the Shiʿites to have been "false caliphs."[30] Since the Shiʿites believed the "true caliph" to be inspired by God and able to read His will, they taught that he was therefore entitled to unquestioned obedience and absolute authority. The Shiʿites' special usage of the term *imām* is grounded in a messianic and eschatological belief in the imminent coming of the last *imām* to restore the true and legitimate caliphate before the end of the world.[31] The last *imām* is known as *al-mahdī*, or the "one who is (divinely) guided."

The Shiʿites have never been a single, unified sect.[32] ʿĀrif (1987) identifies eighty-two Shiʿite groupings which scholars have classified into four main categories.[33] Differences in doctrine, teachings, and ritual form the basis for these necessarily rough and overlapping categorizations. If the Shiʿites differ from the Sunnites because of their belief that the leader of the Community must meet a number of strict criteria, the different Shiʿite groupings are distinguished by their disagreements over the specifics of these criteria and the identities of the *imāms* after al-Ḥusayn. Of the Shiʿite sects, the largest, comprising thirty-four subgroups, is the Imāmites, usually known as the Twelver

30. See Goldziher 1901 for a number of disparaging names given by the Shiʿites to the "false caliphs."

31. The Zaydites, it should be noted, adopted other criteria for the *imām*.

32. For the complexities involved in the term "Shiʿites," see Van Ess 1991–, 1:233–403 and cf. 1:233. A good introduction to Shiʿism is Halm 1988. *See Anthony 2012, Bernheimer 2013, Dakake 2007, and Haider 2011.

33. Besides the Twelver Shiʿites and the Zaydites, there are two other umbrella groups, the extreme Shiʿites and the Seveners (cf. Halm 1988). *See Kohlberg 2003.

Shiᶜites. According to this group, which includes the vast majority of modern Shiᶜites, the *mahdī* went into hiding and occultation around the year 260/873–874. They are called the "Twelvers" because this *mahdī* is the twelfth *imām*.[34]

The other Shiᶜite sect of importance to this study is the Zaydites, a category that embraces some twenty groups. Generally speaking, the Zaydites differ from the Twelvers in that they do not believe that the *imām* is free from error or claim one specific line of succession for the imāmate. Instead, any member of the House of ᶜAlī is acceptable as leader of the Community, for some Zaydites any member of the House of the Prophet. The *imām* can be known by his personal merit and by his willingness to take up the sword to assume authority.

It is an article of faith for most Shiᶜites that the caliphate is a hereditary office which is restricted to ᶜAlī and his descendants from his marriage to Fāṭima. Al-Ḥasan and al-Ḥusayn have also been granted a special status by the Shiᶜites due to their parentage and their martyrdom. Shiᶜite doctrine generally teaches that the special powers and qualities of the Prophet descended to them via their mother Fāṭima, Muḥammad's daughter. Accordingly, they and their progeny are regarded as preeminently able to interpret the will of God. The special knowledge of the *imām* is one of the most important features distinguishing Shiᶜite from Sunnite Islam; where the Sunnites vest ultimate interpretive authority in the hands of the Community, by means of its doctors of law, the Shiᶜites place interpretive authority in the hands of the *imāms* with their special knowledge of God's will.

1.7. The Muᶜtazilites

The Arabic word *iᶜtizāl*, from which the term "Muᶜtazilite" is derived, has a variety of meanings. Of these, "separatism" or "standing apart" (from taking a position on certain issues or choosing the side of one group against another) is a traditional explanation given for the name of the Muᶜtazilite school, referring to an episode in which Wāṣil ibn ᶜAṭāʾ (d. 131/748), the founder of the Muᶜtazilite movement, distanced himself from al-Ḥasan al-Baṣrī (d. 110/728) due to a disagreement over the status of the grave sinner. Influenced by Greek writings, the Muᶜtazilites are said to have created "the speculative dogmatics of Islam."[35]

34. To be sure, the concept of *imām* is not foreign to the Sunnites, but it means something very different to them, certainly not carrying the connotations of "infallibility and immaculateness" which the Twelvers consider characteristic of the *imām*. For most of the Sunnites, the word *imām* stands simply for any pious man who leads the prayer. The Sunnites use *imām* also as an honorific title for eminent religious figures of Islam such as the founders of the schools of law.

35. *EI1* s.v. "Muᶜtazila" (Nyberg). *See *EI2* s.v. "Muᶜtazila" (Gimaret).

The Muʿtazilites asserted that reason (*ʿaql*) is capable of deriving some truths independently of revelation (*naql*).[36] In addition to elevating the role of reason, Muʿtazilite thought rests on five fundamental principles (*uṣūl*, singular *aṣl*). These are:

(I) *Aṣl al-tawḥīd* (the principle of absolute unity). This principle asserts the strict unity of God and His absolute indivisibility. It affirms the oneness of God in the strictest possible sense by rejecting any form of anthropomorphism, such as the notion of a God who sees and hears or has eyes and ears as humans do. It also denies that anyone or anything could share the attributes of God. It is from this principle that the Muʿtazilites deduce the createdness of the Qur'an, as we will see below (1.8.).

(II) *Aṣl al-ʿadl* (the principle of justice). God is just and does what is best for His creation. He neither desires nor ordains evil, which is the product of man's own choices and conduct. Because we know that God is just and that He punishes humans for their sins, man must have free will such that he may deserve reward or punishment for his actions.

(III) *Aṣl al-waʿd wa-l-waʿīd* (the principle of the promise and the threat). This principle is primarily one of practical theology. God must fulfill the promises (*al-waʿd*) He has made to reward human actions as well as His threats (*al-waʿīd*) to punish disobedience. This principle is linked to the principle of *ʿadl* above, because it details the consequences of human exercise of free will.

(IV) *Aṣl al-manzila bayn al-manzilatayn* (the principle of the intermediate position). This principle holds that the grave sinner (*fāsiq*) can be counted neither a believer (as the Murjiʾites held) nor a disbeliever (as the Khārijites claimed).

(V) *Aṣl al-amr bi-l-maʿrūf wa-l-nahy ʿan al-munkar* (the principle of commanding right and forbidding wrong). This principle makes it incumbent upon the Muslim to command (*amr*) that which is right (*maʿrūf*) and to forbid (*nahy*) that which is wrong (*munkar*). This duty is generally considered a *farḍ kifāya* (collective obligation) that may be satisfied for all Muslims as long as it is undertaken by some of them.[37] Although this principle is not unique to the Muʿtazilites and is enshrined word for word in the Qur'an, the Muʿtazilites' emphasis on it provoked controversy concerning who has the authority to undertake it, how far Muslims are permitted to go in "forbidding" evil, what is and is not evil, and whether or not revolt against an unjust yet legitimately appointed ruler is permitted (Watt 1985, 52).

36. For an analysis of the Muʿtazilite concept of *ʿaql*, see Bernand 1972–73.

37. For more information on the general meaning given to this duty, see *Encyclopaedia Iranica* 1:992–95, s.v. "*Amr be maʿrūf*" (Madelung), Bercher 1955, Lambton 1981, 310–15, and Van Ess 1991–, 2:387–90. *See the comprehensive study by Cook (2000).

The Muʿtazilites meticulously elaborated these five assertions and their ramifications with reference to a great many Qur'anic verses and Prophetic hadiths within the framework of rational argument.[38] Their primary focus was on God's unity and justice (principles I and II), since these were considered fundamental; it is for this reason that the Muʿtazilites are sometimes referred to as *ahl al-ʿadl wa-l-tawḥīd* (proponents of justice and absolute unity).

1.8. The Doctrine of the Createdness of the Qur'an

The debate over whether the Qur'an is an object created by an act of God or God's uncreated speech antedates al-Maʾmūn by perhaps more than a century (Madelung 1974).[39] Evidence reported by Watt (1950), Abusaq (1971) and Vajda (*EI2*, s.v. Ibn Dirham), among others, suggests that the tenth Umayyad caliph, Hishām (r. 105–125/724–743), ordered that Jaʿd ibn Dirham be put to death in 124/742 or 125/743 for advocating the doctrine of the createdness of the Qur'an. According to Amīn (1933–36, 3:162) and Sourdel (1962, 32), Hārūn al-Rashīd's threat to behead the noted *mutakallim* (speculative theologian) Bishr ibn Ghiyāth al-Marīsī for teaching that the Qur'an was created drove him into hiding for twenty years, although this story is probably apocryphal.[40]

Proponents of the doctrine of the createdness of the Qur'an argued that the Qur'an, although divine, cannot be deemed uncreated, an idea associated with the traditionists. According to the Muʿtazilites, one of the primary groups associated with this doctrine, such a claim would violate God's absolute unity (*aṣl al-tawḥīd*) and thus constitute polytheism. Their argument is straightforward: we know that God is one and eternal. To claim that the Qur'an is also eternal would imply that God's eternity is shared by an object, the Qur'an, and that God is therefore no longer a Unity. The Muʿtazilites employed the same argument to refute the Christian concept of the Trinity as similarly violating the Oneness of God. Furthermore, they labeled Muslims who claimed that the Qur'an is God's uncreated speech as *mushrikūn* (polytheists), likening them to Christians who claimed that "Jesus was not created because he is the word of God" (Madelung 1974, 517).

1.9. The *Miḥna*

Al-Maʾmūn's command in 218/833 to institute the *miḥna* had the express aim of securing acquiescence in the doctrine of the createdness of the Qur'an. The word *miḥna* has

38. On the relationship between the Muʿtazilites and Hadith, see Van Ess 1982.

39. *See *EI3*, s.v. "createdness of the Qurʾān" (Martin). A short summary of classical Muslim views on the doctrine of the createdness of the Qur'an is Heydorn 2006.

40. Later, Bishr returned and acquired much influence at the court of al-Maʾmūn. See *EI2*, s.v. "Bishr ibn Ghiyāth (Carra de Vaux-Nader-Schacht).

several connotations.[41] The most relevant is that which comes closest to the "Inquisition" of the European Middle Ages, although certainly not in terms of its scope and excesses. However, it should be noted that the caliph himself only used the verb *imtaḥana* ("to interrogate" or "to examine"). It was later Arab chroniclers who introduced the word *miḥna* to describe the caliph's order. Over time, after the doctrine of the createdness of the Qur'an had become almost universally rejected, the term acquired emotional connotations, suggesting that this episode was an ordeal which confronted the entire Muslim Community.

The caliph wrote a series of five letters giving his instructions for the *miḥna*. The fullest text of these appears in al-Ṭabarī's (d. 310/923) universal history in his discussion of the reign of al-Maʾmūn. The first letter, which gives the initial order for the *miḥna*, was written in Rabīʿ I 218/March-April 833; the others, undated, followed in rapid succession. All five letters are addressed to Isḥāq ibn Ibrāhīm, who was the governor of Baghdad and also chief of police. Many of those whom al Maʾmūn wanted interrogated are mentioned by name. They include Aḥmad ibn Ḥanbal (d. 241/855), eponym of one of the four classical schools of legal thought (*madhhabs*). The questioning was carried out by Isḥāq ibn Ibrāhīm, occasionally in the presence of others. He was instructed to keep the caliph informed of the course of the interrogations, apparently by means of verbatim transcripts sent to the caliph, but these have not survived. Al-Maʾmūn further instructed Isḥāq to have the men, who assented, interrogate those in their service.

The preamble of the first letter affirms the caliph's right, indeed duty, to issue the *miḥna* order. The letter also contains detailed arguments for the createdness of the Qur'an. The caliph supports his claim with numerous Qur'anic verses, discussing the rhetorical questions those verses evoke and the inferences which can be drawn from them. All such verses, wrote al-Maʾmūn, speak with one voice, and loudly: the Qur'an is incontrovertibly a creation of God, not His uncreated speech. While much of this first letter

41. One of the connotations is certainly negative. It is, however, not known when the word acquired this negative connotation except that it was apparently coined by Sunnite chroniclers reporting the events of al-Maʾmūn's reign (see below). Wensinck (*EI1*, s.v. "*miḥna*") says that the noun *miḥna* is "derived from the root *m-ḥ-n*, appearing in the Arabic verb *maḥana*, "to smooth," and in some Aethiopic derivations, trial (e.g., the trials to which the prophets and especially the family of Muḥammad, the ʿAlids, are exposed in this world; ... inquisition)." Patton (1897, 1, n. 1) states that the term generally means a "testing" or "trial." This can be due to "accidents of fortune or the actions of men." Patton adds that *miḥna* is often used together with the VIIIth form of *maḥana* (*imtaḥana*) to refer to "a religious test with a view to obtaining assent to some particular belief or system of beliefs." Hinds (*EI2*, s.v. "*miḥna*") adds to Patton's remarks a citation from Abū al-ʿArab al-Tamīmī's *Kitāb al-miḥan* to illustrate a general meaning which refers to someone who has "been afflicted (*ubtuliya*) by being killed, imprisoned, flogged, or threatened...." Dozy (1881) reflects both views given above: «persecution» and «le tourment, la torture.» Lane (1863–93) does not add anything substantial. Finally, while the foregoing definitions tend to stress the negative, the verb *imtaḥana* also means "to look into" or "to examine an issue or a person such as a student" (Ibn Manẓūr, *Lisān al-ʿArab*, sub "*m ḥ n*").

rests on reasoned argument, some parts of it contain attacks on and threats against those who disagree or refuse to concede that the Qur'an was created. The subsequent letters consist entirely of such attacks and threats. At the caliph's request, Isḥāq ibn Ibrāhīm dispatched in chains to Tarsus (in present-day southern Turkey)—where the caliph was pausing in a campaign against the Byzantine Empire—those whom al-Maʾmūn wanted to interrogate personally. However, when they were near al-Raqqa in northern Syria, news reached them of the caliph's death, and they were sent back to Baghdad.

The *miḥna* later became almost synonymous with al-Maʾmūn's name, not merely because he initiated it, but because it represented a systematic attempt to enforce a religious doctrine of his selection.[42] The *miḥna* lasted some sixteen years. After al-Maʾmūn's death in 218/833, it was continued by al-Muʿtaṣim (r. 218–227/833–842)[43] and al-Wāthiq (r. 227–232/842–847),[44] al-Maʾmūn's two immediate successors. According to most reports, the *miḥna* was terminated in 234/848–849 by al-Mutawakkil (r. 232–247/847–861), who succeeded his brother al-Wāthiq.[45]

In the course of the interrogations, men were beaten, imprisoned, humiliated, and lost their official positions. At the outset, a few were perhaps tortured, but none was put to death under al-Maʾmūn, although some were threatened with the sword. As far as we can tell from the surviving sources, approximately the same range of pressures was applied during the regimes of al-Muʿtaṣim and al-Wāthiq, although a few men may well have been executed for their continued resistance during their reigns. The available information does not permit us to make detailed statements about the total number of people subjected to interrogation, the methods used to obtain their assent or the motivations of al-Muʿtaṣim and al-Wāthiq.

Al-Muʿtaṣim (r. 218–227/833–842) was a good soldier but did not have the intellectual prowess of his brother al-Maʾmūn. In all probability, he lacked his predecessor's appreciation of the subtle arguments on the createdness of the Qur'an. He may have simply felt

---

42. Contrary to the impression one gains from reading the otherwise careful Patton (1897), there is no evidence to substantiate the claim (p. 1, n. 1) that the nineteenth ʿAbbāsid caliph al-Qāhir (r. 320–322/932–934) initiated an inquisition. The best explanation I can offer is that Patton probably confused this caliph with al-Qādir. On the religious policies of the latter, see Makdisi (1963, 299 ff.). There are two other episodes in the annals of classical Islamic history which bear some resemblance to the *miḥna*. In 323/935 the twentieth ʿAbbāsid caliph al-Rāḍī (r. 322–329/934–940) issued an edict condemning the doctrine and activities of the Ḥanbalites. There is, however, no evidence that this order led to an inquisition; it simply banned gatherings by the Ḥanbalites. The second event occurred during the reign of the twenty-fifth ʿAbbāsid caliph al-Qādir (r. 381–422/991–1031), who forbade non-traditionists from spreading their ideologies. Again, as in the case of al-Rāḍī, an inquisition was apparently not carried out. *See Sourdel 1999, ch. 13, «les califes face à la réflexion doctrinale», 195–204.

43. *See Winkelmann-Liebert 2003.

44. *See El-Hibri 2001.

45. *See Turner 2010; for later caliphal religious policies, see Melchert 1996.

it his duty to honor the request al-Maʾmūn made in his will that he continue the *miḥna*.[46] In contrast, al-Wāthiq (r. 227–232/842–847), the son of al-Muʿtaṣim, was nicknamed al-Maʾmūn "*al-ṣaghīr*" (the young al-Maʾmūn) for his intellectual brilliance and breadth of knowledge. He pursued the *miḥna* with much vigor and a brutality of which nobody ever accused al-Maʾmūn. Provocatively, al-Wāthiq ordered that "there is no deity but God, the Creator of the Qur'an" be inscribed on the entrances of mosques (Amin 1933–36, 3:184). Again, however, the sources do not permit us to discover his motives.[47]

We know slightly more about the motives which led the tenth ʿAbbāsid caliph, al-Mutawakkil (r. 232–247/847–861), to end the *miḥna* and release from prison those who remained to be interrogated. His decision was not an act of religious tolerance, nor was it an act of mercy or an expression of piety. Al-Mutawakkil's religious policy was marked by hostility to Christians and Jews[48] as well as to the Shiʿites.[49] By the time he ascended to power, the opponents of the doctrine of the createdness of the Qur'an had gained strength. To appease the populace and gain popularity, especially in Baghdad, al-Mutawakkil put an end to the *miḥna* by prohibiting any form of disputation about the Qur'an at all. Additionally, the caliph dismissed his chief judge (*qāḍī al-quḍāt*), the Muʿtazilite Aḥmad ibn Abī Duʾād, and replaced him with a non-Muʿtazilite. He also gave a position to Bishr ibn al-Walīd al-Kindī, who had refused to assent both during the time of al-Maʾmūn and later (Watt 1973, 281). To further curry favor with the emerging Sunnites, al-Mutawakkil demolished the tomb of al-Ḥusayn and threatened to imprison anyone who made a pilgrimage to Karbalāʾ.[50]

The *miḥna* had a lasting impact on developments in Islamic thought. Those who opposed the doctrine of the createdness of the Qur'an felt compelled to come up with cogent answers to the challenge posed by it. As a result, Sunnite theological formulations gained a systematic approach to the issue from that time onward.[51]

---

46. *See Nawas 2010, which argues that al-Muʿtaṣim's appointment was primarily due to pressure from the ʿAbbāsid family and that al-Maʾmūn was forced to this decision, even though his son al-ʿAbbās was an established and popular military commander.

47. *See El-Hibri 2001, which refers to al-Wāthiq's reign as a "riddle."

48. Lichtenstädter 1943, esp. 47–49.

49. For an account of his reign, see Miah 1969. Abbott (1938) has also scrutinized papyri from his reign. *On the end of the *miḥna*, see Turner 2010. For how *the miḥna* contributed to the canonization of Sunnism, see Turner 2013.

50. *For an analysis of the religious policies of the caliphs al-Mutawakkil to al-Muqtadir, see Melchert 1996.

51. A classic Sunnite position on the uncreatedness of the Qur'an was to be formulated toward the end of the fourth/tenth century by the theologian al-Bāqillānī (d. 403/1013), although others before him had written on the subject. A presentation of al-Bāqillānī's views regarding the Qur'an is given by Bouman (1959). An overview of the development of Muslim theological views on the Qur'an is found in *EI2*, s.v. "*al- Ḳurʾān*", section 8: "The *Ḳurʾān* in Muslim life and thought" (Welch). *See also Heydorn 2008.

CHAPTER 2
ʿABDALLĀH AL-MAʾMŪN: HIS LIFE AND REIGN

2.1. Early Life

ʿAbdallāh ibn Hārūn al-Rashīd, known by his caliphal name of al-Maʾmūn, was born on 15 Rabīʿ I, 170/14 September 786.[1] He was the eldest of al-Rashīd's eleven sons. His mother Marājil, who died soon after his birth, was a concubine from Bādhghīs, a province of Khurasan.[2] Zubayda, granddaughter of the second ʿAbbāsid caliph al-Manṣūr and the favorite wife of al-Rashīd, oversaw the upbringing of both her stepson al-Maʾmūn and her own son, Muḥammad al-Amīn, who was born approximately six months after al-Maʾmūn in Shawwāl 170/April 787.

As was customary for the children of the ʿAbbāsid rulers,[3] al-Maʾmūn received a thorough education in the most important fields of learning of the day. Al-Kisāʾī[4] was his tutor in the Arabic language, while al-Yazīdī[5] taught him *adab* ("the humanities"), music, and poetry.[6] With regard to the religious sciences, al-Maʾmūn was trained in Hadith and became a traditionist himself.[7] He studied *fiqh* (Islamic law) under al-Ḥasan ibn Ziyād al-Luʾluʾī[8] and was counted an expert in Ḥanafite jurisprudence. Throughout his life,

1. His *kunya* (patronymic) was either Abū al-ʿAbbās or Abū Jaʿfar.

2. *Madelung (2002) argues that al-Maʾmūn's mother, Marājil, was the daughter of a Khurasanian rebel, Ustādhsīs; cf. Crone 2012, 156.

3. On the education of ʿAbbāsid nobles, see Dietrich 1976.

4. Al-Kisāʾī (d. 189/805) was a well-known Arab philologist and Qur'an reader. The caliph al-Mahdī had made him the tutor of his son al-Rashīd, who in turn appointed him tutor of his two sons al-Amīn and al-Maʾmūn; *EI2*, s.v. "al-Kisāʾī" (Sellheim).

5. Al-Yazīdī (d. 202/817) was, like al-Kisāʾī, a philologist and Qur'an reader. According to Abbott (1946, 174–75), al-Yazīdī taught the Qur'an to al-Maʾmūn, while al-Amīn learned the Qur'an from al-Kisāʾī.

6. *For a collection of poetry attributed to al-Maʾmūn, see Ḥusayn 2002 and al-Ṣamad 1998.

7. *On al-Maʾmūn's participation in scholarly life, see Zaman 1997, 70.

8. A companion of the famous jurist Abū Ḥanīfa and erstwhile judge of al-Kūfa. He transmitted

al-Maʾmūn valued learning and intellectual pursuits, and it appears that he had outstanding mental abilities that set him far above his brother al-Amīn.

When al-Maʾmūn was eighteen years old, he married his cousin Umm ʿĪsā, daughter of al-Hādī, the fourth ʿAbbāsid caliph, who ruled briefly in 169/785.[9] Like his father, al-Maʾmūn had numerous concubines, some of whom bore him children. His most famous son was al-ʿAbbās, who became known as a capable military leader.

Al-Maʾmūn's first significant encounter with politics occurred in 183/799, when al-Rashīd[10] made him second in line to the caliphate after his younger brother al-Amīn, who was an ʿAbbāsid on both sides of his family and who had already been designated in 175/792 as successor. Third in line was another son of al-Rashīd, al-Qāsim, who was given the title al-Muʾtaman.

This arrangement for the succession was solemnly proclaimed and signed by the parties concerned, and formally witnessed in Mecca during the pilgrimage of 186/802. This "Meccan Accord"[11] stipulated the following: Al-Amīn was to be caliph, with Baghdad as his capital; Khurasan was to be governed autonomously by al-Maʾmūn; and the war-front with the Byzantine Empire[12] was to be given to al-Muʾtaman. The troops of al-Amīn and al-Maʾmūn were entitled to enter the other's territory in pursuit of enemies without implying infringement or revocation of the Accord.

Even before the Accord, Jaʿfar ibn Yaḥyā al-Barmakī[13] had been appointed advisor to al-Maʾmūn, a position that he held until the downfall of the Barmakid family in Ṣafar 187/January 803, just after al-Rashīd returned from the pilgrimage during which these arrangements for his succession had been formalized. From that time al-Maʾmūn's close advisor was al-Faḍl ibn Sahl, about whom more will be said below.

---

hadiths from Abū Hanīfa. He died in 204/819–820: al-Khaṭīb al-Baghdādī, *Tārīkh Baghdād*, 7:314–17 and Wakīʿ, *Akhbār al-quḍāt*, 3:188–89.

9. On al-Hādī's short reign, see Moscati 1946.

10. For the reign of al-Rashīd, see Bittermann 1929, Canard 1962, el-ʿAlī 1971, Ahsan 1976, and Bonner 1988, 1989. *See Ḍannāwī 2001, which contains much material on various aspects of al-Rashīd's reign.

11. Also called the "Kaʿba Accord" because it was hung on the Kaʿba, For an in-depth analysis of this document and its significance see Kimber 1986. *See El-Hibri 1992.

12. An overview of the tug of war between the Islamic and Byzantine Empires is given by Canard (1966). *See al-ʿAdawī 1994, El Cheikh 2004, Kaegi 1995, and esp. Kaegi 2010.

13. Member of the Barmakid family who, together with his father, Yaḥyā ibn Khālid, and brother, al-Faḍl ibn Yaḥyā, played a very important role in the administration of the empire under al-Rashīd until he had them removed. On the Barmakids, see Bouvat 1912, Sourdel 1959–60, 127–81, and Meisami 1989. *See *EI3*, s.v. "Barmakids" (Van Bladel).

2.2. The Civil War

Al-Rashīd died on 2 Jumādā II 193/24 March 809 at Ṭūs[14] on his way to subdue a rebellion in Khurasan. Among those accompanying him were his chamberlain and vizier al-Faḍl ibn al-Rabīᶜ,[15] al-Faḍl ibn Sahl, and al-Maʾmūn, who had preceded his father to the Khurasanian city of Marw with an advance contingent. Upon the death of al-Rashīd, al-Amīn became caliph while al-Maʾmūn assumed responsibility for Khurasan, as stipulated in the Meccan Accord. Al-Amīn appears to have been unsatisfied with the specified division of power, however. He first ordered the army and treasury to be returned to Baghdad, after which al-Faḍl ibn al-Rabīᶜ led the army back to the capital. Despite the withdrawal of the army, al-Maʾmūn was nevertheless able to pacify the region by securing the support of a number of Khurasanian chieftains and their troops by recognizing their autonomy; the Khurasanian troops were to remain the backbone of al-Maʾmūn's power base throughout the greater part of his caliphate.

Al-Amīn's recall of the army from Khurasan was only the first of a series of actions, some in direct violation of the Meccan Accord, which were to culminate in a civil war. Al-Amīn further strained relations with his brother in 194/810 by making his young son Mūsā another heir to the caliphate after al-Maʾmūn and al-Muʾtaman.[16] He ordered al-Maʾmūn to return to Baghdad to become his adviser, an order which al-Maʾmūn refused. Al-Amīn responded by trying to tighten his fiscal control over the eastern provinces. He first demanded that revenues be sent to him directly and later dispatched his own agents to the province, contravening the spirit if not the letter of the Meccan Accord. Al-Maʾmūn reacted to these measures by having al-Amīn's name removed from the coinage and the *ṭirāz* of Khurasan.[17]

A complete break between the two brothers came when al-Amīn removed al-Maʾmūn and al-Muʾtaman as heirs to the caliphate in favor of two of his own sons, Mūsā and ᶜAbdallāh. This action brought to an end the Meccan Accord, which all parties had sworn to uphold. In response, al-Maʾmūn initiated what he called "the second ᶜAbbāsid *daᶜwa*" (call) in order to reclaim power, echoing his ancestors' *daᶜwa* against the Umayyads six decades earlier. A civil war would follow.[18]

---

14. City in the Naysābūr region of Khurasan: Le Strange 1930, 388 and Yāqūt, *Muᶜjam al-buldān*, 4:49–50.

15. For his career, see Chejne 1962. *See *EI3* s.n. "al-Faḍl ibn Sahl" (Yücesoy).

16. On this fraternal and divisive war, see Gabrieli 1928 and Samadi 1958. *Jurjī Zaydān's romanticized account of the civil war between al-Maʾmūn and his brother al-Amīn has been translated into English: see Cooperson and Zaidan 2011.

17. A *ṭirāz* is a garment with embroidered bands bearing inscriptions worn by rulers and high officials. On this term, see Ahsan 1979, 68–70. *For an elaborate numismatic history of the reign of al-Maʾmūn, see Shammā 1995; see also El-Hibri 1993.

18. This conflict is sometimes identified in Muslim tradition as the fourth civil war, or *fitna*, in early Islamic history (e.g., Hodgson 1974). In this view the three previous civil wars consisted of the struggles

Preparations for war commenced in Jumādā II 195/March 811 when ʿAlī ibn ʿĪsā ibn Māhān, chief of the *abnāʾ al-dawla* (sons of the dynasty)—the descendants of Arab Khurasanians who had settled in the western part of the empire (especially in Baghdad) after aiding the ʿAbbāsids in taking over the caliphate from the Umayyads[19]—and governor of Khurasan under al-Rashīd, was appointed by al-Amīn as governor of Jibāl[20] with the mission of restoring caliphal authority in Khurasan. The forces under ʿAlī ibn ʿĪsā ibn Māhān were opposed by al-Maʾmūn's forces under the command of Harthama ibn Aʿyan and Ṭāhir ibn al-Ḥusayn.[21] The war was short but bitter. In the course of the decisive battle at Rayy in Shaʿbān 195/May 811, al-Amīn's troops were defeated, ʿAlī ibn ʿĪsā ibn Māhān was killed, and al-Maʾmūn was proclaimed caliph. On the night of 24–25 Muḥarram 198/24–25 September 813, Ṭāhir ibn al-Ḥusayn is reported to have ordered the execution of al-Amīn in Baghdad.

2.3. Al-Maʾmūn's Reign

The reign of al-Maʾmūn, which lasted some twenty-one years, can be divided into the periods before and after his return to Baghdad from Marw on 15 Ṣafar 204/11 August 819. The eight years preceding his return to the capital were characterized by a series of revolts in Baghdad and the province of Iraq. The civil war had created a power vacuum in the heart of the empire. Consequently, various groups including some Shiʿite factions sought to gain leadership over the Community. Although ʿAbbāsid policy concerning the emerging Shiʿites had not been consistent, earlier caliphs, including al-Manṣūr and al-Mahdī, had distanced themselves from the Shiʿites, while al-Hādī's one-year reign included a massacre of Shiʿite rebels at Fakhkh. Al-Rashīd also displayed intolerance of the Shiʿites, especially toward the end of his reign. Given the ʿAbbāsids' ambivalent attitude toward the Shiʿites, their rebellions under al-Maʾmūn are not surprising.

The most prominent Shiʿite uprising during al-Maʾmūn's caliphate was that of Abū al-Sarāyā,[22] who during the civil war is reported to have first fought against the army of Harthama ibn Aʿyan, one of the two major commanders who supported al-Maʾmūn, and

---

between: (a) the forces of ʿAlī and those of ʿĀʾisha, al-Zubayr and Ṭalḥa (35–41/656–661); (b) the forces of Yazīd I and those of Ibn al-Zubayr (59–73/680–692); (c) the forces of the Umayyads and pro-ʿAbbāsid forces (125–133/744–750), which ended with the ascension of the victorious ʿAbbāsid dynasty to the caliphate.

19. *See *EI3* s.n. "*Abnāʾ*" (Turner).

20. A province located between Iraq and Khurasan just below the Caspian Sea, i.e. central-western Iran. It included the important city of Rayy (close to present-day Tehran): Le Strange 1930, 185–231 and Yāqūt, *Muʿjam al-buldān*, 2:99–100.

21. *The composition of al-Maʾmūn's army has now been extensively discussed in Elad 2005, 2010, and 2013.

22. On this man and his revolt, see Tornberg 1868, esp. 706–7 and Arioli 1974.

then later to have become a lieutenant in Harthama's army.[23] After the civil war, Abū al-Sarāyā supported a rebellion in favor of Muḥammad ibn Ibrāhīm ibn Ṭabāṭabā's claim to the imāmate. On 10 Jumādā II 199/26 January 815 Ibn Ṭabāṭabā, a descendant of al-Ḥasan ibn ʿAlī ibn Abī Ṭālib, was heralded at al-Kūfa as *al-riḍā min āl Muḥammad*,[24] a designation tantamount to proclaiming him caliph. One month after this proclamation, Ibn Ṭabāṭabā died either from battle wounds or from poison administered by Abū al-Sarāyā himself, who no longer found him politically useful. Immediately after Ibn Ṭabāṭabā's death, Abū al-Sarāyā proclaimed a new *imām*, a descendent of al-Ḥusayn named Muḥammad ibn Muḥammad ibn Zayd. He was the son of Mūsā al-Kāẓim, who was later to become known as the seventh *imām* of the Twelver Shiʿites.

The major objective of the rebels under Abū al-Sarāyā was to spread the nascent Shiʿite movement to the whole of Iraq. At al-Baṣra and al-Kūfa, Muḥammad ibn Muḥammad ibn Zayd attacked ʿAbbāsid property, earning the sobriquet "Zayd al-Nār" (Zayd the "firebrand" or "agitator"). The rebels then proceeded to Baghdad. As they approached the capital, the caliphal army under the command of al-Ḥasan ibn Sahl was so weak that al-Ḥasan was forced to ask for the help of his rival, Harthama ibn Aʿyan, to oppose them. Harthama initially declined to intervene but was finally persuaded. He was able to put an end to the revolt, which concluded with the decapitation of Abū al-Sarāyā in Rabīʿ I 200/October 815. Al-Kūfa and al-Baṣra were recaptured, and Muḥammad ibn Muḥammad ibn Zayd was arrested and sent to al-Maʾmūn at Marw.

The threat of Shiʿite rebellion did not end with the death of Abū al-Sarāyā, however. In Rabīʿ I 200/November 815, shortly after Abū al-Sarāyā's execution, his envoy in Mecca was successful in proclaiming as *imām* Muḥammad al-Dībāja, a descendant of Jaʿfar al-Ṣādiq, who would eventually become known as the sixth *imām* of the Twelver Shiʿites. Al-Maʾmūn ordered Ḥamdawayh, a son of ʿAlī ibn ʿĪsā ibn Māhān who had helped command the faction of the *abnāʾ* that supported al-Maʾmūn during the civil war, to put down this revolt. He succeeded in recapturing Mecca, and Muḥammad al-Dībāja eventually went into exile in the province of Jurjān.[25]

In Ṣafar 200/September 815, Ibrāhīm, another son of Mūsā al-Kāẓim, initiated yet another Shiʿite revolt in Yemen which was so bloody that he earned the nickname "al-

23. Harthama ibn Aʿyan was one of the chief commanders under al-Rashīd as well. He remained an important military figure until his execution at the court of al-Maʾmūn at Marw in 200/816 probably due to the machinations of al-Faḍl ibn Sahl.

24. "The pleasing-one within the family of [the Prophet] Muḥammad." This was also one of the slogans used by ʿAbbāsid propagandists against the Umayyads in an attempt to woo the Shiʿites to their side. *See Crone 1989; and discussed further below.

25. Province located northwest of Khurasan along the Caspian Sea: Le Strange 1930, 376–81 and Yāqūt, *Muʿjam al-buldān*, 2:119–22.

Jazzār" (the Butcher). This revolt, too, was suppressed by Ḥamdawayh.[26] In the course of the rebellion, Ibrāhīm induced a descendant of ʿAlī ibn Abī Ṭālib's elder brother, ʿAqīl ibn Abī Ṭālib, to lead a military force to control the pilgrimage in 200/816. After being captured by the soldiers of al-Maʾmūn's brother Abū Isḥāq (later the caliph al-Muʿtaṣim), the rebels were sent back to Yemen.

The challenges al-Maʾmūn faced during this period were not limited to Shiʿite, ʿAlid or Ṭālibid rebellions in the provinces. In Baghdad itself fighting broke out in the year 200/816–817 between soldiers of the Ḥarbiyya district of the city[27] and al-Maʾmūn's troops, which were led by al-Ḥasan ibn Sahl. The cause of this unrest seems to have been al-Ḥasan's failure to pay wages, which were likely delayed by the government's preoccupation with suppressing revolts and the consequent fall in revenue. The protest of the Ḥarbiyya troops spread, leading to civil strife throughout the entire city. In response, some power brokers in the city appointed a son of the caliph al-Hādī, Isḥāq ibn Mūsā, as a representative of al-Maʾmūn to replace the appointees of al-Ḥasan ibn Sahl. Soon thereafter, in 201/816, this opposition movement came under the leadership of Muḥammad ibn Abī Khālid, the son of a very prominent *abnāʾ* commander who had a power base in the Ḥarbiyya quarter. Muḥammad ibn Abī Khālid's supporters included al-Manṣūr ibn al-Mahdī, who was a son of the caliph al-Mahdī, and al-Faḍl ibn al-Rabīʿ, who had been a vizier under al-Amīn.

Increasingly, the unrest focused on the position of the Sahlid family in al-Maʾmūn's administration, including al-Ḥasan ibn Sahl, who was then governing Baghdad, and his brother al-Faḍl ibn Sahl, the caliph's vizier. Many inhabitants of Baghdad as well as a number of ʿAbbāsids were unwilling to accept their influence on a caliph they already distrusted. Harthama ibn Aʿyan, a prominent leader of the *abnāʾ*, deemed the situation perilous for the caliph. In consequence, he declined to take up the governorship of Syria and the Ḥijāz, opting instead to lead a large contingent of his troops to Marw to inform al-Maʾmūn personally of the unrest in Iraq and of the prevailing antipathy to the Sahlids. Al-Maʾmūn's regard for al-Faḍl ibn Sahl, however, was apparently so strong that Harthama ibn Aʿyan, a loyal supporter of al-Maʾmūn and his family, was thrown into prison and subsequently executed in Dhū al-Qaʿda 200/June 816, probably on the orders of al-Faḍl.

The ʿAbbāsid family's resentment of the rule of al-Ḥasan ibn Sahl in Iraq and the influence of his brother al-Faḍl on al-Maʾmūn gradually reached a crisis point. On 25 Jumādā II 201/18 January 817 al-Maʾmūn's paternal uncle, al-Manṣūr ibn al-Mahdī, conceded to ʿAbbāsid pressures to become the "representative" of al-Maʾmūn in Baghdad,

---

26. After Ḥamdawayh had suppressed these Shiʿite revolts he tried to set himself up as an independent ruler in Yemen and was only removed by force (Van Arendonk 1919, 94–95).

27. Located northwest of the Round City ("the City of al-Manṣūr") of Baghdad just past the Syria Gate: Le Strange 1900, 122–35.

without the caliph's order.[28] Civil strife in Baghdad did not abate, however. Especially among the lower classes,[29] resentment led not only to massive support for the dissident ʿAbbāsids but also for a figure named Sahl ibn Salāma al-Anṣārī, who in the Ḥarbiyya quarter preached the popular Islamic slogan of strict adherence to the Qur'an and the ways of the Prophet. Subsequently, Sahl ibn Salāma became an opponent of the dissident ʿAbbāsids in a further illustration of the chaotic situation in the city.[30]

Al-Maʾmūn meanwhile did nothing to allay concerns about the influence of the Sahlids or to mend his relationship with the ʿAbbāsids and the populace of Baghdad. Instead, on 2 Ramaḍān 201/24 March 817 he designated ʿAlī ibn Mūsā al-Kāẓim, later known as the eighth *imām* of the Twelver Shiʿites, as his heir and gave him the title of *al-riḍā min āl Muḥammad* (the chosen one from the family of Muḥammad), from which his title ʿAlī al-Riḍā is derived.[31] The timing of this action is curious, because it is clear that it would only further offend the ʿAbbāsids. Again courting his family's anger, the caliph next replaced the traditional ʿAbbāsid color black with green. He gave one of his daughters in marriage to ʿAlī al-Riḍā and another to ʿAlī's son Muḥammad.

In response, a number of prominent ʿAbbāsids and *abnāʾ* leaders declared open rebellion against the caliph. On 28 Dhū al-Ḥijja 201/17 July 817 Ibrāhīm ibn al-Mahdī, another paternal uncle of al-Maʾmūn, was proclaimed caliph and adopted the regnal name of al-Mubārak.[32] Isḥāq ibn Mūsā al-Hādī, the anti-caliph's nephew as well as first cousin and brother-in-law of al-Maʾmūn, was designated his heir.[33] After this investiture, fighting broke out between al-Ḥasan ibn Sahl and the forces of Ibrāhīm ibn al-Mahdī, the anti-caliph. In Jumādā I 202/November 817 al-ʿAbbās, the governor of al-Kūfa, who was the brother of al-Maʾmūn's designated heir, ʿAlī al-Riḍā, was expelled from that city by the anti-caliph. ʿAlī al-Riḍā is reported to have informed al-Maʾmūn of the continuing war in Iraq between the forces of al-Ḥasan ibn Sahl and the anti-caliph, since his vizier al-Faḍl ibn Sahl had not represented the full gravity of the situation. It was at this time that al-Maʾmūn decided to leave Marw for Baghdad; he departed for the capital on 10 Rajab 202/22 January 818.

28. Initially, the ʿAbbāsids in Baghdad had asked him to assume greater authority, but al-Manṣūr refused, saying that he would only represent the caliph and no more.

29. On the *ʿayyārūn* (= lower classes) of Baghdad see Sabari 1981, esp. pp. 77 ff. *See Tor 2007.

30. Lapidus 1975. *A "Khurasanian connection" hypothesis revolving around these events has been suggested by Lapidus and empirically tested and rejected by Nawas (1996a), and Addendum to section 4.7.2. below; for Sahl ibn Salāma, see Cooperson 2000, Van Ess 1991–1997, 3:171–73, and Cook 2000, 104, 107.

31. *Al-Amīn 1995, Tor 2001, *EI3* s.n. "ʿAlī al-Riḍā" (Bayhom-Daou).

32. He received allegiance in the Great Mosque of Baghdad on 5 Muḥarram 202/24 July 817.

33. On this anti-caliphate, see Barbier de Meynard 1869. *For a biography of Ibrāhīm ibn al-Mahdī, see Fahd 2007.

Two important events occurred during the sixteen months it took al-Maʾmūn to arrive in Baghdad. On 2 Shaʿbān 202/13 February 818, the caliph's vizier al-Faḍl ibn Sahl was murdered at Sarakhs while taking a bath. It is unknown who ordered this assassination, but some reports indicate that it was al-Maʾmūn. Soon after al-Faḍl ibn Sahl's death, al-Maʾmūn wrote to al-Ḥasan ibn Sahl expressing his condolences over the murder of his brother. By writing to him, al-Maʾmūn was seeking the good will of the man who was then the commander-in-chief of the caliphal forces in the west, whose support he needed to unseat the anti-caliph and put an end to the ʿAbbāsid uprising. Despite the caliph's need for al-Ḥasan ibn Sahl, however, al-Faḍl ibn Sahl's death marked the end of Sahlid preeminence in the caliphal administration.[34] Shortly after his brother's death, al-Ḥasan ibn Sahl withdrew from the political arena, for unknown reasons.

Approximately seven months later, on 29 Ṣafar 203/5 September 818, ʿAlī al-Riḍā died; here, too, the cause of death remains uncertain.[35] ʿAlī al-Riḍā's disappearance from the political stage was timely in that it made possible a reconciliation with the dissident ʿAbbāsids and *abnāʾ* of Baghdad. Upon al-Maʾmūn's entrance to the capital on 11 Ṣafar 204/7 August 819, support for the anti-caliph Ibrāhīm ibn al-Mahdī melted away. Virtually the only resistance he encountered was the disapproval by the ʿAbbāsids and the bulk of the military of the replacement of ʿAbbāsid black by the color green. This objection was voiced by the military commander Ṭāhir ibn al-Ḥusayn, among others, leading al-Maʾmūn to revert to the traditional ʿAbbāsid black.

After his return to Baghdad in 204/819, al-Maʾmūn was confronted with an entirely new set of circumstances. The influence formerly held by the Sahlids was seized by the Ṭāhirids during this period. On account of their excellence as military leaders, the Ṭāhirids became increasingly influential within the caliphate. Toward the end of 205/820, Ṭāhir ibn al-Ḥusayn was made governor of Khurasan. In the following years the Ṭāhirids established themselves as an almost autonomous dynasty in this key province.[36] When Ṭāhir ibn al-Ḥusayn died in Jumādā II 207/October-November 822, he was succeeded by his son Ṭalḥa ibn Ṭāhir (d. 213/828–829 or 214/829). Another son of Ṭāhir ibn al-Ḥusayn, the very successful ʿAbdallāh ibn Ṭāhir who was greatly admired by al-Maʾmūn, was transferred to Khurasan after Ṭalḥa's death. Before leaving for the province, ʿAbdallāh appointed his cousin Isḥāq ibn Ibrāhīm to replace him as head of the *shurṭa* (security

34. Some eight years later (in Ramaḍān 210/December 825–January 826), the caliph consummated his marriage to al-Ḥasan ibn Sahl's daughter Būrān. Al-Ḥasan ibn Sahl died in 236/850–851.

35. *Al-Mamūn had ʿAlī al-Riḍā buried alongside his own father, Hārūn al-Rashīd; Nawas (1996b), using methods from psychohistory, suggests that this was no coincidence but the result of an unresolved Oedipus complex al-Maʾmūn may have acquired as he was passed over when his father appointed his younger brother al-Amīn, an ʿAbbāsid on both sides, as first heir to the caliphate.

36. On the Ṭāhirids, see Sourdel 1958, Bosworth 1969, 1970, and 1975 and Kaabi 1972. *See Abū l-ʿAlā 2005, 3–37.

forces, police) of Baghdad.[37] The Ṭāhirids played a pivotal role in suppressing the revolts of this period, including that of Naṣr ibn Shabath. By doing so they helped to buttress the authority of al-Maʾmūn's administration.

The first challenge facing al-Maʾmūn upon his return to Baghdad was a series of three major uprisings. For many years, Naṣr ibn Shabath had been agitating in Syria, where he had come to pose a threat to the central government in Baghdad. Taking advantage of the chaos brought about by the civil war, Naṣr began repeatedly raiding parts of northern Syria. Although Ṭāhir ibn al-Ḥusayn had been sent to al-Raqqa to quell the uprising in 199/813 at the beginning of al-Maʾmūn's reign, he had achieved very little. It was only after al-Maʾmūn came to Baghdad that Ṭāhir ibn al-Ḥusayn took decisive action against this uprising. After fighting that dragged on for almost a decade, Ṭāhir ibn al-Ḥusayn's son ʿAbdallāh was able to force Naṣr ibn Shabath to accept a truce in 209/824–25.

Immediately following this victory, al-Maʾmūn ordered ʿAbdallāh ibn Ṭāhir to end the mutiny of ʿUbaydallāh ibn al-Sarī ibn al-Ḥakam, who had been head of the security forces (*ṣāḥib al-shurṭa*) in Egypt since 205/820–821 and became governor of the province in Shaʿbān 206/January 822. After repeatedly resisting al-Maʾmūn's attempts to replace him as governor, he openly rebelled. Upon ʿAbdallāh's arrival in Egypt in 211/826, however, ʿUbaydallah negotiated his surrender and return to Iraq, while ʿAbdallāh became governor of Egypt in his stead.

The third major rebellion was that of Bābak in the eastern part of the empire.[38] This religiously inspired rebellion dated from about 201/816–817 and did not prove easy to quell. Al-Maʾmūn sent multiple expeditions to end the rebellion, including one led by Yaḥyā ibn Muʿādh[39] in 204/819–20 and another led by Muḥammad ibn Ḥumayd ibn al-Ṭūṣī[40] in 213/828. None of these expeditions succeeded, however, and the revolt was not crushed until many years later during the caliphate of al-Muʿtaṣim.

A second major focus of al-Maʾmūn's reign after his return to Baghdad concerned the relationship between religion and politics. During these final fourteen years of his reign, the caliph made four public statements about issues of religio-political significance. First, around 211/826 he had proclaimed that there was to be no protection for anyone who spoke favorably of the Umayyad caliph Muʿāwiya or granted him a status

37. Isḥāq ibn Ibrāhīm conducted the *miḥna* interrogations of 218/833 in Baghdad. He maintained his position as head of the *shurṭa* until his death in 235/850.

38. Bābak was a leader of the movement of the "Khurramiyya." The exact origin and teachings of this group are still unclear despite the existence of extensive relevant literature. For a survey of views on this matter, see *EI2*, s.n. "Khurramiyya" (Madelung); cf. also Rekaya 1974 and Wright 1948. *See Crone 2012, 40–42 and, especially for Bābak, 46–76.

39. This military leader had been in al-Maʾmūn's service since the Civil War.

40. Muḥammad ibn Ḥumayd was the son of the prominent military commander Ḥumayd ibn ʿAbd al-Ḥamīd who had fought the rebellious Baghdadis while serving under al-Ḥasan ibn Sahl in 201–203/816–819 and who had died in 210/825–826.

above the other Companions of the Prophet. Then, in Rabīʿ I 212/June 827, the caliph publicly declared the preeminence of ʿAlī ibn Abī Ṭālib (*tafḍīl ʿAlī*) by asserting that ʿAlī was the best of mankind after the Prophet. Simultaneously, he declared that the Qur'an was created by God. Six years later, he imposed the *miḥna*, aimed at forcing acquiescence in the doctrine of the createdness of the Qur'an. This fourth and final statement appeared only four months before his sudden death.

Toward the end of his reign, the caliph also undertook a reorganization of the army on a grand scale.[41] For reasons that remain obscure, in 213/828 he divided the army into three units. The leader of each unit was given authority over military matters in one region of the empire: the Ṭāhirid Isḥāq ibn Ibrāhīm, head of police and governor of Baghdad, was put in charge of Iraq, Jibāl and Fārs;[42] al-ʿAbbās, the son of al-Maʾmūn, was assigned the region encompassing the frontier with the Byzantine Empire (the border area between modern Turkey and Syria), the Jazīra and the rest of northern Syria; Abū Isḥāq, the brother of al-Maʾmūn who later became the caliph al-Muʿtaṣim, was put in charge of Egypt.

Despite this delegation of military authority, the caliph continued to lead campaigns himself. For example, in Muḥarram 217/February 832 he led an expedition to put down a major uprising of Muslims and Copts in Egypt which Abū Isḥāq had been unsuccessfully combating since 214/829. This campaign followed two others in 215/830 and 216/831 in which al-Maʾmūn had personally led troops into the Byzantine Empire from the region under the charge of al-ʿAbbās.

No sooner had al-Maʾmūn returned from Egypt than he found himself forced to move against the Byzantine Empire for the third time in the space of a couple of years. Indeed, the campaigns against the Byzantine Empire were a major preoccupation of the last years of al-Maʾmūn's reign. It was during this final campaign after his return from Egypt that al-Maʾmūn died near Tarsus in Rajab 218/August 833, reportedly because he had eaten spoiled dates. On his deathbed, al-Maʾmūn appointed as his successor his brother, Abū Isḥāq, henceforth to be known as al-Muʿtaṣim. In doing so he passed over his own sons, including the otherwise apparently trusted and competent al-ʿAbbās.[43]

---

41. On ʿAbbāsid military organization, see Hoenerbach (1950). *See Kennedy 2001 and Elad 2013.

42. Fārs was located between Khurasan and the Persian Gulf: Le Strange 1930, 248–99 and Yāqūt, *Muʿjam al-buldān*, 4:226–28.

43. After al-Maʾmūn's death there were at least two attempts to make al-ʿAbbās caliph, mainly by troops of the Byzantine frontier area. These failed, however, and al-ʿAbbās died in prison in 223/838. *See Nawas (2010), Turner (2013), *EI3* s.n. "al-ʿAbbās ibn al-Maʾmūn" (Turner).

CHAPTER 3
THE MUᶜTAZILISM, THE SHIᶜISM, AND THE ᶜALID HYPOTHESES

3.1. The Muᶜtazilism Hypothesis

The first theory I examine concerning al-Maʾmūn's motives is the Muᶜtazilism hypothesis. This view holds that it is al-Maʾmūn's affinities with the Muᶜtazilites or their ideas that led him to declare the doctrine of the createdness of the Qur'an and to introduce the *miḥna*. Scholars who take this position stress that he had strong and intimate ties with notable Muᶜtazilites and that he held certain important views which aligned with mainstream Muᶜtazilite thought. Inasmuch as the consensus on these points is broad and the variation in opinion quite narrow, I will rely principally on the works of Amīn (1933–36) and Watt (1973).

3.1.1. Patronage of Prominent Muᶜtazilites

The first point of convergence between the Muᶜtazilites and al-Maʾmūn mentioned in the literature is his patronage of many men noted for their interest in "rational theology" (*kalām*), of whom the Muᶜtazilites were the most prominent group at the time (Watt 1973, 145). Scholars repeatedly mention three influential Muᶜtazilite thinkers as having had a particular impact on the caliph: Abū al-Hudhayl al-ᶜAllāf, Thumāma ibn Ashras, and Aḥmad ibn Abī Duʾād.

Abū al-Hudhayl al-ᶜAllāf (d. 227/841 or 235/849)[1] belonged to the so-called Baṣra school of Muᶜtazilism, which interested itself more in theories than in the practical applications to which the Baghdadi school was inclined. Abū al-Hudhayl is notable for his diligence in adapting Greek philosophy to Islamic thought. He also questioned the valid-

1. *EI2*, s.n. Abū 'l-Hudhayl al-ᶜAllāf (Nyberg).

ity of astrology despite its widespread appeal. Abū al-Hudhayl, who came to be known as the *shaykh al-muʿtazila* (doyen of the Muʿtazilites) (Marwah 1978, 1:679), is said to have been a teacher (*ustādh*) of al-Maʾmūn, though it would perhaps be more accurate to describe him as a counselor and guide to the caliph in theological debates and disputations (Amīn 1933–36, 3:98).[2] His association with al-Maʾmūn dates to 202–3/818, the year Thumāma ibn Ashras introduced him to the caliph (Watt 1973, 219). Ibn al-Murtaḍā, a ninth/fifteenth-century writer who composed a biographical work on the Muʿtazilites, quotes verses reportedly recited by al-Maʾmūn in praise of Abū al-Hudhayl.[3] Less directly, Abū al-Hudhayl contributed to the intellectual development of two other distinguished Muʿtazilite thinkers, al-Naẓẓām (d. 231/845)[4] and al-Jāḥiẓ (d. 255/868–69),[5] who, although not part of al-Maʾmūn's entourage, were greatly admired by him. Al-Jāḥiẓ also enjoyed the caliph's patronage.

Thumāma ibn Ashras (d. 213/828)[6] is the second of the Muʿtazilites with whom al-Maʾmūn was associated.[7] He was a man of great learning who was especially noted for his wit and his unusual ability to articulate arguments. On two occasions separated by several years, al-Maʾmūn invited him to become his vizier (Sourdel 1959–60, 220–21 and 238). Although the offer was declined, Thumāma continued to enjoy the caliph's favor, and al-Maʾmūn is reported to have held him in higher esteem than he did his viziers. Al-Maʾmūn's regard for him is also evident from the fact that he was one of the two Muʿtazilite leaders asked to witness the 201/817 document in which al-Maʾmūn named ʿAlī al-Riḍā as his heir.[8]

2. Al-Dīnawarī, 396.

3. Ibn al-Murtaḍā, 49.

4. Al-Masʿūdī, *Murūj*, 4:227. Abū Isḥāq Ibrāhīm ibn Sayyār al-Naẓẓām (d. 231/845) is noted, among other things, for the severity of his criticism of the *muḥaddithūn* (traditionists) (Van Ess 1982, esp. 218–19) for their literalism, narrow-mindedness and insufficient use of their critical faculties. A thoroughgoing skeptic and an experimentalist at heart (he tested, for example, the tolerance of different species of animals for alcoholic drink), al-Naẓẓām was an outspoken opponent of what he considered superstition. His skepticism extended to the notion of *jinn*, even though they are mentioned in the Qur'an (Amīn 1933–36, 3:114). Al-Naẓẓām also dared to criticize the Companions of the Prophet (early supporters of Muḥammad from Mecca and Medina), according them no special status.

5. Abū ʿUthmān ʿAmr ibn Baḥr (d. 255/869), known as al-Jāḥiẓ (the goggle-eyed), was also critical of the *ahl al-ḥadīth* (traditionists); when they attacked his treatise on the createdness of the Qur'an as propagating a notion that had not been held by *al-salaf* (early distinguished Muslims), he challenged them to name a *salaf* who had said that the Book was uncreated. Al-Jāḥiẓ reportedly wrote books on the caliphate which pleased al-Maʾmūn (*Rasāʾil*, Editor's Introduction, p. 13). Al-Jāḥiẓ is also said to have started a Muʿtazilite sub-school of his own (Van Ess 1966).

6. Cf. Van Ess 1968, esp. 1–3.

7. Ibn Khallikān, 6:177; al-Shahrastānī, 71.

8. The other being Bishr ibn al-Muʿtamir (d. between 210–226/825–840), founder of the Baghdadi branch of Muʿtazilism (Watt 1973, 178).

The third Muʿtazilite who had intimate ties with al-Maʾmūn, Aḥmad ibn Abī Duʾād (d. 240/854), was reportedly a wealthy man of many talents. A judge and administrator at the caliphal court, he was also a profound thinker, noted poet, and an exceedingly generous man.[9] He was, according to Watt (1973, 223), a "primarily political figure... who was greatly honoured at the court of al-Maʾmūn." Patton (1897) sees Ibn Abī Duʾād as the primary force behind the *miḥna*. Amīn (1933–36, 3:159) agrees with this evaluation; he considers Ibn Abī Duʾād as "the greatest impetus behind the initiation of the *miḥna*." The eminent status accorded him by al-Maʾmūn is attested to by the fact that the caliph asked in his will that al-Muʿtaṣim take to heart Ibn Abī Duʾād's counsel—a recommendation with which al-Muʿtaṣim complied, as did the caliph al-Wāthiq after him.[10] It is apparent from the above that the caliph had close ties to a number of leading Muʿtazilite thinkers.[11]

Such relationships, however, do not necessarily translate into adherence to Muʿtazilite ideology. The caliph was also close to many men who were not Muʿtazilites or were even anti-Muʿtazilite. For example, he prayed over the corpse of Bishr al-Marīsī,[12] thought to have been a follower of Ḍirār ibn ʿAmr, whom the Muʿtazilites considered an opponent (Van Ess 1967–68, 30 ff.). Another example is Yaḥyā ibn Aktham,[13] a foe of the Muʿtazilites whose counsel al-Maʾmūn valued.[14] The caliph appointed him chief judge and permitted him to continue in that post during the *miḥna*, despite Yaḥyā's sympathy for the views of those interrogated.

---

9. See *EI2*, s.n. Aḥmad b. Abī Duʾād (Zetterstéen-Pellat). *See also *EI3*, s.n. Aḥmad b. Abī Duʾād (Turner).

10. Al-Ṭabarī, iii:1139. Also recorded in Ibn Khallikān's account of the life of Ibn Abī Duʾād, 1:84. The statement is omitted in Ibn al-Athīr's summary of the testament (5:226–27), as well as in Ibn al-ʿImād's heavily edited version (2:43). *See *EI3* s.n. "Aḥmad ibn Abī Duʾād" (Turner). Van Ess intriguingly suggests that the will of al-Maʾmūn may have been a forgery, perhaps orchestrated by Ibn Abī Duʾād himself (Van Ess 1991–1997, 3:487–89). Important documents, especially wills, of the first ʿAbbasid caliphs up through al-Mutawakkil are collected in al-Ḥadīthī (2002), who also annotates and analyzes them.

11. For the Muʿtazilite al-Fuwaṭī (d. before 218/833), who is also reported to have enjoyed the caliph's high regard, see Ibn al-Murtaḍā, 61.

12. *Kitāb al-ʿuyūn*, 380.

13. Yaḥyā ibn Aktham (159/775–242/857) was born in Marw. He was introduced to al-Maʾmūn when the latter arrived in Khurasan. After serving as judge of al-Baṣra, he became chief judge (*qāḍī al-quḍāt*) of Baghdad. He was reportedly very close to al-Maʾmūn and advised the caliph on many occasions. Yaḥyā ibn Aktham lost his position when al-Muʿtaṣim became caliph (he was replaced by Ibn Abī Duʾād), but he was reinstated after al-Mutawakkil came to power. He likely did not believe in the doctrine of the createdness of the Qur'an and was supportive of the traditionists (cf. Ibn Khallikān, 1:84 and 6:147–65).

14. This esteem is reflected in two episodes. In one, Yaḥyā ibn Aktham dissuades al-Maʾmūn from cursing Muʿāwiya by warning of the hazards of arousing passions needlessly (Ibn Abī Ṭāhir Ṭayfūr, 91–92; cf. Nagel 1975, 150). On another occasion, he was able to persuade the caliph not to sanction *mutʿa* marriage (al-Khaṭīb al-Baghdādī, 14:199–200).

3.1.2. *Muʿtazilite Ideology*

A second argument for the Muʿtazilism hypothesis links al-Maʾmūn to Muʿtazilism on grounds of shared convictions and is somewhat more credible than that based on personal contacts, but it is also circumstantial. A number of sources describe the caliph as a Muʿtazilite. The heresiographer al-Baghdādī (d. 429/1037) states that al-Maʾmūn was enticed to Muʿtazilism by Thumāma ibn Ashras.[15] Similarly, the Ḥanbalite compiler Ibn al-ʿImād (d. 1089/1679) explicitly states that al-Maʾmūn was a Muʿtazilite.[16] According to a list in Ibn al-Murtaḍā's (d. 840/1437) *Ṭabaqāt al-muʿtazila*, al-Maʾmūn is counted among the caliphs who held Muʿtazilite views. Indeed, this work reports that the caliph boasted that none of his ʿAbbāsid predecessors held the Jabrite position that God determines human actions,[17] which challenges the Muʿtazilite emphasis on indeterminism. The chroniclers, especially later ones, appear too keen to assign a label to al-Maʾmūn's thought and, in some cases, at least their purpose may have been polemical.

A number of earlier sources give somewhat more nuanced portrayals of al-Maʾmūn's beliefs. Al-Masʿūdī (d. 345/956) states that after al-Maʾmūn came from Khurasan to Baghdad, he professed divine unity (*al-tawḥīd*) as well as the promise and the threat (*al-waʿd wa-l-waʿīd*), both Muʿtazilite principles, as we have seen.[18] Al-Yaʿqūbī (d. 284/897) reports that, while in Damascus in 218/833, the caliph commenced interrogating people about the Muʿtazilite principles of "unity and justice"[19] and related issues.[20] In his letters ordering the *miḥna*, al-Maʾmūn stresses the absolute unity of God, from which he deduces the createdness of the Qur'an, among other things.[21] The same theme is repeated in his testament.[22]

15. Al-Baghdādī, 103.

16. lbn al-ʿImād, 2:39.

17. Ibn al-Murtaḍā, 122 and 127. *The Jabriyya, literally "compulsionists," refers to a theological current that denied free will and attributed everything to divine will. The oppositie current was known as the Qadariyya.

18. Al-Masʿūdī, *Murūj*, 4:227. An interesting detail of al-Masʿūdī's account of al-Maʾmūn's intellectual orientation is his report that the caliph was interested in the works of the Sassanian rulers, in ancient books and in astrology. He reports that the caliph acquired this interest under the influence of al-Faḍl ibn Sahl. After al-Maʾmūn moved from Khurasan to Baghdad following the death of his vizier, he abandoned these subjects in favor of Muʿtazilite teachings and held court debates with speculative theologians (*mutakallimūn*). This report is conveyed also by al-Yaʿqūbī in his essay on Islamic history, *Mushākalat al-nās li-zamānihim*, 27–28.

19. Al-Yaʿqūbī, *Tārīkh*, 2:467–68.

20. According to Miskawayh (p. 465), the topics of interrogation included the createdness of the Qur'an and anthropomorphism. In Muʿtazilite theology, both anthropomorphism (*tashbīh*) and the view that the Qur'an is uncreated are incompatible with the absolute unity of God.

21. Ibn Abī Ṭāhir Ṭayfūr, 338–43 and 344–46; al-Ṭabarī, iii:1113–15 and iii:1118, 1126 and 1130.

22. Al-Ṭabarī, iii:1136.

One of our earliest sources, the *Kitāb Baghdād* of Ibn Abī Ṭāhir Ṭayfūr (d. 280/893), provides the most detail on al-Maʾmūn's theological positions. This work casts doubt on al-Maʾmūn's supposed Muʿtazilism. Ibn Abī Ṭāhir Ṭayfūr reports that Thumāma ibn Ashras, the Muʿtazilite intimate of the caliph, stated that al-Maʾmūn had abandoned the Qadarite belief in indeterminism[23] which is central to Muʿtazilite thinking.[24] That this statement was reportedly made by a prominent Muʿtazilite thinker adds weight to the idea that al-Maʾmūn's views were opposed to those of the Muʿtazilites. Additionally, Ibn Abī Ṭāhir Ṭayfūr reports on two different occasions that al-Maʾmūn considered himself a Murjiʾite,[25] an affiliation incompatible with Muʿtazilism.[26]

In short, the available information gives us no certain grounds to conclude that al-Maʾmūn was a Muʿtazilite.[27] He associated with Muʿtazilites, but also with others. And while al-Maʾmūn and the Muʿtazilites had some views in common, he was by no means

23. Ibn Abī Ṭāhir Ṭayfūr, 66.

24. See the introduction by S. Diwald-Wilzer to the *Ṭabaqāt al-muʿtazila*, p. v-vii, for the intimate connection between the two.

25. Ibn Abī Ṭāhir Ṭayfūr, 82 and 86. Interpreted similarly by Van Ess (1967–68, 34). While the first of these statements (on p. 82) is clear, I question Van Ess's interpretation of the second statement. The text is as follows: "One of the companions of al-Maʾmūn informed me: I heard Ibrāhīm ibn Rashīd say: I was informed by someone who had heard al-Maʾmūn say: *al-Irjāʾ* [i.e., the creed of the *murjiʾa*] is the religion of kings (*dīn al-mulūk*)." It is doubtful that al-Maʾmūn would refer to himself as a "*malik*" (king, pl. *mulūk*). The use of this word was generally restricted to pro-ʿAbbāsid writers referring to the Umayyads, who were considered to have followed irreligious policies and were hence equivalent to secular "*mulūk*." As such, a "*malik*" was the opposite of a true *imām* in al-Maʾmūn's thought, as I discuss below. Nonetheless, the first of the two statements—in which al-Maʾmūn himself declares that he is of the Murjiʾites—is straightforward enough to justify the conclusion that al-Maʾmūn did espouse Murjiʾite views. *Geert-Jan van Gelder has suggested that *mulūk* simply referred to "the elite" and should not be taken literally (personal communication March 29, 1993).

26. A clear example of the clash of views between the Murjiʾites and the Muʿtazilites concerns the principle of "the promise and the threat," which the latter group used in attacking the Murjiʾites. Believing in determinism ("predestination"), the Murjiʾites were of the opinion that even a grave sinner could still go to Paradise. The Muʿtazilites, on the other hand, believed in indeterminism, and thus held that people would be punished or rewarded in accordance with the life they chose to lead (Madelung 1965, 11).

27. Cf. Van Ess 1967–68. In this article, he argues that al-Maʾmūn was a "Ḍirārit" (p. 34), a follower of Ḍirār ibn ʿAmr, a *mutakallim* (rational theologian) with whom the Muʿtazilites were at odds due to the fact that he allowed God some control over the deeds of men. While I agree with Van Ess's conclusion that al-Maʾmūn cannot be counted within the ranks of the Muʿtazilites, I disagree with his labeling the caliph a Ḍirārite. Al-Maʾmūn cannot be unreservedly classified as a Ḍirārite because the two men disagreed strongly on an issue of vital importance to the caliph, namely, leadership of the Islamic Community. Ḍirār ibn ʿAmr, was of the opinion that not only non-Qurashites but also non-Arabs could in principle become caliph. Al-Maʾmūn held the firm view that the leader of the Community had to be at least a member of the Family of the Prophet.

so thoroughly Muʿtazilite as some scholars have suggested.[28] At best, al-Maʾmūn's views were eclectic.

Most likely, the tendency to depict al-Maʾmūn as a Muʿtazilite is due to his public declaration of the createdness of the Qur'an, a doctrine held by the Muʿtazilites, even if its alleged originator, al-Jaʿd ibn Dirham, may or may not have been a Muʿtazilite himself. This tendency was further strengthened by al-Maʾmūn's enforcement of the doctrine through the *miḥna*; together, these acts left an indelible imprint upon posterity. The depiction of al-Maʾmūn as a Muʿtazilite also owes much to the writings of several late Sunnite chroniclers from the sixth/twelfth to the eighth/fourteenth centuries who, looking back at events in the distant past, sought to reconcile what they considered al-Maʾmūn's errors with their otherwise positive image of him. The Muʿtazilites had lost their political power after al-Mutawakkil abandoned the *miḥna*, and their rationalist orientation had subsequently been found repellant by generations of traditionists. They therefore may have served as a convenient vehicle and scapegoat for harmonizing later writers' conflicting views on al-Maʾmūn.

Ibn al-Jawzī (d. 597/1200), for instance, dwelling on the caliph's hesitancy to speak publicly of the doctrine and the *miḥna* order, concludes that the caliph only professed the doctrine of the createdness of the Qur'an under the sway of the Muʿtazilites.[29] Al-Ṣafadī (d. 764/1363), noting the caliph's learning in the sciences and philosophy—an interest which the Muʿtazilites fully shared—adopts the position that it was this sophistication which had attracted al-Maʾmūn to the doctrine of the createdness of the Qur'an. Ibn al-Taghrībirdī (d. 874/1470) concurs.[30] In a different formulation, al-Subkī (d. 771/1370) blames the shallowness of al-Maʾmūn's knowledge in the sciences and philosophy for his adoption of the doctrine.[31]

The views of these chroniclers and of many others who preceded and followed them emphasize the convergence of views between al-Maʾmūn and the Muʿtazilites on the doctrine of the createdness of the Qur'an. Such a congruence of views, however, does not make al-Maʾmūn a Muʿtazilite, especially since this doctrine was by no means restricted to the Muʿtazilites at the time. It was shared by others,[32] including many Ḥanafites.[33] In fact, in his letters on the *miḥna* al-Maʾmūn adduced not only arguments current among

28. For instance, Laoust (1965), who holds that al-Maʾmūn's reign initiates what he calls "le califat muʿtazilite." In addition to Amīn and Watt, scholars who label al-Maʾmūn a Muʿtazilite include Hitti (1968, 89), Shaban (1976, 54) and Sourdel (1962, 43).

29. Ibn al-Jawzī, 309. Al-Maʾmūn's hesitancy is noted also by al-Dhahabī (d. 748/1348, *Tarjamat*, 40). *Cf. *Tārīkh al-islām*, for the full biography.

30. Al-Ṣafadī, 17:655; Ibn Taghrībirdī, 2:225.

31. Al-Subkī, 2:56–57.

32. For variants of the doctrine held by non-Muʿtazilite *mutakallimūn*, see Van Ess (1967; translated into French, Van Ess 1990).

33. Madelung (1974, 509), Van Ess (1967–68, 51) and Watt (1973, 283–84). I argue below that al-Maʾmūn

the Muʿtazilites,[34] but also an argument from the teachings of the school of Abū Ḥanīfa,[35] then dominant in Iraq and a school in which the caliph was well-versed.[36] In more than one letter al-Maʾmūn adduced Abū Ḥanīfa's argument that the Qur'an must be created, because all things other than God are by definition created.[37] This argument is different from the Muʿtazilite claim.[38] The Muʿtazilite doctrine of the created Qur'an is grounded in their beliefs about the nature of God, while the Ḥanafite position is a claim about the status of objects. Al-Maʾmūn also interpreted Qur'anic verses syllogistically to affirm that the Qur'an was an object which was "made" (*jaʿala*) and therefore created by God (e.g., Q Zukhruf 43:3 *innā jaʿalnāhu qurʾān*[an] *ʿarabiyy*[an], "we have made it an Arabic Qur'an/ recitation"). The evidence in the primary sources for an exclusive connection between the Muʿtazilites and al-Maʾmūn's declaration of the *miḥna* is thus lacking.[39] This lack of evidence does not prove that Muʿtazilism made no contribution at all to al-Maʾmūn's profession of the doctrine of the createdness of the Qur'an or his declaration of the *miḥna*; rather, it simply suggests that Muʿtazilism is not a sufficient explanation for al-Maʾmūn's actions, and that we must look elsewhere for his motives.

3.2. The Shiʿism Hypothesis

The second theory proposed by modern scholars holds that al-Maʾmūn's affinities with Shiʿism or the ʿAlids motivated his declaration of the doctrine of the createdness of the

---

did not construe the dogma of the createdness of the Qur'an as an issue of doctrinal significance that had to be accepted for its own sake.

34. The Muʿtazilites and al-Maʾmūn took the position that those who do not profess a created Qur'an are putting an object (the Qur'an) on par with God and hence allowing an object to share in an attribute which belongs to God alone (namely, His eternity), thus violating the idea of God's absolute unity (Madelung 1974, 516–17).

35. The prominent jurist and theologian Abū Ḥanīfa lived from 80/699 till 150/767.

36. According to Ibn al-Taghrībirdī (2:225) al-Maʾmūn "had distinguished himself (*baraʿa*) in *fiqh* (law) according to the school of Abū Ḥanīfa."

37. Al-Ṭabarī, iii:1113–14 and 1118. See also below, section 4.6.

38. On Abū Ḥanīfa's argument for the createdness of the Qur'an and the differences between his argument and the Muʿtazilite stance, see Madelung (1974, esp. 511).

39. Patton (1897, 55) thinks differently. He cites the very late Sunnite writer al-Subkī (2:38), who alleges that Aḥmad ibn Abī Duʾād had encouraged the caliph to introduce the *miḥna* in 218/833. Nowhere could I find evidence to corroborate al-Subkī's narrative. The evidence is also contrary to Amīn's (1933–36, 3:159) undocumented claim that Ibn Abī Duʾād was the "greatest impetus behind the *miḥna*" (*akbar sabab fī hādhihi l-miḥna*), since Aḥmad ibn Abī Duʾād only became prominent under al-Muʿtaṣim and his successor. Cf. Van Ess (1967–68, 35 ff.), who presents evidence that the Ḍirārite Bishr al-Marīsī was possibly "der geistige Kopf der frühen Inquisition" ("the spiritual leader of the early inquisition").

Qur'an and his introduction of the *miḥna*. ʿAlid and Shiʿite are often used interchangeably but, as will be clear below, maintaining a distinction is crucial.[40]

3.2.1. The Shiʿites

Sourdel (1962) has identified three issues which he believes indicate a close affinity between the views of the caliph and mainstream Shiʿite views: *mutʿa* marriage, a temporary form of marriage that may be contracted for pleasure or convenience ;[41] the *takbīr* ritual, that is, uttering the formula "God is great" (*Allāh*[u] *akbar*); and the imāmate. First, Sourdel (1962, 41) argues that al-Maʾmūn's contemplation of a decree permitting *mutʿa* marriage signifies Shiʿite inclinations. However, this argument assumes that *mutʿa* was an exclusively and consistently Shiʿite institution. In reality, attitudes toward *mutʿa* were complex; some Shiʿite groups opposed it, while at times some Sunnite groups sanctioned it.[42] In light of this information, the caliph's stance on *mutʿa* tells us very little. Heffening (*EI2* s.v. "*mutʿa*") supports Sourdel's interpretation. After presenting the differing views on *mutʿa* during the first two centuries of Islamic history, he states in effect that al-Maʾmūn's stance on *mutʿa* can "certainly" be construed as reflecting "his Shīʿī sympathies," since by that time *mutʿa* had come to be firmly associated with them. But al-Khaṭīb al-Baghdādī[43]—a source used by Sourdel—reports that the caliph abandoned his plan of permitting *mutʿa* upon learning from Yaḥyā ibn Aktham that ʿAlī ibn Abī Ṭālib was opposed to it. Thus, one might argue that the caliph's "contemplation" of permission for *mutʿa* reflects not so much a Shiʿite leaning as reverence for ʿAlī ibn Abī Ṭālib.

Second, Sourdel interprets two episodes related to *takbīr* reported by the chroniclers as an indication of al-Maʾmūn's Shiʿite leanings. In the year 216/832, al-Maʾmūn ordered his governor in Baghdad to instruct the troops to pronounce three additional *takbīr*s after their daily prayers.[44] Sourdel (1962, 41–42) views this supplementary *takbīr* as a Shiʿite practice. He bases his interpretation on a report by the Fāṭimid legal expert al-Qāḍī al-Nuʿmān stating that three *takbīrs* after the final *taslīm*[45] were recommended by Jaʿfar al-Ṣādiq, the sixth Shiʿite *imām*.[46] This report also tells us, however, that the three *takbīrs* constituted only part of Jaʿfar's elaborate formula for ending the prayer, which was to be repeated ten times in its entirety. There is no mention of this extended formula in al-

40. Notably, indiscriminate use of these terms may lead one to automatically read into al-Maʾmūn's pro-ʿAlid policy partiality to Shiʿism.

41. *Sourdel's classic article has now been translated into English (Kohlberg 2003).

42. *EI2* s.v. "*mutʿa*" (Heffening). A number of Zaydites, for instance, did not permit *mutʿa*.

43. Al-Khaṭīb al-Baghdādī, 14:199–200.

44. Al-Ṭabarī, iii:1105; al-Azdī, 405 and Ibn al-Athīr 5:220. *On this episode, see Aerts 2014.

45. The salutation which ends the usual prayer.

46. *Daʿāʾim al-Islām*, 1:205. *English translation: Poonawala 2002, 2004.

Maʾmūn's order. Moreover, according to several representative Shiʿite texts, the number of *takbīrs* after the *taslīm* was not fixed and could range from one to seven.[47] Without evidence to the contrary, it is safer to accept the more cautious interpretation that the caliph's command was simply intended to arouse religious zeal among the troops on the eve of a great campaign, not to proselytize on behalf of the Shiʿites.[48]

The second episode related to *takbīr* concerns the funeral ritual. Sourdel (1962, 45) writes that al-Maʾmūn requested in his will that five *takbīrs*, a hallmark of the Shiʿites,[49] be said at his funeral.[50]

Third, Sourdel (1965, 43–44) argues that al-Maʾmūn ascribed to the caliph qualities which the Shiʿites associate with the *imām*, the leader of the Community. Sourdel is correct in making this observation. Such an ascription is evident throughout al-Maʾmūn's reign, especially in the preambles to the first and third letters of the *miḥna* (discussed in section 4.4.). Nagel and Watt generally agree, but with important nuances. Nagel (1975, 386 ff.) finds al-Maʾmūn's conception of the caliphate closest to the Zaydite theory of the imāmate, especially in its emphasis on "personal merit" as a criterion for selecting the caliph; Watt (1973, 177–79) sees it as reflecting a Shiʿite vision, and further speculates that al-Maʾmūn's theory of the caliphate is linked to the doctrine of the createdness of the Qur'an. He argues that there is a great difference between the "prestige" of a created and an uncreated Qur'an. One cannot tamper with an uncreated Qur'an, since that would be equivalent to tampering with God Himself. However, "a created Qurʾān had not the same prestige [as an uncreated one], and there could not be the same objection to its provisions being overruled by the decree of an inspired *imām*" (p. 179).[51] Hinds (*EI2* s.v. "*miḥna*") disagrees and takes issue with Watt largely on theological grounds. He states that Watt's argument fails to recognize that the doctrine of the createdness of the Qur'an

47. Al-Kulaynī, *al-Kāfī*, 3:310, nos. 3 and 7; al-Sharīf al-Murtaḍā, *al-Intiṣār*, 40. My thanks to Etan Kohlberg who was kind enough to help me on this matter. *See Van Ess, *TG*, who in a postscript (4:758) retracts his original argument and concurs with the above.

48. I am indebted to Gual Juynboll for suggesting this interpretation of the episode. Perhaps al-Maʾmūn was preparing his troops for the impending attack on the Byzantines. Lapidus (1975, 378) interprets this order as a measure taken by al-Maʾmūn to enhance the religious authority of the caliph: see 4.1 below.

49. The Shiʿites derived the prescribed five *takbīrs* from their belief that Seth had prayed over Adam five times (Kohlberg 1980, 62–63). The Sunnite schools of law reject this account, and their prescription calls for four *takbīrs*. For the standard Sunnite version see Grütter 1954 and 1957, especially part V ("Das Gebet über dem Toten"; 1957:87 ff.). *See Halevi 2007.

50. Al-Ṭabarī, iii:1136. Cf. Van Ess 1961, 94 = 1990, 177.

51. If we are to understand from this that by declaring the Qur'an created al-Maʾmūn (who claimed for himself superhuman qualities) was of a Shiʿite coloring, such a conclusion overreaches the facts. There is no record to be found in which al-Maʾmūn places himself above the Book or questions the Qur'an—or the Prophet's Hadith for that matter—and all the Qur'anic verses which he cites in his *miḥna* letters are interpreted by him with impeccable logic and fidelity to the text.

is not about the Qur'an as such, but about the nature of God, or more properly, God's Unity.

Proponents of the Shiʿism hypothesis point out that al-Maʾmūn employed the title "*imām*," a term which the Shiʿites preferred over that of "caliph." Several modern scholars claim that al-Maʾmūn was the first caliph to use "*imām*" as his official title (Sourdel 1962, 37; Watt 1973, 177 and ʿUmar 1977, 222). In at least three formal documents he uses the terms caliph and *imām* interchangeably. They include the *Risālat al-Khamīs* of ca. 198/813–14,[52] the proclamation of ʿAlī's designation as heir in 201/817,[53] and the document which initiated the *miḥna*.[54] Three poems also refer to al-Maʾmūn as the *Imām*.[55] However, he was neither the only nor the first ʿAbbāsid caliph officially to use the title of *imām*.[56] Arazi and Elad[57] provide a long list of references in major historical sources (including al-Ṭabarī, al-Jahshiyārī, al-Azdī and al-Yaʿqūbī) showing that al-Maʾmūn's ʿAbbāsid predecessors referred to themselves as "*imāms*" both officially and informally. A coin issued in the year 193/808–809 with the inscription "*al-imām Muḥammad* [al-Amīn]" has also been discovered.[58]

Another argument made by the proponents of this hypothesis is that the createdness of the Qur'an was accepted by mainstream Shiʿites (Amīn 1933–36, 3:267; Watt 1950) and more specifically by the Zaydites (ʿĀrif 1987, 182–86), whom Sourdel (1962) and Nagel (1975) see as having been particularly closely associated with al-Maʾmūn. According to Madelung's (1965) thorough analysis of the ideologies of representative Shiʿite theologians, however, at the time of al-Maʾmūn most groups followed the teachings of Jaʿfar al-Ṣādiq, who held that the Qur'an was uncreated. Aḥmad ibn Ḥanbal even later cited Jaʿfar's view during the *miḥna* in his defense against his interrogators.[59]

---

52. Ṣafwat, 3:377–97.

53. Al-Irbilī, 3:123 ff.

54. Al-Ṭabarī, iii:1112 ff.; Ibn Abī Ṭāhir Ṭayfūr, 338 ff.

55. The first, reported by al-Iṣfahānī (*al-Aghānī*, 20:266), was composed for al-Maʾmūn at the request of Zubayda, al-Amīn's mother, at a time coinciding with the caliph's entry into Baghdad in 204/819. Al-Ṣafadī (659–60) quotes verses from three love poems attributed to al-Maʾmūn, wherein the caliph refers to himself as *imām*. In the third poem al-Maʾmūn is referred to as "the seventh *imām*", i.e., the seventh ʿAbbāsid caliph (Ibn Abī Ṭāhir Ṭayfūr, 204; al-Ṭabarī, iii:1080; al-Azdī, 371).

56. That al-Maʾmūn was the first to use the title is claimed by al-Dūrī (1945, 153, n. 5), Sourdel (1962, 37), Watt (1973, 177), and ʿUmar (1977, 222).

57. 1988, 47–48, n. 155.

58. Miles (1938, 90). Al-Maʾmūn also used the title of *imām* on a number of his coins, some of which date back to 203/818–819 (Miles 1938, 105). *See El-Hibri 1993 and Shammā 1995.

59. Madelung's analysis is part of an exhaustive study of the relationship between the views of the Shiʿites, especially the Zaydites, and the Muʿtazilites. In this (pp. 153 ff.) as well as later works, Madelung (1970, 1989a, 1989b) presents much evidence to indicate that it was only during the period that *followed* al-Maʾmūn's death that the Shiʿites/Zaydites incorporated into their systems Muʿtazilite ideas, presumably including the doctrine that the Qur'an was created.

Yet, scholars who stress the Shiʿite/Zaydite hypothesis might have argued their case on more substantive grounds: namely, the issue of the caliph's authority. This question touches the core of the caliphal institution and is one in which all groups had a stake. The Shiʿites, the Zaydites included, held that the *imām* was entitled to unquestioned authority in matters both spiritual and worldly. The title of *khalīfat Allāh*, which al-Maʾmūn asserted as his birthright (see section 4.3.) and had struck on coins,[60] also asserted this all-encompassing authority. On this core issue of the limitless authority of the leader of the Community, whether called caliph or *imām*, al-Maʾmūn and the Shiʿites agreed. That said, the primary sources do not, however, support the view that the caliph's declaration of the doctrine of the createdness of the Qur'an or his institution of the *miḥna* were directly motivated by Shiʿite leanings, either political or religious. Had deference to Shiʿite views been his motivation, the caliph would have declared the Qur'an uncreated, since that in fact appears to have been the prevailing view among mainstream Shiʿites at the time. Hence, a Shiʿite "connection" does not serve as a satisfactory explanation of the caliph's actions.

3.3. The ʿAlid Hypothesis

If the bond between al-Maʾmūn and the Shiʿites is based upon a partial convergence of views, the bond between the caliph and the ʿAlids had manifold and deep roots. Below I consider three pieces of evidence demonstrating al-Maʾmūn's ʿAlid leanings: the fact that al-Maʾmūn held ʿAlī ibn Abī Ṭālib in the highest esteem; the fact that he was manifestly partial to ʿAlī's progeny; and the fact that he sought to designate an ʿAlid as his successor.

Perhaps the clearest indication of al-Maʾmūn's reverence for ʿAlī ibn Abī Ṭālib was his public declaration in 212/827 that ʿAlī was the best of mankind after the Prophet, echoing a common Shiʿite claim.[61] This declaration reaffirmed al-Maʾmūn's argument from more than a decade earlier that the preeminence of ʿAlī (*tafḍīl ʿAlī*) did not necessarily entail a demeaning of other early Muslims (*al-salaf*).[62]

About the same time as his public declaration of the preeminence of ʿAlī, the caliph proclaimed that anyone who spoke favorably of Muʿāwiya did so at his own peril.[63] Most

60. Crone and Hinds (1986, 94–96) emphasize al-Maʾmūn's use of the title *khalīfat Allāh*. Miles (1938, 103–7) identifies coins on which al-Maʾmūn is referred to by that title.

61. Al-Ṭabarī, iii:1099; al-Azdī, 373; Miskawayh, 463; *Kitāb al-ʿuyūn*, 370.

62. A discussion of this issue took place around 204/819 (Ibn Abī Ṭāhir Ṭayfūr, 75–79). The later chronicler al-Suyūṭī (247) preserves a report that al-Maʾmūn considered ʿAlī preeminent over the first two caliphs, Abū Bakr and ʿUmar. Other later chroniclers (Ibn al-Athīr, 5:216, Ibn Taghrībirdī, 2:201–3, Ibn al-ʿImād, 2:25 and al-Ṣafadī, 658–59) only mention the preeminence of ʿAlī.

63. Al-Ṭabarī, iii:1098, Ibn al-Athīr, 5:215, al-Suyūṭī, 247, and Ibn al-ʿImād, 2:25 record this event as occurring in the year 211/826–827. Others date it a year later (al-Masʿūdī, *Murūj*, 3:454–55; al-Maqdisī, 112; Miskawayh, 463; and *Kitāb al-ʿuyūn*, 370—which closely resembles Miskawayh's account). Al-Ṣafadī,

Shiᶜites had a distaste for Muᶜāwiya, whom they considered to have usurped the caliphate from ᶜAlī and his progeny. The Zaydites shared this general opinion without, however, going as far as their fellow-Shiᶜite groups in denouncing as illegitimate the caliphates of the three men who preceded ᶜAlī. Scholars, including Sourdel (1962) and Nagel (1975), note that al-Maʾmūn was in agreement with the Zaydites, who justified their position first on the grounds that ᶜAlī himself accepted the caliphates of his predecessors and, second, by arguing that it is legitimate to accept an *imām* who is "inferior" (*mafḍūl*), even when someone of greater excellence (*afḍal*) is available.[64] Al-Masᶜūdī, himself probably of Shiᶜite leanings, is the only chronicler who gives an explanation for al-Maʾmūn's decision. In the course of a rather intricate story he implies that al-Maʾmūn took offense because Muᶜāwiya had omitted to mention ᶜAlī ibn Abī Ṭālib when speaking of the first caliphs, as if he had never existed.[65]

Nowhere have I found evidence against al-Maʾmūn's favorable stance toward ᶜAlī ibn Abī Ṭālib. Ibn Abī Ṭāhir Ṭayfūr[66] even preserves a report that al-Maʾmūn gave ᶜAlī ibn Abī Ṭālib precedence (*qaddama*) over his own ancestor al-ᶜAbbās; the chronicler notes that it is a "remarkable report" (*khabar ᶜajīb*). Considering, however, the degree to which al-Maʾmūn was committed to the whole of the Hāshimite family, rather than to any one branch of it (see below), the report may not be as peculiar as it sounds. Other narratives encountered in a number of Shiᶜite writings include a report in Ibn Bābawayh that al-Maʾmūn ascribed healing powers to ᶜAlī and his descendants.[67]

The second piece of evidence is that the progeny of ᶜAlī enjoyed the caliph's favor: he consistently spoke of the ᶜAlids as his family. On his way to Baghdad from Khurasan, for example, al-Maʾmūn told a number of ᶜAlids that they and the ᶜAbbāsids were one

---

17:658, dating the event to 212/827–28, adds that people were warned against beseeching God to grant Muᶜāwiya mercy. There is evidence that al-Maʾmūn conceived of this "cursing of Muᶜāwiya" before he actually issued the warning (Ibn Abī Ṭāhir Ṭayfūr, 91–92; Ibn al-Murtaḍā, 64–65).

64. ᶜĀrif (1987, 326) and Amīn (1933–36, 275). While some Zaydite groups had qualms about this doctrine, the sect's eponym (Zayd, the great-grandson of ᶜAlī ibn Abī Ṭālib) did not disapprove of Abū Bakr's caliphate, even though he did emphatically consider ᶜAlī to have been "*al-afḍal*" (the most excellent) (ᶜĀrif 1987, 341).

65. Al-Masᶜūdī, *Murūj*, 3:454–55. This naturally corresponds with the official Umayyad version of events.

66. Ibn Abī Ṭāhir Ṭayfūr, 16–17.

67. Ibn Bābawayh, 2:145. Other examples include Al-Yaᶜqūbī, *Tārīkh*, 2:454, in which al-Maʾmūn declares that he wedded his daughter to the descendant of ᶜAlī ibn Mūsā al-Riḍā because the caliph longed to be the grandfather of a child from the lineage of ᶜAlī ibn Abī Ṭālib (the couple remained childless). Al-Iṣfahānī, another Shiᶜite, narrates a dream in the *Kitāb al-aghānī* (10:133) which Ibrāhīm ibn al-Mahdī is said to have had about ᶜAlī leading al-Maʾmūn to make a highly disparaging remark to Ibrāhīm ibn al-Mahdī (al-Maʾmūn's uncle). This "dream story" is repeated in al-Ṣafadī (17:660–61), who supplies an additional anecdote in which al-Maʾmūn decides against legalizing *mutᶜa* upon hearing that ᶜAlī ibn Abī Ṭālib did not approve of it (al-Ṣafadī, 17:659).

and the same.[68] On another occasion, he explicitly identified himself with them.[69] The caliph's favoritism found expression in other ways as well. He appointed ʿAlids to lead the pilgrimage;[70] he prayed over the bodies of deceased ʿAlids,[71] including Muḥammad ibn Jaʿfar, who had previously led an uprising against him;[72] and, in 210/825–826, he restored their ownership of Fadak, a disputed property in the Ḥijāz.[73] This favoritism extended until the end of his life, as Sourdel (1962) and others have noted.[74] In his testament, al-Maʾmūn asked al-Muʿtaṣim, his brother and successor, to "surround the ʿAlids with care." He spoke highly of them while deprecating his own family, the ʿAbbāsids.[75]

The third line of evidence revealing al-Maʾmūn's strong pro-ʿAlid leanings concerns his designation of ʿAlī ibn Mūsā as heir on 2 Ramaḍān 201/24 March 817.[76] Whether the caliph made his choice out of a feeling of obligation to the ʿAlids (Gabrieli 1929) or for "political motives," such as striking a compromise between conflicting factional interests, punishing his ʿAbbāsid family for its hostility to him, appeasing the constant ʿAlid

68. Ibn Abī Ṭāhir Ṭayfūr, 10. In this meeting with ʿAlid notables, al-Maʾmūn also urged them to "let bygones be bygones," probably referring to previous discord with the ʿAbbāsid wing of the family and to more recent rebellions by some disgruntled ʿAlids.

69. Ibn Abī Ṭāhir Ṭayfūr, 86. Ibn Bābawayh and al-Masʿūdī offer explanations for al-Maʾmūn's attachment to the ʿAlids. Ibn Bābawayh, 75–76, says the caliph had acquired his ʿAlid leanings at his father's court while still a child. Al-Masʿūdī, *Murūj*, 4:242–43, contains a narrative in which al-Maʾmūn explains that he favors the ʿAlids because ʿAlī ibn Abī Ṭālib had supported the ʿAbbāsids. This theme of "repaying an old debt" is stressed by Zaydān (1902–6) and Gabrieli (1929), who consider al-Maʾmūn's partiality to the ʿAlids genuine.

70. Al-Khalīfa ibn Khayyāṭ and al-Ṭabarī report that the *ḥajj* was led in the year 202/818 by Ibrāhīm ibn Mūsā, the brother of ʿAlī ibn Mūsā al-Riḍā; in 204/820, 205/821 and 206/822 it was led by ʿUbaydallāh ibn al-Ḥasan ibn ʿUbaydallāh ibn ʿAbbās ibn ʿAlī ibn Abī Ṭālib. Al-Masʿūdī (*Murūj*, 4:309) adds that Ibrāhīm ibn Mūsā was the first Ṭālibid ever to lead the pilgrimage. For a complete list of those who led the pilgrimage from the beginning of Islam to the year 335/947, see al-Masʿūdī, *Murūj*, 4:301–13.

71. Around 203/818–819, for instance (al-Masʿūdī, *Murūj*, 3:447).

72. Al-Iṣfahānī, *Maqātil*, 541; Ibn al-Athīr, 5:195; Ibn al-ʿImād, 2:7. The man died in 209/824–25.

73. The property of Fadak changed hands more than once. Al-Yaʿqūbī, *Tārīkh*, 2:469, and al-Balādhurī, *Futūḥ al-buldān*, 33–38, report that upon the death of the Prophet, Fāṭima pressed her claim to it, but Abū Bakr withheld it on grounds that the Prophet intended its income for charity. Al-Balādhurī adds that al-Maʾmūn's decision was reversed again by al-Mutawakkil when he came to power.

74. Also recorded by Marquet (1972, 127–28).

75. Al-Ṭabarī, iii:1136–40. As stated earlier, this will is summarized by Ibn al-Athīr, 5:226–27, and carefully edited by the very late Ḥanbalite writer Ibn al-ʿImād (2:43). Ibn al-ʿImād deemphasized both al-Maʾmūn's pro-ʿAlid stance and the caliph's position on the createdness of the Qur'an.

76. Al-Khalīfa, 764; Ibn Qutayba, *al-Maʿārif*, 388; al-Yaʿqūbī, *Tārīkh*, 2:448; al-Ṭabarī, iii:1012–13; al-Maqdisī, 110; Ibn Bābawayh, 2:146; Ibn al-Athīr, 5:183; Ibn Khaldūn, 1:281; al-Khaṭīb al-Baghdādī, 10:184; Ibn Khallikān, 1:39–40; Ibn al-ʿImād, 2:2; al-Iṣfahānī, *Kitāb al-aghānī*, 10:52–53. For contemporary scholars' account of the designation, see Hasan 1933; Donaldson 1933, 161–67; Abbott 1946, 224; Cahen (1968, 91–92; Marquet 1972, 111; Watt 1973, 176–78; Kennedy 1981, 157 ff. and 1986, 153–54; and Huddāra 1985, 136 ff.

revolts, or any combination of these, is not important.[77] What is significant is that scholars consider the designation of ʿAlī al-Riḍā as heir by al-Maʾmūn a manifestation of his affinities with, if not partiality to, the ʿAlids. The caliph gave the heir-apparent the title "*al-riḍā min āl Muḥammad*," or 'the pleasing-one within the family of Muḥammad (the Prophet),'[78] a title which the Zaydites consider the most appropriate designation for the *imām* (ʿĀrif 1987, 327). Coins were struck with ʿAlī al-Riḍā's name to formalize the occasion,[79] and the dynastic color of the ʿAbbāsids, black,[80] was replaced by green,[81] probably to emphasize that the caliph was intent on breaking with the past. The event also caught the imagination of a number of Shiʿite chroniclers, who seized upon the occasion to inflate the status of ʿAlī al-Riḍā. Ibn Bābawayh (2:138–39), for example, preserves a report which states that the caliph was so eager to gain ʿAlī al-Riḍā's consent to the designation that he was willing to use force to secure it.[82]

There were other affirmations of the caliph's determination to reunite the two wings of the Hāshimite family. Amongst these was al-Maʾmūn's insistence that his oldest son,

77. Mentioned by Sourdel (1962), Watt (1973), Rifāʿī (1927), al-Dūrī (1945), and ʿUmar (1977), among others.

78. Al-Ṭabarī, iii:1012–13; Ibn Bābawayh, 2:146; Miskawayh, 435–36; Ibn al-Athīr, 5:183; Ibn al-ʿIbrī, 233; al-Irbilī, 3:50; Ibn Ṭiqṭaqā, 217; Ibn Kathīr, 10:247; al-Suyūṭī, 246; al-Khaṭīb al-Baghdādī, 10:184; Ibn al-ʿImād, 2:2. The slogan of '*al-riḍā min āl Muḥammad*' was used by the ʿAbbāsids during the takeover from the Umayyads (Shaban 1970, 155; Sharon 1983, 147), primarily to acquire the support of the *shīʿat ʿAlī* who restricted leadership of the Community to the Prophet's family. For a description of some variations on the meaning of the slogan, see Nagel 1972, 107–16; Crone 1989; and Madelung 1989b.

79. Al-Yaʿqūbī, *Tārīkh*, 2:448; al-Masʿūdī, *Murūj*, 3:440–41; al-Iṣfahānī, *Maqātil*, 563–64; Ibn Bābawayh, 2:146; al-Irbilī, 3:66; al-Suyūṭī, 246; Ibn Khallikān, 3:269–70; al-Iṣfahānī, *Kitāb al-aghānī*, 10:52–53. The first coins bearing ʿAlī's name were minted in 202/817–818 and the last in Muḥarram 204/June-July 819, probably just a few weeks after ʿAlī's death (Miles 1938, 103–8).

80. Black was decreed as the official color of the ʿAbbāsid dynasty by al-Manṣūr in 145/762–63 (Athamina 1989, 318).

81. Al-Khalīfa, 764; Ibn Qutayba, *al-Maʿārif*, 388; Ibn Abī Ṭāhir Ṭayfūr, 2; al-Yaʿqūbī, *Tārīkh*, 2:448; al-Ṭabarī, iii:1013; al-Jahshiyārī, 312; al-Maqdisī, 110; al-Azdī, 341–42 and 353; al-Masʿūdī, *Murūj*, 4:440–41; al-Iṣfahānī, *Maqātil*, 563–64; Ibn Bābawayh, 2:146; Miskawayh, 435–36; *Kitāb al-ʿuyūn*, 353; Ibn al-Athīr, 5:183; Ibn al-ʿIbrī, 233; al-Irbilī, 3:66–67; Ibn Kathīr, 10:247; Ibn Khaldūn, 4:18; al-Suyūṭī, 246; al-Khaṭīb al-Baghdādī, 10:187; Ibn Khallikān, 3:269–70; al-Ṣafadī, 17:657; Ibn al-ʿImād, 2:2. The color green did not stand for the ʿAlids exclusively (Sourdel 1970, 122; ʿUmar 1977, 252–53; ʿAthamina 1989, 325) or any other particular group (Weil 1848, 2:216–17, n. 3; ʿAthamina 1989, 325). The only source which has anything to say about the meaning of the color green is Ibn Ṭiqṭaqā (p. 217) who says that it stands for the color of Paradise. He is probably alluding to Qur'anic verses 18:31 and 76:21.

82. Other examples of accounts inflating the status of ʿAlī include al-Iṣfahānī's report (*Maqātil*, 561) implying that the caliph cherished ʿAlī al-Riḍā more than he did Abū Bakr, Islam's first caliph. The Sunnite Ibn al-Taghrībirdī, 2:169 and 2:174–75, is among those who described the occasion in terms which portray al-Maʾmūn as subservient to his designee. Another Sunnite, Ibn Kathīr (10:247) informs us that al-Maʾmūn transmitted hadiths from ʿAlī al-Riḍā.

al-ʿAbbās,[83] and other military leaders pledge allegiance to ʿAlī al-Riḍā.[84] As successor to the caliphate, ʿAlī al-Riḍā's name was added to the Friday prayer.[85] The bond between al-Maʾmūn and ʿAlī al-Riḍā was further strengthened by the marriage of one of the caliph's daughters to ʿAlī al-Riḍā and another to his son Muḥammad.[86]

ʿAlī al-Riḍā died in 203/818 under disputed circumstances,[87] yet his death by no means put an end to the caliph's interest in the ʿAlids. Al-Maʾmūn ordered that ʿAlī al-Riḍā be buried next to his own father, Hārūn al-Rashīd, at Ṭūs.[88] The chroniclers also report that al-Maʾmūn publicly displayed grief over the death of ʿAlī al-Riḍā and that he personally prayed over his grave.[89] A decade after ʿAlī al-Riḍā's death (probably in 215/825–826), al-Maʾmūn ordered that the marriage between his daughter Umm al-Faḍl and ʿAlī al-Riḍā's son Muḥammad be consummated.[90] The later Ḥanbalite writer, Ibn Kathīr[91] dismisses this command as simply a fulfillment of the marriage contract, and yet it also indicates an ongoing commitment to the family of the deceased ʿAlī al-Riḍā.

Al-Maʾmūn did make some concessions to his ʿAbbāsid relatives. When in 204/819 the caliph arrived at the town of al-Nahrawān northeast of Baghdad after returning from Khurasan, his family, leading commanders, and other notables came to greet him attired in green, as he had commanded. Responding to their pleas, he permitted them to resume wearing the traditional ʿAbbāsid black,[92] a step which appears to have eased at least any open opposition.

83. Al-Iṣfahānī, *Maqātil*, 563–64; al-Irbilī, 3:66–67.

84. Al-Iṣfahānī, *Maqātil*, 563–64. The military leaders were subsequently granted one year's provisions.

85. Al-Ṭabarī, iii:1029; Ibn Kathīr, 10:249.

86. Al-Yaʿqūbī, *Tārīkh*, 2:454; al-Ṭabarī, iii:1029; al-Maqdisī, 110; al-Azdī, 343; al-Masʿūdī, *Murūj*, 3:440–41; al-Iṣfahānī, *Maqātil*, 565; Ibn Bābawayh, 2:146; Miskawayh, 444; *Kitāb al-ʿuyūn*, 357; Ibn al-Athīr, 5:193; Ibn al-ʿIbrī, 233; Ibn Kathīr, 10:249; Ibn Khaldūn, 3:532; al-Suyūṭī, 246; Ibn Khallikān, 3:269–70; Ibn al-ʿImād, 2:3.

87. Al-Khalīfa ibn Khayyāṭ, 766; al-Ṭabarī, iii:1030; al-Azdī, 352; al-Masʿūdī, *Murūj*, 3:441. Al-Masʿūdī reports that ʿAlī was either poisoned or died from indigestion. Both possibilities are also found in al-Iṣfahānī, *Maqātil*, 565–67 and 571–72. The Shiʿite al-Yaʿqūbī (*Tārīkh*, 2:453) adduces a report that ʿAlī al-Riḍā was killed by the prominent Khurasanian ʿAlī ibn Hishām, who gave him a poisoned pomegranate to eat. Cf. also Ibn al-Athīr (5:193) who, after reporting the claim that al-Maʾmūn poisoned ʿAlī, states that he thinks this unlikely (*wa-hādhā ʿindī baʿīd*).

88. Al-Azdī, 352; al-Iṣfahānī, *Maqātil*, 567; Miskawayh, 444; *Kitāb al-ʿuyūn*, 357; Ibn al-Athīr, 5:193; Ibn al-ʿIbrī, 233; Ibn Kathīr, 10:249; Ibn Khallikān, 3:270; Ibn al-ʿImād, 2:6; al-Thaʿālibī, 117–18. *See Nawas 1996b.

89. Al-Yaʿqūbī, *Tārīkh*, 2:453; al-Azdī, 352; al-Masʿūdī, *Murūj*, 3:441; al-Iṣfahānī, *Maqātil*, 567; al-Irbilī, 3:72; Ibn al-Athīr, 5:193; Ibn Kathīr, 10:249; Ibn Khallikān, 3:270; Ibn al-ʿImād, 2:6.

90. Ibn Abī Ṭāhir Ṭayfūr, 263–63; al-Ṭabarī, iii:1102–3; al-Azdī, 399; al-Yaʿqūbī, *Tārīkh*, 2:454; Ibn al-Athīr, 5:219; Ibn Kathīr, 10:269; Ibn Khaldūn, 3:544 and Ibn Qutayba, *al-Maʿārif*, 391, who, however, gives the date as 210/825–826.

91. Ibn Kathīr, 10:269.

92. Al-Khalīfa ibn Khayyāṭ, 767; Ibn Abī Ṭāhir Ṭayfūr, 3–4 and 28; al-Yaʿqūbī, *Tārīkh*, 2:453–54; al-Ṭabarī, iii:1037–38; al-Maqdisī, 110; al-Azdī, 353; al-Masʿūdī, *Murūj*, 3:442–43; Ibn al-Athīr, 5:195; Ibn Ṭiqṭaqā,

According to some scholars, the caliph's pro-ʿAlid policies did come to an end with the death of ʿAlī al-Riḍā.[93] Gabrieli (1929) construes events after al-Riḍā's death such as al-Maʾmūn's declaration in 212/827 of the preeminence of ʿAlī ibn Abī Ṭālib and the cursing of Muʿāwiya as mere expressions of "sentiment," rather than a restoration of the old policy. The caliph's affectionate words about the ʿAlids at his deathbed in 218/833 can likewise be seen as expressions of sentiment. Yet, an attachment that manifested itself throughout al-Maʾmūn's reign and which endured until the caliph's death calls for an explanation that is both internally consistent and encompasses all relevant facts.

3.3.1. An Explanation of al-Maʾmūn's Partiality for the ʿAlids

It may well be true, as Gabrieli (1929) argues, that al-Maʾmūn venerated ʿAlī ibn Abī Ṭālib because he felt the ʿAbbāsids owed him a debt.[94] This explanation may also at least partially account for the caliph's repeated leniency in dealing with the numerous rebellions the ʿAlids and their supporters had staged against the ʿAbbāsids in general and al-Maʾmūn's own regime in particular. After the rebellion of Abū al-Sarāyā was put down, for instance, the only punishment meted out to Muḥammad ibn Muḥammad, the ʿAlid in whose name the revolt had been fought, was house arrest[95] in Khurasan.[96] Such acts of forgiveness, as well as al-Maʾmūn's honoring of dead ʿAlids by praying personally over their bodies, demonstrate more than sentimental attachment to the memory of ʿAlī ibn Abī Ṭālib.

Chroniclers' explanations for ʿAlī al-Riḍā's designation as heir are similarly inadequate. Al-Jahshiyārī, al-Iṣfahānī and al-Ṣafadī claim that the caliph was fulfilling an earlier pledge.[97] Ibn al-Qifṭī says that the designation was a calculated decision intended to undermine the popularity that the ʿAlids enjoyed among the populace; the caliph wanted to show that they were by no means immune to worldly ambitions and pursuits.[98] These

---

219; Ibn Kathīr, 10:250; Ibn Khaldūn, 3:533; Ibn Taghrībirdī, 2:175; al-Suyūṭī, 247; al-Khaṭīb al-Baghdādī, 10:184; Ibn Khallikān, 1:40; Ibn al-ʿImād, 2:3. Miskawayh, 447–48, and the *Kitāb al-ʿuyūn*, 358–59, supply the interesting detail that al-Maʾmūn ordered the change to black only after he was satisfied that his initial order (for change of color to green) had been duly heeded, despite the resistance to it.

93. Though they differ on minor details, Gabrieli (1929), Daniel (1979, 181) and Hamdi (1956) take the view that the ʿAlid-Maʾmūn relationship faded with the death of al-Riḍā. Geddes (1963–64) agrees but dates the end of the relationship to 207/823, the year in which the rebellion in Yemen by the ʿAlid ʿAbd al-Raḥmān was put down and the ʿAlids were forbidden to enter the presence of al-Maʾmūn (al-Ṭabarī, iii:1062–63), though the rebel leader was given a guarantee of safety (*amān*).

94. Ibn Ṭiqṭaqā, 219; al-Suyūṭī, 247; Ibn al-ʿImād, 2:3.

95. "*ʿAlā sabīl al-iʿtiqāl wa-l-tawkīl*," al-Iṣfahānī, *Maqātil*, 549. Of course, the caliph's action may also have been prompted by a practical need to appease the ʿAlids.

96. Al-Ṭabarī, iii:987.

97. Al-Jahshiyārī , 312; al-Iṣfahānī, *Maqātil*, 563–64; al-Ṣafadī, 17:657.

98. Ibn al-Qifṭī, 221–23.

interpretations treat ʿAlī al-Riḍā's designation as an isolated event, yet it must fit within a framework that also explains the caliph's esteem for ʿAlī ibn Abī Ṭālib, his inordinate accommodation of the ʿAlids, and his deathbed request that his successor care for them.[99]

Gibb (1961, 118) emphasizes that, even had al-Maʾmūn hoped to appease rebellious Shiʿite groups through the designation of ʿAlī al-Riḍā, it is nonetheless unclear which of these, if any, supported him. ʿAlī al-Riḍā was about fifty-four years old when al-Maʾmūn made him his heir. Reports agree that he had led a retired life unencumbered with political entanglements. If al-Maʾmūn wanted to win over a Shiʿite group, he would have surely done better choosing one of their pretenders over a quietist like ʿAlī al-Riḍā. Ḥasan (1933) points to the caliph's need to win over Khurasanian support as his motivation in appointing al-Riḍā his heir; however, the Khurasanians had already put al-Maʾmūn on the throne about half a decade before the designation, so his need to win their support is not clear.

Nagel (1975, 254–55) and Madelung (1981) take a different approach. Without dismissing other interpretations, they call attention to a belief circulating during al-Maʾmūn's reign that the ʿAbbāsid caliphate was coming to an end, to be followed by the apocalypse and the appearance of the *mahdī*. Madelung argues that al-Maʾmūn "must certainly have been aware of such predictions and expectations when he invited ʿAlī al-Riḍā from Medina in the year 200 H."[100] Al-Riḍā's designation may thus have been the result of al-Maʾmūn's belief that such an appointment was necessary to prepare the caliphate for the end of times.

I contend that al-Maʾmūn was partial to the ʿAlids for two related reasons. One may, for lack of a better term, be termed "political": the designation of al-Riḍā as heir was an attempt to bring the ʿAlids into the ʿAbbāsid fold. The second reason is al-Maʾmūn's sincere conviction that the ʿAlids were bona fide members of the House of the Prophet, equal to the ʿAbbāsids, and to al-Maʾmūn himself.

Al-Maʾmūn's ʿAbbāsid ancestors had given scant thanks for the ʿAlid support that helped bring them to power. Yet, however pleasant it may be to think that al-Maʾmūn designated al-Riḍā as heir in order to rectify an injustice, it is more likely that his aim went further. The repeated uprisings were in themselves an ongoing reminder that more needed to be done to pacify the ʿAlids than merely urging them to "let bygones be bygones" or claiming ʿAlī ibn Abī Ṭālib and his progeny as cousins. Repeatedly antagonized by al-Maʾmūn's ancestors—and with the memory of their oppression at the hands of al-Maʾmūn's own father still alive—the ʿAlids' suspicions could only be allayed by positive

99. Al-Ṭabarī, iii:1139.

100. Madelung 1981, 346. For more on this theme, see Abel 1935, esp. pp. 8–9; Lewis 1950 esp. p. 331; al-Dūrī 1981; and Madelung 1986. *For the theme of eschatology as a contributive factor in al-Maʾmūn's behavior, see the extensive analysis in Yücesoy 2009.

action. The designation of al-Riḍā as heir may have been one such means of incorporating the ʿAlids into the ʿAbbāsid sphere.

It is also the case that this dramatic step, like other deeds and statements by al-Maʾmūn which modern scholars regard as showing unmistakable favoritism for the ʿAlids, was in full accord with his view that the ʿAlids were just as integral a part of the Hāshimite family[101] and the House of the Prophet as their cousins, the ʿAbbāsids.[102] In his letter of designation, al-Maʾmūn says as much. In it we read that the caliph had "given consideration to the members of the two houses of al-ʿAbbās and ʿAlī but had not found anyone more excellent, more pious or more learned than ʿAlī [al-Riḍā]"[103] to be the future caliph. Two points are worth noting. First, by such an assertion, al-Maʾmūn seems to have taken to heart Ibn al-Muqaffaʿ's counsel to his great-grandfather al-Manṣūr (*Risāla fī l-saḥāba*, 57), which stressed that the caliph's family ("*ahl baytihi*") included not only the ʿAbbāsids but the ʿAlids as well. Second, al-Maʾmūn's assertion in effect reversed al-Mahdī's moving away from the *waṣiyya*, a measure with which the ʿAlids naturally had taken issue. The doctrine known as the *waṣiyya* (bequest) pertained to an early claim to legitimacy made by the ʿAbbāsids and their partisans prior to and during the anti-Umayyad revolution. In it, the ʿAbbāsids maintained that the imāmate had been designated to a grandson of ʿAlī ibn Abī Ṭālib, Abū Hāshim, but that he, in turn, had designated an ʿAbbāsid as his successor. Under al-Mahdī, a new propagandistic meaning which excluded the ʿAlids was assigned to the *waṣiyya* doctrine. The new version held that the legitimate succession to the Prophet had been through al-ʿAbbās and his descendants, not through ʿAlī ibn Abī Ṭālib and his grandson.

The ʿAbbāsids, of course, saw matters differently. They regarded the appointment of al-Riḍā as a threat to ʿAbbāsid supremacy and feared that the caliphate would pass to the House of ʿAlī ibn Abī Ṭālib. However, al-Maʾmūn never decreed what would happen after the death of this "most excellent" of living men within the House of the Prophet. If the ʿAbbāsid family's concern was self-perpetuity, that of al-Maʾmūn was the perpetuity of the caliphate. Its importance outweighed the rising and falling fortunes of the ʿAbbāsids and ʿAlids, and its survival could only be assured if the caliph continued to be a man of merit from the family of the prophet Muḥammad. This is perhaps the reason why al-Maʾmūn on his deathbed chose as successor not his own son, al-ʿAbbās, but al-Muʿtaṣim, a man he presumably deemed better able to carry the burden of the caliphate.[104]

---

101. For the term "Hāshimite" including both ʿAlids and ʿAbbāsids, see Nagel 1972, 70 ff., esp. p. 80 and Madelung 1989a, esp. pp. 7–8. See also *EI2*, s.v. "Hāshimiyya" (Lewis). Cf. Crone 1980, 76.

102. See Watt 1973, 154–55 and 1985, 33 and also *EI2* s.v. "Kaysāniyya" (Madelung) esp. p. 837 b. *See also al-Qāḍī 1973.

103. Bosworth 1987, 61 = al-Ṭabarī, iii: 1013, this theme is elaborated on in the complete designation text given by al-Irbilī, 3:124–25.

104. We have no concrete information on why al-Maʾmūn made this choice. *For a possible explanation, see Nawas 2010. It is a fact, however, that the appointment of al-Muʿtaṣim was the first

The seriousness with which al-Maʾmūn took his mission as guardian of the caliphate and his quest to strengthen the caliph's authority are the subject of the next chapter.

time an ʿAbbāsid caliph chose as successor someone other than his own son since the time of al-Manṣūr. Al-Ṣaffāḥ outlived his male descendants (Ibn Ḥazm, *Jamharat ansāb al-ʿArab*, 20) and therefore could not have passed the caliphate on to any of his sons. While al-Hādī was succeeded by his brother, al-Rashīd, and al-Amīn by his brother, al-Maʾmūn, both of them had tried unsuccessfully to place their sons on the throne.

CHAPTER 4
THE CALIPHAL AUTHORITY HYPOTHESIS

4.1. Modern Scholars' Formulations of This Hypothesis

Some modern scholars propose that al-Maʾmūn's conception of the caliphal institution and caliphal authority was what prompted him to declare the doctrine of the createdness of the Qur'an and to introduce the *miḥna*. This proposition, the caliphal authority hypothesis, can be found in the works of Sourdel (1962), Nagel (1975) and Watt (1973), but is more explicit in the works of Lapidus (1975), Hinds (*EI2*, s.v. "*miḥna*") and Crone and Hinds (1986).

In general, scholars argue that al-Maʾmūn developed his vision of the caliphate in response to the challenges the ʿAbbāsid Empire was facing at the time. The ʿAbbāsids' grip on power was under strain. Although the decline is generally dated to the reign of al-Mutawakkil (r. 232–247/847–861), the disintegration had begun earlier. There were clear signs of it during the days of al-Rashīd, if not earlier. By the time of al-Rashīd's reign control of the far western flank of the empire had been lost; the Umayyads had control of al-Andalus, and the Aghlabids of North Africa had become autonomous.[1] The eastern flank fared somewhat better, but Bābak was proving far stronger than anybody had expected, and the Ṭāhirids were becoming more deeply entrenched as a dynastic regime. Moreover, various rebellions were beginning to threaten the empire's central provinces. Al-Rashīd's division of the empire between al-Amīn and al-Maʾmūn failed to bring about the stability he sought and instead resulted in the chaos of the fourth Civil War. The proponents of the caliphal authority hypothesis argue that al-Maʾmūn sensed that strong political and religious, or better, politico-religious, leadership of the Community was the only viable means to reclaim ʿAbbāsid power.

Nagel (1975) stresses the importance of al-Maʾmūn claiming the title of *imām*, which may have been an attempt to gain support by appealing to religious sentiment. Al-

1. See Talbi 1966.

Maʾmūn's focus on the imāmate can be dated to around the year 198/813–814 with his "letter to the army" (*Risālat al-Khamīs*), which Nagel (1975, 136 ff.) analyzes at length. He argues that in this letter al-Maʾmūn develops the concept of the caliphate into a full-fledged politico-religious institution. Al-Maʾmūn writes of the caliph as an "*imām al-hudā*"[2] (*imām* of right guidance), possessing faculties inspired by God. Not everybody can be an *imām*. God chooses him, and the choice is confined to those like al-Maʾmūn, who come from the family of the Prophet. In this conception of the caliphate, Nagel continues, man is portrayed as weak, neither endowed with the talent to choose an *imām* nor with the ability to conduct his affairs without guidance. It is the duty of the *imām*, whom God endows with superhuman knowledge, to educate people and guide them onto the right path, so that they may obey the divine law and lead a praiseworthy life. To "guide rightly," the *imām*/caliph relies on the revealed law of God and on his personal qualities as a political leader (Nagel 1975, 145).

Having elevated the status of the *imām* by these arguments, al-Maʾmūn placed himself "über den Zwist der Theologen und über die Kämpfe der religiös-politischen Strömungen ..." ("above the theologians' quarrel and above the struggles of religio-political currents"; Nagel 1975, 150). Consequently, he could claim complete authority to educate and to dictate. In Nagel's opinion, al-Maʾmūn in this way laid the basis for theocratic rule. In so doing, he hoped to achieve the unity of the Community in both the religious and political spheres. In sum, Nagel argues that the *Risālat al-Khamīs*, written so early in al-Maʾmūn's reign, laid the foundation for his vision of the caliph as a God-inspired, God-chosen, God-heeding figure—an *imām* held to be infallible and immaculate, at least by those who venerated the institution of the imāmate.[3]

According to others, elevating the status of the imāmate was not sufficient to affirm al-Maʾmūn's power. To ensure success, al-Maʾmūn needed to defeat those who would challenge his self-portrayal and question the authority he was arrogating to himself. These were the *ʿulamāʾ*, learned men of influence and traditionists for whom the literalist Ibn Ḥanbal became a symbol during the *miḥna*. Lapidus draws attention to the opposition of the *ʿulamāʾ* by describing "the enormous political and ideological problems" (1975, 378) which the caliph faced. To counteract their opposition, al-Maʾmūn extended the claims of the caliphate by "vesting it with ... extensive religious authority and control of ritual and doctrine" (Lapidus 1975, 378). The changes which the caliph introduced were separated by stretches of years. Thus, "in the ... year [212/827] al-Maʾmūn ... announced his support for the doctrine of the created Qurʾān." Three years later, he "declared new

2. ʿUmar (1977, 222) suggests that the notion of "*hudā*" as used by al-Maʾmūn and his ancestors may have been based on Qur'anic verse 21:73, which says "We appointed them to be leaders guiding by Our command ..." (*wa-jaʿalnāhum aʾimmat*[an] *yahdūna bi-amrinā ...*).

3. For a similar argument, see Sourdel 1962, esp. 44.

variations in the standard prayer sequence and ordered that three '*takbīr*'[4] be said" (Lapidus 1975, 378). Naturally, "this religious policy caused consternation in *ʿulamāʾ* circles," notes Lapidus, and the caliph's answer was to enact what he hoped would be the coup de grâce, the *miḥna* of 218/833 (Lapidus 1975, 379).

Lapidus is of the opinion—and others including Abusaq (1971, 28) concur—that the *miḥna* had a wider objective than simply quelling opposition to the doctrine of the createdness of the Qur'an. Its purpose went even beyond signaling in no uncertain terms the caliph's authority over the *ʿulamāʾ*, whose growing independence pointed ominously toward a growing "separation of state and religion" (Lapidus 1975, 365). The *miḥna*, asserts Lapidus, "was also a response," if not a challenge, to those "who asserted the priority of *kitāb* [the Book] and sunna against the authority of the Caliph" (Lapidus 1975, 379).

The views of Nagel and Lapidus are congruent with opinions formulated by other scholars, although they differ in detail and emphasis. The issues stressed by Lapidus, for example, are in harmony with Watt's (1973) reading, though Watt reads less confrontation and more conciliation into the caliph's maneuvers than Lapidus does. While both agree that the caliph was eager to unite the Community, Watt sees al-Maʾmūn's measures as a many-sided attempt to neutralize factionalism, while Lapidus understands them as having been targeted at suppressing the "Khurasanian tradition of militant opposition to the Caliphate" (Lapidus 1975, 382). Similarly, Sourdel's remark that "... jamais auparavant on n'avait vu un calife se présenter comme un 'docteur', chargé par Dieu d'éclairer la communauté et de lui communiquer la science qui lui avait été confiée" ("... never before had we seen a caliph present himself as a 'doctor' charged by God to enlighten the community and to communicate to it the knowledge entrusted to him"; Sourdel 1962, 44), is another way of stating what Nagel was to expand on later.

The views of Hinds (*EI2*, s.v. "*miḥna*") and Crone and Hinds (1986) are similar, although they do not consider al-Maʾmūn's claim to authority an innovation. According to Hinds, al-Maʾmūn's maneuvers were intended "to reestablish... that type of caliphal religious authority... which had... been familiar in the time of the Umayyad caliphate." Crone and Hinds (1986, 21) agree with Lapidus that the caliphal authority which al-Maʾmūn sought would indeed "leave no room for *ʿulamāʾ*: if God manifests His will through caliphs here and now, there is no need to seek guidance from scholars" whose stock in trade was to "remember what a prophet had said in the past."

In sum, the above works maintain that the caliph's adoption of the doctrine of the createdness of the Qur'an and his declaration of the *miḥna* were attempts on his part to define the caliphate, thereby giving it that spirit of worldly and sacred authority which would allow the incumbent to rule supreme over a strong and united Islamic Community.

4. Utterance of the formula *Allāh*[u] *akbar* (God is great).

4.2. The Argument of This Study

I concur with the general hypothesis that al-Maʾmūn's conception of caliphal authority and the caliphal institution was the primary motive for his declaration of the doctrine of the createdness of the Qur'an and the proclamation of the *miḥna*. I differ, however, with other studies concerning certain aspects of al-Maʾmūn's actions and political thought. Al-Maʾmūn made a concerted effort to reunite the two branches of the Banū Hāshim tribe, a policy which he saw as an effective means to restore a secure foundation to a caliphate that the long history of Shiʿite and/or ʿAlid antagonisms and grievances had helped to undermine. It is reasonable to assume that al-Maʾmūn was especially sensitive to the hazards of a vulnerable caliphate and caliph because of his personal experience of nearly being removed by al-Amīn prior to the Civil War, the anti-caliphate of Ibrāhīm ibn al-Mahdī, the loss of a good part of the empire to the Aghlabids and Idrīsids (not to mention the Ṭāhirids, for whom the caliph had become little more than a nominal leader), the ever-present menace of the Byzantine Empire, and a great number of uprisings in various regions of the Islamic empire, especially toward the end of his reign.

Having failed to secure stable power for himself and his posterity through such measures as his aborted attempt to bring the ʿAlids into the mainstream, al-Maʾmūn took another path, the *miḥna*. Through it he sought to restore to the caliph that measure of all-encompassing authority which had allegedly given the early caliphs maximal leverage, but had later been lost. He probably saw no other option; that this was the case is indicated by his request in his testament to his successor, al-Muʿtaṣim, that he "follow [his] brother's line regarding the Qur'an,"[5] even though al-Maʾmūn had shortly before received information which suggested that this was not to be an easy task.

In this chapter I argue that a clear and coherent vision of the caliphate is manifest in texts written by or for al-Maʾmūn over the course of his reign, appearing well before the *miḥna*. The evidence consists of four documents which the sources claim to be copies of originals written by or for al-Maʾmūn. The first of these documents, the *Risālat al-Khamīs* (written around 198/813–814), continued a long tradition in which the ʿAbbāsid caliphs sought to cement their power and its legitimacy through epistles addressed to their ʿAbbāsid subjects.[6] The second text contains the caliph's designation in 201/817

5. Al-Ṭabarī, iii:1137.

6. In Ṣafwat, 377–97. Also found in Rifāʿī (1927, 3:26–37) with very minute editorial differences from Ṣafwat's version. Ṣafwat's note (p. 377) on this *risāla* ("epistle") translates as follows: "The early ʿAbbāsid caliphs charged their most eloquent clerks to compose the *Risālat al-Khamīs* in support of their cause (*al-daʿwa al-ʿAbbāsiyya*) and of their claim that the sons of the Prophet's uncle al-ʿAbbās and his descendants have the first priority in inheriting Muḥammad's caliphate. Each *risāla* urged support also for the ruling caliph, enumerated and lauded his attributes and legitimized his personal status as caliph. The caliphs used to dispatch the *risāla* to Khurasan where it was read to the throngs who gathered to hear it. Its dispatch to Khurasan itself symbolized the ruling caliph's appreciation for past Khurasanian support

of ʿAlī al-Riḍā as his heir.[7] The *miḥna* letters, especially the first[8] and third[9] in the series, form the third main source. The fourth text is the caliph's testament.[10] While other studies have taken up these texts separately, the combined use here of sources spanning his entire reign throws greater light on al-Maʾmūn's conception of the caliphate and his motivations for the *miḥna*.

It is probably because of the drama attending the *miḥna* decree and its implementation that al-Maʾmūn's early interest in asserting the authority of the caliphate has tended to be overlooked, although it is very much in evidence as far back as 198/813–814, just after he had assumed the caliphal office. That said, it should be noted that al-Maʾmūn's vision did not differ greatly from that of his predecessors. Indeed, I argue that al-Maʾmūn was in fact attempting to restore to the leader of the Muslim Community a position which he assumed previous caliphs had enjoyed—a view which fits well with the overall interpretation given by Crone and Hinds (1986) of the development of the caliphal institution—though al-Maʾmūn added a few personal touches to make it conform to his own conception of the caliphate.

As al-Maʾmūn saw it, the caliphal institution protected Islam and the Muslim community. Any weakening of it was therefore bound adversely to affect the fortunes of "God's religion." Given these stakes, such a drastic measure as the *miḥna* was justified. A milder course such as a decree asserting that the caliph was the ultimate authority on all matters of concern to his subjects would not do. After all, his designation of ʿAlī al-Riḍā was by decree—one solemnly signed by the two parties involved, witnessed by others and formally sealed by pledges of allegiance—yet it only succeeded in provoking opposition to the caliph. This time words alone would not suffice; they had to be backed by resolute action, and the steps had to be carefully planned. The caliph thus first identified

---

and a prod to renewal of their allegiance and partiality to the ʿAbbāsids. The first of these *risālas* was composed for al-Manṣūr. The *risāla* under consideration [on behalf of al-Maʾmūn] was composed by the eloquent Aḥmad ibn Yūsuf, a clerk (*kātib*) in al-Faḍl ibn Sahl's office in Khurasan. It relates the support for the ʿAbbāsid *daʿwa*, praises al-Maʾmūn and justifies the overthrow of al-Amīn ..." The letter was probably written in 198/813–814, some time after the death of al-Amīn. For more specifics on the "genre" of *risālat al-khamīs*, see Arazi and Elad (1988), who also include a French translation of al-Maʾmūn's *Risālat al-Khamīs*. Cf. Nagel (1975, 140 ff.), who gives an analysis of the *risāla*.

7. The text used here is the version given by al-Irbilī, 3:123 ff. The designation by al-Maʾmūn appears in English in Crone and Hinds (1986, as appendix 4, 133–39). Crone and Hinds based their translation on al- Qalqashandī's *Ṣubḥ al-aʿshā* and Sibṭ ibn al-Jawzī, *Mirʾāt al-zamān* (using this last-mentioned manuscript's variations as given by Gabrieli in the footnotes to his Italian translation [1929, 38–43]). There are some very minor and inconsequential differences in the Arabic texts of al-Qalqashandī and al-Irbilī.

8. Al-Ṭabarī, iii:1112–17.

9. Al-Ṭabarī, iii:1117–21.

10. Al-Ṭabarī, iii:1136–40.

his opponents and then deployed the issue of the createdness of the Qur'an as a challenge from which his targets could not escape.

These opponents were the emerging class of learned men (*ʿulamāʾ*), including experts in law (*fuqahāʾ*), judges, and traditionists (*muḥaddithūn*), who by this time held such authority and exerted such influence and power over the public as to make the caliph appear irrelevant in matters of faith. These men had to be forced to accept, on pain of torture or death if necessary, that it was the caliph, not they, who held the highest spiritual authority. After all, as al-Maʾmūn argued in the *miḥna* letters, the caliph was the sole recipient of special gifts from God and only he had the knowledge necessary to save the souls of Muslims. Al-Maʾmūn ordered the *miḥna*, then, for no other reason than to safeguard the caliphal institution whose head he envisaged as having the birthright, indeed, the duty, to exercise an authority in spiritual matters that was as supreme, undisputed and universally acknowledged as the authority he exercised as the Community's political leader.[11]

4.3. Al-Maʾmūn's Vision of the Caliphate

Al-Maʾmūn's theory of the caliphate holds that the caliph possesses special ties to God and the Prophet on one hand and to the Muslim Community on the other. Concerning his position in relation to God and the Prophet, al-Maʾmūn referred to himself on three occasions as the deputy or representative of God (*khalīfat Allāh*). The first of these was in 201/817, the year in which he designated ʿAlī al-Riḍā as heir.[12] The second was probably shortly after the year 202/817–818, in the context of a letter the caliph wrote to al-Ḥasan ibn Sahl.[13] The third was in the *miḥna* order[14] in 218/833.[15] The caliph saw himself not only as the representative of God, but of the Prophet as well. He refers to himself as the

11. *Four years after completing my dissertation, I came across Fahmī Jadʿān's *al-Miḥna: Baḥth fī jadaliyyat al-dīnī wa-l-siyāsī fī al-islām*, published in 1989, a book filled with original insights and information. Though Jadʿān's approach is quite different from mine, his conclusions are similar. Jadʿān also argues that it is too simple to say that the Muʿtazilites were behind the *miḥna*, the more so, he says, because the Muʿtazilites were not then a united group but consisted rather of a number of subgroups at odds with each other. Furthermore, as Van Ess had earlier pointed out and as I emphasize here, the Muʿtazilites were not the only intellectuals at the time who adhered to the doctrine of the createdness of the Qur'an. Jadʿān's main conclusion is that the *miḥna* was a result of a confrontation between "people of religion" (*ahl al-dīn*) and "people of state" (*ahl al-dawla*). My argument, as I develop below, is that the *miḥna* was an attempt to draw religion into the state. See also Hildebrandt 2007, whose focus is a possible neo-Muʿtazilite trend in modern and contemporary Islam, but who also compares my work with Jadʿān's, carefully pointing out similarities and differences (474–483 and 495).

12. Al-Irbilī, 3:124.

13. Ṣafwat, 426–27.

14. Al-Ṭabarī, iii:1117.

15. Somewhat removed from the immediate context which concerns us here is another episode in

successor of his forefather, Muḥammad, around 210/825–26,[16] and in the *miḥna* order the caliph goes so far as to describe himself as the inheritor of prophethood.[17]

Al-Maʾmūn also claimed for himself a uniquely personal relationship with God. In the letter to al-Ḥasan ibn Sahl mentioned above, the caliph stated that God had inspired him with His views, intent and zeal.[18] Around roughly the same time, although in a different context, the caliph stated that the choice of ʿAlī ibn Mūsā as heir was inspired by God.[19] Finally, in the year 218/833, al-Maʾmūn wrote in his first letter of the *miḥna* that God had entrusted him with special and hidden knowledge in addition to political power.[20] He further claimed that he, unlike others, was able to recognize God as He really is (*ḥaqq qadrihi*).[21]

Al-Maʾmūn's perception of himself as the *khalīfa* of both God and the Prophet fits well with a portrayal from quite early in his reign of the caliphal institution as wrought by God.[22] Having directly linked to God and the Prophet his person as well as the institution, it should come as no surprise that al Maʾmūn saw himself as the bulwark of Islam and its protector.[23] While portraying the caliphal institution as intrinsically tied to God and the Prophet in ways which transcended human agency, his vision also stressed the merits of the holder of the caliphal office,[24] as we see in both al-Maʾmūn's statement that his brother, al-Amīn, did not merit the office and in the designation text of ʿAlī al-Riḍā.[25]

---

which all the ʿAbbāsid caliphs are referred to by a poet as God's representatives. The poem in question is recorded by al-Iṣfahānī in his *Kitāb al-aghānī*, 19:331.

16. Al-Balādhurī, 37.

17. Al-Ṭabarī, iii:1112. The claim of having been made the recipient of the heritage of prophethood ("... *wa-mawārīth al-nubuwwa allatī awrathahum*") seems extravagant. Sourdel (1962, 44) and others interpret this as one of the indications that al-Maʾmūn was the first ʿAbbāsid caliph to make such a claim of authority and in doing so resembled a Shiʿite *imām*. Pointing to references from, among others, al-Iṣfahānī's *Kitāb al-aghānī* and Ibn al-Qalānisī's *Dhayl tārīkh Dimashq*, Goldziher (1981, 183, n. 43), however, maintains that this manner of expression was a favorite one amongst the ʿAbbāsid caliphs. If one accepts Goldziher's statement, this would mean that al-Maʾmūn was no exception in using this language. Addressing themselves to the spirit, not the letter, of the expression being discussed, Crone and Hinds (1986) go even further by arguing that, from the very beginning of the caliphate through to the Umayyads and early ʿAbbāsids, the self-perception of the caliph as the supreme spiritual leader was the rule rather than the exception.

18. Ṣafwat, 426–27.

19. Al-Irbilī, 3:124–25.

20. Al-Ṭabarī, iii:1112–13.

21. Al-Ṭabarī, iii:1113.

22. Ṣafwat, *Risālat al-Khamīs*, 383 ff. and al-Irbilī, 3:124–25.

23. Ṣafwat, *Risālat al-Khamīs*, 383 ff.

24. Ṣafwat, *Risālat al-Khamīs*, 385.

25. Al-Irbilī, 3:125. See also Ibn Bābawayh, 2:138–39; Miskawayh, 435–56.

Al-Maʾmūn's vision also specified the caliph's duties to both God and the Prophet and to his subjects. The caliph was assigned by God as guardian of His religion and laws.[26] It was his duty to combat the unbelievers, protect the unity of the state, stem the tide of civil discord, maintain public order and security and ensure access to the Holy Places.[27] Accountable to God for his actions,[28] the caliph served as the executor of His ordinances[29] and of the Prophet's commands.[30]

In his conduct, the caliph must follow the path of the Prophet[31] and serve as a model of good behavior for his subjects.[32] He must seek God's favor through his actions while fearing His punishment.[33] Fearing God and obeying Him are themes that recur throughout al-Maʾmūn's reign.[34]

The caliph must place the well-being of his subjects above his personal inclinations,[35] and he must be guided by the principle of justice.[36] Among the caliph's recommendations to his brother who was to succeed him were to treat his subjects with gentleness[37] and to take from the strong to give to the weak.[38]

Al-Maʾmūn repeatedly stressed his subjects' duty to obey their caliph.[39] He held that he was entitled to a wide-ranging authority over them. In his *miḥna* order, for example, al-Maʾmūn claimed that he was justified in using the sword to secure compliance with his wishes.[40] He also considered it within his jurisdiction to determine who was and who was not entitled to transmit hadiths.[41] A report recorded by al-Jahshiyārī[42] dating to 201/816–17 shows al-Maʾmūn first overruling a judge and then summarily dismissing him because his verdict went against the caliph's vizier, al-Faḍl ibn Sahl.

---

26. Al-Masʿūdī, *Murūj*, 4:332–34; al-Ṭabarī, iii:1112; Ṣafwat, Letter to al-Ḥasan ibn Sahl, 426–27.
27. Al-Masʿūdī, *Murūj*, 4:332–34.
28. Al-Irbilī, 3:124–25.
29. Al-Ṭabarī, iii:1117.
30. Al-Balādhurī, 37.
31. Al-Balādhurī, 33.
32. Al-Irbilī, 3:124–25.
33. Al-Ṭabarī, iii:1137.
34. Al-Yaʿqūbī, *Tārīkh*, 2:438; al-Irbilī, 3:124–25; al-Ṭabarī, iii:1117 and 1138–39.
35. Al-Ṭabarī, iii:1138.
36. Al-Irbilī, 3:124–25.
37. Al-Ṭabarī, iii:1138.
38. Al-Ṭabarī, iii:1138.
39. Al-Ṭabarī, iii:1117; Miskawayh, 447–48; *Kitāb al-ʿuyūn*, 358–59; al-Irbilī, 3:124–25; Ibn Kathīr, 10:250–51.
40. Al-Ṭabarī, iii:1126.
41. Al-Ṭabarī, iii:1125.
42. Al-Jahshiyārī, 315–16.

Claiming for the caliph a superior knowledge of what is best for the Community, al-Maʾmūn portrayed himself as providing religious instruction[43]—a role he also claimed as far back as 198/813–814 in the *Risālat al-Khamīs*.[44] His aim as an educator was to save the souls of his subjects by ensuring that they tread the right path as he defined it for them.[45]

Al-Maʾmūn's conception of the caliphate may thus be summarized as follows. The caliph is uniquely linked to God and the Prophet and is the representative of both on earth. This bond bestows special authority on him and enjoins upon him duties including guardianship of Islam and spiritual and secular leadership of the Community. This conception dates to about 198/813–814 and did not change over time. It was, however, only at the end of his reign that al-Maʾmūn took concrete measures to ensure that his vision became a reality.

4.4. The *Miḥna* Letters

The caliph ordered the *miḥna* while sojourning near Tarsus, where he was either engaged in or planning a military campaign against the Byzantine Empire.[46] The order was conveyed to his governor in Baghdad, Isḥāq ibn Ibrāhīm, in a series of five letters written in the last four months of the caliph's life, and of which only the first bears a date—Rabīʿ I 218/March–April 833.[47]

In the first of these letters al-Maʾmūn indicated the groups to be interrogated. In later letters, he specified particular individuals to be questioned by Isḥāq ibn Ibrāhīm in Baghdad as well as men whom he wanted dispatched to him for personal interrogation. In the first letter, too, the caliph made plain that he had both the right and the duty to order the *miḥna*. Ignorance of God's ways was widespread, and the men who were supposed to guide the public had failed to do so.[48]

Equating "religious faith" with the doctrine of the createdness of the Qur'an, the caliph instructed his governor to secure assent to the doctrine and to keep him informed of the outcome of the proceedings. This task the governor fulfilled by sending what may have been verbatim transcripts of the interrogations. Isḥāq ibn Ibrāhīm was further instructed to make public the names of those who assented to the doctrine and to continue to observe them—presumably to forestall possible retractions or "double talk"—but otherwise to allow them to retain their jobs.

43. Al-Ṭabarī, iii:1117.

44. Ṣafwat, *Risālat al-Khamīs*, 383 ff.

45. Ṣafwat, *Risālat al-Khamīs*, 383 ff.; al-Irbilī, 3:124–25; al-Ṭabarī, iii:1117. And, from a passage in al-Yaʿqūbī (*Mushākalat*, 28), we learn also that the caliph was no less concerned about the need to contribute to the advancement of secular learning as well.

46. Al-Ṭabarī, iii:1132.

47. Al-Ṭabarī, iii:1116.

48. Al-Ṭabarī, iii:1112–13.

The caliph was fully determined that the *miḥna* succeed and spared no means in pursuing this goal. The tactics used varied to suit individual cases. Al-Maʾmūn sometimes dangled the "carrot"—as in the case of al-Wāsiṭī, who was to be told by Isḥāq ibn Ibrāhīm that he would be permitted to transmit hadiths if he assented to the doctrine[49]—but far more often he used the "stick" approach. The caliph denigrated, embarrassed, and blackmailed his targets, cut off their means of support and threatened them with imprisonment and the sword in order to ensure success.

The *miḥna* order does not appear to have been an impulsive act, but rather a calculated step. Considering that al-Maʾmūn's first letter is strikingly ambiguous (see below), that he decided to have the first stage of the *miḥna* carried out by his governor Isḥāq ibn Ibrāhīm as proxy, and that he hand-picked a group of seven men whom he himself first wanted to interrogate, it is safe to assume that the caliph was acting strategically. The goal of asserting the supreme authority of the caliph in all matters demanded such care.

We may now turn to a comparison of the five letters. Two letters, the second and the fifth, are quite brief. The second merely instructs the governor to dispatch seven men to be interrogated by the caliph in person.[50] The fifth letter[51] commands Isḥāq ibn Ibrāhīm to tell Bishr ibn al-Walīd, one of the men interrogated, that he had erred in interpreting a particular Qur'anic verse, and further asks Isḥāq to dispatch to Tarsus all those already interrogated by the governor, except for Aḥmad ibn Ḥanbal and Muḥammad ibn Nūḥ, who had been sent to al-Maʾmūn already.[52]

The first and the third letters, in contrast, are of approximately the same length at some 660 words each. They are similar in other ways, too. The most striking feature of the first letter is its vagueness. This vagueness is probably intentional, reminiscent of a "trial balloon" floated in order to discover what the best next step might be. The letter does not specify the rationale for the interrogation, who is to be subjected to questioning, or the specific measures to be taken against those who refuse to acquiesce in the doctrine. The threat against those who resist is tentative and vague: "The Commander of the Faithful will not seek the assistance of... those whose faith is in doubt" (*inna amīr al-muʾminīn ghayr mustaʿīn fī ʿamalihi ... bi-man lā yūthaq bi-dīnihi*).[53]

Speaking in generalities, al-Maʾmūn states that he considers it his solemn duty to correct the wrong views of those who are "sunk in ignorance and in blindness about God, plunged into error regarding the true nature of His religion, His unity and faith in Him ... people who fall short of being able to grasp the reality of God as He should be recognized

49. Al-Ṭabarī, iii:1126.
50. Al-Ṭabarī, iii:1116.
51. Al-Ṭabarī, iii:1131–32.
52. Al-Ṭabarī, iii:1132.
53. Al-Ṭabarī, iii:1116.

... and to distinguish between Him and His creation,"[54] i.e., the Qur'an. Finally, the bulk of the letter is devoted to damning the self-serving "group of adherents of the false way"[55] and setting forth evidence from the Book which, the caliph says, can only be interpreted to mean that the Qur'an is finite in time, a created object.

The third letter describes in detail what was only vaguely stated in the first. Here, instead of the "judges and court functionaries"[56] mentioned in the first letter, the caliph specifies the names of some of those to be interrogated and implies others by listing the positions they would have to relinquish were they to refuse to assent to the doctrine. His threat in the third letter is also more specific:

> [The Commander of the Faithful] does not regard any of them [who deny the doctrine] suited for holding an office of trust as depositories, authorized legal counsel, witnesses, men whose words or reports are to be construed as reliable, or men to exercise authority over any aspect of the lives of our subjects (*wa-lā yarā [amīr al-muʾminīn] an yaḥill aḥad*[an] *minhum maḥall al-thiqa fī amāna wa-lā ʿadāla wa-lā shahāda wa-lā ṣidq fī qawl wa-lā ḥikāya wa-lā tawliya li-shayʾ min umūr al-raʿiyya*).[57]

The link between the doctrine and "God's unity" is also made quite explicit. Unlike the first letter, this letter summarily accuses those who disbelieve in the createdness of the Qur'an of being infidels.[58]

The first and third letters also share three important features. First, both are heavily loaded with arguments—generally well-reasoned—that are supported by adducing numerous Qur'anic verses. Second, in contrast to the fourth letter, these have a more elegant and coherent style and flow smoothly. Third, they both contain a detailed exposition of the qualities required of the occupant of the caliphal office as well as of his privileges and duties.

The fourth letter is the longest, and its tone and style are at great variance with all the others.[59] It rests on combative argumentativeness rather than reasoning, and in it the caliph no longer concerns himself with the dispute over doctrinal issues. To be sure, al-Maʾmūn's confrontational and non-conciliatory stance is very much in evidence in all of the letters, but it is most evident here. In this letter the issue of the createdness of the Qur'an is relegated to the background, to be replaced by a repeated insistence that

54. Bosworth 1987, 200 = al-Ṭabarī, iii:1113.
55. Bosworth 1987, 202 = al-Ṭabarī, iii:1114.
56. Al-Ṭabarī, iii:1115–16.
57. Al-Ṭabarī, iii:1120.
58. Al-Ṭabarī, iii:1120.
59. Al-Ṭabarī, iii:1125–31.

the caliph must be obeyed and his ex cathedra pronouncements accepted without any qualification whatsoever.

All in all, the fourth letter reads as though it was not written by the same man who wrote the other letters. Also, its style is not in keeping with other texts written by (or for) al-Maʾmūn previously.[60] Why the tone of the fourth letter has hardened and its focus shifted is open to speculation. It is quite possible that al-Maʾmūn was reacting to the messages he received from his governor and had realized that he had underestimated the degree of opposition he would encounter. This could explain why the caliph's threats became increasingly harsh and specific and why he dispatched this letter with a special courier,[61] as though he were intent on bringing *miḥna* proceedings to a swift conclusion with maximal speed and efficiency.

The seven men whom al-Maʾmūn summoned for personal interrogation via the second letter had all declared their assent to the doctrine. If the caliph was surprised by the recalcitrance he faced, he had good reason to be.

4.4.1. The Polarity of Good against Evil in the Miḥna Letters

In the *miḥna* letters al-Maʾmūn seeks to depict an unbridgeable gulf between himself and the rest of the Community. Especially in the preambles to the first and third letters, he emphatically sets himself far above the Muslim Community as the supreme head to whose will all others must bow. In order to maximize the distance between the ruler and the ruled, al-Maʾmūn portrays the caliph as a paragon of wisdom, virtue and knowledge whose position is deeply rooted in no less than the realm of God and the Prophet. Standing in contrast with the caliph are the "*siflat al-ʿāmma*" ("base elements") and the evil ones. Al-Maʾmūn writes:

> The Commander of the Faithful has realized that the broad mass of the people, and the overwhelming majority of the base elements and lower strata of society

60. It is true that one cannot expect the fourth letter to conform to the style in which al-Maʾmūn wrote to al-Amīn (then a caliph), even though he was furious at his brother's unprovoked betrayal; nor does one expect to encounter in a *miḥna* order that tenderness and poetic elegance one sees for instance in a letter he wrote to Zubayda, since the circumstances were different and she was his ʿAbbāsid stepmother. It is perfectly understandable that the fourth letter, indeed all the *miḥna* letters, would not be a match for other letters in which the caliph sought to woo potential allies or gain their favor. Still, the fourth letter stands out as an oddity when compared with everything else that was penned by or for al-Maʾmūn. It is also an oddity in that it violates everything we know about the caliph's presentation of himself. Al-Maʾmūn had always maintained decorum and did not hesitate to defer to the opinions of others, inferiors included, when their positions made more sense than his own, as we saw above.

61. "*Kharīṭa bundāriyya*" (al-Ṭabarī, iii:1130). The Persian "*bundār*" means here "rapid courier" (al-Ṭabarī, Glossarium, cxli-cxlii; cf. Bosworth 1987, 220, n. 678).

> (*al-sawād al-akbar min ḥashw*[62] *al-raʿiyya wa-siflat al-ʿāmma*) are those who—in all the regions and far horizons of the world—are... sunk in ignorance... and have no foresight or vision or faculty of reasoning.[63]

From this summary judgment, which is the only mention of the masses in all of al-Maʾmūn's letters, the caliph immediately turns his ire against the people "of the false way" who "deliberately lead astray" the masses and who are even "more deeply sunk in ignorance and blindness" than they.[64] The caliph's contempt for the men he sought to subjugate through the *miḥna* is in abundant evidence in all his letters. They are called liars, evil, thieves, of corrupt honor, usurers, deceitful, stupid and worse.

Upon scrutinizing these letters in succession, two noticeable developments emerge in the nature of the caliph's attack, which reaches its apex in the fourth letter. One transforms the men from opponents of a doctrine to opponents of the religion of Islam in its entirety. The other shift portrays his opponents as renegades hurling defiance at their caliph.

Initially, al-Maʾmūn made arguments to counter dissent regarding the doctrine of the createdness of the Qur'an, adducing evidence that such a stand violated logic and Scripture. Having failed to convince his opponents, al-Maʾmūn begins to make accusations and issues open threats. He accuses his opponents of "polytheism"[65] and "anthropomorphism,"[66] and likens them to "Christians who say of Jesus, the son of Mary, that he was not created because he is the Word of God."[67] He sees resistance as outright enmity to Islam. By refusing to acknowledge that the Qur'an was created, the men involved were portrayed as having perverted the Qur'anic text and committed a "heresy" (*ilḥād*),[68] thereby aiding Islam's enemies (*sahhalū al-sabīl li-ʿaduww al-islām wa-iʿtarafū bi-l-tabdīl wa-l-ilḥād*).[69] The "utterances [of these men that the Qur'an is not created] ... have enlarged the breach in their religion and the defect in their trustworthiness."[70] Not only are they of "depraved nature... and vessels of ignorance" but they are the "tongue of *Iblīs*" (the devil) as well.[71] These men "have forsaken the divine truth for their own delusions and have adopted for themselves a supporter for their error to the exclusion of God" (*fa-tarakū al-ḥaqq ilā bāṭilihim wa-ttakhadhū dūn Allāh waliyyat*[an] *ilā ḍalālatihim*).[72]

62. On "*ḥashwiyya*," see Houtsma 1912 and Halkin 1934.
63. Al-Ṭabarī, iii:1112–13.
64. Al-Ṭabarī, iii:1113.
65. Al-Ṭabarī, iii:1126.
66. Al-Ṭabarī, iii:1125.
67. Al-Ṭabarī, iii:1118.
68. On this term, see *EI2*, s.v. "*mulḥid*" (Madelung).
69. Al-Ṭabarī, iii:1119.
70. Bosworth 1987, 208 = al-Ṭabarī, iii:1119.
71. Al-Ṭabarī, iii:1115.
72. Bosworth 1987, 202 = al-Ṭabarī, iii:1114.

The theme of obedience to the caliph underlies the second shift in the letters. Whereas in the earlier communications the caliph expressed an expectation that the men interrogated would recognize the truth of the doctrine, his fourth letter states that these men must "fully concur with the views of the Commander of the Faithful"[73] concerning the Qur'an. Obedience, it may be recalled, was the only duty al-Maʾmūn required of his subjects. He viewed refusal to assent to the doctrine as disobedience and a violation of the hierarchical relationship between the ruler and the ruled, rather than a disagreement on a discrete issue. This defiance constituted such an insult to the caliphal institution and to the man appointed by God as guardian of His religion, as to fully justify al-Maʾmūn's threat of the sword. Violence was a fitting threat for a *miḥna* whose purpose was to assert the caliph's all-encompassing authority.

4.4.2. The Caliph as the Embodiment of Virtue and Illumination in the Miḥna Letters

"God made it incumbent upon the *imāms* and caliphs of the Muslims," al-Maʾmūn said in the first letter,

> that they should be zealous: in establishing God's religion, which He has asked them to guard faithfully; in the heritage of prophethood of which He has made them inheritors of the tradition of knowledge which He has entrusted to their keeping; in acting justly in the government of their subjects; and in being diligent in obeying God's will in their conduct towards those subjects. Now the Commander of the Faithful asks God to direct him to firmness and resolution... in the exercise of the authority over his people which God, in His compassion and grace, has entrusted to him.[74]

The third letter expands on the role of the caliph and also emphasizes the special knowledge which God inspires in the caliphs that makes them uniquely qualified to be the Community's guides and educators—a theme already in evidence as far back as 198/813–814, the year in which the *Risālat al-Khamīs* is believed to have been composed. Additionally, the caliph portrays himself as educator not only of the common man but also of those who "... lead an ascetic life... thereby acquiring for themselves glory... and securing for themselves leadership."[75] The preamble to the third letter reads as follows:

> That which God has a right to expect from His representatives on earth and from those entrusted by Him with authority over His servants, upon whom He has been pleased to lay the establishing of His religion and upon whom He has laid the burden of caring for His creatures, the application of His ordinances

73. Bosworth 1987, 216 = al-Ṭabarī, iii:1127.
74. Bosworth 1987, 199–200 = al-Ṭabarī, iii:1112.
75. Bosworth 1987, 202 = al-Ṭabarī, iii:1114.

> and His laws, and the conscious imitation of His justice among His creatures, is that they should exert themselves earnestly for God; render Him sincere service in that which He has asked them to keep safe and has laid upon them, make Him known through that excellence of learning which He has entrusted to them and the knowledge which He has placed within them; guide back to Him the one who has turned aside from Him and bring back the one who has turned his back from His command; demonstrate for their subjects the way of salvation; draw their attention to the limits of their faith and the way to their heavenly success and protection from sin; and reveal to them those of their affairs which are hidden from them and those which are dubious and obscure ... [God also claims from them as of right] that they should bring this about by guiding the subjects aright and giving them clear vision ...[76]

Whether al-Maʾmūn genuinely believed that God inspired him to truth and that his actions were purely in the service of God and the Prophet—even if we were able to answer such a question—is not relevant. What mattered was that the men trying to secure leadership "for themselves"[77] who were subjected to interrogation understand that they must defer to the caliph, who claimed the mission of upholding God's will and religion. The letter does not specify the identity of the men endeavoring to assume "leadership." It is clear, however, both from the letters and al-Maʾmūn's actions, that the reference was to the *ʿulamāʾ*, who he maintained were arrogating to themselves a role that he saw as his birthright. Believing himself endowed with special knowledge inaccessible to such pretenders and committed to guiding his subjects to the path of salvation, it was logical for al-Maʾmūn to give the *miḥna* a strong religious rationale—the doctrine of the createdness of the Qur'an—which he made to seem the ultimate test of fidelity to Islam. He indicated in no uncertain terms that it was he, and he alone, who was qualified to execute God's ordinances and settle religious questions, just as it was he who controlled the affairs of the state. Al-Maʾmūn appears to have been seeking no less than a complete restoration of caliphal supremacy on all matters both sacred and secular which he understood to have existed at the time of his kinsman, Muḥammad, and at the time of the first four caliphs.[78]

4.5. The Timing of the *Miḥna*

The sources say very little about the *miḥna* declaration and nothing whatsoever about the reasons for it or the circumstances surrounding it. Indeed, all that they tell us is that in

76. Bosworth 1987, 205–6 = al-Ṭabarī, iii:1117.

77. Bosworth 1987, 202 = al-Ṭabarī, iii:1114.

78. Crone and Hinds (1986) understand such a conception of caliphal authority to have characterized the Umayyad period as well, contrary to both Sourdel (1962, especially p. 44) and ʿUmar (1977, 111 ff.), who state that a caliph had never before assumed such authority for himself.

the year 212/827, the caliph "made public the view that the Qur'an was created" (*aẓhara l-qawl bi-khalq al-qurʾān*). The timing of the order is curious. We have no knowledge of any special circumstances which may have prompted al-Maʾmūn to order an interrogation so far from home and at such a time. The caliph's campaign was not his first against the Byzantine Empire, and there is nothing in the sources, old or new, to suggest that the issuance of the *miḥna* decree could have contributed to a military victory, or that the two events are otherwise related.[79]

The observations below rest on the assumption that the declaration of the doctrine of the createdness of the Qur'an and the *miḥna* order were indeed separated by six years, as al-Ṭabarī reports. Having perused the sources, I find this assumption dubious and consider it more logical that they occurred in the same year, that is in 212/827 or 218/833, even though there is no known evidence to support my theory. Be that as it may, it is also not unthinkable that al-Maʾmūn's issuance of the *miḥna* order, allegedly in 218/833, was the culmination of some "unfinished business" which he may have started on the eve of his departure for the front. What that unfinished business could have been, if indeed there was any, is not known. The reason for issuing the *miḥna* decree in Rabīʿ I of the year 218/March-April 833 and so far from the capital and during a campaign against the Byzantines, remains a mystery.[80]

Viewed from a broader perspective, however, the issuance of the order was not untimely. Around the time of al-Maʾmūn's reign, men of learning, the *ʿulamāʾ*, including the *fuqahāʾ* (jurists), were gaining authority and becoming more intellectually sophis-

---

79. We might speculate that the caliph's proximity to the Byzantine Empire may have led him to learn that Theophilus (ruled 829–42 AD) was at the time taking determined steps against idolaters in his empire (Vasiliev 1964, 286). This knowledge may have given him the impetus to do a similar "housekeeping" job at home.

80. *Discrepancies in the totality of our source material remain. For instance, we are told that the well-known grammarian, al-Naḍr ibn Shumayl, had also been interrogated during the *miḥna*, by Isḥāq ibn Ibrāhīm in 218/833 (Bosworth [1987, 210] = al-Ṭabarī, iii:1121). But al-Naḍr ibn Shumayl had died in 203 or 204/818–820, "he is said to have died in D̲h̲u 'l-Ḥid̲j̲d̲j̲a 204/May–June 820, but the year 203 is also mentioned" *EI2* s.n. (Pellat) as in Ibn Saʿd, *Ṭabaqāt* 7:373, al-Khalīfa ibn al-Khayyāṭ, *Ṭabaqāt*, 324 and al-Dhahabī, *Siyar*, 9:328–32. In *Theologie und Gesellschaft*, Josef van Ess presents material, some of it circumstantial yet intriguing, which seems to indicate that Ibrāhīm ibn al-Mahdī—after having become anti-caliph in the wake of al-Maʾmūn nominating ʿAlī al-Riḍā as his heir (see 2.3)—took steps to calm the unrest in Baghdad: Van Ess describes a trial held in the Great Mosque of Baghdad against Bishr al-Marīsī who, as stated above (1.8), had supposedly already been questioned by Hārūn al-Rashīd on the doctrine of the status of the Qur'an. This issue requires more scrutiny with stress on any role Ibrāhīm ibn al-Mahdī may have played (Van Ess 1992, *TG* 3:173–90). The more so since al-Maʾmūn also ordered his governor Ibrāhīm ibn Isḥāq to have Ibrāhīm ibn al-Mahdī declare in public that he upheld the doctrine of the createdness of the Qur'an because he had once proclaimed the oppositie (Bosworth [1987, 216] = al-Ṭabarī, iii:1126–27).

ticated.[81] It was in all likelihood precisely this freedom and expanding influence which al-Maʾmūn sought to curtail. The caliph may have felt that, if this trend were to continue unchecked, it would eventually lead to a "house divided."[82] He envisioned a community with a single head who commanded strong and decisive authority over Muslim affairs both secular and sacred. Islam had enemies enough. After all, al-Maʾmūn himself had been a witness, indeed a party, to a great *fitna* (the fourth civil war). Further, the insurrections and rebellions during his tenure were incessant, his own family could not be counted on to support him as the Community's head, his father al-Rashīd had been dispossessed of a good portion of the empire, and the Byzantines were not weakening. Plausibly, only a return to the time when a caliph allegedly held unquestioned authority in all spheres of life could restore the preeminence of the caliphal institution.

4.6. The Strategic Value of the Doctrine of the Createdness of the Qur'an

The sources do not indicate why al-Maʾmūn selected the doctrine of the createdness of the Qur'an for his declaration, or why he made any declaration of doctrine at all. I argue, however, that the doctrine was not an end in itself, but only a pretext for conducting a *miḥna*, a view that corresponds with the silence of the sources on the matter. A *miḥna* naturally required an issue about which men might be questioned. The doctrine of the createdness of the Qur'an was an eminently suitable issue, since it met three important and overlapping criteria which gave the caliph, who set the rules of the "debate," a decided advantage over his opponents. First, the doctrine of the createdness of the Qur'an was a theological issue. As such it had the advantage of challenging those who claimed for themselves knowledge of and expertise in theological matters on a question within their own sphere of authority. It would be inconceivable that these experts in theology would refuse to give an opinion about a matter so intimately tied to their claims to authority. Were they to do so, they would be revealed as impostors or ignoramuses, as the caliph called them, and damage their own interests. Further, an outright refusal to give an opinion was likely to be construed by non-scholars as an act of insubordination to the authority of the caliph—which even Aḥmad ibn Ḥanbal, one of those interrogated, ruled impermissible.

Second, the doctrine of the createdness of the Qur'an was advantageous as a test issue because it lent itself to the type of straightforward, cause and effect rhetoric which characterizes the caliph's letters.[83] The caliph cast the doctrine in the form of a ques-

81. Humphreys 1991, 187 ff.; cf. Lapidus 1975. For the position of the ʿ*ulamāʾ* in society at the time see Cohen 1970.

82. *Echoing Ibn al-Muqaffaʿ, as noted below (3.3.1) (Ibn al-Muqaffaʿ, *Risāla fī l-saḥāba*, 24–28 in particular).

83. Argued similarly by Crone (1980, 258, n. 608), who is additionally of the opinion that the only

tion that the men interrogated were expected to answer by saying "agree" or "disagree." There was no room for equivocation, since answers which did not respond directly were dismissed by repeating the same question again and again. Refusal to give a direct affirmative answer was also portrayed as a refusal of the Islamic religion in toto.[84]

The third criterion which made this doctrine particularly suitable as a test case was the difficulty of rebutting it. Neither on grounds of logic nor on the authority of the Book could the doctrine be refuted within the framework of interrogation that the caliph imposed. In essence, the caliph argued syllogistically in his letters: God created all things; the Qur'an is a thing; therefore, the Qur'an is created.[85] Such an argument left little room for his opponents to disagree. Responding to al-Maʾmūn's insistence that "God made the Qur'an" (*jaʿala al-qurʾān*)[86] meant nothing other than "God created the Qur'an," the best that anyone could produce was a denial of the equivalence of *khalaqa* (to create) and *jaʿala* (to make), yet he could not or would not say what else "*jaʿala*" could mean.

The men interrogated were thus given few options. Some simply acquiesced. A second group took cover under *taqiyya* (dissimulation; caution; insincere compliance with a demand under duress).[87] A third group, at once soothing their own consciences and appeasing the caliph, gave implied consent by responding that, if the Commander of the Faithful wanted them to say that the Qur'an was created, then "*al-samʿ wa-l-ṭāʿa*:"[88]

---

other important issue open to al-Maʾmūn at the time was the determinism/free will debate—a theme which, however, would far too easily lead to ambiguity. By this Crone means that "... free will and divine omnipotence may be compatible to theologians, but the doctrines whereby this compatibility is achieved never make simple shibboleths." Stated differently, had al-Maʾmūn used the free will/determinism issue as the basis of the *miḥna*, he would have begun a debate which could not easily be settled, since there are numerous verses in the Qur'an which can be interpreted as supporting the idea of free will and many others which support determinism.

84. The caliph made such an assertion on numerous occasions in his correspondence to his governor, who was in turn instructed to convey the message to opponents. The following is a sampling. In the third letter, al-Maʾmūn wrote that those who did not hold the view that the Qur'an was created "lay themselves open to the risk of rejecting God's own creative power ... [and] His primordial existence" (Bosworth 1987, 206 = al-Ṭabarī, iii:1118). Later on in the same letter, al-Maʾmūn described those who denied the doctrine as men who did not have "any share in the true religion, nor any part in the real faith and the certainty of revealed truth" (Bosworth 1987, 208 = al-Ṭabarī, iii:1120). In the fourth letter, disbelief in the doctrine was equated with "anthropomorphism ... unalloyed infidelity and sheer polytheism" (Bosworth, 214 and 216 = al-Ṭabarī, iii:1125–26). Repeatedly, the caliph stressed that a denial of the doctrine was a direct violation of the belief in God's oneness.

85. As we saw above, Abū Ḥanīfa employed this argument, too.

86. Al-Ṭabarī, iii:1124. Reference was made to Qur'anic verse 43:2.

87. On this concept in general see Goldziher 1906; for its meaning among the Twelver Shiʿites, see Kohlberg 1975.

88. Al-Ṭabarī, iii:1123.

to hear is to obey (the caliph's command).[89] (This last is also a form of *taqiyya*, through linguistic ambiguity.)

It could not have been lost on a man of al-Maʾmūn's intelligence that members of the latter two groups were circumventing the issue and did not give the unequivocal answer demanded by the form of the question. This was of little consequence, however, since the doctrine of the createdness of the Qur'an was a pretext. Indeed, the counterfeit acquiescence of those who hid behind *taqiyya* and especially "hearing is obeying" was probably of greater service to the caliph than genuine consent, since the message of feigned consent went further to legitimize the caliph's own claims to be the arbiter of spiritual matters. It is therefore unsurprising that al-Maʾmūn lost no time in making public the names of those who were considered to have passed the test. On basis of the above, it would be reasonable to surmise that his goal was to tame and subjugate men rather than to correct their views on doctrinal questions, although of course such a conclusion can only be speculative. The real issue was not a particular theological doctrine, but rather the authority of the caliph versus the authority of those who saw themselves as the legitimate repository of religious knowledge and heritage and as the authentic transmitters of such knowledge.[90]

4.7. Interrogated Individuals

The men subjected to interrogation form two major groups. The larger group consists of unnamed interrogated individuals about whom we cannot say much but who should not be ignored. The second group comprises those whom chroniclers identified by name. Until now, researchers have exclusively focused on this second group.

The vast majority of the unnamed interrogated individuals represent two positions within the judiciary: the judges and the *shuhūd* (plural of *shāhid*), court functionaries trained in law.[91] Isḥāq ibn Ibrāhīm, the governor and chief of police in Baghdad, was ordered to interrogate the judges within his jurisdiction, including Jaʿfar ibn ʿĪsā and ʿAbd al-Raḥmān ibn Isḥāq, the only two men named in the third letter about whom I was able to find any information. These two men held judgeships in the eastern and western sectors of Baghdad during the reign of al-Maʾmūn, posts in which they likely remained dur-

89. *The claim that disagreement with a particular doctrine entails a person's lack of knowledge about Islam in general is also used by some contemporary Islamist groups. This tactic obstructs dialogue by casting complex issues as simple, black and white alternatives: see Nawas 2004 and 2013. For a skillful comparison of Islam with other religions in today's world, noting Islam's special continuity with its intellectual past, see Cook 2014.

90. Cf. Lapidus 1975, 379; Crone and Hinds 1986, 93–96.

91. The current translation of *shāhid* is "witness," a term that falls short of reflecting the functions of the *shāhid* at the time of al-Maʾmūn.

ing the *miḥna*.[92] Their interrogation suggests that the caliph initially sought methodically to secure consent to the doctrine in Baghdad. Al-Maʾmūn instructed Isḥāq ibn Ibrāhīm that once the judges had assented to the doctrine, they, in turn, were to interrogate those under their jurisdiction.[93] Later, in the fourth letter, al-Maʾmūn appears to broaden the scope of the interrogation by asking his governor to question the "judges in the outlying areas of [Isḥāq's] administrative jurisdiction."[94] This letter also repeats the order that judges who have assented to the doctrine should in turn question those under them. Specifically, the judges were to interrogate "those who are in their courts for purposes of giving evidence about the claimant's rights,"[95] meaning the *shuhūd*. We do not know how many unnamed judges and *shuhūd* were interrogated. Their number must, however, have been considerable, especially since a *qāḍī* might have more than one *shāhid*, as may be surmised from al-Maʾmūn's letters. Certainly, their number must have greatly exceeded that of the men who were named in the letters.

In contrast, the group of named interrogated individuals consists of forty-four men. Except for al-Ḥārith ibn al-Miskīn, who is mentioned by Ibn Khallikān, their names all appear in al-Ṭabarī's history.[96] This section analyzes the available information on these interrogated individuals and asks whether anything sets them apart from the rest of the Muslim Community and from their peers. To answer these questions, this study gathered information about the identity, background and affiliations of each of these men. The information appears in appendix 2 in the last column of the table. The table also identifies the men involved in the successive stages of the *miḥna* as indicated by the sequence of al-Maʾmūn's letters to his governors. It indicates the men who acquiesced in the doctrine, those who initially refused to assent but later did, those who steadfastly refused to assent, and, finally, those who were at any time dispatched to the caliph at Tarsus. Listed separately, too, are the men who gave assent but were for unknown reasons still sent to Tarsus on the orders of the caliph. Unfortunately, very limited information is available on most of the named interrogated individuals; for about a quarter of them, no information could be found, and the information on several others must be taken as tentative, since it is not possible to be certain that the biographical literature located concerns the correct individuals.

Everyone interrogated was a man of some learning. Judging by the text of his letters, al-Maʾmūn knew most if not all of the interrogated individuals personally. The evaluations al-Maʾmūn made in his letters of some twenty of these men, sometimes including quite intimate details, indicate two things. First, the caliph must have known a great deal

92. These two men have been added to the list of named individuals below.
93. Al-Ṭabarī, iii:1120.
94. Bosworth (1987, 215) = al-Ṭabarī, iii:1125.
95. Bosworth (1987, 209) = al-Ṭabarī, iii:1120.
96. Ibn Khallikān, 2:56–57.

about them and, second, they must have been prominent enough for the caliph to want to stay informed of their doings and alleged machinations.[97]

There is no particular pattern to the geographical distribution of the forty-four named interrogated individuals. On the basis of the information available, it appears that seven were from Baghdad and four or five from Khurasan (notably Marw). We have far more information about their intellectual pursuits and professions. The largest group—nineteen or twenty—were *muḥaddithūn* (hadith transmitters). Three men were both *muḥaddithūn* and judges, while two others can be identified as *muḥaddithūn* and *fuqahāʾ* (jurists). The group included six judges of whom two were also *fuqahāʾ*. Two men were designated as "*min ahl al-sunna*" (one of the Sunnites) and one as a "*mutakallim*" (speculative theologian). Three were Ḥanafites, and one other, described as "*min ahl al-raʾy*" (one of the proponents of reasoned opinion), may be taken as a *faqīh* or added to the three Ḥanafites, who were often so described.

In all, the forty-four men interrogated were quite heterogeneous in terms of their callings, geographic origins and residential locations.[98] The information available does, however, allow us to draw two conclusions. The first is an obvious one, namely, that they all must have possessed eminence and learning to a degree that brought them to the notice of the caliph. The second conclusion is that the two largest groups, the traditionists and the judiciary, share a common devotion to what may be termed the codified life of the Prophet. While the *muḥaddithūn* concerned themselves with the transmission of the traditions of the Prophet and his close associates, many jurists increasingly interpreted and applied hadiths in their discussions of the law.

Among the forty-four named interrogated individuals, the *muḥaddithūn* formed the largest group, followed by the judiciary. Viewed, however, from the perspective of all the named and unnamed men who were subjected to the *miḥna* under al-Maʾmūn, interrogated individuals who were *muḥaddithūn* outnumbered those who were members of the judiciary. Judging by the qualifications I found, such as "famous" or "reliable" *muḥaddith*s, as well as by the caliber and length of the lists of men who taught or studied under the *muḥaddithūn* in our sample, nearly everyone was a *muḥaddith* of distinction.

That it was the caliph's intent to target the *muḥaddithūn* as well as members of the legal profession is evident in the second letter, even though the first and third letters speak only of *qāḍī*s and *shuhūd*. The caliph's second letter ordered seven men to Tarsus. Of the six on whom we have information, five were *muḥaddithūn*; one was also a judge and a second also a *faqīh*. Perhaps taking his cue from this, Isḥāq ibn Ibrāhīm went beyond the caliph's explicit instructions in the first and third letters by including *muḥaddithūn*

97. *Indeed, the caliph apparently had a reputation for knowing minute personal details of people he knew well: see Ibn Abī Ṭāhir Ṭayfūr, 101.

98. Contrary to Lapidus (1975, 380), who implies a Khurasanian common denominator. *And see 4.7.2. below, where I take issue with the notion of a Khurasanian common denominator.

among the first group he interrogated (column B of the table). That the caliph did not object is reflected, among other things, in his criticism of the various men listed in column E. In sum, while no single factor unites the named interrogated individuals, most were members of the judiciary or *muḥaddithūn*.

4.7.1. Al-Maʾmūn's Targeting of the Judiciary and Traditionists

By the time of al-Maʾmūn, the judgeship had developed into an influential profession responsible for maintaining social order through such functions as fending for the weak (e.g., orphans) and supervising the operation of *waqf*s (pious foundations) in addition to its role administering justice.[99] As the Muslim Community grew, so did the judiciary.[100] Furthermore, Juynboll (1983, 89) informs us that the *qāḍī*s of Baghdad "more so than anywhere else, are identified with transmitting traditions." As a consequence, the judiciary came to acquire an aura of divine legitimacy alongside the de facto power it had over the lives of a large segment of the population. Not only was the Muslim Community subject to the *qāḍī*s and their functionaries, but the caliph himself increasingly lost authority to the near-autonomous judiciary. This trend al-Maʾmūn sought to reverse in order to achieve his vision of the caliph as supreme head of the Community.

Concurrent with the expansion of the judgeship, the number of jurists (*fuqahāʾ*) elaborating the law also grew, and many of the teachings that would evolve into the doctrines of the later schools of jurisprudence spread.[101] Furthermore, the need for legal officials became more urgent in a society that was undergoing rapid change and becoming multiethnic, leading to the development of bureaucracies. One important element of this bureaucracy is represented by the *shuhūd*, young notaries appointed and dismissed by the judge in whose court they worked, who busied themselves drawing up contracts or otherwise handling the work of the court. The first *shuhūd* appeared about 100 years before al-Maʾmūn's era, and they gradually developed into a recognized profession within the judiciary. As extensions of the *qāḍī*'s power, the *shuhūd*, too, played an important role in the maintenance of social order. Together, the judges and the *shuhūd* oversaw the implementation of the *sharīʿa* within the Muslim Community.

The *muḥaddithūn*, in contrast, preserved knowledge of the Prophet, his Companions and other important early figures in Islam. They based their claims to legitimacy on their

99. Various reports on the identity of the first judge in Islam are found in Juynboll 1983, 77–78.

100. On courts and their functionaries, see Juynboll 1983, 77–95; Humphreys 1991, 209–27; *EI2* s.v. "*ḳāḍī*" (Tyan) and s.v. "*fiḳh*" (Schacht); *EI1* s.v. "*shāhid*" (Heffening); Makdisi 1981; Cahen 1970; and Amedroz 1910. For a list of judges in Baghdad see Massignon 1948, and in al-Baṣra see Sourdel 1955.

101. On this process, see Schacht 1964, 23–56 and Coulson 1964, 36–52. *An empirical study of the geographic distribution of the schools of law during the first four centuries of Islam is Bernards and Nawas 2003.

special link with the Messenger, a link which granted them considerable prestige and influence. The number of *muḥaddithūn* was also increasing, likely at an even faster rate than the growth of the judiciary, since hadith transmission required no official appointment. It should also be pointed out that at the time of al-Maʾmūn the boundary between Hadith and *fiqh* was in many ways still indistinct.[102]

No evidence suggests that al-Maʾmūn was opposed to the *muḥaddithūn* as mere collectors of hadiths. He was, however, opposed to their growing influence and collective power within Islamic society.[103] The caliph sensed that his position as "guardian of Islam" and inheritor of the "heritage of prophethood" was threatened by the expanding number and influence of the *muḥaddithūn*.[104] The *miḥna* can thus be understood as an attempt to counter this threat by removing undesirable *muḥaddithūn*. This view finds some support from the caliph's own statements in his letters. On at least two separate occasions, al-Maʾmūn let it be known that he intended to screen the *muḥaddithūn*, taking for granted that he had the authority to do so. Acknowledging receipt of a message from Isḥāq ibn Ibrāhīm, the caliph wrote:

> [You also mention] ordering those who would not profess that the Qur'an was created to refrain from transmitting traditions... whether in private or in public.[105]

4.7.2. Other Patterns

I searched for further patterns in the biographies of the forty-four named interrogated individuals by looking to the ways in which they are grouped within the *miḥna* letters and in other sources (see the columns of appendix 2 for these groupings), yet none emerged. The absence of patterns may simply affirm my earlier suggestion that, beyond the intent to subdue those who challenged his claims to spiritual authority, the judiciary and *muḥaddithūn*, the caliph had no further targets in the *miḥna*.

The one pattern that could be identified concerns the group of seven men summoned for personal interrogation by the caliph in his second letter, listed in column A of appendix 2. There is biographical information about six of the seven men, all of whom were either very prominent or were associated with very prominent men. Discounting Ismāʿīl ibn Dāwūd, who could not be traced at all,[106] five of the six men were traditionists; one of those, Ibn Saʿd, was also a judge. Whether or not it is merely coincidence that

102. Makdisi 1981, 146.

103. Note in this context the importance assumed by "Prophetic *sunna*" (instead of "living *sunna*") which had been emphasized by al-Shāfiʿī (d. 204/820) as an increasingly important source for Islamic law (see Schacht 1964, 59–60).

104. Cf. Crone and Hinds 1986, 90–92.

105. Bosworth 1987, 214 = al-Ṭabarī, iii:1125.

106. *My thanks go to Christopher Melchert who tried to identify this man and who speculates that

al-Maʾmūn ordered his governor to interrogate a group consisting largely of members of the judiciary while he himself questioned a group of mostly *muḥaddithūn* is a question that must go unanswered.[107]

In addition, the caliph's singling out of these men supports my earlier contention that al-Maʾmūn undertook the *miḥna* methodically and strategically, using the group of seven to set a precedent for how he expected the rest of the *miḥna* to proceed. There are several indications of this. First, it is probably no accident that the entire group of seven assented to the doctrine. Of the 44 named interrogated individuals, 12 persisted in their opposition in defiance of the caliph's threats (see column G). It is probably safe to assume that al-Maʾmūn knew beforehand that these seven men would assent, given that he knew them personally, asked for them by name, knew a good deal about the intimate lives of the majority of those interrogated, and had engaged in discussion of theological issues with some of them, as his letters reveal.

While six of the men do not seem to have any special qualities to set them apart from others subjected to the *miḥna*, one of al-Maʾmūn's select group of seven stands out from all the other named interrogated individuals, probably including even Aḥmad ibn Ḥanbal. The man in question is Yaḥyā ibn Maʿīn, a famous *rijāl* expert, or specialist in the reliability of hadith transmitters. Aḥmad ibn Ḥanbal, who along with two members of his family transmitted from Ibn Maʿīn, said of him, "if Yaḥyā ibn Maʿīn does not know of a particular hadith, then it is not a hadith."[108] Yaḥyā ibn Maʿīn also had connections of some kind with eight of the interrogated individuals—a network wider than that of any other man, with the possible exception of Ibn Ḥanbal. This network includes Ibn Ḥanbal and al-Qawārīrī, two of the four men who were interrogated in fetters after the initial stage of the *miḥna*, implying that their assent to the doctrine was considered especially important.

It is tempting to conclude from the above that the caliph's choice of seven men, of whom six were "typical" and one, Yaḥyā ibn Maʿīn, a towering figure, was designed to set a precedent. Their assent, probably anticipated by al-Maʾmūn, would lead others to submit and end the *miḥna* quickly. That the caliph sought to use the group of seven as a model for others to emulate is supported by a message he sent to his governor instructing him to put the seven men on display. Al-Ṭabarī records:

> After they all replied... that the Qur'an was created... [al-Maʾmūn] dispatched them to the City of Peace [i.e., Baghdad], and Isḥāq ibn Ibrāhīm summoned them together at his house. He announced *publicly* their opinion and their judgment to a gathering of *experts in the religious law* (*fuqahāʾ*) *and senior traditionists,*

"he was a locally notable man of religion, hence not found in standard reference works" (personal communication July 9, 2015).

107. *See, however, the addendum at the end of section 4.7.2.

108. Al-Khaṭīb al-Baghdādī, 14:180.

> and they affirmed exactly what the seven persons had replied to al-Maʾmūn. So Isḥāq let them go. What Isḥāq ibn Ibrāhīm did in this matter was by command of al-Maʾmūn[109] [emphasis mine].

To summarize, most of the men subjected to the *miḥna* fall into two major groups, a larger group of traditionists and a smaller group of members of the judiciary. These two groups were influential in society, the judiciary because of their role in elaborating the *sharīʿa* and administering its laws, and the *muḥaddithūn* because they preserved and transmitted knowledge about the Prophet and those close to him, a body of knowledge which at the time was in the process of being canonized. Al-Maʾmūn had no personal quarrel with the men he subjected to the *miḥna*, and he freed unharmed anyone who submitted to his will. What the caliph sought was the restoration of the spiritual authority which he understood the first caliphs to have possessed, but which he now saw claimed by the groups he sought to subdue. The interrogation of the judiciary and the *muḥaddithūn* was a means to achieve that end, just as the initial interrogation of seven handpicked men whom he expected to submit without resistance had served that end at an earlier stage of the *miḥna*.

*Addendum to 4.7.2.

In 1996 I published an article analyzing the interrogated individuals on many more additional counts to see if any common factors or patterns existed among them (Nawas 1996a). I was able to identify and collect of meaningful data for twenty-eight of the forty-four men (almost two-thirds, or 63.6%). To bring out any differences or similarities a "control group" was identified consisting of peers of the interrogated individuals who lived during the same time period but were not interrogated. This control group included 56 men, twice as many as the number of interrogated individuals about whom information could be found. The interrogated individuals and the control group were compared and statistically tested using a wide range of variables. The only significant differences that emerged lay in their intellectual and social spheres—the interrogated individuals were more eminent thinkers and had greater social influence—emphasizing that the caliph wanted his authority over religious matters to be acknowledged by the elite of the *ʿulamāʾ*. If they would yield to the caliph, so would their less eminent counterparts. Moreover, the caliph seemingly wanted to make the interrogated *ʿulamāʾ* an example to all traditionists, with the aim of censoring the hadith enterprise, which supports the hypothesis that explains the *miḥna* as a design on the part of al-Maʾmūn to secure for the caliphal institution full control over religious matters.[110] This article furthermore

109. Bosworth 1987, 205 = al-Ṭabarī, iii:1116–17.

110. *Lucas suggests that by focusing on al-Maʾmūn in my research I did not demonstrate in any way that the Hadith-scholars (cf. my broader focus on the *ʿulamāʾ*) were indeed seeking political authority. Lucas (2004, 196–97 and esp. n. 142), further remarks, "While al-Nawas' [*sic*] argument that the primary

casts doubt on an alternative hypothesis expounded by Lapidus (1975), which explains the *miḥna* as an attempt to quell opposition amongst the Khurasanian *abnāʾ* (i.e., the earliest supporters of the ʿAbbāsid caliphate) since no statistical predominance of (Arab-) Khurasanians within the ranks of the opposition to the *miḥna* was found.

goal of the *miḥna* was to strengthen the caliphal authority is more convincing than the "Muʿtazilite/ Shiʿite" genre of hypotheses, it must be admitted that al-Maʾmūn made a strikingly poor selection of interrogatees, since Nawas was able to find information on merely twenty-eight of the purported "hundreds" of men subjected to the *miḥna*. Clearly al-Maʾmūn missed many of the best and brightest Hadith scholars! How Nawas arrives at the number of victims of the *miḥna* in the "hundreds" is also a mystery, since he does not offer any source for this figure..."

It is true that I could only find information for twenty-eight of the forty-four men who were *named* as interrogated. Lucas skips over the important point that al-Maʾmūn first ordered a group of seven respected *ʿulamāʾ* (six of whom could straightforwardly be identified and who were very prominent) to be interrogated and forced to subscribe to the doctrine of the createdness of the Qur'an. Only after the caliph had received their assent did he order his governor to start questioning other *ʿulamāʾ*. The "hundreds" I refer to I deduce from the fact that al-Maʾmūn decreed that all judges and *shuhūd*—the primary court functionaries—throughout the entire realm must assent to the doctrine before being allowed to perform their official duties. Of course, we do not know how many men belonged to the judiciary, but a figure in the hundreds is not unlikely. Hinds (*EI2* s.n. "*miḥna*") proposes an analytical distinction. On the one hand he speaks of the *miḥna* as a test beyond the confines of the courtroom (the main topic discussed in this study). On the other hand, he also speaks of "*miḥna* as a regular formality in courts of law." Hinds provides a concrete example of what a *miḥna* in the courtroom implied: "...we are told that in Miṣr [Egypt] the *ḳāḍī* would accept the testimony only of those witnesses who acknowledged that the Ḳurʾān had been created...." Hinds gives more examples but notes that we do not have much material on the *miḥna* in courts or in the provinces. The most elaborate description of the *miḥna* outside Baghdad is given by Van Ess (1991–1997, 3:473–81).

CHAPTER 5
CONCLUSION

In 212/827 the seventh ʿAbbāsid caliph, ʿAbdallāh al-Maʾmūn, declared publicly that the Qur'an was created. Six years later, according to surviving sources, he ordered what came to be known as the *miḥna*, a form of inquisition—though on the basis of the available information, it would be a gross exaggeration to equate the *miḥna* with the Inquisition of the European Middle Ages—to force compliance with this doctrine. The caliph's actions have puzzled modern scholars for two main reasons. First, the *miḥna* represents the first time in Islamic history that a caliph declared a religious doctrine and enforced that doctrine upon the Community. Second such actions are not congruent with the typical portrayal of al-Maʾmūn as an accessible man who glorified the intellect and advocated the supremacy of reason as an arbiter of truth.

Modern scholars have proposed several interpretations of the caliph's actions. The most widely accepted theories posit that al-Maʾmūn was motivated by (1) his Muʿtazilite affinities, (2) his Shiʿite or ʿAlid leanings or (3) his perception of caliphal authority. Yet even the proponents of these theories have been uncertain of their explanatory power, singly or in combination.

This study has evaluated these theories on the basis of three strategies: (a) separating the issue of the declaration of the doctrine of the createdness of the Qur'an from the *miḥna* order; (b) focusing specifically on the motives which may have prompted the caliph first to declare the doctrine and then to order the *miḥna*; and (c) using a wide range of Arabic primary sources (72 in all). The results of this study permit the following conclusions to be drawn.

First, al-Maʾmūn's affinities with the Muʿtazilites and their views were not sufficient to cause him to issue the doctrine of the createdness of the Qur'an and impose the *miḥna*. There is evidence that al-Maʾmūn was indeed close to a number of Muʿtazilites. However, he was also close to both non-Muʿtazilites and anti-Muʿtazilites. The very little that is known about the caliph's theological positions does not indicate that he was a Muʿtazilite. Moreover, the idea that the Qur'an was created was not an exclusively Muʿtazilite doctrine at the time. The foregoing does not rule out the possibility that Muʿtazilite influences may have contributed in some way to his actions, but there are no grounds for construing such influences, if any, as the main motivational force behind the *miḥna* or for otherwise linking them causally to his actions.

Second, al-Maʾmūn's presumed affinity for the Shiʿites is not a sufficient explanation for his actions. It is true that the views of the Shiʿites and the caliph converged on a number of issues, most notably the attributes of the *imām*. Such confluence is not remarkable, however. Shiʿism, amorphous though it was at the time, was a widespread movement associated with numerous ideas. That al-Maʾmūn would be receptive to ideas which were relevant to his concerns as a political and religious leader is not surprising. In contrast, al-Maʾmūn displayed a strong regard for the ʿAlids throughout his reign. His affinity for the ʿAlids was not the motivation for the *miḥna*; rather, both his regard for them and his declaration of the *miḥna* were tied to his conception of caliphal authority.

Third, the sources provide ample evidence for the argument that al-Maʾmūn's actions were prompted by his determination to assert the caliph's equal entitlement to religious and political authority in the affairs of the Muslim Community. The careful examination of a series of letters and other documents brought together for the first time here reveals that al-Maʾmūn held this view with impressive consistency throughout his reign.

From al-Maʾmūn's perspective, it was probably a useful coincidence that the Shiʿites of his time had a theory of the "*imām*" that aligned with his own definition of the "caliph." Similarly, the doctrine of the createdness of the Qur'an was likely the more suited to his purposes because it was being debated in Muʿtazilite and other circles. His theory of caliphal authority, however, was fully "Maʾmūnite." It combined what he may have perceived of as an echo from a time, when the Prophet and his successors supposedly personified Islam in all its facets, with the needs of his own time in which many ideas were in a state of ferment and the decline in the fortunes of the empire had to be arrested.

This Maʾmūnite conception of the caliphate is evident in (1) his decision to institute a *miḥna*; (2) his singling out of the *ʿulamāʾ* as its target; (3) the use to which he put the doctrine of the createdness of the Qur'an; and (4) his noted partiality for the ʿAlids, which has long intrigued scholars. While no discussion of these issues can be free from speculation, given the limited range of solid facts available, the analysis below offers a straightforward, internally consistent account that accommodates these four factors within the framework of the theory that al-Maʾmūn's vision of the caliphate was the primary motive for his actions.

Miḥna. The goal of the *miḥna* was not the enforcement of a particular religious doctrine, nor was al-Maʾmūn's primary motivation in declaring that the Qur'an was created the settling of a theological question about the status of the Book. Instead, the *miḥna* aspired to return the Muslim Community to a time when the authority of Muḥammad was allegedly supreme by claiming that absolute authority for Muḥammad's successors, the caliphs. The doctrine of the createdness of the Qur'an was merely a convenient pretext for achieving this objective, as is evident in the shift in the caliph's rhetoric after he encountered resistance to the doctrine. From that point in the *miḥna* the doctrine was relegated to the background and replaced by the theme of "obedience" to the caliph. To secure this obedience, al-Maʾmūn subjected his opponents to a barrage of threats and accused them of undermining "God's religion" and the cause of Islam.

ʿUlamāʾ. The caliph's targets in the *miḥna* were not landowners, artisans, military leaders, tax collectors or partisans, but rather the *ʿulamāʾ*—judges and *shuhūd* (court functionaries), traditionists and *fuqahāʾ* (jurists). By the time of al-Maʾmūn, the *ʿulamāʾ* had succeeded in establishing themselves as the Muslim Community's de facto spokesmen on religious matters, thereby restricting the authority of the caliph to political affairs. This, al-Maʾmūn was determined to undo by means of the *miḥna*. When his initial efforts in the first, somewhat vague, *miḥna* letter failed, the caliph employed stronger tactics, including threats, orders to interrogate specific men, and instructions to the governor to publicize promptly the names of the *ʿulamāʾ* who acquiesced in the doctrine.

The caliph had no need to involve other groups in the *miḥna*, since only the *ʿulamāʾ* stood in the way of his attaining the all-encompassing authority he sought. He further benefited from targeting them because their public acquiescence as the community's de facto religious spokesmen was tantamount to an acknowledgement that the caliph did indeed have the authority to rule on religious matters. In acquiescing to his authority, they would condemn themselves to irrelevance.

The doctrine. It remains unknown why the caliph introduced the doctrine of the createdness of the Qur'an in 212/827 specifically. We similarly lack evidence as to why al-Maʾmūn chose this issue as the one through which he would stake his claim to authority. The doctrine does have special merits, however. First, it was well suited for entrapping the caliph's opponents within the narrow rules he had established for interrogation. Interrogated individuals were permitted to respond only to the question, "tell me if you agree or disagree," which left little room for discussion or nuance. Second, it was a theological issue, which the test had to address since al-Maʾmūn's goal was to assert his authority in religious matters by challenging those who claimed such expertise for themselves. Finally, the doctrine of the createdness of the Qur'an was uniquely suited for al-Maʾmūn's purposes because the Qur'an says nothing about the matter directly, and the indirect evidence which al-Maʾmūn adduced from the Qur'an was perfectly consistent and could scarcely be opposed on grounds of logic. Unable to refute the caliph's logic by means of logic, the *ʿulamāʾ* laid themselves bare to al-Maʾmūn's accusations of ignorance, thereby appearing to be the incompetent spokesmen on religious matters he claimed they were. Their apparent ignorance vindicated his claim that only the caliphs, to whom God granted special knowledge, could be the authentic spokesmen of Islam.

ʿAlids. Al-Maʾmūn venerated ʿAlī ibn Abī Ṭālib, acted leniently toward the repeated ʿAlid insurrections against even his own regime, and in many other ways showed unmistakable favoritism to members of the ʿAlid wing of the Banū Hāshim throughout his life. While al-Maʾmūn's affection for the ʿAlids may have been genuine, his purpose in seeking to reintegrate them into the caliphal institution was in all likelihood to strengthen the caliphate and to stress its link to the sacred. It is in this light that we may view al-Maʾmūn's designation as heir in 201/817 of ʿAlī al-Riḍā, the "most excellent, most pious and most learned" man within the "House of the Prophet."[1] Al-Maʾmūn's cataloging of the merits of a future caliph and his acceptance of the ʿAlids as potential candidates for the caliphate are directly relevant to my contentions. In the first place, they served to remind Muslims, including his ʿAbbāsid family, that the foremost criterion of legitimacy for a caliph was his tie to Muḥammad, rather than narrow dynastic considerations—a theme the caliph was to dwell on further some seventeen years later in his testament. And second, the introduction of the idea of "merit" was meant to secure the survival of "Islam's guardian," the caliphal institution, by ensuring that only those capable of wielding its authority wisely would become caliph.

A number of questions remain. If the *miḥna* was indeed initiated to strengthen the caliphal institution and enhance the authority of the caliph, was this also its main purpose under al-Maʾmūn's successors, al-Muʿtaṣim, al-Wāthiq, and later al-Mutawakkil, who reversed the policy soon after his accession?[2] Why did al-Mutawakkil honor Aḥmad ibn Ḥanbal and ask him to write about the status of the Qur'an? What connections, if any, did the high rank which Aḥmad ibn Ḥanbal attained under al-Mutawakkil have with this caliph's repressive policies against the Jews and Christians and with his persecution of the Shiʿites and ʿAlids?

It would be worth undertaking a close scrutiny of the circumstances surrounding al-Muʿtaṣim's succession as well as his religious policy.[3] Did the Muʿtazilite Aḥmad ibn Abī Duʾād play any role in al-Maʾmūn's choice of al-Muʿtaṣim rather than his son, al-ʿAbbās, as his successor? While the results of this study indicate that the Muʿtazilites and Muʿtazilism were not the primary motive for the introduction of the *miḥna*, did they or Ibn Abī Duʾād in particular play any role in shaping the policy of the *miḥna* under

1. Bosworth 1987, 61 = al-Ṭabarī, iii: 1013.

2. *Melchert 1996.

3. *Nawas (2010) looks into the reasons for al-Muʿtaṣim succeeding al-Maʾmūn rather than al-Maʾmūn's otherwise competent son al-ʿAbbās. The main conclusion is that al-Muʿtaṣim became the new caliph as the result of ʿAbbāsid opposition to al-Maʾmūn. The kernel of this opposition had already begun to develop during the civil war between al-Amīn and al-Maʾmūn—al-Muʿtaṣim and Ibrāhīm ibn al-Mahdī had fought on al-Amīn's side—and this opposition continued during al-Maʾmūn's reign. Ultimately, al-Maʾmūn was able to appease the opposition by accepting al-Muʿtaṣim as a member of his own inner circle at a later stage. Al-Maʾmūn's reign nonetheless ended in a victory for the anti-Maʾmūn wing of the ʿAbbasid family. With this change, the Maʾmūnite vision of a strong caliphal institution—the main thesis of this book—receded, and henceforth the ʿAbbasid caliphate commenced its gradual decline, as confirmed later by the lack of an efficient central authority and ensuing chaos. Nawas (2010) also importantly suggests that the collapse of the ʿAbbasid Caliphate started soon after the first three decades of the ninth century CE, not during the second half of that century, contrary to the prevalent view in the field.

al-Muʿtaṣim and al-Wāthiq? This question applies especially to the former, who was a military man whose limited intellectual accomplishments did not make him feel at home with speculative theologians like the Muʿtazilites.

It would be beneficial also to undertake an in-depth study of all the biographical material that can be found on all those who were interrogated during the sixteen years of the *miḥna*—both those who have been studied in the present work and those who were interrogated after the reign of al-Maʾmūn.[4] Such an undertaking could yield two kinds of useful information. First, with a larger body of evidence than was initially available for this study, it might be possible to perceive patterns that do not appear in a smaller sample. Second, it would be illuminating to study the change over time in chroniclers' perceptions of the men who consented, refused to acquiesce, took cover under *taqiyya*, and so forth. Such a study could also throw some light on when the *miḥna* began to be perceived as modern scholarship now perceives it, which is quite different from the way it was reported at the time. It might also illuminate the ways in which writers of different religious groups and ideological persuasions have understood the *miḥna*.

4. Note that Nawas (1996a) only deals with men who were interrogated under al-Maʾmūn, not with interrogees under al-Muʿtaṣim or al-Wāthiq.

APPENDIX 1
CHRONOLOGICAL INFORMATION ON THE COMPILERS OF THE SOURCES USED

The information below is taken from the second and third editions of the *Encyclopaedia of Islam,* as well as from al-Ziriklī's *al-Aʿlām,* Graf's *Geschichte der christlichen arabischen Literatur,* the *Dictionary of the Middle Ages,* and Jarret's introduction to al-Suyūṭī's *Tārīkh al-khulafāʾ.*

	Name of compiler (year of death), *Work(s) cited*	Information about the chroniclers and their orientations
1.	Ibn Saʿd (d. 230/845), *Kitāb al-ṭabaqāt al-kabīr*	Traditionist and client (*mawlā*) of the Hāshimites. Originally from al-Baṣra, he traveled far and studied under several authorities. He was one of the seven men who were ordered to be brought to al-Maʾmūn to secure their acquiescence in the doctrine of the createdness of the Qur'an. This work contains information on more than 4000 transmitters. Preceded by a biography of the Prophet, the entries are arranged geographically. Unlike his teacher al-Wāqidī, Ibn Saʿd was reputed to be a trustworthy transmitter, usually giving a complete *isnād* (chain of transmitters).
2.	al-Khalīfa ibn Khayyāṭ (d. 240/854), *Tārīkh*	Not much is known about this chronicler, genealogist and *muḥaddith.* He probably lived all his life in al-Baṣra, where he was born. His works reflect ʿUthmānī tendencies. This work is probably the oldest surviving *tārīkh* work we have.
3.	al-Azraqī (d. 244/858), *Akhbār Makka*	Historian of Mecca. His family rose to power under the Umayyads and married into the dynasty. The traditions he uses go back to the school of Ibn ʿAbbās and represent his doctrine.

4.	Ibn Ḥabib (d. 245/859–860), *Kitāb al-muḥabbar*	Philologist. Few details are known about his life. In his time he was considered a reliable scholar in matters of poetry, genealogy and history. His main authority is Ibn al-Kalbī.
5.	al-Jāḥiẓ (d. 255/868–869), *Rasāʾil*	Baṣran man of letters who wrote on Muʿtazilite theology and politico-religious polemics. His writings on theology were devoted to reconciling faith and reason; in politics he dealt with the nature of the caliphate. He never held an official appointment, but he was revered due to al-Maʾmūn's praise of him, among other things. Of his *Rasāʾil* (essays), the *ʿUthmāniyya* is the largest. It deals with the legitimacy of the first three caliphs of Islam and attacks the assertions of the Shiʿites. Politically, al-Jāḥiẓ was a Muʿtazilite apologist of the ʿAbbāsids against pro-Umayyad groups, particularly the "*Nābita*," the *Shuʿūbiyya* (Muslims who denied that the Arabs had a privileged position in Islam) and the Shiʿites. He had Muʿtazilite followers of his own.
6.	Ṣāliḥ ibn Aḥmad ibn Ḥanbal (d. 265/878), *Sīrat Aḥmad ibn Ḥanbal*	Son of Aḥmad ibn Ḥanbal, Ṣāliḥ was born in Baghdad. He was appointed judge in Isfahan, where he died.
7.	Ḥanbal ibn Isḥāq ibn Ḥanbal (d. 273/886), *Dhikr miḥnat al-imām Aḥmad ibn Ḥanbal*	Paternal cousin of Aḥmad ibn Ḥanbal as well as his pupil. Memorizer (*ḥāfiẓ*) of hadiths. Died in Wāsiṭ.
8.	Ibn Qutayba (d. 276/889), *Kitāb al-maʿārif*	A Sunnite theologian and writer of *adab*. Born in al-Kūfa. He enjoyed a favored position at the caliphal court after al-Mutawakkil abandoned Muʿtazilism for mainstream Sunnism. He was given official appointments and became judge in Dīnawar. The work is encyclopedic in scope.
9.	Ibn Qutayba (see directly above), *ʿUyūn al-akhbār*	A large *adab* compendium.
10.	Pseudo-Ibn Qutayba, *Kitāb al-imāma wa-l-siyāsa*	A concise history of Islam which ends with the difficulties between al-Amīn and al-Maʾmūn.

11.	al-Fasawī, Yaʿqūb ibn Sufyān (d. 277/890), *Kitāb al-maʿrifa wa-l-taʾrīkh*	A prominent memorizer (*ḥāfiẓ*) of hadiths. Came from Fasā in Fārs. He is said to have transmitted on the authority of around 1000 *shaykhs*. He died in al-Baṣra.
12.	al-Balādhurī (d. 279/892), *Futūḥ al-buldān*	Important historian of the 3rd/9th century. There are very few details on his life, and even the years of his birth and death are uncertain. He spent most of his life in or around Baghdad, where he had contacts with the historians Ibn Saʿd and al-Madāʾinī. He was a boon companion of al-Mutawakkil. He is praised for his critical mind and reliability.
13.	Ibn Abī Ṭāhir Ṭayfūr (d.280/893), *Kitāb Baghdād*	Man of letters and historian of Baghdad. Born to a family of Persian origin. Of his larger *Book of Baghdad* the only extant part is on the reign of al-Maʾmūn. As a source, it is important due to its early date, the inclusion of documents and the compiler's eye for detail and cultural information. Al-Ṭabarī relied on it for al-Maʾmūn's reign.
14.	al-Dīnawarī (d. ca. 282/895), *Kitāb al-akhbār al-ṭiwāl*	Scholar of Persian descent. He was interested in both Hellenistic learning (*ḥikmat al-falsafa*) and Arabic humanities. He was also the composer of mathematical works. The *Accounts* is his only extant work and has been underutilized, perhaps because of its Iranian perspective.
15.	al-Yaʿqūbī (d. 284/897), *Mushākalat al-nās li-zamānihim*	Spent his youth in Armenia and served under the Ṭāhirids until their fall, after which he went to Egypt. His Shiʿism does not affect his writings, though an interest in astrology is prominent. He does not usually mention his sources.
16.	al-Yaʿqūbī (see above), *Tārīkh*	The first volume offers an account of the history of the world before Islam, paying particular attention to the cultural achievements of different peoples. The second volume details the history of Islam, including the ʿAbbāsid caliphs.
17.	al-Nawbakhtī (d. ca. 300/912), *Firaq al-shīʿa*	Astrologer who had some knowledge of philosophy. Of Persian descent (as his name suggests), but lived in Baghdad. He was attracted to both Shiʿism and Muʿtazilism. This work is an early account of the different Shiʿite sects.

18.	al-Khayyāṭ (d. ca 300/912), *Kitāb al-intiṣār*	Theologian and jurist who was a prominent Mu^ctazilite of the Baghdadi school. The book is a refutation of an attack by a renegade Mu^ctazilite and was probably finished around 269/822–3.
19.	Wakī^c (d. 306/918), *Akhbār al-quḍāt wa-tawārīkhuhum*, known as *Ṭabaqāt al-quḍāt*	Historian and geographer. He was the judge of al-Ahwāz, and died in Baghdad. This work is a history of judges organized geographically.
20.	al-Ṭabarī (d. 310/923), *Tārīkh al-rusul wa-l-mulūk*	Commentator on the Qur'an, and premier classical historian. The *Tārīkh* is a history of the world, presenting events with little analysis. Al-Ṭabarī was initially a Shāfi^cite, then founded a school of his own, al-Jarīriyya. His important break was with Aḥmad ibn Ḥanbal, whose authority he only accepted in Hadith but not in *fiqh*. The followers of Ibn Ḥanbal showed their anger toward al-Ṭabarī often.
21.	Ibn ^cAbdrabbihi (d. 328/940), *al-^cIqd al-farīd*	Writer and poet of Cordoba. At one time court poet. Despite his Andalusian origins, this book is an encyclopedic work restricted to information on the Middle East.
22.	al-Jahshiyārī (d. 331/942), *Kitāb al-wuzarā^ʾ wa-l-kuttāb*	Born in al-Kūfa, he succeeded his father in becoming *ḥājib* (chamberlain) at the caliphal court and hence was politically active. Best known for this work, a history of the *kuttāb* (secretaries) and viziers till 296/908. The extant version ends at the beginning of the reign of al-Maʾmūn. The work gives information on the characters and intellectual capabilities as well as the administrative or political qualities of those discussed.
23.	al-Tamīmī (d. 331/944–945), *Kitāb al-miḥan*	Historian, poet, traditionist and Mālikite jurist. Took part in a revolt against the Shi^cite Fāṭimids and died in prison. The work belongs to the *maqātil* genre of works on rebellions, untimely deaths and assassinations.
24.	al-Azdī (d. 334/946), *Tārīkh al-Mawṣil*	Historian of Mosul. This history of the city was written within the broader context of the events of his time.

25.	al-Masᶜūdī (d. 345/956), *Murūj al-dhahab wa-maᶜādin al-jawhar*	Baghdadi of Kūfan descent. His compositions have a historical-geographical framework. He was sympathatic towards the members of the Prophet's family (*ahl al-bayt*) and Twelver Shiᶜism. This work can be divided into two parts. The first concerns "sacred" history up to the time of the Prophet and includes many countries. The second part is a history of Islam which rarely addresses events beyond Islamic lands.
26.	al-Masᶜūdī (see above), *Kitāb al-tanbīh wa-l-ishrāf*	Probably the last work of al-Masᶜūdī. It succinctly summarizes the main points of the author's other historical-geographical writings.
27.	al-Kindī (d. 350/961), *Kitāb al-wulāt wa-kitāb al-quḍāt*	Historian of Egypt. Essentially a local history, this work also contains information on legal institutions and practices.
28.	al-Maqdisī (d. 355/966), *Kitāb badʾ al-khalq wa-l-tārīkh*	Very little is known about the author of this world history which starts with the beginning of time and has philosophical overtones.
29.	al-Iṣfahānī (d. 356/967), *Kitāb al-aghānī*	Historian, man of letters and poet. Of Arab descent and a member of the Marwānid branch of the Umayyads, though a Shiᶜite. This work consists of a collection of songs and poems as well as information on their composers.
30.	al-Iṣfahānī (see above), *Maqātil al-Ṭālibiyyīn*	This work, written in 313/923, is a compilation of biographies of the descendants of Abū Ṭālib ending with accounts of seventy who died during the reign of al-Muqtadir (d. in 320/932).
31.	Ibn Bābawayh (Ibn Bābūya) (d. ca. 381/991), *ᶜUyūn akhbār al-Riḍā*	Known as al-Ṣadūq, he is considered by the Twelver Shiᶜites to be one of their most prominent jurists and traditionists. It is said that he was born in answer to a prayer to the Hidden Imām—and Ibn Bābawayh was proud of this origin. In 355/966 he went to Baghdad, probably from Khurasan, and later died in Rayy. He taught in Baghdad and entered debates on behalf of the Shiᶜite Būyid Rukn al-Dawla.

32.	al-Tanūkhī (d. 994), *Nishwār al-muḥāḍara*	Man of letters and judge. Born and raised in al-Baṣra. His adult life was spent in Baghdad, where he died. The book is a collection of anecdotes.
33.	Ibn al-Nadīm (d. ca. 377/998), *Kitāb al-fihrist*	Little is known of his life; he may have been a bookseller. He was interested in philosophy and the sciences. He was also a Shiᶜite, probably of the Twelver creed. He reports that this work, a list of known books, was completed in 377/987–988. Some of the Shi'ite ideas contained in this book were offensive to non-Shi'ite readers.
34.	Sāwīris (Ibn al-Muqaffaᶜ) (d. before 393–394/1003), *Tārīkh baṭāriqat al-kanīsa al-miṣriyya*	Coptic monk of whom nothing is known. This history of the patriarchs is a very useful source for the history of Egypt and the Egyptian church as well as for Christianity in Nubia.
35.	al-Shābushtī (d. 399/1008), *Kitāb al-diyārāt*	Man of letters affiliated with the ruler of Egypt, who made him his librarian and boon companion. In this work he mentions each monastery in Iraq, the Shām, al-Jazīra and Egypt. He died in Egypt.
36.	Miskawayh (d. 421/1030), *Tajārib al-umam*	Historian and philosopher as well as the librarian and secretary of a number of viziers. He studied the History of al-Ṭabarī closely. His philosophical work, in which he is particularly concerned with ethics, is more elaborate than his historical endeavors. The work is a universal history from the Flood to the year 369/980, but only original in its last part on the Būyids.
37.	al-Baghdādī (d. 429/1037), *al-Farq bayn al-firaq*	Teacher of theology, law and mathematics among other subjects. Lived in Naysābūr. He was a Shāfiᶜite whose work here is a polemic directed against all non-orthodox sects. In *EI2* Tritton observes that "it is fair to say that he draws from doctrines, which he condemns, conclusions never envisaged by their authors."
38.	al-Thaᶜālibī (d. 1038), *Laṭāʾif al-maᶜārif*	Writer of literature and history. Came from Naysābūr. His name of affiliation (*nisba*) is derived from the fact that he was a furrier who sewed the hides of foxes. He wrote a great number of entertaining and enjoyable books, of which the *Laṭāʾif* is one.

39.	Abū Nuᶜaym al-Iṣfahānī (d. 430/1038), *Ḥilyat al-awliyāʾ wa-ṭabaqāt al-aṣfiyāʾ*	Shāfiᶜite authority on law (*fiqh*) and mysticism (*taṣawwuf*). His grandfather was the first of his family to become a Muslim. Abū Nuᶜaym al-Iṣfahānī was once considered one of the best traditionists of his time. He was physically attacked due to frictions between the Ḥanbalites and Shāfiᶜites in his hometown, Iṣfahān. This work, finished in 422/1031, is a collection of the deeds and sayings of about 650 pious people (*nussāk*) beginning with the first four caliphs of Islam.
40.	al-Ṣābī (d. 448/1056), *Rusūm dār al-khilāfa*	Historian and secretary (*kātib*). He converted to Islam at a late age. He came from Baghdad where he studied literature. He was at one time in charge of the chancellery (*dīwān al-inshāʾ*) in Baghdad. This book provides an overview of the proper etiquette of the caliphal court within a historical framework.
41.	al-Māwardī (d. 450/1058), *Kitāb al-aḥkām al-sulṭāniyya.*	Shāfiᶜite jurist. Judge of Baghdad, where he died. He served two caliphs (al-Qādir and al-Qāʾim) who endeavored to restore strict Sunnism. The work used here is considered a classic on public law.
42.	Ibn Ḥazm (d. 456/1064), *Kitāb al-fiṣal fī l-milal*	Andalusian poet, historian, jurist, philosopher and theologian. Ẓāhirite (one who restricts interpretation of the Qur'an to its apparent meaning). The work is a major study of the various Islamic sects and also of other religions. It is regarded as a sound historical source.
43.	Ibn al-Farrāʾ (d. 458/1065), *al-Aḥkām al-sulṭāniyya*	Ḥanbalite judge in Baghdad known also as Abū Yaᶜlā. At one time he was vehemently attacked by some Shāfiᶜite theologians, who accused him of anthropomorphism. He was also on a council charged with stating official caliphal doctrine, especially concerning the nature of God and the uncreated status of the Qur'an. His son is the composer of a *ṭabaqāt* work on the Ḥanbalites, see no. 46. This work concerns public law.

44.	al-Khaṭīb al-Baghdādī (d. 463/1071), *Tārīkh Baghdād*	Shāfiʿite scholar of Hadith and law as well as a preacher in Baghdad. He was a Ḥanbalite, like his father, but later became a Shāfiʿite. The Ḥanbalites were at the time influential in Baghdad, and al-Khaṭīb was subjected to their hostility; he responded by making occasional disparaging remarks about Aḥmad ibn Ḥanbal and his followers. He was forced to flee to Damascus, where he lived for a number of years and where was almost executed by the Fāṭimid governor for angering some Shiʿites. He died in Baghdad. This work is an encyclopedic collection of about 7800 entries on those who played some political or social role in Baghdadi life. The work's scope far exceeded its writer's intent of providing some essentials for Hadith scholars
45.	Anonymous, (ca. end of 5th/11th century), *Kitāb al-ʿuyūn wa-l-ḥadāʾiq fī akhbār al-haqāʾiq*	There is a close resemblance—at least for the reign of al-Maʾmūn—between this work and al-Ṭabarī's History.
46.	Ibn Abī Yaʿlā (d. 526/1131), *Ṭabaqāt al-ḥanābila*	Historian and Ḥanbalite jurist (*faqīh*). Born in Baghdad, where he was also killed by men who sought his money. As its title suggests, the *ṭabaqāt* is a compendium about the Ḥanbalites. (See entry 43 about Ibn al-Farrāʾ, Ibn Abī Yaʿlā's father.)
47.	Mārī ibn Sulaymān (d. ca. 545/1150), "*Commentario*"	The first Nestorian to systematize theology as a whole. The chronicle used here is part of a theological encyclopedia entitled *Al-Mijdal li-l-istibṣār wa-l-jadal,* which contains the Arabic translation of lost Nestorian works on history and provides important material for the history of the caliphs of Baghdad.
48.	al-Shahrastānī (d. 548/1153), *Kitāb al-milal wa-l-niḥal*	Philosopher of Islam from Shahrastān who died in Baghdad. This work is an exposition of the doctrine of various philosophies, religions and Islamic sects.

49.	Michael the Syrian (595–596/1199), *Chronique*	Historian and liturgist as well as Jacobite patriarch of Antioch. Strong proponent of monophysitism. This work starts with the Creation and ends in the year 1195–96. It covers secular and church events and has a third section narrating miscellaneous events. The Seleucid era is used for dating. It is a good source for the history of the twelfth century.
50.	Ibn al-Jawzī (d. 597/1200), *Manāqib Aḥmad ibn Ḥanbal*	A very prominent Baghdadi Ḥanbalite, he was a jurist, traditionist, historian and preacher. His career as a preacher started with the reign of al-Muqtafī (r. 530/1136–555/1160), whose vizier initiated a Sunnite "revival." Ibn al-Jawzī championed Ḥanbalism not only in his sermons but also in his many writings. Toward the end of his life he fell into disgrace due to the fact that the new vizier was a Shiʿite. *Translated by Michael Cooperson (2013 and 2015).
51.	Yāqūt (d. 626/1229), *Muʿjam al-udabāʾ* (*Irshād al-arīb ilā maʿrifat al-adīb*)	Trustworthy historian, geographer, scholar of grammar and literature. Originally a Byzantine captured by the Muslims, he was later released by his master. He earned a living by copying books. He traveled to many places. This work is a collection of biographies of important men of learning.
52.	Ibn al-Athīr (d. 630/1233), *al-Kāmil fī l-tārīkh*	A scholar and soldier who spent most of his adult life in Mosul. He fought in the armies of Ṣalāḥ al-Dīn. Although he wrote on other subjects, his greatest contribution is in history. This annalistic work details history from the beginning of the world to the year 628/1230–31; it is highly regarded.
53.	Ibn al-Qifṭī (d. 646/1248), *Tārīkh al-ḥukamāʾ*	Arab writer, born in Egypt. At one time head of the *dīwān* of finances of the Atabeg of Aleppo. He probably used this position to pursue his scholarly interests. This work contains 414 biographies of physicians, philosophers and astronomers. It is also of value due to its use of Greek works which have not survived in their original form.
54.	Ibn al-Abbār (d. 658/1260), *Iʿtāb al-kuttāb*	Andalusian historian, traditionist, man of letters and poet. When the *amīr* al-Mustanṣir read a satire which Ibn al-Abbār wrote about him, he had the poet executed; his corpse and his works were burnt the next day. In one of his works, this author shows himself to be anti-Umayyad with possible Shiʿite tendencies.

55.	Ibn Khallikān (d. 681/1282), *Kitāb wafayāt al-aʿyān wa-anbāʾ abnāʾ al-zamān*	A Shāfiʿite biographer and scholar. Born in Irbil, he traveled to Mosul, Damascus and Egypt, among other places. He met the historian Ibn al-Athīr. He was appointed judge of Syria by the Mamlūk sultan Baybars, but had a disappointing career. This work contains biographies of notable figures. Only those whose year of death was known were included in the alphabetically-arranged work. This work is a very useful source both because of its detailed descriptions of contemporaries and its use of lost or unpublished sources for earlier figures.
56.	Ibn al-ʿIbrī (Bar Hebraeus) (d. 681/1286), *Mukhtaṣar al-duwal*	Historian and translator. His Jewish father was at one time physician of a Tatar general. He eventually became head of the Jacobite church in the east. He was known for his tolerance and energy in withstanding political and religious pressures. This work was purportedly written at the request of his Muslim friends and is the Arabic adaptation of a larger Syriac universal political history. He is noted for his reliability in conveying, with fidelity, the contents of the sources he used.
57.	al-Irbilī (d. 692/1293), *Kashf al-ghumma bi-maʿrifat al-aʾimma*	Prolific writer and poet. Worked first for the governor of Irbil then for the chancellery (*dīwān al-inshāʾ*) in Baghdad. Considered a reliable source by the Twelver Shiʿites.
58.	Ibn Ṭiqṭaqā (d. 709/1309), *al-Kitāb al-fakhri fī ādāb al-sulṭāniyya wa-l-duwal al-islāmiyya*	Historian of Ḥasanid ʿAlid descent. Like his father, he was an active agent (*naqīb*) of the ʿAlid cause. He wrote his history of Islam for Fakhr al-Dīn ibn ʿĪsa ibn Ibrāhīm of Mosul. The work contains biographies of the caliphs to al-Muʿtaṣim along with the viziers who served them.
59.	al-Dhahabī (d. 748/1348), *Tarjamat al-imām Aḥmad* (which is part of his *Tārīkh al-islām*)	Historian and theologian. His main interests were Tradition and law. He was a Shāfiʿite who spent much of his life in Cairo. His works are notable for their frequent references to his authorities. The *Tārīkh al-Islām* is a large history of Islam to the year 700/1300–1301. It is divided into seventy classes (*ṭabaqāt*) mainly organized by obituary notices. For the first three centuries of Islam it can be considered a short compendium of al-Ṭabarī's History. *See now also al-Dhahabī's *Tārīkh al-islām* and *Siyar aʿlām al-nubalāʾ*.

60.	al-Dhahabī (see above), *Tadhkirat al-ḥuffāẓ*	A compendium for evaluating transmitters of hadiths.
61.	al-Dhahabī (see above), *Mīzān al-iʿtidāl*	A compendium for evaluating the transmission of hadiths.
62.	al-Ṣafadī (d. 764/1363), *al-Wāfī bi-l-wafayāt*	Man of letters and historian. Originally from Ṣafad, he studied in Damascus, where he died. He wrote about 200 works, including the biographical dictionary used here, which consists of thirty-two volumes.
63.	al-Subkī (d. 771/1370), *Ṭabaqāt al-shāfiʿiyya*	Historian, scholar and Shāfiʿite judge. Born in Cairo but moved with his father to Damascus. Some of his fellow judges in Damascus accused him of unbelief, and he was brought in chains to Cairo. He was released, however, and returned to Damascus, where he died of the plague.
64.	Ibn Kathīr (d. 774/1373), *al-Bidāya wa-l-nihāya*	Historian and traditionist. Syrian Ḥanbalite and pupil of al-Dhahabī. He once took part in the inquiry into an "unbeliever" (*zindīq*) who was accused of incarnationism (*ḥulūl*); later, he was a member of a council which condemned a Shiʿite to death for cursing the first three caliphs, Muʿāwiya and Yazīd. This work is a history of Islam; for the caliphate his sources included al-Ṭabarī, Ibn al-Jawzī, Ibn al-Athīr and al-Dhahabī. It is a principal source for the Mamlūk period.
65.	Ibn Khaldūn (d. 808/1406), *ʿIbar* (which includes the *Muqaddima*)	North-African historian, "sociologist" and philosopher. The introduction (*Muqaddima*) to his universal history (*al-ʿIbar*) contains Ibn Khaldūn's philosophy of history. This work is most useful for the history of the western part of the Islamic world, especially the history of the Berbers. At times the writer is not accurate with details.
66.	Ibn al-Murtaḍā (d. 840/1437), *Ṭabaqāt al-muʿtazila*	The author was a Zaydite *Imām* who held this post from 793/1390–91 until 794/1391–92. Though the work is relatively late, it is still considered an important and original source on the Muʿtazilites.

67.	Ibn Ḥajar al-ʿAsqalānī (d. 852/1449), *Tahdhīb al-tahdhīb*	A major Egyptian judge and scholar of *ḥadīth* and history. It was at the age of twenty-three that he decided to specialize in the study of Hadith. A Shāfiʿite, his interest in religious learning was typical of the Muslim higher middle class of the time. Most of the material he used was from older sources, and he aimed at thoroughness and completeness.
68.	Ibn Hajar al-ʿAsqalānī (see directly above), *Lisān al-mīzān*	This work provides information on men associated with hadith transmissions who are not in the canonical collections.
69.	Ibn al-Taghrībirdī (d. 874/1470), *al-Nujūm al-zāhira fī mulūk Miṣr wa-l-Qāhira*	Historian of Egypt who had a military career before he began to write history. This work is a history of Egypt commencing with the year 20/641 and continuing until the writer's own time—written, so he tells us, for his friends and especially the Mamlūk sultan's son.
70.	al-Suyūṭī (d. 911/1505), *Tārīkh al-khulafāʾ*	An author who wrote on many fields. The strength of this work lies not in its originality but in the conciseness of its narrative.
71.	Ibn al-ʿImād (d. 1089/1679), *Shadharāt al-dhahab fī akhbār man dhahab*	A scholar of the Ḥanbalite school. This work is an annalistic biographical history whose entries are usually arranged by year of death. It covers the period from the year 1 of the Islamic calendar until 1000. It was written as a preliminary source for scholars who could not afford more elaborate and expensive works.
72.	Ṣafwat, A.Z., *Jamharat rasāʾil al-ʿArab. Vol. III and IV*	A compilation of important letters and documents of which Volumes III and IV—used in this study—include material relevant to the early ʿAbbāsid period.

APPENDIX 2
INFORMATION ON THOSE INTERROGATED

The columns in the Table headed by letters represent the following categories. An individual's inclusion in a category is represented by an asterisk [*].

A. The seven men summoned by the caliph for personal interrogation as per his second letter.
B. The twenty-six men interrogated *en masse* by Isḥāq ibn Ibrāhīm whose names are reported by al-Ṭabarī immediately following the third letter.
C The fourteen men whom al-Ṭabarī mentions immediately following the third letter as having been individually interrogated by Isḥāq ibn Ibrāhīm, and about some of whom we only have information from the description of the *miḥna* proceedings. (A comparison of columns B and C shows that nine of these fourteen men were previously interrogated *en masse*, the other five presumably individually and for the first time.)
D. The twenty-four men who passed the review of the caliph in his fourth letter and of whom sixteen (see column E) were reviled by him.
E. The sixteen (of the twenty-four men listed in column D) whom al-Maʾmūn subjected to verbal assault on grounds of defective intellect [(I)] or on grounds of personal integrity and character [(P)].
F. The twenty one men who were dispatched to Tarsus as reported by al-Ṭabarī immediately following the text of the fifth letter. (Two other men, Aḥmad ibn Ḥanbal and Muḥammad ibn Nūḥ, were also sent to Tarsus, but on an earlier occasion—hence their names are not listed in column F.)
G. The final list of the twelve men who on no occasion are reported to have given their assent to the doctrine.
For those who did give assent, see (a), (b), (c) in the table:
   a. The fifteen men who gave assent, according to al-Ṭabarī, and were hence not sent to Tarsus.
   b. The twelve men who gave assent and yet were sent to Tarsus.
   c. Though al-Ṭabarī does not say so directly, the five men in this final group may have given their assent as implied by their having been spared dispatch to Tarsus, which, judging by the caliph's orders, would not have been the case had they resisted.

No.	Name	A	B	C	D	E	F	G
1.	ᶜAbbās, *mawlā* of al-Maʾmūn				* (c)			
2.	ᶜAbd al-Aᶜlā ibn Mushir, Abū Mushir al-Dimashqī				* (a)			
3.	ᶜAbd al-Munᶜim ibn Idrīs			* (a)				
4.	ᶜAbd al-Raḥmān ibn Isḥāq ibn Ibrāhīm ibn Salāma al-Ḍabbī		*		* (c)			
5.	Abū Muslim	* (a)						
6.	Aḥmad ibn Shujāᶜ		*		* (b)	* (P)	*	
7.	ᶜAlī ibn Abī Muqātil		*	*	*		*	*
8.	"al-Aᶜmā" (the blind man)			* (a)				
9.	al-Bazzāz, Abu al-ᶜAwwām		*		* (b)	* (I)	*	
10.	Bishr ibn al-Walīd al-Kindī		*	*	*	* (I)	*	*

Biographical information
A *mawlā* (client) of al-Maʾmūn (al-Ṭabarī, III:1125); nothing else is known about him
Muḥaddith from whom the interrogated Yaḥyā ibn Maʿīn and others transmitted; interrogated by al-Maʾmūn personally; from Damascus and very popular there; Ibn Ḥanbal spoke highly of him and said that he was his teacher (al-Khaṭīb al-Baghdādī, 11:72–75).
Muḥaddith who died in Baghdad (al-Khaṭīb al-Baghdādī, 11:131–34).
Influential judge in western Baghdad at the time of al-Maʾmūn (especially after the dismissal of Bishr ibn al-Walīd al-Kindī, who was also interrogated).
Mustamlī (one who dictates traditions as a profession) of the famous Qur'anic commentator and traditionist Yazīd ibn Hārūn; knew Sajjāda, another of those interrogated; possibly had contact with Manṣūr ibn al-Mahdī, who had refused to serve as anti-caliph against al-Maʾmūn (al-Khaṭīb al-Baghdādī, 13:342).
Could not be identified.
Could not be identified.
Al-Ṭabarī reports that he was not a *faqīh* (iii:1124); nothing else is known about him.
A reliable *muḥaddith* who transmitted from several men but transmitted only to his son; may have been a *mustamlī* (one who dictates traditions as a profession) of perhaps the father of Ibn ʿUlayya (al-Khaṭīb al-Baghdādī, 5:227–28).
Judge since 208/823–824; studied *fiqh* under Abū Yūsuf, the chief judge under al-Rashīd; influential at the court of al-Maʾmūn; learned; a Ḥanafite opponent of the doctrine of the createdness of the Qur'an; rather a controversial figure (al-Khaṭīb al-Baghdādī, 7:804).

No.	Name	A	B	C	D	E	F	G
11.	al-Dhayyāl al-Haytham		*	*	*	* (P)	*	*
12.	al-Faḍl ibn Ghānim		*		* (b)	* (P)	*	
13.	al-Ḥasanī, Jaᶜfar ibn ᶜĪsā				*			
14.	Ibn al-Aḥmar			* (a)				
15.	Ibn ᶜAlī ibn ᶜĀṣim		*		* (b)	* (I)	*	
16.	Ibn al-Bakkāʾ al-Akbar			*			*	*
17.	Ibn Dāʾūd, Ismāᶜīl	* (a)						
18.	Ibn al-Dawraqī, Aḥmad	* (a)						
19.	Ibn al-Farrukhān		*		* (b)	* (P)	*	
20.	Ibn Ḥanbal, Aḥmad		*	*	*	* (I)		*

Biographical information
Could not be identified either under this name or that given by Yāqūt (9:18–24), al-Dhayyāl *ibn* al-Haytham.
From Marw; lived and died in Baghdad; traditionist who studied Hadith under numerous men; even more transmitted from him; was considered an authority on Hadith by the Egyptians; appointed judge (possibly chief judge) of Egypt by the territory's governor, but was dismissed after some ten months (al-Khaṭīb al-Baghdādī, 12:357–60).
Judge; at one time (probably 210/825–826) appointed by al-Maʾmūn as judge of eastern Baghdad, probably till at least 218/833–834 (Wakīʿ, 3:273; al-Khaṭīb al-Baghdādī, 7:160–62).
Could not be identified. Uhrig (1988, 271) suggests he was the son of the grammarian ʿAlī b al-Mubārak, known as al-Aḥmar (d. 194/810).
Identity uncertain. He may be Muḥammad or Abū ʿAlī ibn ʿĀṣim or ʿĀṣim ibn Abī al-Ḥusayn or ʿĀṣim ibn ʿAlī ibn ʿĀṣim Ṣuhayb; the latter (the only one on whom information could be found) was a very popular *muḥaddith* who transmitted in al-Ruṣāfa; members of the Ibn Ḥanbal family, including Aḥmad, transmitted from him and another interrogated individual, al-Qawārīrī; may have had contacts with Yaḥyā ibn Maʿīn, who was also interrogated, but whether their relationship was cordial is uncertain (al-Khaṭīb al-Baghdādī, 12:247–50).
Could not be identified. Perhaps he was the brother of Ibn al-Bakkāʾ al-Aṣghar who, as it appears from al-Ṭabarī's report (iii:1124), was an antagonist of Ibn Ḥanbal and may have taken part in the interrogation proceedings.
Could not be identified.
Transmitted from the famous Yazīd ibn Hārūn; reliable traditionist; the son of Aḥmad ibn Ḥanbal and many others transmitted from him (al-Khaṭīb al-Baghdādī, 4:6–7).
Could not be identified.
The famous *muḥaddith* and eponym of the Ḥanbalī school of law.

No.	Name	A	B	C	D	E	F	G
21.	Ibn al-Hirsh		*				*	*
22.	Ibn al-Miskīn, al-Ḥārith, Abū ʿUmar							*
23.	Ibn ʿUlayya al-Akbar		*	* (a)				
24.	Ibrāhīm ibn al-Mahdī				* (c)			
25.	Isḥāq ibn Abī Isrāʾīl		*				*	*
26.	Ismāʿīl ibn Abī Masʿūd	* (a)						
27.	al-Jawharī, ʿAlī ibn Jaʿd		*				*	*
28.	Muḥammad ibn Ḥātim ibn Maymūn		*		* (b)	* (P)	*	
29.	Muḥammad ibn Nūḥ al-Maḍrūb		*		*	* (P)		*
30.	Muḥammad ibn Saʿd ibn Manīʿ al-Baṣrī	* (a)						

Biographical information
Could not be identified; also not found under Hirsh or Harsh as Yāqūt (9:18–24) suggests.
Reliable *muḥaddith*; *faqīh*; transmitted in Baghdad to the son of Ibn Ḥanbal among others; jailed for his refusal to assent, only to be released by al-Mutawakkil (Ibn Khallikān, 2:56–57; al-Khaṭīb al-Baghdādī, 8:216–18).
Identity uncertain; not to be confused with the *mutakallim* Ibn ʿUlayya who was a proponent of the createdness of the Qur'an (contrary to Uhrig 1988, 265); see Van Ess (1991–, 2:420, n. 23) on the confusion between the two.
The paternal uncle of al-Maʾmūn who was installed in 202/817–818 as anti-caliph in the aftermath of the death of al-Amīn due to the ʿAbbāsids' fear that the caliphate might be passed on to the ʿAlids.
Originally from Marw; said to be a reliable transmitter; among the many who transmitted from him are al-Bukhārī and ʿAbdallāh, son of Ibn Ḥanbal (al-Khaṭīb al-Baghdādī, 6:356–62).
Traditionist; *kātib* (clerk) of al-Wāqidī (al-Khaṭīb al-Baghdādī, 6:250).
Transmitted to many, including al-Bukhārī and, from among those interrogated, Isḥāq ibn Abī Isrāʾīl; portrayed as a courageous man, reflected in an anecdote about how he failed to stand up with everyone else when al-Maʾmūn left the room, and then justified his action with a hadith that impressed the caliph (al-Khaṭīb al-Baghdādī, 11:360–66).
Muḥaddith who transmitted from Yaḥyā ibn Hārūn among others, and from whom Muslim and many others transmitted; originally from Marw (al-Khaṭīb al-Baghdādī, 2:266–68).
Famous among the *ahl al-sunna* though his hadiths were not extensive; associated with Ibn Ḥanbal and sent along with him to Tarsus in fetters on the orders of al-Maʾmūn (al-Khaṭīb al-Baghdādī, 3:322–23).
Muḥaddith and famous historian, known as Ibn Saʿd; born in al-Baṣra; *kātib* (clerk) of al-Wāqidī; studied under more than six scholars; three others transmitted from him; had contact with al-Qawārīrī, Yaḥyā ibn Maʿīn, and Ibn Ḥanbal, all interrogated (al-Khaṭīb al-Baghdādī, 5:321).

No.	Name	A	B	C	D	E	F	G
31.	al-Muẓaffar			* (a)				
32.	al-Naḍr ibn Shumayl		*				*	*
33.	al-Qaṭīʿī, Ismāʾīl ibn Ibrāhīm, Abū Maʿmar		*		* (b)	* (P)	*	
34.	al-Qawārīrī, ʿUbaydallāh ibn Maysara		*	*	* (b)	* (P)	*	
35.	Qutayba ibn Saʿīd		*	* (a)				
36.	Saʿdawayh, Saʿīd ibn Sulaymān		*		* (b)	* (P)	*	
37.	Sajjāda, al-Ḥasan ibn Ḥammād ibn Kusayb		*		* (b)	* (P)	*	
38.	*Shaykh* from the progeny of ʿUmar ibn al-Khaṭṭāb		*	* (a)				
39.	al-Sindī				* (c)			
40.	al-Tammār, Abū Naṣr		*		* (b)	* (I)	*	

Biographical information
From Baghdad; possibly a *muḥaddith* (al-Khaṭīb al-Baghdādī, 13:126).
Possibly mistakenly identified since al-Naḍr ibn Shumayl appears to have died 14 or 15 years before the *miḥna*, in 203/818–819 or 204/819–820; a traditionist and grammarian from al-Baṣra who lived in Marw and introduced the *sunna* to Khurasan; a *qāḍī* of impeccable reputation (Juynboll 1983, 23 and 115; Ibn Ḥajar, *Tahdhīb*, 10:390–91).
Muḥaddith from whom al-Bukhārī and Muslim transmitted, as did a son of Ibn Ḥanbal; of Khurasanian origin.
Baṣran who lived in Baghdad; involved in judicial activities (as implied in the fourth letter on the *miḥna*); transmitted from and to many men including Ibn Ḥanbal and another men interrogated.
Traditionist who studied under numerous men and from whom a number of others transmitted, including Ibn Ḥanbal and Zuhayr ibn Ḥarb, also interrogated; al-Bukhārī and Muslim transmitted from him as well (al-Khaṭīb al-Baghdādī, 12:464–70).
Reliable traditionist who, according to al-Khaṭīb al-Baghdādī, was of the *ahl al-sunna*; lived in Baghdad and transmitted there; many transmitted from him, including two who were interrogated, Yaḥyā ibn Maʿīn and Muḥammad ibn Ḥātim ibn Maymūn, as well as a son of Sajjāda; after consenting to the doctrine he described himself as *kāfir* (unbeliever) (al-Khaṭīb al-Baghdādī, 9:84–87).
Considered a reliable traditionist; studied under and transmitted to numerous men; Ḥanafite; according to al-Khaṭīb al-Baghdādī, he allegedly had a woman divorce her husband for having said that the Qur'an was created (a story thought possible by Ibn Ḥanbal) (al-Khaṭīb al-Baghdādī, 7:295-6).
Judge of al-Raqqa, from the progeny of ʿUmar ibn al-Khaṭṭāb; nothing else is known of him (al-Ṭabarī, III:1124).
Possibly al-Sindī ibn Yaḥyā b Saʿīd al-Ḥarashī, a former supporter of al-Amīn (Bosworth 1987, 17, n. 37) who was among those who officiated in the ceremony which declared al-Maʾmūn deposed and Ibrāhīm b. al-Mahdī anti-caliph (al-Ṭabarī, III:1015-6).
Muḥaddith; originally from Khurasan but lived in Baghdad throughout his life; very pious; Muslim was among the many who transmitted from him (al-Khaṭīb al-Baghdādī, 10:420–23).

No.	Name	A	B	C	D	E	F	G
41	Yaḥyā ibn ʿAbd al-Raḥmān al-ʿUmarī		*		* (b)		*	
42.	Yaḥyā ibn Maʿīn	* (a)						
43.	al-Ziyādī, Abū Ḥassān		*	*	*	* (P)	*	*
44.	Zuhayr ibn Ḥarb, Abu Khaythama	* (a)						

Biographical information
Could not be identified under this name or that given by Yāqūt (9:18–24), Yaḥyā ibn ʿAbd al-Raḥmān al-Riyāshī; the *miḥna* letters tell us that he may have claimed to be descended from ʿUmar b al-Khaṭṭāb (al-Ṭabarī, III:1130).
Important traditionist, *faqīh*, *ʿālim* and *rijāl*-expert (someone who has knowledge of the reliability of hadith transmitters); known for his piety and learning; Ibn Ḥanbal, his son and grandson transmitted from him as did Muḥammad ibn Saʿd, Zuhayr ibn Ḥarb, Ibn al-Dawraqī (all interrogated), al-Bukhārī, Muslim and Abū Dāʾūd; he and Ibn Ḥanbal admired each other; Ibn Ḥanbal considered him a most reliable *muḥaddith* (Ibn Saʿd, 7:354; al-Khaṭīb al-Baghdādī, 14:177–87).
Born in Baghdad; died in 242/856–857 or 243/857–858; judge and traditionist closely associated with al-Wāqidī (d. 207/822–823); Ḥanafite; opposed to the doctrine of the createdness of the Qur'an; frequently quoted by Ibn Abī Ṭāhir Ṭayfūr (al-Khaṭīb al-Baghdādī, 7:356–61).
Traditionist; *ʿālim* (al-Khaṭīb al-Baghdādī, 8:482–84).

APPENDIX 3
TIMETABLE OF KEY EVENTS DURING AL-MAʾMŪN'S REIGN

AH	AD	Event
198	813–814	End of Civil War; al-Maʾmūn stays in Khurasan
Ramadan 201	March 817	al-Maʾmūn appoints ʿAlī al-Riḍā heir to the caliphate
Muharram 202	July 817	Ibrāhīm ibn al-Mahdī appointed anti-caliph in Baghdad
202	817–818	al-Maʾmūn decides to leave Khurasan for Baghdad
Shaʿban 202	February 818	al-Faḍl ibn Sahl murdered while taking a bath
Safar 203	September 818	ʿAlī al-Riḍā dies
Safar 204	August 819	al-Maʾmūn enters Baghdad
211	826–827	al-Maʾmūn forbids people to speak favorably about the Umayyad caliph Muʿāwiya
212	827–828	al-Maʾmūn proclaims the doctrine of the createdness of the Qur'an and the pre-eminence (*tafḍīl*) of ʿAlī ibn Abī Ṭālib
Muharram 217	February–March 832	al-Maʾmūn goes to Egypt
Rabiʿ I 218	March–April 833	*Miḥna* starts
Rajab 218	August 833	al-Maʾmūn dies

Chronology according to al-Ṭabarī, *Tārīkh al-rusul wa-l-mulūk*.

APPENDIX

BIBLIOGRAPHY

*Entries added to this edition are marked with an *. Death dates are provided for authors of primary sources.*

Primary sources

Abū Nuʿaym al-Iṣfahānī (430 A.H./1038 A.D.). *Ḥilyat al-awliyāʾ wa-ṭabaqāt al-aṣfiyāʾ*. Beirut: Dār al-kutub al-ʿilmiyya, 1309/1988.

Abū Yaʿlā, see Ibn al-Farrāʾ

al-Azdī (334/946). *Tārīkh al-Mawṣil*. Edited by ʿA. Ḥabība. Cairo: Dār al-taḥrīr li-l-ṭabʿ wa-l-nashr, 1387/1967.

al-Azraqī (244/858). *Akhbār Makka*. Edited by R. Ṣ. Malḥas. Madrid: Dār al-Andalus, n.d.

al-Baghdādī (429/1037). *Al-Farq bayn al-firaq*. Edited by M. al-Kawtharī. Cairo: Maktab nashr al-thaqāfa al-islāmiyya, 1367/1948.

al-Balādhurī (279/892). *Futūḥ al-buldān*. Edited by S. al-Munajjid. Cairo: Maktabat al-nahḍa al-miṣriyya, 1957. English translation: *The Origins of the Islamic State*. Translated by P. K. Hitti. New York: Columbia University, 1916.

Bar Hebraeus, see Ibn al-ʿIbrī

al-Dhahabī (748/1348). *Mīzān al-iʿtidāl fī naqd al-rijāl*. Edited by ʿA. M. and F.ʿ A. al-Bajāwī. N.p.: Dār al-fikr al-ʿarabī, n.d.

——. *Tadhkirat al-ḥuffāẓ*. Hyderabad: Dāʾirat al-maʿārif al-ʿuthmāniyya, 1388/1968.

——. *Tarjamat al-imām Aḥmad* (an abridgement of *Tārīkh al-islām*). Edited by A. M. Shākir. Beirut: Dār al-maʿārif li-l-ṭibāʿa, 1365/1946.

al-Dīnawarī (282/895). *Kitāb al-akhbār al-ṭiwāl*. Edited by H. al-Zayn. Beirut: Dār al-fikr al-ḥadīth, 1988.

al-Jāḥiẓ (255/868–9). *Rasāʾil*. Edited by ʿA. Mulḥim. Beirut: Dār maktabat al-hilāl, 1987.

al-Jahshiyārī (331/942). *Kitāb al-wuzarāʾ wa-l-kuttāb*. Edited by M. al-Saqqā et al. Cairo: M. M. al-Ḥalabī, 1401/1980.

al-Fasawī (277/890). *Kitāb al-maʿrifa wa-l-tārīkh*. Edited by A. D. al-ʿUmarī. Baghdad: Maṭbaʿat al-irshād, 1394–6/1974–76.

Ḥanbal ibn Isḥāq ibn Ḥanbal (273/886). *Dhikr miḥnat al-imām Aḥmad ibn Ḥanbal*. Edited by M. Naghash. Cairo: Dār nashr al-thaqāfa, 1397/1977.

Ibn al-Abbār (658/1260). *Iʿtāb al-kuttāb*. Edited by Ṣ. al-Ashtar. Damascus: Maṭbūʿāt majmaʿ al-lugha al-ʿarabiyya, 1380/1961.

Ibn ʿAbdrabbihi (328/940). *Al-ʿIqd al-farīd*. Edited by M. M. Qumayḥa. Beirut: Dār al-kutub al-ʿilmiyya, 1404/1983.

Ibn Abī Ṭāhir Ṭayfūr (280/893). *Kitāb Baghdād*. Edited and translated by H. Keller. Leipzig: O. Harrassowitz, 1908.

Ibn Abī Yaʿlā (526/1131). *Ṭabaqāt al-ḥanābila*. Edited by M. al-Faqī. Cairo: Maṭbaʿat al-sunna al-muḥammadiyya, n.d.

Ibn al-Athīr (630/1233). *Al-Kāmil fī l-tārīkh*. Beirut: Dār al-kitāb al-ʿarabī, 1403/1983.

Ibn Bābawayh (ca. 381/991). *ʿUyūn akhbār al-riḍā*. Edited by Ḥ. al-Khurāsān. Najaf: al-Maṭbaʿa al-ḥaydariyya, 1390/1970.

Ibn al-Farrāʾ (a.k.a. Abū Yaʿlā) (458/1066). *Al-Aḥkām al-sulṭāniyya*. Edited by M. al-Faqī. Cairo: al-Ḥalabī, 1356/1938.

Ibn Ḥabīb (245/859–60). *Kitāb al-muḥabbar*. Edited by I. Lichtenstädter. Beirut: Dār al-āfāq al-jadīda, n.d.

Ibn Ḥajar al-ʿAsqalānī (852/1449). *Tahdhīb al-tahdhīb*. Beirut: Dār al-fikr, 1404/1984.

——. *Lisān al-mīzān*. Beirut: Muʾassasat al-aʿlamī li-l-maṭbūʿāt, 1406/1986.

Ibn Ḥazm (456/1064). *Kitāb al-fiṣal fī l-milal*. Edited by ʿA. Khalīfa. Cairo: M.ʿA. Ṣubayḥ, 1347/1928–9. Partial English translation: *The Heterodoxies of the Shiites According to Ibn Ḥazm*. Translated by I. Friedländer. New Haven: American Oriental Society, 1909.

——. *Jamharat ansāb al-ʿarab*. Edited by ʿA.M. Hārūn. Cairo: Dār al-maʿārif, 1982.

Ibn al-ʿIbrī (a.k.a. Bar Hebraeus) (681/1286). *Mukhtaṣar al-duwal*. Edited by A. Ṣāliḥānī. Beirut: Dār al-rāʾid al-lubnānī, 1403/1983.

Ibn al-ʿImād (1089/1679). *Shadharāt al-dhahab fī akhbār man dhahab*. Beirut: Dār al-āfāq al-jadīda, n.d.

Ibn al-Jawzī, *Manāqib al-imām Aḥmad b. Ḥanbal/Virtues of the Imām Aḥmad ibn Ḥanbal*, ed. and tr. Michael Cooperson, 2 vols. Library of Arabic Literature. New York: New York University Press, 2013, 2015.

Ibn al-Jawzī (597/1200). *Manāqib al-imām Aḥmad ibn Ḥanbal*. 2nd and revised edition. Edited by M. A. al-Khānjī al-Kutubī. Beirut: Khānjī wa-Ḥamdān, n.d.

Ibn Kathīr (774/1373). *Al-Bidāya wa-l-nihāya*. Beirut: Maktabat al-Maʿārif, 1966.

Ibn Khaldūn (808/1406). *Kitāb al-ʿibar*. Beirut: Maktabat al-madrasa wa-dār al-kitāb al-lubnānī, 1967.

Ibn Khallikān (681/1282). *Wafayāt al-aʿyān wa-anbāʾ abnāʾ al-zamān*. Edited by I. ʿAbbās. Beirut: Dār al-thaqāfa, n.d.

Ibn al-Muqaffaʿ (ca. 140/757). *Risāla fī l-ṣaḥāba*. Edited by Ch. Pellat. Paris: G.-P. Maisonneuve et Larose, 1976.

Ibn al-Murtaḍā (840/1437). *Ṭabaqāt al-muʿtazila*. Edited by S. Diwald-Wilzer. Wiesbaden: Franz Steiner, 1961.

Ibn al-Nadīm (385/995). *Kitāb al-fihrist*. Cairo: al-Maṭbaʿa al-raḥmāniyya, 1348/1929–30. English translation: *The Fihrist of al-Nadīm*. Translated by B. Dodge. New York: Columbia University Press, 1970.

Ibn al-Qifṭī (646/1248). *Tārīkh al-ḥukamāʾ*. Edited by J. Lippert. Leipzig: Dieterich, 1903.

Ibn Qutayba (276/889). *Kitāb al-maʿārif*. Edited by Th. ʿUkāsha. Cairo: Dār al-maʿārif, n.d.

——. *ʿUyūn al-akhbār*. Edited by Yūsuf ʿAlī Ṭawīl. Cairo: al-Hayʾa al-miṣriyya al-ʿāmma li-l-kitāb, 1973.

Ibn Qutayba (Pseudo-). *Kitāb al-imāma wa-l-siyāsa*. Edited by Ṭ. M. al-Zaynī. Cairo: Dār al-maʿārif, n.d.

Ibn Saʿd (230/845). *Kitāb al-ṭabaqāt al-kabīr*. Edited by I. ʿAbbās. Beirut: Dār ṣādir, n.d.

Ibn al-Taghrībirdī (874/1470). *Al-Nujūm al-zāhira fī mulūk Miṣr wa-l-Qāhira*. Cairo: Wizārat al-thaqāfa wa-l-irshād al-qawmī, 1929–72.

Ibn Ṭiqṭaqā (709/1309). *Al-Fakhrī fī l-ādāb al-sulṭāniyya wa-l-duwal al-islāmiyyā*. Beirut: Dār Ṣādir, n.d. English translation: *Al-Fakhrī*. Translated by C. E. J. Whitting. London: Luzac and Company, 1947.

al-Irbilī (692/1293). *Kashf al-ghumma bi-maʿrifat al-aʾimma*. Edited by H. al-Rasūlī. Qumm: al-Maṭbaʿa al-ʿilmiyya, 1381/1961–2.

al-Iṣfahānī (356/967). *Kitāb al-aghānī*. Beirut: Dār al-thaqāfa, 1983.

——. *Maqātil al-ṭālibiyyīn wa-akhbāruhum*. Edited by A. Ṣaqr. Cairo: Dār iḥyāʾ al-kutub al-ʿarabiyya, 1365/1946.

al-Khalīfa ibn Khayyāṭ (240/854). *Tārīkh*. Edited by Suhayl Zakkār. Damascus: Wizārat al-thaqāfa wa-l-siyāḥa wa-l-irshād al-qawmī, 1968.

al-Khaṭīb al-Baghdādī (463/1071). *Tārīkh Baghdād*. Beirut: Dār al-kutub al-ʿilmiyya, n.d.

al-Khayyāṭ (ca. 300/913). *Kitāb al-intiṣār*. Edited by H. Nyberg. Beirut: Dār qābis, 1986.

al-Kindī (350/961). *Kitāb al-wulāt wa-l-quḍāt*. Edited by R. Guest. Leiden: E J . Brill, 1912.

Kitāb al-ʿuyūn wa-l-ḥadāʾiq fī akhbār al-ḥaqāʾiq (End 5th/11th century.) Edited by M. J. de Goeje and P. de Jong. Leiden: E. J. Brill, 1869.

al-Kulaynī (328/939–40 or 329/940–1). *Al-Uṣūl wa-l-furūʿ min al-kāfī*. Edited by ʿA. al-Ghaffārī. Beirut: Dār al-aḍwāʾ, 1405/1985.

al-Maqdisī (a.k.a. al-Muqaddasī) (355/966 or after). *Kitāb al-badʾ wa-l-taʾrīkh*. Port Said: Maktabat al-thaqāfa al-dīniyya, n.d.

Mārī ibn Sulaymān (ca. 545/1150). *Maris Antri et Slibae de patriarchis nestorianorum commentaria. Pars prior: Maris textus arabicus*. Rome: C de Luigi, 1899.

al-Masʿūdī (345/956). *Kitāb al-tanbīh wa-l-ishrāf*. Edited by M. J. de Goeje. Leiden: E. J. Brill, 1894.

——. *Murūj al-dhahab wa-maʿādin al-jawhar*. Beirut: Dār al-andalus, 1983.

al-Māwardī (450/1058). *Kitāb al-aḥkām al-sulṭāniyya*. Edited together with a Latin translation by Enger, *Constitutiones politicae*. Bonn: A. Marcus, 1853. French translation: *Les statuts gouvernementaux*. Translated by E. Fagnan. Algiers: A. Jourdan, 1915.

Michael the Syrian (595–6/1199). *Chronique de Michel le Syrien*. Edited and translated by J. B. Chabot. Paris: Académie des inscriptions et belles-lettres, 1899–1910.

Miskawayh (421/1030). *Tajārib al-umam*. Edited by M. J. de Goeje. Leiden: E. J. Brill, 1871.

al-Muqaddasī, see al-Maqdisī

al-Nawbakhtī (ca. 310/922). *Firaq al-shīʿa*. Beirut: Dār al-aḍwāʾ, 1404/1984. (Based on the edition by H. Ritter).

Pseudo-Ibn Qutayba, see Ibn Qutayba (Pseudo-)

al-Qāḍī l-Nuʿmān ibn Muḥammad (363/974). *Daʿāʾim al-islām*. Edited by Ā. Fayḍī. Cairo: Dār al-maʿārif, 1370/1951.

al-Ṣābī (448/1056). *Rusūm dār al-khilāfa*. Edited by M. ʿAwwād. Beirut: Dar al-rāʾid al-ʿarabī, 1406/1987. English translation: *Rusūm dār al-khilāfa: The Rules and Regulations of the ʿAbbāsid Court*. Translated by E. A. Salem. Beirut: Imprimerie Catholique, 1977.

al-Ṣafadī (764/1363). *Al-Wāfī bi-l-wafayāt*. Part 17 edited by D. Krawulsky. Wiesbaden: Franz Steiner, 1982.

Ṣafwat, A. Z. *Jamharat rasāʾil al-ʿarab. Vols. III and IV*. Cairo: M. al-Ḥalabī, 1356/1937.

Ṣāliḥ ibn Aḥmad ibn Ḥanbal (265/878). "Sīrat Aḥmad ibn Ḥanbal" in A. ʿA.-J. al-Dūmī, *Aḥmad ibn*

Ḥanbal bayn miḥnat al-dīn wa-miḥnat al-dunyā. Cairo: al-Maktaba al-tijāriyya al-kubrā, 1380/1960–61.

Sāwīris (a.k.a. Ibn al-Muqaffaʿ) (before 393–4/1003). *Tārīkh baṭāriqat al-kanīsa al-miṣriyya*. Edited and translated by B. Evetts. *Patrologia orientalis*, x, 5 (1915).

al-Shābushtī (388/998). *Kitāb al-diyārāt*. Edited by K. ʿAwwād. Baghdad: Maṭbaʿat al-maʿārif, 1386/1966.

al-Shahrastānī (548/1153). *Kitāb al-milal wa-l-niḥal*. Edited by M. Kaylānī. Cairo: M. al-Ḥalabī, 1396/1979.

al-Sharīf al-Murtaḍā (436/1044). *Al-Intiṣār*. Bombay, 1315/1897–8.

al-Subkī (771/1370). *Ṭabaqāt al-shāfiʿiyya al-kubrā*. Edited by M. al-Ṭannāḥī and ʿA. al-Ḥilw. Cairo: M. al-Ḥalabī, 1383/1964.

al-Suyūṭī (911/1505). *Tārīkh al-khulafāʾ*. Beirut: Dār al-kutub al-ʿilmiyya, 1408/1988. English translation: *History of the Caliphs*. Translated by H. S. Jarrett. Amsterdam: Oriental Press, 1970. [The translation is a reprint of Calcutta edition of 1881.]

al-Ṭabarī (310/923). *Tārīkh al-rusul wa-l-mulūk*. Edited by M. J. de Goeje et al. Leiden: E. J. Brill, 1879–1901. English translation of the section on the reign of al-Maʾmūn: *The Reunification of the ʿAbbāsid Caliphate. Volume 32 of the history of al-Ṭabari*. Translated by C. E. Bosworth. Albany: State University of New York Press, 1987. German translation: *Das Kalifat von al-Maʾmūn*. Translated by H. F. Uhrig. Frankfurt am Main: Verlag Peter Lang, 1988.

al-Tanūkhī (384/994). *Nishwār al-muḥāḍara wa-akhbār al-mudhākara*. Edited by ʿA. al-Shāljī. N.p.: 1391/1971.

al-Tamīmī (333/944–5). *Kitāb al-miḥan*. 2nd ed. Edited by Y. W. al-Jubūrī. Beirut: Dār al-gharb al-islāmī, 1408/1988.

al-Thaʿālibī (429/1038). *Laṭāʾif al-maʿārif*. Edited by P. de Jong. Leiden: E. J. Brill, 1867. English translation: *The Book of Curious and Entertaining Information*. Translated by C. E. Bosworth. Edinburgh: Edinburgh University Press, 1968.

Wakīʿ (306/918). *Akhbār al-quḍāt wa-tawārīkhuhum*. Beirut: ʿĀlam al-kutub, n.d.

al-Yaʿqūbī (284/897). *Mushākalāt al-nās li-zamānihim*. Edited by W. Millward. Beirut: Dār al-kitāb al-jadīd, 1962. Translated by W. Millward in *Journal of the American Oriental Society* 84 (1964): 329–44.

——. *Tārīkh*. Beirut: Dar ṣādir, n.d.

Yāqūt al-Ḥamawī (626/1229). *Muʿjam al-udabāʾ* (a.k.a. *Irshād al-arīb ilā maʿrifat al-adīb*). Beirut: Dār iḥyāʾ al-turāth al-ʿarabī, n.d.

——. *Muʿjam al-buldān*. Beirut: Dār ṣādir, n.d.

Secondary sources

Abbott, Nabia. "Arabic Papyri of the Reign of Ǧaʿfar al-Mutawakkil ʿala-llāh (A.H. 232–47/A.D. 847–61)." *Zeitschrift der Deutschen Morgenländischen Gesellschaft* 92 (1938): 88–135.

——. *Two Queens of Baghdad. Mother and Wife of Hārūn al-Rashīd*. Chicago: University of Chicago Press, 1946.

Abel, Armand. "LʿApocalypse de Baḥīra et la notion islamique de Mahdī." *Annuaire de l'institut de philologie et d'histoire orientales* 3 (1935): 1–12.

——. "Le Khalife, présence sacrée." *Studia Islamica* 7 (1957): 29–45.

*Abū l-ʿAlāʾ, Ibrāhīm ʿAbd al-Munʿim Salāma. *Fī tārīkh al-dawla al-islāmiyya al-mashriqiyya al-mustaqilla ʿan al-khilāfa al-ʿabbāsiyya*. Alexandria: Markaz al-iskandariyya li-l-kitāb, 2005.

*Abū Ḥabīb, Saʿdī. *Marwān ibn Muḥammad wa-asbāb suqūṭ al-dawla al-umawiyya*. Furn al-Shubbāk, Lebanon: Dār Lisān al-ʿArab, 1995.

Abusaq, Muhammad. "The Politics of the Miḥna." Ph.D. diss., University of Edinburgh, 1971.

*al-ʿAdawī, Ibrāhīm Aḥmad. *Al-Umawiyyūn wa-l-bīzanṭiyyūn*. Fayyum, Egypt: Dār riyāḍ al-ṣāliḥīn, 1994.

*Aerts, Stijn. "The Prayers of Abū Muslim and al-Ma'mūn: An Exercise in Dating *Ḥadīth*." *Journal of Abbasid Studies* 1 (2014): 66–83.

*Agha, Saleh Said. *The Revolution Which Toppled the Umayyads. Neither Arab nor Abbasid*. Leiden: Brill, 2003.

Ahsan, Muhammad M. "A Note on Hunting in the Early ʿAbbasid Period: Some Evidence in Expenditure and Prices." *Journal of the Economic and Social History of the Orient* 19 (1976): 101–5.

——. *Social Life under the Abbasids*. London: Longman/Librairie du Liban, 1979.

*Amabe, Fukuzo. *The Emergence of the ʿAbbāsid Autocracy. The ʿAbbāsid Army, Khurāsān and Adharbayjān*. Kyoto: Kyoto University Press, 1995.

Amedroz, Henry F. "The Office of Kadi in the Ahkam Sultaniyya of Mawardi." *Journal of the Royal Asiatic Society of Great Britain and Ireland* (1910): 761–96.

Amīn, Aḥmad. *Ḍuḥā l-islām*. 3 Vols. Cairo: Maktabat al-nahḍa al-miṣriyya, 1933–6.

*al-Amīn, Ḥasan. *Al-Riḍā wa-l-Maʾmūn wa-wilāyat al-ʿahd. Ṣafaḥāt min al-tārīkh al-ʿabbāsī*. Beirut: Dār al-Jadīd, 1995.

*Anthony, Sean W. *The Caliph and the Heretic. Ibn Sabaʾ and the Origins of Shīʿism*. Leiden: Brill, 2012.

Arazi, Albert, and Amikam Elad. "L'épître à l'armée. Al-Maʾmūn et la seconde *daʿwa*." *Studia Islamica* 66 (1988): 27–70 & 67 (1988): 29–73.

ʿĀrif, Aḥmad ʿA. *Al-Ṣila bayn al-zaydiyya wa-l-muʿtazila*. San'a: al-Maktaba al-yamaniyya and Beirut: Dār āzāl, 1987.

Arioli, Angelo. "La rivolta di Abū Sarāyā: Appunti per una tipologia del leader islamico." *Ann. Fac. Ling. Lett. Stran. ca'Foscari* 5 (1974): 189–97.

ʿAthamina, Khalīl. "The Black Banners and the Socio-Political Significance of Flags and Slogans in Medieval Islam." *Arabica* 36 (1989): 307–26.

Balog, Paul. "Pious Invocations Probably Used as Titles of Office or as Honorific Titles in Umayyad and ʿAbbāsid Times." In *Studies in Memory of Gaston Wiet*, edited by M. Rosen-Ayalon, 61–68. Jerusalem: Institute of Asian and African Studies, Hebrew University of Jerusalem, 1977.

Barbier de Meynard, Charles. "Ibrāhīm fils de Mehdi. Fragments historiques. Scènes de la vie d'artiste au IIIe siècle de l'hégire (778–839 de notre ère)." *Journal Asiatique* ser. 6, 13 (1869): 201–342.

Bercher, Léon. "L'obligation d'ordonner le bien et d'interdire le mal selon al-Ghazali." *Institut de belles lettres arabes* 18 (1955): 53–91 & 313–21.

Bernand, Marie. "La notion de *ʿilm* chez les premiers Muʿtazilites." *Studia Islamica* 36 (1972): 23–45 and 37 (1973): 27–56.

*Bernards, Monique and John Nawas, "The Geographic Distribution of Muslim Jurists during the First Four Centuries AH." *Islamic Law and Society* 10 (2003): 168–81.

*Bernheimer, Teresa. *The ʿAlids. The First Family of Islam, 750–1200*. Edinburgh: Edinburgh University Press, 2013.

Biddle, David W. "The Development of the Bureaucracy of the Islamic Empire during the Late Umayyad and Early Abbasid Period." Ph.D. Diss., University of Texas (Austin), 1972.

Bittermann, Helen R. "Hārūn ar-Rashīd's Gift of an Organ to Charlemagne." *Speculum* 4 (1929): 215–17.

*Black, Antony. *The History of Islamic Political Thought. From the Prophet to the Present*. New York: Routledge, 2001.

Blankinship, Khalid Y. "The Tribal Factor in the ʿAbbāsid Revolution: The Betrayal of the Imam Ibrāhīm b. Muḥammad." *Journal of the American Oriental Society* 108 (1988): 589–603.

Bonner, Michael. "Al-Khalīfa al-Marḍī: The Accession of Hārūn al-Rashīd." *Journal of the American Oriental Society* 108 (1988): 79–91.

——. "The Mint of Hārūnābād and al-Hārūniyya, 168–171." *American Journal of Numismatics* (1989): 171–93.

Bosworth, Clifford E. "An Early Arabic Mirror for Princes: Ṭāhir Dhū l-Yamīnain's Epistle to His Son ʿAbdallāh (206/821)." *Journal of Near Eastern Studies* 29 (1970): 25–41.

——. *The History of al-Ṭabarī. Volume xxxii. The Reunification of the ʿAbbāsid Caliphate*. Albany: State University of New York Press, 1987.

——. "The Ṭāhirids and Arabic Culture." *Journal of Semitic Studies* 14 (1969): 45–79.

——. "The Ṭāhirids and Ṣaffārids." In *Cambridge History of Iran. Volume 4. The Period from the Arab Invasion to the Saljuqs*, edited by R. N. Frye, 90–135. Cambridge: Cambridge University Press, 1975.

Bouman, Johan. *Le conflit autour du Coran et la solution d'al-Bāqillānī*. Amsterdam: Jacob van Campen, 1959.

Bouvat, Lucien. "Les Barmecides d'après les historiens arabes et persans." *Revue du monde musulmane* 20 (1912): 3–131.

Cahen, Claude. *Der Islam I*. Fischer Weltgeschichte 14. Translated from the French by G. Endreß. Frankfurt am Main: Fischer Taschenbuch Verlag, 1968.

——. *Les peuples musulmans dans l'histoire médiévale*. Damascus: Éditions dʿAmérique et d'Orient, 1977.

——. "Points de vue sur la 'revolution ʿAbbāside'" [1963], republished in his *Les peuples musulmans dans l'histoire médiévale* (see above), 105–60.

——. "À propos des *shuhūd*." *Studia Islamica* 31 (1970): 71–79.

*Calder, Norman. "*Ikhtilāf* and *Ijmāʿ* in Shafiʿi's *Risala*." *Studia Islamica* 58 (1983): 55–81.

Canard, Marius. "Byzantium and the Muslim World to the Middle of the Eleventh Century." In *Cambridge Medieval History*, edited by J. M. Hussey, Vol. IV, part 1, 696–735. Cambridge: Cambridge University Press, 1966.

——. "La prise d'Héraclée et les relations entre Hārūn ar-Rashīd et l'empereur Nicéphore Ier." *Byzantion* 32 (1962): 345–79.

Chejne, Anwar G. "Al-Faḍl b. al-Rabīʿ. A Politician of the Early ʿAbbāsid Period." *Islamic Culture* 36 (1962): 163–81 & 237–44.

——. *Succession to the Rule in Islam*. Lahore: Sh. Muḥammad ashrāf, 1960.

Cohen, Hayyim J. "The Economic Background and the Secular Occupations of Muslim Jurisprudents and Traditionists in the Classical Period of Islam." *Journal of the Economic and Social History of the Orient* 13 (1970): 16–61.

*Cook, Michael A. *Ancient Religions, Modern Politics. The Islamic Case in Comparative Perspective*. Princeton, NJ: Princeton University Press, 2014.

*——. *Commanding Right and Forbidding Wrong in Islamic Thought*. Cambridge: Cambridge University Press, 2000.

*Cooperson, Michael. *Classical Arabic Biography: The Heirs of the Prophets in the Age of al-Maʾmun*. Cambridge: Cambridge University Press, 2000.

*——. *Al-Maʾmun*. Makers of the Muslim World Series, edited by Patricia Crone. Oxford: Oneworld, 2005.

*——. "Two ʿAbbasid Trials: Aḥmad Ibn Ḥanbal and Ḥunayn b. Isḥāq." *Al-Qanṭara: Revista de Estudios Arabes* 22, no. ii (2001): 375–93.

*Cooperson, Michael and Jurji Zaidan. *The Caliph's Heirs. Translated from the Arabic with an Afterword and Study Guide*. Novels of Islamic History in Translation Series. Bethesda, MD: The Zaidan Foundation, 2011.

Coulson, Noel J. *A History of Islamic Law*. Edinburgh: Edinburgh University Press, 1964.

*Crone, Patricia. *God's Rule. Government and Islam*. New York: Columbia University Press, 2004.

*——. *The Nativist Prophets of Early Islamic Iran. Rural Revolt and Local Zoroastrianism*. Cambridge: Cambridge University Press, 2012.

*——. ""No Compulsion in Religion:" Q. 2:256 in Mediaeval and Modern Interpretation." In *Le Shīʿisme Imāmite quarante ans après. Hommage à Etan Kohlberg*, edited by M. A. Amir-Moezzi, Meir M. Bar-Asher and S. Hopkins, 131–78. Turnhout, Belgium: Brepols, 2009.

——. "On the Meaning of the ʿAbbasid Call to al-Riḍā." In *The Islamic World. Essays in Honor of Bernard Lewis*, edited by C. E. Bosworth, C. Issawi, R. Savory and A. Udovitch, 95–111. Princeton: The Darwin Press Inc., 1989.

——. *Slaves on Horses. The Evolution of the Islamic Polity*. Cambridge: Cambridge University Press, 1980.

Crone, Patricia, and Martin Hinds. *God's Caliph. Religious Authority in the First Centuries of Islam*. Cambridge: Cambridge University Press, 1986.

Dabashi, Hamid. *Authority in Islam*. New Brunswick: Transaction Publishers, 1989.

*Dakake, Maria Massi. *The Charismatic Community. Shiʿite Identity in Early Islam*. Albany, NY: State University of New York Press, 2007.

*Daniel, Elton L. "The 'Ahl Al-Taqādum' and the Problem of the Constituency of the Abbasid Revolution in the Merv Oasis." *Journal of Islamic Studies* 7, no. ii (1996): 150–79.

——. *The Political and Social History of Khurasan under Abbasid Rule 747–820*. Minneapolis: Bibliotheca Islamica, 1979.

*Ḍannāwī, Saʿdī. *Mawsūʿat Hārūn al-Rashīd*. 3 vols. Beirut: Dār Ṣādir, 2001.

Dictionary of the Middle Ages. New York: Charles Scribner & Sons, 1982–9.

Dietrich, Albert. "Das politische Testament des zweiten ʿAbbāsidenkalifen al-Manṣūr." *Der Islam* 30 (1952): 133–65.

——. "Quelques aspects de l'éducation princière à la cour abbaside." *Revue des études islamiques* 44 (1976): 89–104.

Donaldson, Dwight M. *The Shiʿite Religion*. London: Luzac & Company, 1933.

Donner, Fred M. *The Early Islamic Conquests*. Princeton: Princeton University Press, 1981.

Dozy, Reinhart. *Supplément aux dictionnaires arabes*. 2 Vols. Leiden: E. J. Brill, 1881.

al-Dūri, ʿAbd al-ʿAzīz. *Al-ʿAṣr al-ʿabbāsī al-awwal*. Beirut: Dar al-ṭalīʿa li-l-ṭibāʿa wa-l-nashr, 1945.

——. "Al-Fikra al-mahdiyya bayn al-daʿwa al-ʿabbāsiyya wa-l-ʿaṣr al-ʿabbāsī al-awwal." In *Studia Arabica et Islamica. Festschrift for Iḥsān ʿAbbās*, edited by W. al-Qāḍī, 123–32. Beirut: American University of Beirut, 1981.

El-Ali, Saleh Ahmad. "A New Version of Ibn al-Muṭarrif's List of Revenues in the Early Times of Hārūn al-Rashīd." *Journal of the Economic and Social History of the Orient* 14 (1971): 303–10.

*El Cheikh, Nadia. *Byzantium Viewed by the Arabs*. Cambridge, MA: Harvard University Press, 2004.

*El-Hibri, Tayeb. "Coinage Reform under the ʿAbbāsid Caliph al-Ma'mūn." *Journal of the Economic and Social History of the Orient* 36, no. i (1993): 58–83.

*——. "Harun al-Rashid and the Mecca Protocol of 802: A Plan for Division or Succession?" *International Journal of Middle East Studies* 24 (1992): 461–80.

*——. "The Image of the Caliph al-Wāthiq: A Riddle of Religious and Historical Significance." *Quaderni di Studi Arabi* 19 (2001): 41–60.

*Elad, Amikam. "The Armies of al-Ma'mūn in Khurāsān (193–202/809–817–18): Recruitment of Its Contingents and Their Commanders and Their Social-Ethnic Composition." *Oriens* 38 (2010): 35–76.

*——. "The Ethnic Composition of the ʿAbbāsid Revolution: A Reevaluation of Some Recent Research." *Jerusalem Studies in Arabic and Islam* 24 (2000): 246–326.

*——. "Al-Maʾmūn's Military Units and Their Commanders up to the End of the Siege of Baghdad (195/810–198/813)." In *ʿAbbasid Studies IV. Occasional Papers of the School of ʿAbbāsid Studies, Leuven, July 5-July 9, 2010*, edited by M. Bernards, 245–84. Oxford: Gibb Memorial Trust, 2013.

*——. *Mawālī* in the Composition of al-Ma'mūn's Army: A Non-Arab Takeover." In *Patronate and Patronage in Early and Classical Islam*, edited by M. Bernards and J. Nawas, 278–325. Leiden: Brill, 2005.

——. "The Siege of al-Wāsiṭ (132/749). Some Aspects of ʿAbbāsid and ʿAlid Relations at the Beginning of ʿAbbāsid Rule." In *Studies in Islamic History and Civilization in Honour of Professor David Ayalon*, edited by M. Sharon, 59–90. Jerusalem: Cana, 1986.

Encyclopaedia Iranica. London: Routledge & Kegan Paul, 1982–.

Encyclopaedia of Islam, first edition. Leiden: E. J. Brill, 1913–38.

Encyclopaedia of Islam, second edition. Leiden: E. J. Brill, 1954–2009.

Encyclopaedia of Islam, third edition. Leiden: E. J. Brill, 2007–.

*Fahd, Badrī Muḥammad. *Ibrāhīm ibn al-Mahdī. Al-khalīfa al-mughannī*. Beirut: Al-Dār al-ʿarabiyya li-l-mawsūʿāt, 2007.

Frye, Richard N. "The Role of Abū Muslim in the ʿAbbāsid Revolt." *Muslim World* 37 (1947): 28–38.

Gabrieli, Francesco. *Al-Maʾmūn e gli ʿAlidi*. Leipzig: Verlag Eduard Pfeiffer, 1929.

——. "La successione di Hārūn ar-Rašīd e la guerra fra al-Amin e al-Maʾmūn." *Rivista degli studi orientali* 11 (1928): 341–97.

Geddes, Charles L. "Al-Maʾmūn's Šīʿit Policy in Yemen." *Wiener Zeitschrift für die Kunde des Morgenlandes* 59–60 (1963–4): 99–107.

Gibb, Hamilton A.R. "Government and Islam under the Early ʿAbbāsids. The Political Collapse of Islam." In *L'élaboration de l'islam. Colloque de Strasbourg*, edited by C. Cahen et al., 115–27. Paris: Presses universitaires de France, 1961.

Goldziher, Ignác. "Du sens propre des expressions Ombre de Dieu, Khalife de Dieu pour désigner les chefs dans l'Islam." *Revue de l'histoire des religions* 35 (1897): 331–38.

——. *Introduction to Islamic Theology and Law*. Translated from the German by A. and R. Hamori. Princeton: Princeton University Press, 1981.

——. "Das Prinzip der *taḳijja* im Islam." *Zeitschrift der Deutschen Morgenländischen Gesellschaft* 60 (1906): 213–226.

——. "Spottnamen der ersten Chalifen bei den Schīʿiten." *Wiener Zeitschrift für die Kunde des Morgenlandes* 15 (1901): 321–34.

Graf, Georg. *Geschichte der christlichen arabischen Literatur*. Vatican: Biblioteca apostolica vaticana, 1947.

Grutter, Irene. "Arabische Bestattungsgebräuche in frühislamischer Zeit (nach Ibn Saʿd und Buḫārī)." *Der Islam* 31 (1954): 147–73 and 32 (1957): 79–104 & 168–94.

*al-Ḥadīthī, Muḥammad Jāsim. *Waṣāyā al-Khulafāʾ wa-l-umarāʾ al-siyāsiyya wa-l-idāriyya fī l-ʿaṣr al-ʿabbāsī al-awwal. Dirāsa taḥlīliyya*. Baghdad: Al-Majmaʿ al-ʿIlmī, 2002.

*Haider, Najam. *The Origins of the Shīʿa. Identity, Ritual, and Sacred Space in Eighth-Century Kūfa*. New York: Cambridge University Press, 2011.

*Halevi, Leor. *Muhammad's Grave: Death Rites and the Making of Islamic Society*. New York: Columbia University Press, 2007.

Halkin, Abraham S. "The Ḥashwiyya." *Journal of the American Oriental Society* 54 (1934): 1–28.

* Hallaq, Wael B. "On the Authoritativeness of Sunni Consensus." *International Journal of Middle East Studies* 18:4 (1986): 427–454.

*——. *A History of Islamic Legal Theories: An Introduction to Sunnī Uṣūl al-Fiqh*. Cambridge: Cambridge University Press, 1997.

Halm, Heinz. *Die Schia*. Darmstadt: Wissenschaftliche Buchgesellschaft, 1988.

Hamdi, Sidqi. "The Pro-ʿAlid Policy of al-Maʾmūn." *Bull. Coll. Arts Baghdad* 1 (1956): 96–105.

*Hasan, Ahmad. *Analogical Reasoning in Islamic Jurisprudence: A Study of the Juridical Principle of Qiyas*. Delhi: Adam Publishers and Distributors, 2007.

Ḥasan, I. "Al-Maʾmūn wa-ʿAlī al-Riḍā." *Majallat kulliyyat al-ādāb* 1 (1933): 84–94.

Hassuri, Ali. "On the Epithet of the ʿAbbasid Caliphs." *Der Islam* 59 (1982): 111–13.

Hawting, Gerald R. *The First Dynasty of Islam. The Umayyad Caliphate AD 661–750*. Carbondale, IL: Southern Illinois University Press, 1987. 2nd ed. London: Routledge, 2000.

*Heydorn, Florian. *Ḫalq al-Qur'an. Genese einer frühislamischen Häresie*. Norderstedt, Germany: GRIN Verlag, 2008.

*Hildebrandt, Thomas. *Neo-Muʿtazilismus? Intention und Kontext im modernen arabischen Umgang mit dem rationalistischen Erbe des Islam*. Islamic Philosophy, Theology and Science. Leiden: Brill, 2007.

Hinds, Martin. "Kufan Political Alignments and Their Background in the Mid-Seventh Century A.D." *International Journal of Middle East Studies* 2 (1971): 346–67.

——. "The Murder of the Caliph ʿUthmān." *International Journal of Middle East Studies* 3 (1972a): 450–69.

——. "The Ṣiffīn Arbitration Agreement." *Journal of Semitic Studies* 17 (1972b): 93–129.

Hitti, Philip K. *History of the Arabs*. 10th ed. New York: Macmillan, 1970.

——. "Al-Maʾmun: Radical Caliph and Intellectual Awakener of Islam." In *Makers of Arab History*, 76–94. New York: Harper and Row, 1968.

Hodgson, Marshall. *The Venture of Islam I*. Chicago: The University of Chicago Press, 1974.

Hoenerbach, Wilhelm. "Zur Heeresverwaltung der ʿAbbāsiden." *Der Islam* 29 (1950): 257–90.

Houtsma, Martijn Th. "Die Ḥashwīya." *Zeitschrift für Assyriologie* 26 (1912): 196–202.

Huddāra, M. M. *Al-Maʾmūn. Al-khalīfa wa-l-ʿālim*. Cairo: al-Hayʾa al-miṣriyya al-ʿāmma li-l-kitāb, 1985.

Humphreys, R. Stephen. *Islamic History: A Framework for Inquiry*. London: I.B. Tauris, 1991.

*Hurvitz, Nimrod. *The Formation of Hanbalism: Piety into Power*. London: Routledge Curzon, 2002a.

*——. "*Miḥna* as Self-Defense." *Studia Islamica* 92 (2001a): 93–111.

*——. "The Mihna (Inquisition) and the Public Sphere." In *The Public Sphere in Muslim Societies*, edited by M. Hoexter, S. N. Eisenstadt, and N. Levtzion, 17–29. Albany, NY: State University of New York Press, 2002b.

*——. "Who Is the Accused? The Interrogation of Aḥmad Ibn Ḥanbal." *Al-Qanṭara: Revista de Estudios Arabes* 22, no. ii (2001b): 359–73.

*Ḥusayn, Ṣubḥī Nāṣir. *Shiʿr al-Khalīfa al-Maʾmūn. Dirāsa wa-Nuṣūṣ*. Amman: Dār al-bayt al-ʿatīq, 2002.

Ibn Manẓūr. *Lisān al-ʿArab*. 9 Vols. Cairo: Dār al-maʿārif, n.d.

*Ibrahim, Aiman. *Der Herausbildungsprozeß des arabisch-islamischen Staates. Eine quellenkritische Untersuchung des Zusammenhangs zwischen den staatlichen Zentralisierungstendenzen und der Stammesorganisation in der frühislamischen Geschichte 1-60 H./622-680*. Berlin: Klaus Schwarz Verlag, 1994.

*Jadʿān, Fahmī. *Al-Miḥna. Baḥth fī jadaliyyat al-dīnī wa-l-siyāsī fī al-islām*. Amman: Dār al-Shurūq, 1989.

Jarret, Henry S. See al-Suyūṭī, *Tārīkh al-khulafāʾ*.

Juynboll, Gautier H.A. *Muslim Tradition. Studies in Chronology, Provenance and Authorship of Early Ḥadīth*. Cambridge: Cambridge University Press, 1983.

——. "Some New Ideas on the Development of Sunna as a Technical Term in Early Islam." *Jerusalem Studies in Arabic and Islam* 10 (1987): 97–118.

Kaabi, Mongi. "Les origines Ṭāhirides dans la *daʿwa* ʿAbbāside." *Arabica* 19 (1972): 145–64.

*Kaegi, Walter. *Byzantium and the Early Arab Conquests*. Cambridge: Cambridge University Press, 1995.

*——. *Muslim Expansion and Byzantine Collapse in North Africa*. Cambridge: Cambridge University Press, 2010.

*Kennedy, Hugh. *The Armies of the Caliphs. Military and Society in the Early Islamic State*. London: Routledge, 2001.

——. *The Early Abbasid Caliphate*. London: Croom Helm, 1981.

——. *The Prophet and the Age of the Caliphates*. London: Longman, 1986.

——. "Succession Disputes in the Early Abbasid Caliphate (132/749–193/809)." In *Proceedings, Union européenne des arabisants et islamisants. 10th Congress. Edinburgh 9-16 September 1980*, edited by R. Hillenbrand, 29–33. 1980.

Kimber, Richard A. "Hārūn al-Rashīd's Meccan Settlement of AH 186/AD 802." In *Occasional Papers of the School of Abbasid Studies No. 1*, 55–79. St. Andrews: The School, 1986.

Kohlberg, Etan. "Some Imāmī-Shīʿī Views on *Taqiyya*." *Journal of the American Oriental Society* 95 (1975): 395–402.

——. "Some Shīʿī Views of the Antediluvian World." *Studia Islamica* 52 (1980): 41–66.

*——, ed. *Shīʿism*. The Formation of the Classical Islamic World, vol. 33. Burlington, VT: Ashgate, 2003.

Lambton, Ann K.S. *State and Government in Medieval Islam*. London: Oxford University Press, 1981.

Lane, E. William. *An Arabic-English Lexicon Derived from the Best and Most Copious Eastern Sources*. 8 Vols. London: Williams and Norgate, 1863–93.

Laoust, Henri. *Les schismes dans l'islam*. Paris: Payot, 1965.

Lapidus, Ira M. "The Separation of State and Religion in the Development of Early Islamic Society." *International Journal of Middle East Studies* 6 (1975): 363–85.

Le Strange, Guy. *Baghdad during the Abbasid Caliphate*. London: Oxford University Press, 1900.

——. *The Lands of the Eastern Caliphate*. Cambridge: Cambridge University Press, 1930.

Lewis, Bernard. "An Apocalyptic Vision of Islamic History." *Bulletin of the School of Oriental and African Studies* 13 (1950): 308–38.

——. "The Regnal Titles of the First Abbasid Caliphs." *Dr. Zakir Husain Presentation Volume*. New Delhi, 1968.

——. "Some Observations on the Significance of Heresy in the History of Islam." *Studia Islamica* 1 (1953): 43–63.

Lichtenstädter, Ilse. "The Distinctive Dress of Non-Muslims in Islamic Countries." *Historia Judaica* 5 (1943): 35–52.

*Lucas, Scott C. *Constructive Critics, Ḥadīth Literature, and the Articulation of Sunnī Islam: The Legacy of the Generation of Ibn Saʿd, Ibn Maʿīn, and Ibn Ḥanbal*. Leiden: Brill, 2004.

Madelung, Wilferd. "ʿAbdallāh b. al-Zubayr and the Mahdi." *Journal of Near Eastern Studies* 40 (1981): 291–305.

——. "The Hāshimiyyāt of al-Kumayt and Hāshimī Shiʿism." *Studia Islamica* 70 (1989a): 5–26.

——. *Der Imam al-Qāsim ibn Ibrāhīm und die Glaubenslehre der Zaiditen*. Berlin: Walter de Gruyter & Co., 1965.

——. "Imām al-Qāsim ibn Ibrāhīm and Muʿtazilism." In *On Both Sides of Bab al-Mandab: Ethiopian, South-Arabic and Islamic Studies Presented to Oscar Löfgren on his Ninetieth Birthday. Transactions*, 2. Stockholm: Swedish Research Institute in Istanbul, 1989a.

——. "Imamism and Muʿtazilite Theology." In *Le shīʿisme imāmite. Colloque de Strasbourg*, 13–30. Paris: Presses universitaires de France, 1970.

——. "New Documents Concerning al-Maʾmūn, al-Faḍl b. Sahl and ʿAlī al-Riḍā." In *Studia Arabica et Islamica. Festschrift for Iḥsān ʿAbbās*, edited by W. al-Qāḍī, 333–46. Beirut: American University of Beirut Press, 1981.

——. "The Origins of the Controversy Concerning the Creation of the Koran." In *Orientalia Hispánica sive studia F.M. Pareja octogenario dicata*, edited by J.M. Barrai, 504–25. Leiden: E. J. Brill, 1974.

*——. *The Succession to Muḥammad. A Study of the Early Caliphate*. Cambridge: Cambridge University Press, 1997.

——. "The Sufyānī between Tradition and History." *Studia Islamica* 63 (1986): 5–48.

——. "Was the Caliph al-Maʾmūn a Grandson of the Sectarian Leader Ustādhsīs?" In *Studies in Arabic and Islam*, edited by S. Leder *et al.*, 485–90. Leuven: Peeters, 2002

Makdisi, George. *Ibn ʿAqīl et la résurgence de l'islam traditionaliste au XIe siècle (Ve siècle de l'Hégire)*. Damascus: Institut français de Damas, 1963.

——. *The Rise of Colleges: Institutions of Learning in Islam and the West*. Edinburgh: Edinburgh University Press, 1981.

*Marín-Guzmán, Roberto. *Popular Dimensions of the ʿAbbasid Revolution. A Case Study of Medieval Islamic Social History*. Cambridge, MA: Fulbright-Laspau, 1990.

Marquet, Yves. "Le šiʿisme au IXe siècle à travers l'histoire de Yaʿqūbī." *Arabica* 19 (1972): 1–45 & 101–38.

*Marsham, Andrew. *Rituals of Islamic Monarchy. Accession and Succession in the First Muslim Empire*. Edinburgh: Edinburgh University Press, 2009.

Marwah, Ḥusayn. *Al-nazaʿāt al-māddiyya fī l-falsafa al-ʿarabiyya al-islāmiyya*. 2 Vols. Beirut: Dār al-Fārābī, 1978.

Massignon, Louis. "Cadis et naqībs baghdadiens." *Wiener Zeitschrift für die Kunde des Morgenlandes* 51 (1948): 106–15.

Meisami, Julie S. "Masʿūdī on Love and the Fall of the Barmakids." *Journal of the Royal Asiatic Society* (1989): 252–77.

*Melchert, Christopher. "Aḥmad Ibn Ḥanbal and the Qurʾan." *Journal of Qurʾanic Studies* 6, no. 2 (2004): 22–34.

*——. "Religious Policies of the Caliphs from al-Mutawakkil to al-Muqtadir, A.H. 232–295 / A.D. 847–908." *Islamic Law and Society* 3, no. iii (1996): 316–42.

Miah, M. Shamsuddin. *The Reign of al-Mutawakkil*. Dacca: A.B.M. Habibullah, 1969.

Miles, George C. *The Numismatic History of Rayy*. New York: The American Numismatic Society, 1938.

Millward, William G. See al-Yaʿqūbī, *Mushākalāt al-nās li-zamānihim*.

Moscati, Sabatino. "Le califat d'al-Hādī." *Studia Orientalia* 13 (1946): 3–28.

Mottahedeh, Roy. *Loyalty and Leadership in an Early Islamic Society*. Princeton: Princeton University Press, 1980.

Muir, William. *The Caliphate: Its Rise, Decline and Fall*. London: The Religious Tract Society, 1981.

Nagel, Tilman. *Rechtleitung und Kalifat: Versuch über eine Grundfrage der islamischen Geschichte. Studien zum Minderheitenproblem im Islam 2*. Bonn: Selbstverlag des Orientalischen Seminars der Universität, 1975.

——. *Untersuchungen zur Entstehung des abbasidischen Kalifates*. Bonn: Selbstverlag des Orientalischen Seminars der Universität, 1972.

*Nawas, John A. "All in the Family? Al-Muʿtaṣim's Succession to the Caliphate as Denouement to the Lifelong Feud between al-Maʾmūn and his ʿAbbasid Family." *Oriens* 38 (2010): 77–88.

*——. "Mihna." In *Oxford Bibliographies Online*, edited by A. Rippin. Oxford: Oxford University Press, 2014.

*——. "The Miḥna of 218 A.H./833 A.D. Revisited: An Empirical Study." *Journal of the American Oriental Society* 116, no. iv (1996a): 698–708.

*——. "The Moral Imperative in Contemporary Islamic Movements: An Early Expression in the Structure of al-Maʾmūn's Inquisition (*miḥna*), 833 CE." In *Strategies of Medieval Communal Identity: Judaism, Christianity and Islam*, edited by P. M. Cobb and W. J. van Bekkum, 75–86. Leuven, Belgium: Peeters, 2004.

*——. "A Psychoanalytic View of Some Oddities in the Behavior of the ʿAbbasid Caliph al-Maʾmūn." *Sharqiyyāt. Journal of the Dutch Association for Middle Eastern and Islamic Studies* 8, no. i (1996b): 69–81.

*——. "A Reexamination of Three Current Explanations for al-Maʾmun's Introduction of the Mihna." *International Journal of Middle East Studies*, 26 (1994): 615–29.

*——. *Theoretical Underpinnings of the Construct of Absolutism: A Contribution to the Comparative Study of History*. Occasional Paper 19. MERA / Middle East Research Associates, 1993a.

*——. "Toward Fresh Directions in Historical Research: An Experiment in Methodology Using the Putative 'Absolutism' of Hârûn al-Rashîd as a Test Case." *Der Islam* 70, no. i (1993b): 1–51.

*——. "The *ʿUlamāʾ* as Autonomous Bearers of Religious Authority: Explaining Western Europe's Current Identity Problem with Islam." In *Negotiating Autonomy and Authority in Muslim Contexts*, edited by M. Bernards and M. Buitelaar, 15–28. Leuven, Belgium: Peeters, 2013.

Nicol, Norman D. "Early ʿAbbāsid Administration in the Central and Eastern Provinces, 132–218 A.H./750–833 A.D." Ph.D. diss., University of Washington, 1979.

Omar, Farouk. "Some Aspects of the ʿAbbāsid-Ḥusaynid Relations during the Early ʿAbbasid Period 132–193 A.H./750–809 A.D." *Arabica* 22 (1975): 170–79.

Paret, Rudi. "Ḫalīfat Allah.Vicarius Dei. Ein differenzierender Vergleich." In *Mélanges d'islamologie.*

Volume dédié à la mémoire de Armand Abel par ses collègues, ses élèves et ses amis, edited by P. Salmon, 224–32. Leiden: E. J. Brill, 1974.

——. "Signification coranique de *ḫalīfa* et d'autres dérivés de la racine *ḫalafa*." *Studia Islamica* 32 (1970): 211–17.

*——. "Sure 2, 256: *Lā ikrāha fī d-dīni*. Toleranz oder Resignation?" *Der Islam* 45 (1969): 299–300.

Patton, Walter M. *Ahmed ibn Ḥanbal and the Miḥna*. Leiden: E. J. Brill, 1897.

Petersen, Erling L. "ʿAlī and Muʿāwiya. The Rise of the Umayyad Caliphate 656–661." *Acta Orientalia* 23 (1959): 157–96.

——. "Studies on the Historiography of the ʿAlī-Muʿāwiyah Conflict." *Acta Orientalia* 27 (1963): 83–118.

*Poonawala, Ismail, and al-Nuʿmān ibn Abī ʿAbd Allāh al-Maghribī. *The Pillars of Islam. Volume 1: Acts of Devotion and Religious Observances. Daʿāʾim al-islām /al-Qāḍī al-Nuʿmān; Translated by Asaf A. A. Fyzee; Completely Revised and Annotated by Ismail Kurban Husein Poonawala*. Oxford: Oxford University Press, 2002.

*——. *The Pillars of Islam*. Volume 2: *Muʿāmalāt: Laws Pertaining to Human Intercourse. Daʿāʾim al-islām /al-Qāḍī al-Nuʿmān; Translated by Asaf A. A. Fyzee; Completely Revised and Annotated by Ismail Kurban Husein Poonawala*. Oxford: Oxford University Press, 2004.

al-Qāḍī, Wadād. *Al-Kaysāniyya fī al-tārīkh wa-l-adab*. 1973.

*——. "The Term "Khalifa" in Early Exegetical Literature." *Die Welt des Islams* 28 (1988): 392–411.

Rekaya, Mohamed. "Mise au point sur Théophobe et l'alliance de Bābek avec Théophile (833/4–839/40)." *Byzantion* 44 (1974): 43–67.

Rifāʿī, Aḥmad F. *ʿAṣr al-Maʾmūn*. 3 Vols. Cairo: Maktabat dār al-kutub al-miṣriyya, 1927.

*Robinson, Chase F. *ʿAbd al-Malik. Makers of the Muslim World*. Oxford: Oneworld, 2005.

Sabari, Simha. *Mouvements populaires à Bagdad à l'époque ʿAbbasside, ix-xi siècles*. Paris: Adrien Maisonneuve, 1981.

Ṣamad, al-. Wāḍiḥ. *Dīwān al-Amīn wa-l-Maʾmūn*. Beirut: Dār Ṣādir, 1998.

Samadi, S. B. "The Struggle between the Two Brothers al-Amin and al-Mamun." *Islamic Culture* 32 (1958): 99–120.

Schacht, Joseph. *An Introduction to Islamic Law*. Oxford: Clarendon Press, 1964.

Sezgin, Fuat. *Geschichte des arabischen Schrifttums*. Band I: *Qur'ānwissenschaften, ḥadīt, Geschichte, Fiqh, Dogmatik, Mystik. Bis ca. 430 H*. Leiden: E J. Brill, 1967.

Shaban, Muhammad A. *The ʿAbbāsid Revolution*. Cambridge: Cambridge University Press, 1970.

——. *Islamic History. A New Interpretation. Vol. 2. A.D. 750-1055 (A.H. 132-448)*. Cambridge: Cambridge University Press, 1976.

Shacklady, Helen. "The ʿAbbasid Movement in Khurāsān." In *Occasional Papers of the School of Abbasid Studies. No. 1*, 98–112. St. Andrews: St. Andrews University Press, 1986.

Sharon, Moshe. *Black Banners from the East: The Establishment of the ʿAbbāsid State–Incubation of a Revolt*. Jerusalem: The Magnes Press, 1983.

*Shehaby, Nabil. "*ʿIlla* and *Qiyas* in Early Islamic Legal Theory." *Journal of the American Oriental Society* 102:1 (1982): 27–46.

*Shūfānī, Ilyās. *Ḥurūb al-ridda. Dirāsa naqdiyya fī l-maṣādir*. Damascus: Dār al-ḥiṣād, 1995.

*——. *Al-Riddah and the Muslim Conquest of Arabia*. Toronto: University of Toronto Press, 1973.

Sourdel, Dominique. "The ʿAbbasid Caliphate." In *Cambridge History of Islam. Vol I. The Central Islamic Lands*, edited by P.M. Holt, A.K.S. Lambton, and B. Lewis, 104–39. Cambridge: Cambridge University Press, 1970.

——. "Les cadis de Baṣra d'après Wakīʿ." *Arabica* 2 (1955): 111–14.

——. "Les circonstances de la mort de Ṭāhir Ier au Hurāsān en 207/822." *Arabica* 5 (1958): 66–69.

*——. *L'état impérial des califes abbassides, VIIIe–Xe siècle.* Paris: Presses universitaires de France, 1999.

——. "La politique religieuse du calife ʿabbaside al-Maʾmun." *Revue des études islamiques* 30 (1962): 27–48.

——. *Le vizirat ʿAbbāside de 749 à 936 (132 à 324 de l'Hégire).* Damascus: Institut Français de Damas, 1959–60.

Talbi, Mohamed. *L'émirat aghlabide, 184-296/800-909, histoire politique.* Paris: Adrien Maisonneuve, 1966.

*Tor, Deborah G. "An Historiographical Re-Examination of the Appointment and Death of ʿAlī al-Riḍā." *Der Islam* 78, no. i (2001): 103–28.

*——. *Violent Order: Religious Warfare, Chivalry, and the ʿAyyār Phenomenon in the Medieval Islamic World.* Würzburg, Germany: Ergon Verlag, 2007.

Tornberg, Carl J. "Über muhammedanische Revolutions-Münzen." *Zeitschrift der Deutschen Morgenländischen Gesellschaft* 22 (1868): 700–707.

*Turner, John P. "The Death of al-ʿAbbās b. al-Maʾmūn and a "Thwarted" Coup d'état." *Journal of Near Eastern Studies* 72, no. 1 (2013): 11–23.

*——. "The End of the Miḥna." *Oriens* 38 (2010): 89–106.

*——. *Inquisition in Early Islam: The Competition for Political and Religious Authority in the Abbasid Empire.* London: I. B. Tauris, 2013.

Uhrig, H. Ferdinand. *Das Kalifat von al-Maʾmūn. Aus den Annalen von at-Tabari übersetzt und unter Heranziehung der sonstigen bedeutenden Quellen ausführlich erläutert.* Frankfurt am Main: Verlag Peter Lang, 1988.

ʿUmar, F. *Buḥūth fī l-tārīkh al-ʿabbāsī.* Beirut: Dār al-qalam li-al-ṭibāʿa, 1977.

Van Arendonk, Cornelis. *De opkomst van het zaidietische imamaat in Yemen.* Leiden: E. J. Brill, 1919.

Van Ess, Josef. "LʿAutorité de la tradition prophétique dans la théologie muʿtazilite." In *La notion d'autorité au Moyen Age. Islam, Byzance, Occident*, edited by G. Makdisi, D. Sourdel, and J. Sourdel-Thomine, 212–26. Paris: Presses universitaires de France, 1982.

——. "Ḍirār b. ʿAmr und die "Cahmīya. Biographie einer vergessenen Schule." *Der Islam* 43 (1967): 241–79 and 44 (1968): 1–70 & 318–20.

*——. *Der Eine und das Andere. Beobachtungen an islamischen häresiographischen Texten.* 2 vols. Berlin: De Gruyter, 2011.

——. "Ǧāḥiẓ und die *aṣḥāb al-maʿārif*" *Der Islam* 42 (1966): 169–78.

——. "Ibn Kullāb und die *Miḥna*." *Oriens* 18–19 (1967): 92–142. French translation by Cl. Gilliot: "Ibn Kullāb et la Miḥna." *Arabica* 27 (1990): 173–233.

——. "Les qadarites et la Ġailāniya de Yazīd III." *Studia Islamica* 31 (1970): 269–86.

——. "Skepticism in Islamic Religious Thought." *Al-Abḥāth* 21 (1968): 1–18.

*——. *Theologie und Gesellschaft im 2. und 3. Jahrhundert Hidschra. Eine Geschichte des religiösen Denkens im frühen Islam.* 6 vols. Berlin: Walter de Gruyter, 1991–7.

Vasiliev, Alexander A. *History of the Byzantine Empire. 324–1453.* Madison: The University of Wisconsin Press, 1964.

Watt, W. Montgomery. "Early Discussions about the Qurʾān." *Muslim World* 11 (1950): 27–40 & 96–105.

——. *The Formative Period of Islamic Thought.* Edinburgh: Edinburgh University Press, 1973.

——. *Islamic Philosophy and Theology. An Extended Survey*. Edinburgh: Edinburgh University Press, 1985.

——. "The Political Attitudes of the Muʿtazilah." *Journal of the Royal Asiatic Society* (1963): 38–57.

Weil, Gustav. *Geschichte der Chalifen*. Mannheim: Friedrich Bassermann, 1848.

*Winkelmann-Liebert, Holger. "Die *Miḥna* im Kalifat des al-Muʿtaṣim." *Der Islam* 80, no. ii (2003): 224–83.

Wright, Edwin M. "Bābak of Badhdh and al-Afshīn during the Years 816–41 A.D., Symbols of Iranian Persistence against Islamic Penetration in North Iran." *Muslim World* 38 (1948): 43–59, 124–31.

*Yücesoy, Hayrettin. *Messianic Beliefs and Imperial Politics in Medieval Islam: The ʿAbbasid Caliphate in the Early Ninth Century*. Columbia, SC: University of South Carolina Press, 2009.

* Zaman, Muhammad Qasim. *Religion and Politics under the Early ʿAbbāsids: The Emergence of the Proto-Sunnī Elite*. Leiden: Brill, 1997.

Zaydān, Jūrjī. *Taʾrīkh al-tamaddun al-islāmī*. 5 Vols. Beirut: Dār al-ḥayāt li-al-ṭibāʿa wa-l-nashr, 1902–6.

al-Ziriklī, Khayr al-Dīn. *Al-Aʿlām*. 8 Vols. Beirut: Dar al-ʿilm li-l-malāyīn, 1989.

INDEX

al-ʿAbbās ibn al-Maʾmūn, 19 n46, 22, 30, 45, 48, 80
al-ʿAbbās ibn Mūsā al-Kāẓim (brother of ʿAlī al-Riḍā), 27
ʿAbbāsid Caliphate/Empire, 4, 6 n7–8, 9–11
  decline of, 10–11, 51, 80 n3
ʿAbbāsid *daʿwa*, first, 9, 25, 55 n6
ʿAbbāsid *daʿwa*, second, 24
ʿAbbāsid family, 19 n46, 26–28, 43, 45, 80
  and ʿAlids, 8, 9, 42–43, 46–48
  and Shiʿites, 3, 24–25
ʿAbbāsid predecessors, xiii, 3, 34, 40, 47, 55
ʿAbbāsid Revolution, 9–10, 25 n24, 44 n78
ʿAbbāsids
  color black, 28, 44–45
  color green, 44
  waṣiyya doctrine, 48
ʿAbd al-Malik ibn Marwān, caliph, 8
ʿAbd al-Raḥmān ibn Isḥāq, 69, 96
ʿAbd al-Raḥmān I, Umayyad emir, 10 n21
ʿAbdallāh ibn Ṭāhir ibn al-Ḥusayn, 28–29
Abnāʾ, 24–28, 76
Abū al-Sarāyā, 24–25, 46
Abū Bakr, caliph, xi, 6–7, 42 n64, 43 n73, 44 n82
Abū Ḥanīfa, 21 n8, 37, 68 n85
Abū al-Hudhayl al-ʿAllāf, 31–32
Abū Muslim, 9–10
Abū Ṭālib, 12, 87
adab works,
al-ʿAdl, 15–16
Aghlabids, 51, 54
Ahl al-ḥadīth. See Traditionists
Ahl al-raʾy, 71
Ahl al-sunna, 11, 71, 101, 103
Aḥmad ibn Abī Duʾād, 19, 31, 33, 37 n39, 80
Aḥmad ibn Ḥanbal, xii, 4, 17, 40, 52, 60, 67, 74, 80, 86, 90, 95, 97–99, 101, 103
Aḥmad ibn Yūsuf, 55 n6
ʿĀʾisha bint Abī Bakr, 6, 7, 24 n18
ʿAlī ibn Abī Ṭālib, 6–7, 8, 11–13, 24 n18, 26, 38, 41–42, 43 n69, 46–48, 79
  preeminence of (*tafḍīl ʿAlī*), 30, 42, 107
ʿAlī al-Riḍā (ʿAlī ibn Mūsā al-Kāẓim), 27, 44–45, 47, 66 n80, 107
  death of, 28, 45–46, 107
  designation as heir, 27, 32, 40, 43–48, 54–57, 80
ʿAlī ibn ʿĪsā ibn Māhān, 24–25
ʿAlids, xi, xiii, 3, 8–10, 12, 13, 17 n41, 26, 38 n40, 41–50, 54, 77–80
al-Amīn, caliph, 21–24, 26, 28 n35, 40, 49 n104, 51, 54, 55 n6, 57, 62 n60, 80 n3
al-Amr bi-l-maʿrūf wa-l-nahy ʿan al-munkar, xii, 15
al-Andalus (Spain), 10 n21, 51
Animals, tolerance for alcohol, 32 n4
Anthropomorphism/*tashbīh*, 15, 34 n20, 63, 68 n84
Anti-Caliphate, of Ibrāhīm ibn al-Mahdī (al-Mubārak), 27–28, 54
Apocalypse, 47
ʿAqīl ibn Abī Ṭālib, 26
Arabic language, 8, 21
Arazi, Albert and Amikam Elad, 40, 55 n6
Army, reorganization of, 24 n21, 30
Astrology, 31–32, 34 n18, 85
ʿAyyār, pl. *ʿayyārūn*, 27 n29
al-Azdī, 40, 86

Bābak, 29, 51
Bādhghīs, 21
Baghdad, x, 10, 12, 17–19, 22–29, 30, 33 n13, 34, 38, 40 n55, 42, 45, 59, 66 n80, 69–72, 74, 76 n110, 107
al-Baghdādī, 34, 88

Banū Hāshim, 8–9, 42, 44, 48, 54, 79
Banū Kalb, 8
al-Bāqillānī, 19 n51
Barmakids, 10, 22
al-Baṣra, 7, 25, 33 n13, 72 n100
biographical dictionaries, 5, 32, 70, 73, 81
Bishr al-Marīsī, 33, 37 n39, 66 n80
Bishr ibn al-Muʿtamir, 32 n8
Bishr ibn al-Walīd al-Kindī, 19, 60, 96–97
Bundār (Persian), 62 n61
Būrān (daughter of al-Ḥasan ibn Sahl), 28 n34
Byzantine Empire, 4, 10, 18, 22, 30, 39 n48, 54, 59, 66–67

Caliph/*khalīfa*, as title, 5–7, 41, 56–57
Christians, 19, 63, 80
Christian Trinity, 16, 63
Chronicles (Universal and local histories), 5, 17, 34, 36, 38, 41 n62, 42, 44, 45–46, 69, 81, 83–94
Civil war (between al-Amīn and al-Maʾmūn), 23–24, 25, 29, 51, 54, 67, 80 n3, 107
Coins, 8, 23, 40–41, 44
Commander of the Faithful/*amīr al-muʾminīn*, 7, 60–62, 64, 68–69
Companions of the Prophet, 30, 32 n4, 72–73
Copts, 30
Cordoba, 10 n21, 12
Createdness of the Qur'an, doctrine, 1–5, 15–19, 30–31, 32 n5, 33 n13, 34, 36–37, 39–41, 43 n75, 51, 53–54, 56, 59, 61, 63, 65–69, 76 n110, 77–79, 107
Crone, Patricia, 1 n2, 67 n83
Crone, Patricia and Martin Hinds, 2–3, 6 n7, 41 n60, 51, 53, 55, 65 n78

Damascus, 8, 12, 34
Ḍirār ibn ʿAmr, 33, 35 n27, 37 n39

Egypt, xi, 4, 7, 29–30, 76 n110, 107
Eschatology, 47 n100
Ess, Josef van, 33, 35 n25, 35 n27, 37 n39, 39 n47, 56 n11, 66 n80, 76 n110

Fadak, 43
al-Faḍl ibn al-Rabīʿ, 23, 26
al-Faḍl ibn Sahl, 22–23, 25 n23, 26–28, 34 n18, 55 n6, 58, 107
al-Faḍl ibn Yaḥyā al-Barmakī, 22 n13
Faqīh, pl. *fuqahāʾ*, 56, 66–67, 71–72, 74–75, 79
Fārs, 30
Fāṭima bint Muḥammad, 7, 14, 43 n73
Fāṭimid, 38
Fiqh/Jurisprudence, 3, 12, 21, 37 n26, 73
Fitna, pl. *fitan*, 23 n18, 67
Funeral rituals, 39
al-Fuwaṭī, 33 n11

Genealogical works, 5
Ghaylān al-Dimashqī, 1 n1
Gibb, Hamilton, 47
Great Mosque of Baghdad, 27 n32, 66 n80

al-Hādī , caliph, 1 n1, 10, 22, 24, 26, 48 n104
Hadith, 11–12, 16, 21, 39 n51, 44 n82, 58, 60, 71, 73–75
Ḥamdawayh ibn ʿAlī ibn ʿĪsā ibn Māhān, 25–26
Ḥanafites, 12, 21, 36–37, 71
Ḥanbalites, 4, 12, 18 n42, 34, 43 n75, 45
Ḥarbiyya district of Baghdad, 26–27
al-Ḥārith ibn al-Miskīn, 70, 100
Harthama ibn Aʿyan, 24–26
Hārūn al-Rashīd, caliph, 1, 10, 16, 28 n35, 45, 66 n80
al-Ḥasan al-Baṣrī, 14
al-Ḥasan ibn Sahl, 25–28, 29 n40, 56–57
al-Ḥasan ibn Ziyād al-Luʾluʾī, 21
al-Ḥasan ibn ʿAlī ibn Abī Ṭālib, 7, 12–14, 25
Ḥasanids, 12
Ḥashwiyya, 63 n62
Heresy/*ilḥād*, 1, 63
Ḥijāz, 26, 43
Hinds, Martin, 2, 17 n41, 39–40, 51, 53, 76 n110
Hishām ibn ʿAbd al-Malik, caliph, 1 n1, 16
Hudā, 52
Ḥumayd ibn ʿAbd al-Ḥamīd, 29 n40
al-Ḥusayn ibn ʿAlī ibn Abī Ṭālib, 12–14, 19, 25
Ḥusaynids, 12

Iblīs/the Devil, 63
Ibn Abī Ṭāhir Ṭayfūr, 35, 42, 85
Ibn Bābawayh, 42, 43 n69, 44, 87
Ibn al-ʿImād, 5, 33 n10, 34, 43 n75, 94
Ibn al-Jawzī, 36, 91
Ibn al-Muqaffaʿ, 48, 67 n82
Ibn al-Murtaḍā, 32, 34, 93
Ibn Kathīr, 44 n82, 45, 93
Ibn Saʿd, 5, 73, 83, 100
Ibn Ṭabāṭabā (Ḥasanid), 25

Ibn Taghrībirdī, 36, 37 n36, 44 n82, 94
Ibn al-Zubayr, 24 n18
Ibrāhīm ibn al-Mahdī (al-Mubārak), 27–28, 42 n67, 54, 66 n80, 80 n3, 100, 107
Ibrāhīm ibn Mūsā, brother of ʿAlī al-Riḍā, 43 n70
Ibrāhīm ibn Rashīd, 35 n25
Idrīsids, 54
Ijmāʿ, 12
Imām, 13–14, 25, 27, 35 n25, 38–42, 44, 51–52, 57 n17, 64, 78
Imām al-hudā, 52
Imāmate, 6 n7, 13–14, 25, 38–39, 48, 52
Imāmites. *See* Twelver Shiʿites
Inquisition, ix, xii–xiii, 1, 17–18, 37 n39, 77
Iraq, 13, 24–27, 29–30, 37
Isḥāq ibn Ibrāhīm, 17–18, 28, 29 n37, 30, 59–60, 66 n80, 69–71, 73–75, 95
Isḥāq ibn Mūsā al-Hādī, 26–27
Ismāʿīl ibn Dāwūd, 73

Jabriyya ("determinism"), 34 n17, 35 n26, 68 n83
al-Jaʿd ibn Dirham, 36
Jaʿfar al-Ṣādiq, 25, 38, 40
Jaʿfar ibn ʿĪsā, 69, 98
Jaʿfar ibn Yaḥyā al-Barmakī, 22
al-Jāḥiẓ, 32, 84
al-Jahshiyārī, 40, 46, 58, 86
al-Jazīra, 30
Jerusalem, 8
Jesus, son of Mary, 16, 63
Jews, 19, 80
Jibāl, 24, 30
Jinn, 32 n4
Jurjān, 25
Juynboll, Gautier, 39 n48, 72

Kaʿaba Accord. *See* Meccan Accord
Kairouan, 12
Karbalāʾ, 13, 19
Khalīfat Allāh, 41, 56
Khalq al-Qurʾān. *See* Createdness of the Qur'an, doctrine
al-Khaṭīb al-Baghdādī, 38, 90
Khurasan, Khurasanians, xi, 9–10, 21–24, 27 n30, 28, 33 n13, 34, 42, 45–47, 53, 54 n6, 71, 76, 107
Khurramiyya, 29 n38
al-Kisāʾī, 21
al-Kūfa, 7, 9–10, 13, 21 n8, 25, 27

Madelung, Wilferd, 21 n2, 40, 47
al-Mahdī (Savior), 9, 13–14, 47
al-Mahdī, caliph, 1 n1, 10, 21 n4, 24, 26, 48
Mālikites, 12
al-Maʾmūn
  and ʿAbbāsids, 19 n46, 26–27, 43–45, 47–48, 67, 80
  and ʿAlī ibn Abī Ṭālib, 41–42, 48, 79–80
  and ʿAlids, 27, 41–49, 54, 78–80
  and astrology, 34 n18
  and Byzantine Empire, 4, 18, 30, 39 n48, 59, 66
  and death of ʿAlī al-Riḍā, 45
  and al-Faḍl ibn Sahl's murder, 28
  and Murjiʾism, 35–36
  and Muʿtazilism, 31–37
  and Shiʿism, 37–41
  as homo politicus, 3
  as military leader, 24 n21, 30
  death of, 30
  education of, 21–22
  fragmentary subjective labels in secondary literature, 2–3, 5
  kunya of, 21 n1
  last will and testament, 18–19, 30, 33-34, 43, 54–55, 80
  marriage to Būrān, 28 n34
  personality, 21–22
  reign of, 24–30
  religio-political issues, 29–30
al-Manṣūr, caliph, 3, 9, 10, 21, 24, 44 n80, 48, 55 n6
al-Manṣūr ibn al-Mahdī, 26–27
al-Manzila bayn al-manzilatayn, 15
Marājil, mother of al-Maʾmūn, 21
Marw, 23–27, 71
Marwān II, caliph, 6, 10
al-Masʿūdī, 34, 42, 43 n69, 45 n87, 87
Mecca, 22, 25, 32 n4
Meccan Accord, 22–23
Medina, 7, 13, 32 n4, 47
Miḥna
  and "Khurasanian connection," 53, 71 n98, 75–76
  duration of, 18
  meaning and connotations of, xii, 17 n41
Muʿāwiya, caliph, 6–8, 13, 42
  cursing of, 29–30, 33 n14, 41–42, 46, 107
  personality, 8
Muḥaddithūn. *See* Traditionists
Muḥammad. *See* Prophet Muḥammad

Muḥammad al-Dībāja, 25
Muḥammad ibn Abī Khālid, 26
Muḥammad ibn ʿAlī al-Riḍā, 45
Muḥammad ibn Ḥumayd ibn al-Ṭūsī, 29
Muḥammad ibn Jaʿfar, 43
Muḥammad ibn Muḥammad ibn Zayd (al-Nār, Ḥusaynid), 25, 46
Muḥammad ibn Nūḥ, 60, 95, 100
Murjiʾa /Murjiʾites, 15, 35
Mūsā al-Kāẓim, 25
Mūsā ibn al-Amīn, 23
Mutʿa marriage, 33 n14, 38, 42 n67
Mutakallimūn, 34 n18, 36 n32
al-Muʾtaman. *See* al-Qāsim ibn Hārūn al-Rashīd
al-Muʿtaṣim (Abū Isḥāq), caliph, 18, 26, 29–30, 33, 37 n39, 43, 48, 54, 80–81
  personality, 18–19
al-Mutawakkil, caliph, 6, 18–19, 33 n10, 33 n13, 36, 43 n73, 51, 80
Muʿtazilism /Muʿtazilites, xii, 3, 16, 19, 31–37, 56 n11, 77–78, 80–81
  and al-Jāḥiẓ, 32 n5, 84
  Baghdadi school of, 32 n8
  Baṣra school of, 31–32
  doctrine, 14–16, 34–37

Nagel, Tilman, 2–3, 6 n7, 39, 40, 42, 47–48, 51–53
al-Nahrawān, 45
Najaf, 13
Naṣr ibn Shabath, 29
Naysābūr, 23 n14
al-Naẓẓām, 32

Patton, Walter, ix, 2, 4–5, 17 n41, 18 n42, 33, 37 n39
Philosophy, Greek, 31–32, 36
Pilgrimage, 19, 22, 26, 43
Polytheism, 16, 63, 68 n84
Prayer, *takbīr* in, 38–39, 52–53
Prophet Muḥammad, 5–7, 9, 11–12, 14, 17 n41, 25 n24, 27, 32 n4, 44, 48, 54 n6, 57, 65, 78, 80
Prophethood/*nubuwwa*, 57, 64, 73

Qadariyya ("indeterminism"), 1 n1, 34–35
Qāḍī, 70–72
Qāḍī al-quḍāt, 19, 33 n13
al-Qāḍī al-Nuʿmān, 38–39
al-Qādir, caliph, 18 n42
al-Qāhir, caliph, 18 n42
al-Qāsim ibn Hārūn al-Rashīd (al-Muʾtaman), 22
al-Qawārīrī, 74, 102
Qiyās, 12
Qur'an, 6 n7, 11–12, 15–16, 19, 21 n5, 27, 32 n4, 37, 54, 60–61, 68 n83. *See also* Createdness of the Qur'an
  2:256, 1 n2
  18:31, 44 n81
  21:73, 52 n2
  43:2, 68 n86
  43:3, 37
  76:21, 44, n81
  as object, 16, 37, 68
  as word of God, 16
Quraysh, 6–9

al-Rāḍī, caliph, 18 n42
al-Raqqa, 18, 29
Rayy, 24
al-Riḍā min āl Muḥammad, 9, 25, 27, 44
Ridda, 6
Rightly-Guided Caliphs, 6
Risālat al-Khamīs, 40, 52, 54, 59, 64
Round City (City of al-Manṣūr), 26 n27
Rulership, theocratic, 52

al-Ṣafadī, 36, 40 n55, 42 n67, 46, 93
Siflat al-ʿāmma, 62–63
al-Saffāḥ, caliph, 3, 6, 9–10
Sahl ibn Salāma al-Anṣārī, 27
Sahlids, 26–28
al-Salaf, 32 n5, 41
Sarakhs, 28
al-Shāfiʿī/Shāfiʿites, 12, 73 n103
Shāhid, shuhūd, 69–72, 76 n110, 79
Shīʿat ʿAlī/Shiʿa/Shiʿites, 3, 6–7, 9–13, 19, 24–26, 38–42, 44, 45 n87, 47, 54, 57 n17, 77–80
  extreme (*ghulāt*), 13 n33
  Seveners, 13 n33
  Twelvers, 13–14, 25, 27, 68 n87
  Zaydites, 13 n33, 14, 40–42
Shurṭa (security forces, police), 28–29
Sourdel, Dominique, 2–3, 16, 38–40, 42–43, 52 n3, 53, 57 n17, 65 n78
al-Subkī, 36, 37 n39, 93
Succession to Caliphate, 8 n16, 12, 22, 80
Sunna, 6 n7, 11–12, 73 n103
Sunnites, 11, 71
Syria, 7, 10, 18, 26, 29–30

al-Ṭabarī, 17, 43 n70, 66, 70, 86, 95
Tafḍīl ʿAlī. *See* ʿAlī ibn Abī Ṭālib, preeminence of
Ṭāhir ibn al-Ḥusayn, 24, 28–29
Ṭāhirids, 28–29, 51, 54
Takbīr. *See* Prayer, *takbīr* in
Ṭalḥa ibn Ṭāhir ibn al-Ḥusayn, 28
Ṭalḥa ibn ʿUbaydallāh, 24 n18
Ṭālibids, 12, 26, 43 n70
Taqiyya, 68–69, 81
Tarsus, 4, 18, 30, 59–60, 70–71, 95
Tashayyuʿ, 12 n29
Taslīm, 38–39
Tawḥīd, 15–16, 34
Theophilus (Byzantine emperor), 66 n79
Thumāma ibn Ashras, 31–32, 34–35
Ṭirāz, 23
Traditionists/*muḥaddithūn*, xiii, 11, 16, 18 n42, 21, 32 n4, 32 n5, 33 n13, 36, 52, 56, 71, 72–75, 79
Ṭūs, 23, 45

ʿUbaydallāh ibn al-Ḥasan ibn ʿUbaydallāh ibn ʿAbbās ibn ʿAlī ibn Abī Ṭālib, 43 n70
ʿUbaydallāh ibn al-Sarī ibn al-Ḥakam, 29
ʿUlamāʾ, 3, 12, 52–53, 56, 65–66, 67 n81, 75–76, 78–79
ʿUmar ibn al-Khaṭṭāb, caliph, 6–7, 8, 41 n62
ʿUmar ibn ʿAbd al-ʿAzīz, caliph, 8
Umayyads, xi, 1 n1, 3, 6–10, 13, 16, 23–25, 29, 35 n25, 42 n65, 44 n78, 48, 51, 53, 57 n17, 65 n78
Umm al-Faḍl, daughter of al-Maʾmūn, 45
Umm ʿĪsā, wife of al-Maʾmūn, 22
ʿUthmān ibn ʿAffān, caliph, 6–7, 12

Van Gelder, Geert Jan, 35 n25

al-Waʿd wa-l-waʿīd, 15, 34
Wāṣil ibn ʿAṭāʾ, 14
al-Wāsiṭī, 60
al-Wāthiq, caliph, 18–19, 33, 80–81
Watt, Montgomery, 31–33, 36 n28, 39–40, 51, 53

Yaḥyā ibn Aktham, 33, 38
Yaḥyā ibn Khālid al-Barmakī, 22 n13
Yaḥyā ibn Maʿīn, 74, 104
Yaḥyā ibn Muʿādh, 29
al-Yaʿqūbī, 34, 42 n67, 43 n73, 59 n45, 85
Yazīd I, caliph, 8, 13, 24 n18
al-Yazīdī, 21
Yemen, 25–26, 46 n93

Zaydites. *See* *Shīʿat ʿAlī*/Shiʿa/Shiʿites
Zubayda, wife of Hārūn al-Rashīd, 21, 40 n55, 62 n60

AHMED IBN HANBAL AND THE MIHNA

A BIOGRAPHY OF THE IMAM INCLUDING AN ACCOUNT OF THE MOHAMMEDAN INQUISITION CALLED THE MIHNA, 218–234 A.H.

Walter Melville Patton

INTRODUCTORY REMARKS.

The following pages contain the record of the Imâm Aḥmed ibn Ḥanbal and of a struggle [1]) with which he stood connected, whose issues were so great as to warrant a close study of all that is involved in the movement. The history of Dogma in Islâm as written by Western writers has given us an idea of the questions which were being disputed at this time, and the outward history of events has recorded in very meagre outline the most important public occurrences of our narrative; but there has been, so far, no use made of the rich opportunity presented in the biography of Aḥmed ibn Hanbal to see the theological controversies of Islâm in their connection with the outward history of the State. This kind of historical study is the more interesting, because from it we are enabled to understand the relation of the State to religion at that time, and the place occupied by religion and its teachers in the State.

1) The Mihna This term, meaning in general usage a 'testing' or 'trial', whether by the accidents of fortune or the actions of men, is often used, (together with the VIII Form of the verb مَحَنَ) with reference to a religious test with a view to obtaining assent to some particular belief or system of beliefs. We find this special usage largely illustrated in the records of the Mu'tazilite inquisition, the account of which is to appear in the sequel. It is also found in the accounts of the Orthodox inquisition under the Khalif Ḳâhir 200 years later. Most commonly, the whole persecution extending from the year 218 A. H. to 234 A. H. is called the Miḥna.

We have referred above to the issues of the Miḥna, as the persecution inaugurated by al-Maʾmûn is called. The importance of them lies in the fact that they settled the orthodox character of Islâm for all following ages; and in the preservation of orthodoxy lies the preservation of Islâm itself, in our judgment. Had Rationalism succeeded in bringing about by persecution a general abandonment of orthodoxy, it is probable that the principle of free thought, without recognition of authority, would have had a disintegrating effect within Islâm itself, and would have made it much more susceptible to modifying and reforming influences from without; so that, in time, we should have seen standards of faith and life, which contravene our reason as the Ḳorân and Tradition do, given up for something more satisfying to reason and moral judgment. We need not enter into the question whether any good came from the preservation of orthodoxy, further than to say that if Islâm was to continue to be Islâm, to preserve orthodoxy was the best way to accomplish such a result.

We ought to give Rationalism credit for having asserted the principle, un-Islâmic though it be, that thought must be free in the search for truth. The abuse of free-thinking, however, in a love of speculation for speculation's sake, and in an inordinate desire of controversial victory is, in the history of this period, abundantly exemplified.

Ahmed ibn Hanbal during his whole career subsequent to the death of the Imâm al-Shâfiʿî (204 A. H.) was the most remarkable figure in the camp of Mohammedan orthodoxy, and during the course of the Mihna did more than any other individual to strengthen the resistance of his party to the repressive efforts of the Khalifs and their officers. He stood for the standing or falling of orthodoxy in its time of trial; and there is little exaggeration in the statement, made more than once concerning him, that 'all men were looking to him for an example, that as he decided on the test as to the Ḳorân being applied to him, so they might follow'.

We have some interesting circumstantial evidence of

Aḥmed's position and influence among the people from the way in which he was treated by the Khalifs. Al-Ma'mûn had made up his mind to cite him to appear with the first seven men to whom he put the test, but even the violent bigot Aḥmed ibn Abû Dowâd the Chief-Kâḍî advised his master not to summon him, doubtless recognizing that success with the seven men would be much more difficult should Aḥmed be with them, and feeling that the result of their trial would better determine whether or not it would be wise to attack one greater than they. Al-Ma'mûn's letter to his governor in Baghdâd after the latter had examined the doctors treats with gentleness Aḥmed ibn Ḥanbal, when one reads what he had to say about most of the other doctors there alluded to. In the case of al-Muʿtaṣim, we must bear in mind that he did not scourge Aḥmed until he had exhausted every means to save him, by threats, arguments and entreaties. He declared that had al-Ma'mûn not ordered him to deal with him and such as he, he would have had nothing to do with the infliction of the punishment. Furthermore, the scourging took place in the court-yard of the palace unknown to the mass of the people, who stood outside waiting for the announcement as to how the trial had ended. As soon as they suspected that their Imâm was being tortured, there was a tremendous excitement; and it seemed as if the Khalif's palace would become an object of assault, when al-Muʿtaṣim had Aḥmed's uncle 'Isḥâḳ brought out, and had this man falsely intimate to them that he had not harmed his nephew in the least. To make himself still more secure against the danger of a popular uprising, al-Muʿtaṣim kept Aḥmed within the precincts of the palace until the evening, and then dressed him up in gala costume and sent him under cover of dusk to his dwelling. We may consider it as significant of Aḥmed's standing among the people that there were no further attempts to coerce him during the remaining fifteen years of the Miḥna, though we are assured that he was active in teaching and as popular as he ever had been, or even more so. Al-Wâthiḳ's treatment furnishes some evidence to shew how he regarded Aḥmed's influence. We are told that, despite the urging of Ibn Abû Dowâd, he would not cite Aḥmed for examination before him, but sent word to the Imâm to remove from his country; a good proof that Aḥmed had great power with the people. The biographer adds that he does not know whether the Khalif refrained from dealing with Aḥmed because of admiration for his steadfastness, or because of fear that evil consequences might come upon him should he lay violent hands upon so holy a man. For al-Mutawakkil we need say little here. His attention to Aḥmed and the messages which he sent him point clearly to his popularity and influence.

The religious sentiment in the Muslim populace had not much sympathy with the loose views and free living of the liberal teachers. Hence it was that they idolized as they did a man like Aḥmed ibn Ḥanbal. His intense devotion to the things most venerated and cherished by the people: God, the Prophet, the Ḳorân, the Tradition, the Sunna of the Prophet, and the Communion of the Faithful, endeared him to the mass of the common folk. He was, also, a remarkable example of an effort which always excited reverence in the breast of the Muslim, namely, the effort 'to bring himself near to God and thus secure a good reward from him'. Those who are familiar with the stock expressions of Mohammedan piety will understand what this means in the case of a sincere and earnest religionist. Judging by the record of a host of extravagant visions of blessedness in Paradise which men had of the Imâm Aḥmed after his departure from the world, one cannot doubt that all good Muslims believed him to have obtained even more than the good reward for which he had hoped.

That Aḥmed ibn Ḥanbal has come to be regarded as the founder of the Ḥanbalite Madhhab, or School, is not to be wondered at, though it is not because of any intention on his part, as far as I can see. He was a great saint and defender of orthodoxy, and it is due to this fact that his pupils and admirers, after his death, sought to give form to their master's teachings and compacted themselves into a sect or school of theology. I do not believe that Aḥmed himself had the idea that such would occur. That a school was formed spontaneously is a testimony to the powerful impression of the man's personality upon his own age and that following. The things which the Muslims reckon to Aḥmed's praise are his personal life, his intensely orthodox teaching, and his maintenance of his teaching in the face of persecution. He was learned in only one direction, that is, in the Ḳorân, Tradition, the Consensus of usage and opinion among the Faithful. These things he knew thoroughly; of worldly learning he does not appear to have had any great store. The kind of knowledge he had, supplementing great courage and firmness and much natural shrewdness, was his effective weapon in the controversial warfare which he had to wage. Aḥmed's great book the Musnad is the best monument to that knowledge in which he especially excelled. It exercised such an influence, in itself and in the works derived from it, for the maintenance of Tradition in its worthy place as a basis of theology, that its author's career ought to be known. We will then see the real life which was so steadying in its effect upon Mohammedan religious thought, and which was but followed up in its effect by the book which it produced.

Some native biographers and historians have noticed the man and the persecution in which he suffered for his faith with too flattering recognition of Aḥmed's worth and services. Others whose interest is more secular and who record, for the most part, only the outward events of civil history have often passed over the religious movement of Aḥmed's time with little or no notice. But there is a significance about the man and the movement which the greatest of the chroniclers, such as Ṭabarî, have not been slow to recognize. Abu'l-Maḥâsin, who professes to be writing the annals of Egypt, but whose interest in religious persons and events is evident on almost every page of his work, has done full justice to the general course of events in connection with the Miḥna and to the public career of Aḥmed ibn Ḥanbal.

In the narrative which follows, I have sought to give the connected story of my subject's life from its beginning to its close. The account expands, however, at that point where his life becomes a factor in the public history of the time, in order that we may have a fair impression of the whole course of religious events then transpiring, and may, also, see more clearly Aḥmed ibn Ḥanbal in the arena where he, more than elsewhere, won for himself that great fame which has placed him among the chief heroes and saints of his faith.

It should be remarked that European writers have too often written their accounts in a spirit of antipathy toward the orthodox theology of Mohammedanism, and have given more than a due share of commendation to the Muʿtazilites (Rationalists). They were, it is true, advocates of the freedom of thought, but were, none the less, in many cases, too self-indulgent and pleasure-loving to be credited with the highest moral aims or earnestness. It is doubtful whether, in most instances, their championship of free thinking was from any lofty conception of what constitutes true freedom. It would appear to be rather the motive of convenience that moved them to take the course they took. They preached the gospel of Freedom because they felt the Law and the Commandment to impose an inconvenience upon them, so that they could not do as they wished. All praise is due to the sincere men who loved freedom and sought it as the right of every man, but the sequel will shew not many of such men in that field of history which it covers.

The characters of the four Khalifs al-Maʾmûn, al-Muʿtaṣim, al-Wâthiḳ and al-Mutawakkil will receive some additional light from the narrative which follows; as a result, probably that of the first and last named will receive a different judgment from that which has been passed hitherto. Al-Maʾmûn, the scholar and patron of scholars, the first free-thinking Khalif who took a real interest in religion, will be more fully discovered as a man intolerant toward those who differed from him, even to the degree of becoming an intense persecutor. As to his liberal tendencies, it is not likely we shall find any reason to change our judgment. He had a quick and very capable mind, and hated to be fettered. He believed he had the right to think to the full extent of his opportunity, and to make opportunity for mental ranging where he had none. Had he stopped at this point, he would have presented to us a record of great service to his fellow men accomplished by moral means; but when he rejected what he deemed a spiritual tyranny, only to turn spiritual and physical tyrant himself, the pure quality of his early aspirations is for us sadly spoiled.

Al-Mutawakkil is a Khalif whose character cannot possibly be what European historians have made it out to be darker than the plague of darkness itself. He was orthodox, but his treatment of liberals will easily bear comparison with his predecessors' treatment of the orthodox theologians; while the attitude he assumed toward Aḥmed ibn Ḥanbal does not present to us a man without redeeming qualities. It is not to be understood that we condone his terrible treatment of individuals, and the gloating satisfaction with which he sometimes related his own barbarities. Nor would we soften terms over his treatment of Jews and Christians. But the man was a fanatical religionist, and many of his deeds must be viewed from the religious standpoint to a greater extent than they have been heretofore.

It will be seen that, in regard to some other points, I have indicated in a footnote here and there a difference of opinion from some of the modern authorities whose works have been consulted. But, none the less, I avail myself of the present opportunity to say that the books of scholars like Steiner, von Kremer, Houtsma and Goldziher have been of great service to me, and that I am fully appreciative of the service their contributions have rendered to our knowledge of that period of Mohammedan history with which my sketch professes also to deal.

In my work I have derived most of the material used

from three manuscripts in the Library of the University of Leiden; 1) Cod. 311*a*, which, with its companion Cod. 311*b*, represents the 5th and 4th vols, respectively, of a five volume Ms. of the حلية الاولياء or حلية الابرار of Abû Nuᶜaim Aḥmed ibn Abdallah al-ʾIspahânî (d. 450). 2) Cod. 73*a*, which was not in the University collection of Mss. at the time that Dozy prepared his Catalogue, and is, therefore, not described. Its companion volume, Cod. 73*b* Gol., is however described. The two volumes form together one transcript of the work of Tâjuʾd-Dîn Abduʾl-Wahhâb ibnuʾl-Subkî (d. 771), entitled طبقات الشافعية: 3) Cod. 1917, which is likewise not described in the University Catalogue, but will be found in the Catalogue of Landberg, "Catalogue de Manuscrits arabes provenant d'une Bibliothèque privée à el-Medîna et appartenant à la Maison E. J. Brill, Leide", p. 53, Cod. 188, Aḥmed el-Maqrîzî († 845) مناقب احمد بن حنبل *Autographe de l'auteur.*

The biography of Aḥmed ibn Ḥanbal in Abû Nuᶜaim is found pp. 138—161 and in al-Subkî pp. 132—143. I have made most extensive use of the former of these two, as being the most detailed and circumstantial account of my subject's life. It is the oldest account of the three, and shews that fact in the amount of gossip and personal detail which it records, and which the later accounts have omitted. The narrative in al-Subkî affords a great deal of matter touching Aḥmed's part in the Miḥna, but not so much for the biography before and after that time. Al-Maḳrîzî's contribution is almost sure to be a portion of his Mokaffa, and is a good piece of biographical writing, well-arranged, concise in expression, and covering fully the life and relations of Aḥmed. Considered as a literary production, it is a better account than that of Abû Nuᶜaim, because of its compactness and system; but, for one who is gathering materials to compose a sketch having itself a similar purpose to Maḳrîzî's, as might be expected, the more diffuse narrative of Abû Nuᶜaim, with its accumulation of traditional accounts bearing on many minor points in Aḥmed's career, has much more to offer.

As is pointed out in a footnote Ṭabarî's Annales have been followed for the letters of the Khalif al-Ma'mûn. The same source, also, has afforded some useful information touching matters of more public interest during the progress of the Miḥna.

My endeavor has been to use the materials gathered from these and other sources in such a way as to make many witnesses contribute each something complementary to the testimony of his fellows, and yet have the whole convey the impression of a continuous narration.

To my greatly esteemed Professor, Doctor M. J. De Goeje, Professor of Arabic in the University of Leiden, I am indebted for direction, advice, and encouragement without which it would have been impossible to have accomplished the result that is here presented. I am very thankful to him for this, as also for his great courtesy as Interpres Legati Warneriani in placing at my disposal the three manuscripts which have been used in the preparation of the work.

Leiden, Feby 4th, 1897.

WALTER M. PATTON.

AḤMED IBN ḤANBAL AND THE MIḤNA.

I.

Aḥmed's Birth and Family Connections.

Aḥmed ibn Hanbal was born in the month of Rabiʿ the first, 164 A. H.[1]. The home of his parents was in Khorasân[2]. His father Moḥammed ibn Ḥanbal was one of the descendants of a captain in the Abbaside army in Khorasân which fought to overthrow the Omayyads[3]. The family left Khorasân to take up residence in Baghdâd, however, and Aḥmed was born a few days or months after their arrival in the latter city[4]. We are not informed what family his parents had beside himself, and in none of the sources of information to which I have had access is there, excepting of a brother of his father's, ʾIsḥâḳ ibn Ḥanbal[5] and a son of this man, Ḥanbal ibn ʾIsḥâḳ ibn Ḥanbal[6], any mention of a relative of his father's or his own generation. His lineage was of pure Arabic stock[7] from the family of Shaibân of the great tribe of Bekr ibn Wâʾil. Aḥmed is rarely called 'ibn Moḥammed', the name

1) Ibn Chall. N°. 19, Dhahabî, Liber Class. 8, N°. 18, Abuʾl-Maḥâsin I, 735 ff.

2) Jâcût II, 777.

3) Abû Nuʿaim, Leiden Ms. 311*a*, 150*b*, وكان ابوه من ابناء قواد خراسان

4) Ibn Chall. N°. 19, Dhahabî, Liber Class. 8, N°. 18, Al-Nawawî, Biog. Dicty. p. ١٤٩.

5) Abuʾl-Maḥ. I, 771.

6) Abuʾl-Maḥ. II, 76; cf. p. 26, l. 5 infra.

7) Al-Maḳrîzî, Leiden Ms, 1917, p. 1, واصله من العرب قال يحيى بن معين ما رايت خيرًا من احمد ما افتخر علينا قط بالعربية ولا ذكرها

of his paternal grandfather taking the place of that of his father, probably from the fact that the latter died at thirty years of age while his son was still in infancy. On the death of the father, the responsibility for Aḥmed's care and training devolved upon his mother, whose name and history we do not know [1]).

Years of Study and Teachers.

We are without any details of his early years and know merely that he continued to reside in Baghdâd until the year 179 A. H. In this year, when fifteen years of age, he began the study of the Tradition [2]). He first went to the lecture-room of Abdallah ibn al-Mubârak, who came to Baghdâd for the last time in 179 A. H. He was too late in going, however, as Ibn al-Mubârak had left the city to take part in an expedition to Tarsus [3]). Mâlik ibn ʾAnas, too, died in the very year in which Aḥmed began to study; and the latter used to say that he had been deprived of Mâlik ibn ʾAnas and Hammâd ibn Zaid, but that God had given him in their place Sofyân ibn ʿUyaina and ʾIsmâʿîl ibn ʿUlayya [4]). His first teacher was Hushaim ibn Bashîr al-

1) That Aḥmed's father did not die before his boy was born will appear from the following: Abû Nuʿaim, p. 138 *b*, وتُوفّى ابوه محمد بن حنبل ولهُ ثلثون سنة فوليَتْه أمه قال ابى كان قد ثقب أذنيّ الخ

2) Dhahabî, Lib. Class. 8, N°. 18.

3) Abû Nuʿaim, 138 *a*, وكان ابن المبارك قدِمَ فى هذه السَّنة وهى اخر قدمة قدِمَها وذهبتُ الى مجلسه فقالوا خرج الى طرسوس فتوفّى سنة احدى وثمانين

Abdallah ibn al-Mubârak d. 181 A. H., al-Nawawî Biog. Dicty ٣٦٥.

4) Al-Maḳrîzî, p. 2, وكان رضه يتأسّف على عدم اجتماعه بالامام مالك لان مالك رضه توفى السنة التى طلب الامام احمد فيها الحديث وهى سنة تسع وسبعين ومائة فكان يقول فاتنى مالك فأخلف الله

Sulamî, to whom he went in the year 179. With Hushaim he studied in this year and, then, to receive more particular instructions in difficult traditions, he continued to study with him three years longer and part of a fourth year up to the time of Hushaim's death, which occurred in the year 183 A. H. From Hushaim's dictation he wrote the كتاب الحج, containing about 1000 traditions, a part of the تفسير, the قضاء and some minor writings. He is said to have learned from this teacher in all more than three thousand traditions [1]). For the study of tradition he visited Kûfa and Baṣra, Mecca, Medîna, Yemen, Syria and Mesopotamia [2]) and among the other teachers under whom he studied were Sofyân ibn ʿUyaina († 198), ʾIbrâhîm ibn Saʿd († 183), Yaḥya ibn Saʿîd al-Kaṭṭân († 198), Wakîʿ († 196), Ibn ʿUlayya († 193), Ibn Mahdî († 198), Abd al-Razzâḳ († 211), Jarîr ibn Abd al-Ḥamîd († 188), al-Walîd ibn Muslim († 194), ʿAlî ibn Hishâm ibn al-Barîd, Muʿtamar ibn Suleimân († 187), Ghundar († 193), Bishr ibn al-Mufaḍḍal († 186), Ziyâd al-Bakâʾî, Yaḥya ibn Abû Zâʾida († 182), Abû Yûsuf the Kâḍî († 182), Ibn Numair († 234), Yazîd ibn Hârûn († 206), al-Ḥasan ibn Mûsâ al-ʾAshyab († 209), ʾIsḥâḳ ibn Râhawaih († 238), ʿAlî ibn al-Madînî († 234), and Yaḥya ibn Maʿîn († 233) [3]).

على سفيان بن عيينة وفاتنى حماد بن زيد فأخلف الله على اسمعيل بن علية

1) Abû Nuʿaim, 139 *a*, [قال ابو الفضل صالح] قال ابى وكتبت عن هشيم سنة تسع وسبعين الا انى لم اعتقد بعض سماعى ولزمناه سنة ثمانين واحدى وثنتين وثلاثة ومات فى سنة ثلاثة وثمانين كتبنا عنه كتاب الحج نحوا من الف حديث وبعض التفسير والقضاء وكتبا صغارا قال قلت تكون ثلاثة آلاف حديث قال اكثر

2) On the subject of travelling about to acquire a knowledge of traditions cf. Goldziher, Moh. Studien II, p. 176.

3) Cf. al-Nawawî Biog. Dict. ١٤٢ f.; al-Subkî, p. 133; Dhahabî, Lib. Class. 8, N°. 18. Dhahabî adds Bahr ibn ʾAsad. Abu'l-Maḥ. I, 638, makes Ḳubaisa

He studied with al-Shâfiʿî the Fiḳh and the ʾUsûl al-Fiḳh [1]). We do not know much of the history of Aḥmed until the year 218 A. H. is reached. In that year the Miḥna was begun by the Khalif al-Maʾmûn and Aḥmed comes at once into prominence. He must have been studying with Abû Yûsuf the Kâḍî before 182 A. H. when Abû Yûsuf died. His personal intercourse with al-Shâfiʿî began in 195 A. H., when the latter came to Baghdâd, and lasted till 197 A. H., when al-Shâfiʿî went to Mecca. After a break it was renewed in Mecca, and after that, probably, for a brief space of time in Baghdâd, when al-Shâfiʿî returned there for a month in 198 A. H. before finally taking his departure from ʿIrâḳ [2]). We know that Aḥmed was in Baghdâd in this year. Wakîʿ ibn al-Jarrâh he knew very intimately before his death in 197 A. H. Aḥmed had such familiarity with this man's traditions that he gave his son liberty to take any of Wakîʿ's books that he pleased, and told him that, if he would give him any tradition whatever from it, he would give him the ʾIsnâd for it, or, if he would give him the ʾIsnâd, he would give him the tradition. Wakîʿ had his tradition from Sofyân from Salama, but Aḥmed seems to have been able to add to his own teacher's knowledge in respect to the traditions of Salama [3]). With Sofyân ibn ʿUyaina he studied in Mecca

---

ibn ʿOḳba one of Aḥmed's teachers; I, 681, Khalaf ibn Hishâm al-Bazzâr; I, 715, ʾIsmâʿîl ibn ʾIbrâhîm ibn Bistam; I. 734, Ḳutaiba ibn Saʿîd ibn Jamîl. By Shahrastânî Wakîʿ and Yazîd ibn Hârûn are classed as Shyites, Haarbr. Trans. I. 218.

1) al-Maḳrîzî, p. 2, واجتمع بالامام الشافعى رضّه واخذ عنه الفقه واصوله

2) De Goeje, Z. D. M. G. XLVII, p. 115; Ibn Chall. N°. 569.

3) al-Subkî, p. 132, وقال قتيبة بن سعيد كان وكيع اذا كانت العتمة ينصرف معه احمد بن حنبل فيقف على الباب فيذاكره فاخذ ليلة بعضادتى الباب ثم قال ياابا عبد الله [احمد] اريد ان القى عليك حديث سفيان قال هات قال تحفظ عن سفيان عن سلمة بن كهيل

before 198 A. H., in which year Sofyân died. We have no means of fixing the exact date when he studied with Sofyân. It was, no doubt, on the occasion of a pilgrimage, for Aḥmed performed the Hajj five times in all [1]). It was also during the residence of al-Shâfi'î in Mecca, in all likelihood, for we have it recorded that 'Isḥâḳ ibn Râhawaih on two occasions disputed there with al-Shâfi'î during Aḥmed's residence there, and it would seem also in his presence [2]).

The following incident is characteristic of the man. While in Mecca, Aḥmed's clothes and effects were stolen during his absence from his lodgings in the hours when he was engaged in study with his teacher (Sofyân). On his return, the woman of the house told him of the theft, but his only enquiry was as to whether the writing-tablets had been preserved. On learning that they had, he asked for nothing more. Still, owing to the torn state of his clothes, he was forced

كذا قال نعم ثنا يحيى فيقول سلمة كذا وكذا فيقول ثنا عبد الرحمن فيقول وعن سلمة كذا وكذا فيقول انت حدثنا حتى تفرغ من سلمة ثم يقول احمد فتحفظ [عن] سلمة كذا وكذا فيقول وكيع لا فياخذ فى حديث شيخ شيخ قال فلم يزل قائما حتى جاءت الجارية فقالت قد طلع الكوكب او قالت الزهرة وقال عبد الله قال لى ابى خذ اى كتاب شئت من كتب وكيع فان شئت ان تسألنى عن شىء (الكلام .marg) حتى اخبرك بالاسناد وان شئت بالاسناد حتى اخبرك عن الكلام

1) al-Nawawî Biog. Dict., p. ١٤٤, l. 16.

2) al-Subkî, pp. 157, 158, مناظرة بين الشافعى واسحاق رضهما روى عن اسحاق بن راهويه قال كنا بمكة والشافعى بها واحمد بن حنبل ايضا بها الخ

مناظرة اخرى بينهما ...... فسكت الشافعى فلما سمع ذلك احمد بن حنبل الخ

to remain away for several days from the lecture-room, until the anxiety of his fellow-students led them to seek him out and put him in the way of earning a little money to procure a change of garments. Their proferred gifts or loans he would not on any account accept [1]).

Abd al-Razzâḳ Aḥmed first met in Mecca. On one of his

1) Abû Nuʿaim, 143 *a*, [قال ابو نعيم] حدثني ابى ثنا احمد قال املى على عبد الله بن احمد [بن حنبل] من حفظه قال نزلنا بمكة دارا وكان فيها شيخ يكنى بابى بكر بن سماعة وكان من اهل مكة قال نزل علينا ابو عبد الله فى هذه الدار وانا غلام قال فقالت امى الزم هذا الرجل فاخدمه فانه رجل صالح فكنتُ اخدمه وكان يخرج يطلب الحديث فسرق متاعه وقماشه فجاء فقالت له أُمى دخل عليك السُراق فسرقوا قماشك فقال ما فعلت الالواح قالت له أُمى فى الطاق قال وما سأل عن شىء غيرها (142 *a* حدثنا سليمان بن احمد ثنا عبد الله بن احمد بن حنبل ثنا على بن الجهم بن بدر قال كان لنا جار فاخرج الينا كتابا فقال اتعرفون هذا الخط قلنا نعم هذا خط احمد بن حنبل فقلنا له كيف كتب ذلك قال كنا بمكة مُقيمين عند سفيان بن عيينة ففقدنا احمد بن حنبل اياما لم نره ثم جئنا اليه نسأل عنه فقال لنا اهلُ الدار التى هو فيها هو فى ذلك البيت فجئنا اليه والباب مردود عليه واذا عليه خلقان فقلنا يابا عبد الله ما خبرُك لم نرك منذ ايام قال سُرِقَتْ ثيابى فقلت له معى دنانير فان شئت خذ قرضا وان شئت صلة فابى ان يفعل فقلت تكتب لى باجرة قال نعم فاخرجت دينارًا وابى ان ياخذه وقال اشتر لى ثوبا واقطعه نصفين فأوماً انه يأتزر بنصف ويرتدى بالنصف الآخر وقال جئنى ببقيته ففعلتُ فجئتُ بورق فكتب لى فهذا خطه

pilgrimages Yaḥya ibn Maʿîn accompanied Aḥmed [1]), and they made up their minds that, after the completion of the pilgrimage, they would go to Sanʿâ in Yemen and study Tradition with Abd al-Razzâḳ. On arriving at Mecca they met with the teacher, who had, like themselves, come to perform the Hajj. Yaḥya ibn Maʿîn introduced Aḥmed to him, and, after making known their wish to study with him, an appointment was made by Ibn Maʿîn in accordance with which they should receive his instructions in Mecca instead of going to Sanʿâ. Ibn Maʿîn told Aḥmed of this and the latter asked him why he had made such an arrangement. His reply was that it would save a month's journey each way and all the expenses of the trip. Aḥmed, however, declared that he could not allow such considerations to overcome his pious resolutions, and, in the end, they did go to Sanʿâ and received there the traditions. He suffered great hardships on the way thither, for, though offered money sufficient to enable him to travel in comparative comfort, he refused to take it and hired himself to one of the camel drivers of a caravan going to the place. At Sanʿâ, likewise, he lived in penury and suffering, though help was tendered him such as would have secured him against anything of the kind. Abd al-Razzâḳ himself said that Aḥmed remained with him almost two years, and that when he came he offered him money, saying that the country was one where trading was difficult and to gain his livelihood would be impossible. Aḥmed was inflexible, however, saying that he had a sufficiency for his needs. The traditions which he had from this teacher were those of al-Zuhrî from Sâlim ibn Abdallah from his father and the traditions of al-Zuhrî from Saʿîd ibn al-Musayyib from Abû Huraira. Aḥmed was fortunate in having studied with Abd al-Razzâḳ before the year 200 A. H., for his reputation as a sound traditionist was impaired after that date. It is in keeping with Aḥmed's character that he should, as we are informed, have put into practice every tradition which he

1) Abu'l-Feda, Annales, Reiske ed, II. 186.

learned from Abd al-Razzâk, even to one in which the Prophet is represented as giving to Abû Ṭaiba, a surgeon, a dinâr for cupping him. Following this example Aḥmed, too, asked to be cupped and gave the surgeon a dinâr [1]).

1) al-Makrîzî, p. 7, حجّ احمدُ حجّات رافق فى بعضها يحيى بن معين واتفقا على انهما بعد انقضاء الحج يمضيان الى صنعاء اليمن ياخذان الحديث عن عبد الرزاق فوجداه فى الطواف فلما فرغ اجتمعا عليه وكان احمدُ لا يعرف شخصه وانما يعرفه باسمه فقال له يحيى بن معين هذا اخوك احمد بن حنبل فقال حيّاهُ الله انه ليبلغنى عنه كلّ ما أسَرّ به ثبّته الله تعالى على ذلك ثم واعد يحيى الشيخ على قراءة فلما انصرفا عنه قال احمدُ لابن معين لمَ اخذتَ على الشيخ الموعدَ فقال له يحيى قد اراحك الله مسيرة شهر ورجوع شهر والنفقة فقال الامام احمد ما كان الله ليرانى وقد نويت نية أفسِدها بما تقول ثم سافرا الى صنعاء اليمن واخذ عنه بها وصحّ عن الامام احمد انه قال ما كتبت حديثا الا وقد عملت به حتى مرّ بى ان رسول الله صلعم احتجم واعطى ابا طيْبة الحَجّام دينارًا فاحتجمتُ واعطيت الحجام دينارا. Abû Nuʿaim, 141 b, لما خرج احمد بن حنبل الى عبد الرزاق انقطعت به النفقة فاكرى نفسَه من بعض الجمّالين الى ان وافى صَنعآء وقد كان اصحابُه عرضوا عليه المواساةَ فلم يَقبل من احد شيئا.... يقول (عبد بن حُمَيْد) سمعت عبد الرزاق يقول قدم علينا احمد بن حنبل هاهنا فاقام سنتين الا شيئا فقلت له يابا عبد الله خذ هذا لِشَىْء دفعه اليه فانتفعْ به فانّ ارضنا ليست بارض متّجر ولا مَكْسَب واراناا عبد الرزّاق كفّه مدها فيها دنانير فقال احمد انا بخير ولم يقبل منى. Abû Nuʿaim, 144 a, لما قدم احمد ابن حنبل مكّة من عند عبد الرزاق رأيت به شحوبا وقد تبيّن

With Isḥâḳ ibn Râhawaih, who is called in the Kitâb al-Fihrist (I. 230) a leading Ḥanbalite, he corresponded for a length of time, until Isḥâḳ took a letter of recommendation which Yaḥya ibn Yaḥya had written for him to Abdallah ibn Ṭâhir, and received from the latter because of it both money and high position [1]).

Aḥmed's Period of Teaching. When still a youth Aḥmed ibn Ḥanbal was held in reverence as an authority on the Tradition, and in the assemblies of the sheikhs was looked up to with great respect [2]). We do not know when his most

عليه اثر النصّب والتعب فقلت [اى احمد بن ابراهيم الدورقى] يابا عبد الله لقد شققت على نفسك فى خروجك الى عبد الرزاق فقال ما اهون الشقّة فيما استفدنا من عبد الرزاق كتبنا عنه حديث الزهرى عن سالم بن عبد الله عن ابيه وحديث الزهرى عن سعيد بن المسيّب عن ابى هريرة رضه .... قال ابى [اى ابو عبد الله] ما كتبنا عن عبد الرزاق من حفظه شيئًا الا مجلس الاول وذلك انا دخلنا بالليل فوجدناه فى موضع جالسا فاملى علينا سبعين حديثا ثم التفت الى القوم فقال لو لا هذا ما حدثتكم يعنى ابى [اى ابو عبد الله] قال ابى [ابو عبد الله] وجالس عبد الرزاق معمرا [مات سنة ١٥٣] تسع سنين فكان يكتب عنه كلّ شىء يقول قال عبد الله وكل من سمع من عبد الرزاق بعد المائتين فسماعه ضعيف وسمع منه ابى قديما

1) al-Nawawî Biog. Dict. ١٤٤ f. cf. al-Subkî, p. 156, فدخل الحاجب [الى ابن طاهر] فقال له رجل بالباب زعم ان معه رقعة يحيى بن يحيى الى الامير فقال يحيى بن يحيى قال نعم قال ادخله فدخل اسحق وناوله الرقعة فاخذها عبد الله وقبلها واقعد اسحق بجنبه وقضى دينه ثلاثين الف درهم وصيره من ندمائه

2) Abû Nuʿaim, 144 *b*, قال ابو نصر سمعت عبد بن حميد يقول كان فى مسجد اظنه ببغداد واصحاب الحديث يتذاكرون واحمد يومئذ شاب الا انه المنظور اليه من بينهم الخ

active period of teaching and literary work occurred, but he was established as the greatest traditionist of his time when al-Ma'mûn introduced the Miḥna, and continued to teach until shortly after al-Wâthiḳ came to the Khalifate when he was forced to give up teaching. He may have resumed teaching for a year or so after al-Mutawakkil came to power, but in 237 A. H. when he went to the camp he took an oath never to tell a tradition in its integrity as long as he lived, a vow which he appears to have kept[1]).

His Works. In regard to his books we know on the whole very little. He left at his death twelve loads and a half of books all of which he had memorized[2]). The names which have come down to us are the following: كتاب العلل - كتاب الزهد - كتاب الناسخ والمنسوخ - كتاب التفسير - الفرائض - كتاب الفضائل - كتاب المسائل - كتاب الاشربة - كتاب الايمان - كتاب المناسك - كتاب الردّ على الجهميّة - كتاب طاعة الرسول - كتاب المسند[3]).

The Musnad. Of one book, his great work, the Musnad, we have more definite particulars. It comprised the testimonies of more than 700 Companions of the Prophet, and was selected and compiled from 700,000 traditions (or according to another account from 750,000) and contained 30,000 (in some accounts 40,000) traditions. Aḥmed boasted that whatever was in it was a reliable basis for argument, and that what was not contained in it was not to be regarded as a sound basis. He looked upon this book as an imâm which was to settle all differences of opinion about any Sunna of the Prophet[4]). It has always had the greatest reputation in Mo-

1) Cf. Chapter II near the end; Chapter III near the beginning.

2) al-Nawawî, Biog. Dict. ١٤٣.

3) Kitâb al-Fihrist I, ٢٢٩.

4) al-Subkî, p. 133, l. 20, والف مُسنده وهو اصل من اصول هذه الامة. l. 27 قال لنا [الامام] ان هذا الكتاب قد جمعته وانتقيته من اكثر من سبعمائة وخمسين الفا فيما اختلف فيه المسلمون من حديث رسول

hammedan theological circles, and has been used as a basis of many smaller works and as a source of information by many authors. Its immense size and the very inconvenient method of its arrangement have, however, done a great deal to prevent its becoming much more used than it actually has been. In fact, it has been rarely mastered by any one individual, and perhaps as rarely transcribed by one person. Hence it is that, whereas there are a number of partial copies of the work, only one complete manuscript is known to-day [1]).

The Musnad as compiled by Aḥmed ibn Ḥanbal is no longer extant [2]), nor does it seem to have survived his own age; for Abû Abd al-Raḥmân Abdallah Aḥmed's son, who edited, with some additions of his own, the work of his

الله صلعم فارجعوا اليه فان كان فيه والا ليس بحجة.... فقال عملت هذا الكتاب امامًا اذا اختلف الناس فى سنّة عن رسول الله صلعم رجع اليه وقال ايضا خرّج ابى المسند من سبعمائة الف حديث قال ابو موسى المدينى ولم يخرج الا عمّنْ ثبت عنده صدقه وديانته دون من طَعَنَ [Cod. has these points. Read ?طُعِنَ] فى امانته ثم ذكر باسناده الى عبد الله ابن الامام احمد رحمة الله عليهما قال سالت ابى عن عبد العز[يز] ابن ابان فقال لم اخرج عنه فى المسند شيًا لـمّـا حدّث بحديث المواقيت تركته قال ابو موسى فلما عدد احاديث المسند فلم ازل اسمع من افواه الناس انها اربعون الفا الى ان قرات على ابى منصور بن زريق ببغداد قال انا ابو بكر الخطيب قال قال ابن المنادى لم يكن فى الدنيا اروى عن ابيه منه يعنى عبد الله ابن الامام احمد لانه سمع المسند وهو ثلاثون الفا والتفسير وهو مائة الف وعشرون الفا الخ

The sum 40000 for the traditions is that given in the Kitâb al-Fihrist I, ٢٢٩, l. 22.

1) Goldziher, Z. D. M. G., L, 466 f.
2) Goldziher, Z. D. M. G., L, 473.

father after his death [1]), speaks of what he heard from his father, what he read to his father from his own copy of the original page, and what he had gathered from books and papers belonging to his father, as being embodied in the edition which he had made [2]). In some cases he says that he 'thinks' he had a tradition from his father in such and such a form, in such and such a manner of communication, or under such and such a heading. These evidences seem to point to the absence of any book which could have been used to verify what he had in mind. The Musnad as now preserved to us is in the revised form given it by the editorial labours of Abdallah ibn Aḥmed. It is mentioned, further, that an edition of the Musnad with certain supplementary traditions by the editor was made by Abû ʿOmar Moḥammed ibn Abd al-Wahîd († 345). A commentary in eighty sections making together ten volumes was prepared by Abu ʾl-Ḥasan ibn Abd al-Hâdî al-Sindî († 1139); an epitome called al-Durr al-Muntacad min Musnad Aḥmed was compiled by Zain ad-Dîn ʿOmar ibn Aḥmed al-Shammâ al-Ḥalabî [3]) and, finally, an edition of the Musnad ordered alphabetically according to the names of the Companions of the Prophet from whom the traditions take their origin was made by the Jerusalem scholar Abû Bekr Moḥammed ibn Abdallah al-Maḳdisî: ترتيب مسند احمد بن حنبل على حروف المعجم [4]). A printed edition of the work, based chiefly on a manuscript in the Library of the Sâdat Wafâʾîya at Cairo was issued in 1896 [5]).

The great work according to the boast of Aḥmed himself was intended to be encyclopaedic in its aim, as far as traditions related to the Sunna of the Prophet were concerned. It apparently attempts to comprehend everything which in

1) Goldziher, Z. D. M. G., L, 472, 504.
2) Goldziher, Z. D. M. G., L, 497.
3) Ḥaj. Ḫal. V, 534 f.
4) Goldziher, Z. D. M. G., L, 470.
5) Goldziher, Z. D. M. G., L, 468.

the author's judgment could possibly contribute to a complete notion of what the Sunna was. All the reliable materials coming down from the Companions were meant to be included within the book. Hence, only the very broadest tests were applied to the traditions which were accepted by the author. The main criterion was that the Isnâd must be sound; that is, no man whose reputation for truthfulness or religious character was deemed unsatisfactory could be allowed to validate a tradition [1]). The test of conflict with clear teaching of the Prophet elsewhere found was also applied, but not with the most thorough consistency [2]); and, finally, the duplicate traditions were excluded, though here, also, Aḥmed's practice was not uniform [3]). In a work of such an aim we expect to find and in this work do find all kinds of traditions: those relating to ritual, legal precedents, moral maxims, fables, legends, historical incidents and biographical anecdotes [4]). Furthermore, we cannot find the same order which is observed in the great collections of al-Bokhârî and Muslim. Their material was much less in quantity than Aḥmed ibn Ḥanbal's and much narrower in its scope. They had a purpose much more special in view, which permitted of a real system being observed. But Aḥmed's aim was simply to store up genuine traditions and nothing more [5]).

In such a collection, too, as that found in the Musnad any one acquainted with the genesis of Mohammedan tradition can understand that there would appear all sorts of inconsistencies and contradictions. Such, in fact, are found in the book. Sayings are attributed to the Prophet which never could have been uttered by him. He is represented as having prescience of events occurring long after his time, and as lending his countenance to views whose later origin

1) Goldziher, Z. D. M. G., L, 478 & note 1); v. note 4, p. 19.
2) Goldziher, Z. D. M. G., L, 480; v. note 4, p. 19.
3) Goldziher, Z. D. M. G., L, 481.
4) Goldziher, Z. D. M. G., L, 474.
5) v. note 4, p. 19.

is clearly known; opposite opinions and parties alike find their support in distinct traditions of the Musnad [1]). It might seem that there was room to question the honesty of the author who would thus leave all kinds of discrepancies in his work; but reflection will shew that a dishonest man would hardly admit or allow to remain in his compilation such things, and that the aim of Aḥmed, comprehensive and unscientific as it was, sufficiently accounts for whatever of miscellaneous or contradictory character there appears. It is quite likely, too, that the Musnad was a collection brought together during many years, and one to which labor was not continuously devoted by the compiler. In the use of the work, also, after its completion there probably was no continuity observed. He would read a portion now and a portion again, a portion to this one and a portion to that one (only three persons are said to have heard it complete from Aḥmed himself). These facts would make it difficult for him to have in mind and eye the whole work at one time, so as to perceive the mutual harmony or discrepancy of the parts of which it was composed. He, thus, might easily admit and with difficulty correct such inconsistencies as those of which we have spoken. With his aim, as we conceive it, however, inconsistencies made very little difference. He was but collecting sound traditions, and not supporting particular opinions or movements. It was not his idea to constitute himself a harmonist. Dishonesty in connection with any of the contents of the Musnad lies properly with other and earlier authorities than Aḥmed. We have no record of his having been charged with fabricating traditions during his lifetime [2]). His great fault was the uncritical aim and method. Even in the Isnâds, where he was supposed to be an excellent critic,

---

1) Goldziher, Z. D. M. G., L, 478, 489 f.

2) During the trial before al-Muʿtaṣim it was not objected that any of his traditional arguments were unsound. When he was charged with plagiarizing a tradition (which he had not there cited), he was angry and took pains to put his adversaries to confusion. Cf. a passage in the long Arabic note in Chapter II.

he appears to have been rather liberal. There are found lists of authorities with anonymous individuals even as the first sources of the traditions cited; a few names are given credit, also, who do not stand as reputable authorities in the opinion of many theologians. In the cases of most of the latter Aḥmed, however, makes a special note to the effect that he sees no reason to refuse the traditions furnished by them. And, lastly, he favours at times the Ḳuṣṣâṣ, who, while not altogether discountenanced as authorities, were not held in great repute [1]).

Abdallah, Aḥmed's son, did his part as editor with great conscientiousness, noting carefully his own additions to the materials gathered by his father, and inserting corrections and glosses with explicit statement of his own authorship of them. The traditions which he added to the Musnad appear to have been afterwards brought together by him in a separate book which bore the title زوائد مسند الامام احمد بن حنبل لولده عبد الله الزاهد. In some cases where Abdallah had heard a tradition found in the Musnad from another teacher as well as his father, he wrote a note to that effect when putting in the tradition concerned [2]).

During his lifetime Aḥmed read the Musnad to his sons Ṣâliḥ and Abdallah and to his uncle Isḥâḳ ibn Ḥanbal, and they alone formed the favoured circle who heard the complete work from the lips of its author [3]).

As may be inferred from what has been already said,

---

1) Goldziher, Z. D. M. G., L, 471 f, 478 f; Cf. De Goeje, Gloss. Belâdhori and Gloss. Fragm. Hist. Ar. قصّ. The Ḳuṣṣâṣ having as storytellers no very serious aim were naturally enough in discredit with serious traditionists, but it may well have been that such men actually furnished some sound traditions. According to the critical method then in vogue, the soundness of such traditions would depend upon their contents to some extent, but more upon the Isnâds.

2) Goldziher, Z. D. M. G., L, 501 ff. Abdallah is said to have made additions, likewise, to his father's كتاب الزهد.

3) v. note 4, p. 19.

the great work of Aḥmed is not arranged with any reference whatever to the subjects of the traditions it includes. Such an arrangement is found rather in that kind of tradition-collections called Musannafs, a class of works which properly belongs to a later development of Arabic literature than these Musnads. The latter class, of which Aḥmed's book is representative, is ordered according to the earliest authorities or first sources of the traditions cited, and according to the localities where the author obtained his materials. In such an arrangement we would expect to find traditions bearing a particular colour and evincing a similar tendency brought together, according to the predilection or bias of the original authorities or of the localities made responsible for the traditions. This feature, which is almost inevitable in employing such a method, is a mere accident of the classification, and forms no part of the author's intention. Such a miscellaneous arrangement and the mass of the materials brought together made these Musnads of little general value as works of reference on account of their inconvenience, and led to such an undertaking as that of al-Maḳdisî to bring a more convenient order into the book of Aḥmed ibn Ḥanbal. It does not diminish the awkwardness of his work, either, that the traditions of the same primitive authority should be found, some in a section classified according to the names of the men, and others in one or more sections classified according to the places in which the materials were gathered [1]).

The order of the Musnad of Aḥmed ibn Ḥanbal, as found in the recently published Cairo edition, is as follows;

Vol. I, pp. 2—195, Traditions of ten Companions of the Prophet, including the first four Khalifs.

Vol. I, pp. 195—199, Four other Companions (principle of separate classification not given).

Vol. I, pp. 199—206, The Ahlu 'l-Bait.

---

1) Goldziher, Z. D. M. G., L, 469 ff.

Vol. I, p. 206 to the end, Vol. II and Vol. III to p. 400, The well-known Companions.
Vol. III, pp. 400—503, Traditions of Meccans.
Vol. IV, pp. 2—88, Traditions of Medînans.
Vol. IV, pp. 88—239, Traditions of Syrians.
Vol. IV, pp. 239—419, Traditions of Kûfans.
Vol. IV, p. 419—Vol. V, p. 113, Traditions of Baṣrans.
Vol. V, p. 113—Vol. VI, p. 29, The Anṣâr.
Vol. VI, pp. 29—467, The Women. (In pp. 383—403 of this section are put in some traditions (من) مسند القبائل [1]).

It should be carefully borne in mind that each one of the sections enumerated, as well as the whole work, is called a Musnad, e. g. The Musnad of the Meccans, the Musnad of the Anṣâr etc. [2]). Such is a general description of the long famous Musnad of the Imâm Aḥmed.

Aḥmed's Pupils. We have the names of some of those who heard the Tradition from him, among whom were his teachers Abd al-Razzâḳ, Ibn Mahdî and Yazîd ibn Hârûn. Other pupils were Abu'l-Walîd, ʿAlî ibn al-Madînî, al-Bokhârî, Muslim, Abû Dâûd, al-Dhuhlî, Abû Zurʿa al-Râzî, Abû Zurʿa al-Dimashkî, Ibrâhîm al-Ḥarbî, Abû Bekr Aḥmed ibn Moḥammed ibn Hânî al-Ṭâ'î al-Athram, al-Baghawî, Obaidallah ibn Moḥammed Abu 'l-Ḳâsim (his last pupil آخرهم [3]), Ibn Abî Dunya, Moḥammed ibn Isḥâḳ al-Ṣaghânî, Abû Ḥâtim al-Râzî, Aḥmed ibn Abi 'l-Hawârî, Mûsâ ibn Hârûn, Ḥanbal ibn Isḥâḳ, Othmân ibn Saʿîd al-Dârimî, Hajjâj ibn al-Shâʿir, Abd al-Malik ibn Abd al-Hamîd al-Maimûn, Baḳî ibn Makhlad al-Andalusî, Yaʿḳûb ibn Shaiba, Duḥaim al-Shâmî and his own sons Abdallah and Ṣâliḥ [4]). His method of teaching was to read the tra-

---

1) Goldziher, Z. D. M. G., L, 470.

2) Goldziher, Z. D. M. G., L, 472. On the Musnad cf., also, Goldziher, Moh. Studien II, 228, 230, 266, 270.

3) Dhahabî, Liber Class. 8, N°. 18.

4) al-Nawawî, Biog. Dict. ١٤٣. The name مخلد in al-Nawawî's list should be متخلد; v. de Jong's ed. of Dhahabî's Muschtabih 74, Ḳamûs, and Abu'l-

ditions from a book rather than recite them [1]). He is not known to have taught in any other way except in the case of about one hundred traditions [2]). He adopted this method notwithstanding the fact that he had everything committed to memory and was generally regarded as being almost the first ḥâfiẓ of his time. On one occasion when he was delivering the tradition to some of his pupils, after they had learned it by heart, and were preparing to write it, Aḥmed exclaimed, 'the book is the best ḥâfiẓ' and with that he started up and brought a book [3]). His wish probably was to verify his memoriter recitation.

Aḥmed does not appear to have taken money from his disciples, either for his services as a teacher or for the writing materials etc. which he furnished [4]).

Relations with al-Shâfiʿî. For al-Shâfiʿî he always entertained the most affectionate regard. His testimony to him was that none in his day carried an ink-bottle or touched a pen but there was resting upon him an obligation to al-Shâfiʿî [5]). For thirty years he declared he had never prayed a prayer without offering in it a petition for his friend, and on his son's asking him what kind of a man al-Shâfiʿî was that he should pray for him so regularly, he replied that al-Shâfiʿî was like the sun to the world and like good health to mankind [6]). Al-Shâfiʿî, too, seems to have had a great

---

Maḥâsin II. ٣٢٨. دحيم الشامى I have added from al-Subkî, p. 133, l. 18, cf. Dhahabî Liber Class. 8, N°. 69.

1) al-Nawawî, Biog. Dict. ١٤٣.

2) Abû Nuʿaim, 139 *a*, يقول (عبد الله بن احمد بن حنبل) ما رايتُ ابى فى حفظه حدّث من غير كتاب الا باقلّ من مائة حديث

3) al-Nawawî, Biog. Dict. ١٤٤, cf. Goldziher, Moh. Stud. II, 196, 197.

4) al-Nawawî, Biog. Dict. ١٤٥, cf. Goldziher, Moh. Stud. II, 181.

5) al-Nawawî, Biog. Dict. ٩٣.

6) al-Nawawî, Biog. Dict. ٧٩. al-Maḳrîzî, p. 2, وقال الامام احمد ما صليت صلاة منذ ثلاثين سنة الا وانا ادعو للشافعى كذا فى الحلية

respect and affection for Aḥmed. He is said to have declared, 'O Abû Abdallah, whenever a tradition from the Messenger of God is sound in your judgment, tell it to us that we may conform to it'. Aḥmed is reported as saying that al-Shâfiʿi told him that he (Aḥmed) was more learned in the sound traditions than himself, and that his (al-Shafiʿi's) desire was to know from him what he regarded as sound that he might adopt it. Aḥmed's son Abdallah declared that, wherever al-Shâfiʿi says in his book 'a trustworthy person told me that', or 'a trustworthy person related that to me', he refers to his father. Abdallah said, further, that the book which al-Shâfiʿi composed in Baghdâd was more correct than the book which he composed in Egypt, because, when he was in Baghdâd, he asked Aḥmed and the latter suggested corrections to him, but when he was in Egypt and was inclined to adopt a weak tradition there was no one to correct him [1]). Al-Shâfiʿi

---

للحافظ ابى نعيم وقال الامام الغزالى فى الاحياء اربعين سنة ولكثرة دعائه له قال له ابنه اىّ رجل كان الشافعى حتى تدعو له كل هذا الدعاء فقال يا بنى كان الشافعى كالشمس للدنيا وكالعافية للناس

1) Abû Nu'aim, 140*b*, حدثنا سليمان بن احمد قال سمعت عبد الله بن احمد بن حنبل يقول سمعت ابى يقول قال محمد بن ادريس الشافعى يابا عبد الله اذا صحّ عندكم الحديث عن رسول الله صلعم فاخبرونا به حتى نرجع اليه   حدثنا سليمان [ابن احمد] قال سمعت عبد الله بن احمد يقول سمعت ابى يقول قال لى محمد بن ادريس الشافعى انت اعلم بالاخبار الصحاح منا فاذا كان خبر صحيح فأعلمنى حتى اذهب اليه كوفيا كان او بصريا او شاميا قال عبد الله جميع ما حدث به الشافعى فى كتابه فقال حدثنى الثقة او اخبرنى الثقة فهو ابى رحمه الله، قال عبد الله وكتابه الذى صنّفه ببغداد هو اعدل من الكتاب الذى صنفه بمصر وذلك انه حيث

went to Egypt in the year 198, stayed probably two or three months and then returned to Mecca, whence he took his final journey to Egypt in the end of 199 or the beginning of 200. In ʿIrâḳ he composed the Book of the Hajj. His first visit to Baghdâd was in the year 195; he left there for Mecca in 197 and returned for a month to Baghdâd in 198 [1]). Al-Shâfiʿî said, 'I left Baghdâd and did not leave behind in it any one greater as a fakîh, or one more pious, self-denying, or learned than Aḥmed' [2]).

Other Contemporaries. Al-Haitham ibn Jamîl, one of Aḥmed's teachers in Baghdâd, thought highly of his pupil's authority. On one occasion he was told that Aḥmed ibn Ḥanbal differed from him in regard to a certain tradition and his reply was, 'My wish is that it may shorten my life and may prolong Aḥmed ibn Ḥanbal's life' [3]). It is worthy of note that Aḥmed gave apparently unreserved credit to *Yazîd ibn Hârûn.* Yazîd ibn Hârûn as a traditionist. At one time Mûsâ ibn Ḥizâm al-Tirmidhî was on his way to Abû Suleimân al-Jûzajânî to ask him some question about the books of Moḥammed ibn al-Ḥasan when Aḥmed met him and enquired whither he was going. On learning his object, Aḥmed remarked

---

كان هاهنا يسال الشيخ فيُغيِّر عليه ولم يكن بمصر مَنْ يُغيِّر عليه اذا ذهب الى خبر ضعيف قل وسمعت ابى يقول استفاد منّا الشافعى ما لم نستفد منه

1) De Goeje, Z. D. M. G. XLVII. 115; Ibn Chall. N°. 569.

2) al-Subkî, p. 132, l. 9, قل فيه الشافعى فيما رواه حرملة خرجت من بغداد وما خلفت بها افقه ولا اورع ولا ازهد ولا اعلم من احمد cf. Ibn Chall. N°. 19.

3) Abû Nuʿaim, 141 *a*, حدّث الهيثم بن جميل بحديث عن هشيم فوهم فيه فقيل له خالفوك فى هذا قل مَن خالفنى قلوا احمدُ بن حنبل قل وددتُ انّه نقص من عُمرى وزاد فى عمر احمد بن حنبل

that it was a very strange thing that Ibn Ḥizâm should be ready to accept the testimony of three persons leading up to Abû Ḥanîfa, and yet refuse that of three authorities forming a chain of tradition to the Prophet. Ibn Ḥizâm did not grasp Aḥmed's meaning and asked for an explanation. Aḥmed answering said, "You will not receive the Isnâd 'Yazîd ibn Hârûn in Wâsiṭ said, Ḥomaid told me from Anas, saying, the Messenger of God said'; and, yet, you receive the Isnâd 'Such an one said, Moḥammed ibn al-Ḥasan told us from Yaʿkûb from Abû Ḥanîfa". Mûsa adds that he was so impressed by the force of what Aḥmed said that he engaged a boat at once and went to Wâsiṭ to receive the Tradition from Yazîd ibn Hârûn [1]). When Aḥmed himself went to study with Yazîd, on the other hand, Yazîd ibn Saʿîd al-Ḳaṭṭân enquired for him, and, on learning where he had gone, exclaimed, 'What need has he of Yazîd?' This was interpreted to mean that Aḥmed was more fit to be the teacher than the scholar of Yazîd ibn Hârûn [2]).

---

1) Abû Nuʿaim, 144 *b*, (يقول موسى بن حزام الترمذى بترمذ) كنت اختلف الى ابى سليمان الجُوزَجانى [الخُوزجانى .Cod] فى كتب محمد بن الحسن فاستقبلنى احمد بن حنبل عند الجسر فقال لى الى اين فقلت الى ابى سليمان فقال لى احمد العجب منكم تركتم الى النبى صلعم ثلاثة واقبلتم على ثلاثة الى ابى حنيفة فقلت كيف يابا عبد الله قال يزيد بن هارون بواسط يقول حدثنا حميد عن انس قال قال رسول الله صلعم وهذا يقول ثنا محمد بن الحسن عن يعقوب عن ابى حنيفة قال موسى بن حزام فوقع قوله فى قلبى فاكتريت زورقا من ساعتى فانحدرت الى واسط فسمعت من يزيد بن هارون

2) Abû Nuʿaim, 140 *a*, قال (عبد الله) سمعت ابى يقول كنت مقيما على يحيى بن سعيد القطان ثم خرجت الى واسط فسال يحيى بن سعيد عنى فقالوا خرج الى واسط فقال اىُّ شىء يصنع

ʿAlî ibn al-Madînî. ʿAlî ibn al-Madînî not only shewed great respect for Aḥmed, but received it, likewise, from him. It is said that when ʿAlî came to Baghdâd he took a leading place among the traditionists, and at such times as men like Aḥmed and Yaḥya ibn Maʿîn and Khalaf and al-Muʿaiṭî were in difference of opinion on any point the voice of ʿAlî was regarded as decisive. Aḥmed out of respect never called ʿAlî by his proper name, but always by his kunya Abu ʾl-Ḥasan [1]). While Aḥmed was regarded as the best faḳîh of his time, Ibn al-Madînî was said to have superior knowledge of the different views held as to traditions [2]), and to be the most learned of the doctors of his day, as Yaḥya ibn Maʿîn was the one who wrote the most, and Abû Bekr ibn Abû Shaiba was the greatest ḥâfiẓ [3]).

Yaḥya ibn Maʿîn. Of Yaḥya ibn Maʿîn Aḥmed said, that the hearing of Tradition from Yaḥya was healing for troubled breasts. He said, also, that Yaḥya ibn Maʿîn was a man whom God created for the express purpose of exposing the lies of liars; and any tradition which Yaḥya did not know was no tradition. When he died Yaḥya left behind him one hundred and fourteen cases and four casks of books. This is in harmony with what has just been said as to his having written more traditions than any of his contemporaries [4]).

بواسِط قالوا يُقيم على يزيد بن هارون قال واى شىء يصنع عند يزيد ابن هارون قال ابو عبد الرحمن يعنى ابى هو اعلم منه

1) al-Nawawî, Biog. Dict. ٤٤٣, cf. Goldziher Moh. Stud. I. 267.

2) al-Subkî, p. 185, l. 1, وقيل لابى داود احمد اعلم ام على قال على اعلم باختلاف الحديث من احمد

3) al-Nawawî, Biog. Dict. ١٤٤.

4) " " ٦٢٨; the word جبات should probably be read حِبَابٌ, *jars*, (sg. حُبّ) vid. De Goeje, Gloss. Bibl. Geog.

Al-Ḥusain ibn ʿAlî al-Karâbîsî. One of the contemporaries of Aḥmed ibn Ḥanbal was al-Ḥusain ibn ʿAlî ibn Yazîd Abû ʿAlî al-Karâbîsî († 245 A. H.) This man was well known both as a faḳîh and as a traditionist. At first, he was a disciple of the Ra'y school, but, later, inclined to the views of al-Shâfiʿî, became a student of his teachings and received authorization [1]) to teach what he had learned. The Khatîb al-Baghdâdî tells that he was much disesteemed (lit. was very rare) as a traditionist because he had acquired a bad name with Aḥmed ibn Ḥanbal. This was owing to his strong leaning toward dialectical theology (علم الكلام) [2]), in general, and, more particularly, to his application of dialectics in order to come to his conclusions touching the Ḳorân. He was a professed believer in the uncreated existence of the Ḳorân, but could not satisfy Aḥmed ibn Ḥanbal by his profession of this doctrine, and much less by his utterances on the symbolic expression of the Ḳorân in articulate human sounds (لفظ القرآن) [3]). He appears to have trifled somewhat in his treatment of subjects that were to minds such as that of Aḥmed in the highest degree sacred and serious. For example, his declared faith in the created nature of the Lafẓ al-Ḳorân was on one occasion told to Aḥmed, who, though the profession was in full accord with his own conviction, declared it heresy, because the process by which it had been reached was that of reasoning and not that of submission to traditional authority. Aḥmed's judgment on him was made known to al-Karâbîsî, who changed his declaration of faith and professed that the Lafẓ al-Ḳorân was uncreated as well as the Ḳorân itself. Naturally enough,

---

1) اجازة cf. Goldziher, Moh. Stud. II. 189.

2) For origin and use of the term كلام vid. Houtsma, De Strijd over het Dogma, 87 f.; cf. Shahrastânî, Haarbr. transl'n II. 388 f.

3) The Lafẓ al-Ḳorân is used here with reference to the enunciation of the Ḳorân in human speaking; in the following paragraph we have taken it to have a wider scope.

this pleased Aḥmed no better and he vigorously declared that this, too, was heresy. The whole quarrel, as one can readily see, was with the method of al-Karâbîsî, far more than with his theological conclusions [1]).

---

1) al-Subkî, p. 172, الحسين بن على بن يزيد ابو على الكرابيسى كان اماما جليلا جامعا بين الفقه والحديث تفقه اولا على مذهب اهل الرأى ثم تفقه للشافعى . . . . (قال داود الاصبهانى) قال لى حسين الكرابيسى لما قدم الشافعى الى بغداد قدمته فقلت له تأذن لى ان اقرا عليك الكتب فابا. وقال خذ كتب الزعفرانى فقد اجزتها لك فاخذها اجازة قال الخطيب حديث الكرابيسى يعز جدا وذلك ان احمد بن حنبل كان يتكلم فيه بسبب مسئلة اللفظ وهو ايضا كان يتكلم فى احمد فتجنب الناس الاخذ عنه لهذا السبب قلت كان ابو على الكرابيسى من متكلمى اهل السنة استاذ فى علم الكلام كما هو استاذ فى الحديث والفقه ولهُ كتاب فى المقالات قال ابو الخطيب الامام فخر الدين فى كتاب غاية المرام على كتابه فى المقالات معول المتكلمين فى معرفة مذاهب الخوارج وسائر اهل الاهواء قلت المروى انه قيل للكرابيسى ما تقول فى القران قال كلام الله غير مخلوق فقال له السائل فما تقول فى لفظى بالقران فقال لفظك به مخلوق فمضى السائل الى احمد بن حنبل فشرح له ما جرى فقال هذه بدعة والذى عندنا ان احمد رضه اشار بقوله هذه بدعة الى الجواب عن مسئلة اللفظ اذ ليست مما يعنى المرء وخوض المرء فى ما لا يعنيه من علم الكلام بدعة فكان السكوت عن الكلام فيه اجمل واولى ولا يظن باحمد رحمه الله انه يدّعى ان اللفظ الخارج من بين الشفتين قديم ومقالة الحسين هذه قد نقل مثلها عن البخارى والحارث بن اسد المحاسبى ومحمد بن نصر المروزى وغيرهم وسيكون لنا عودة فى ترجمة البخارى الى الكلام فى ذلك ونقل ان احمد لما قال هذه بدعة رجع السائل الى الحسين

Al-Bokhârî. We have interesting evidence of the doctrinal sympathy between al-Bokhârî and Aḥmed ibn Ḥanbal. A jealous rival of al-Bokhâri in Nîsâbûr charged the latter with heresy on the point of the Lafẓ al-Ḳorân, and the imputation was taken up by many. But it is clear that al-Bokhârî's silence on the question, from reluctance to be drawn into any reasoning on a point for which there was so little evidence pro or con in Tradition, was the only ground for suspecting his orthodoxy. His belief, as well as that of Aḥmed ibn Ḥanbal, was that the Ḳorân itself was not created, but the Lafẓ al-Ḳorân, by which he understood the human acts of writing,

---

فقال له تلفظك بالقران غير مخلوق فعاد الى احمد نعرفه مقالة الحسين ثانيا فانكر احمد ايضا ذلك وقال هذه ايضا بدعة وهذا يدلك على ما نقوله من ان احمد انما اشار بقوله هذه بدعة الى الكلام فى اصل المسئلة والا فكيف ينكر اثبات الشىء ونفيه فافهم ما قلناه فهو الحق ان شاء الله تعالى وبما قال احمد نقول فنقول الصواب عدم الكلام فى المسئلة راسا ما لم يدع الى الكلام حاجة ملسّة ومما يدلك ايضا على ما نقوله وان السلف لا ينكرون ان لفظنا حادث وان سكوتهم انما هو عن الكلام فى ذلك لا عن اعتقادة ان الرواة رووا ان الحسين بلغه كلام احمد فيه فقال لاقولن مقالة حتى يقول احمد بخلافها فيكفر فقال لفظى بالقران مخلوق وهذه الحكاية قد ذكرها كثير من الحنابلة وذكرها شيخنا الذهبى فى ترجمة الامام احمد وفى ترجمة الكرابيسى فانظر الى قول الكرابيسى فيها ان مخالفها يكفر والامام احمد فيما يعتقده لم يخالفها وانما انكر ان يتكلم فى ذلك فاذا تاملت ما سطرناه ونظرنا قول شيخنا فى غير موضع من تاريخه ان مسئلة اللفظ مما يرجع الى قول جهم عرفت ان الرجل لا يدرى فى هذه المضايق ما يقول وقد اكثر هو واصحابه من ذكر جهم بن صفوان وليس قصدهم الا جعل الخ

reading, reciting and all other acts connected with the use or preservation of the revelation, was created [1]).

---

1) al-Subkī, p. 214, قال الحسن بن محمد بن جابر قال لنا الذهلى لما ورد البخارى نيسابور اذهبوا الى هذا الرجل الصالح فاسمعوا منه فذهب الناس اليه واقبلوا على السماع منه حتى ظهر الخلل فى مجلس الذهلى فحسده بعد ذلك وتكلم فيه قال ابو احمد بن عدى ذكر لى جماعة من المشايخ ان محمد بن اسمعيل لما ورد نيسابور واجتمعوا عليه حسده بعض المشايخ فقال لاصحاب الحديث ان محمد بن اسمعيل يقول اللفظ بالقران مخلوق فامتحنوه فلما حضر الناس قام اليه رجل فقال يابا عبد الله ما تقول فى اللفظ بالقران مخلوق هو ام غير مخلوق فاعرض عنه ولم يجبه فاعاد السؤال فاعرض عنه ثم اعاد فالتفت اليه البخارى وقال القران كلام الله غير مخلوق وافعال العباد مخلوقة والامتحان بدعة فشغّب الرجل وشغّب الناس وتفرقوا عنه وقعد البخارى فى منزله قال محمد بن يوسف الفربرى سمعت محمد بن اسمعيل يقول اما افعال العباد فمخلوقة حدثنا على بن عبد الله ثنا مروان بن معاوية ثنا ابو ملك عن ربعى عن حذيفة قال قال النبى صلعم ان الله يصنع كل صانع وصنعته وسمعت عبيد الله بن سعيد يقول ما زلت اسمع اصحابنا يقولون ان افعال العباد مخلوقة قال البخارى حركاتهم واصواتهم واكسابهم وكتابتهم مخلوقة فاما القران المتلو المثبت فى المصاحف المسطور المكتوب الموعى فى القلوب فهو كلام الله ليس بمخلوق قال الله تعالى بل هو ايات بينات فى صدور الذين اوتوا العلم وقال يقال فلان حسنُ القراءة ولا يقال حسن القران ولا روىّ القران وانما ينسب الى العباد القراءة لان القران كلام الرب والقراءة فعل العبد وليس لاحد ان يشرع فى امر الله بغيرِ علم كما زعم بعضهم ان القران بالفاظنا والفاظنا به شىء واحد والتلاوة هى المتلو او القراءة

Moḥammed ibn Aslam. Another of Aḥmed's companions, whose highest compliment was that he resembled the great Imâm, was Moḥammed ibn Aslam Abû Ḥusain al-Kindî al-Tûsî

هى المقروءة فقيل له ان التلاوة فعل القارئ وعمل التالى فرجع وقال ظننتهما مصدرين فقيل له هل لا امسكت كما أمسك كثير من اصحابك ولو بعثت الى من كتب عنك واستردت ما اثبت وضربت عليه فزعم ان كيف يمكن هذا وقال قلتَ ومضى فقلت له كيف جاز لك ان تقول فى الله شيئا لا يقوم به شرحا وبيانا اذا لم تميّز بين التلاوة والمتلو فسكت اذ لم يكن عنده جواب وقال ابو حامد الاعمش رايت البخارى فى جنازة سعيد بن مروان والذهلى يساله عن الاسماء والكنى والعلل ويمر فيه البخارى مثل السهم فما اتى على هذا شهر حتى قال الذهلى الا من يختلف الى مجلسه فلا يأتنا فانهم كتبوا الينا من بغداد انه تكلم فى اللفظ ونهيناه فلم ينته فلا تقربوه قلت كان البخارى على ما روى وسنحكى ما فيه ممن قال لفظى بالقران مخلوق وقال محمد بن يحيى الذُهلى من زعم ان لفظى بالقران مخلوق فهو مبتدع لا يجالس ولا يكلّم ومن زعم ان القران مخلوق فقد كفر وانما اراد محمد بن يحيى والعلم عند الله ما اراده احمد بن حنبل كما قدمناه فى ترجمة الكرابيسى من النهى عن الخوض فى هذا ولم يرد مخالفة البخارى وان خالفه وزعم ان لفظه الخارج من بين شفتيه المحدثتين قديم فقد باء بغضب واثم عظيم والظن به خلاف ذلك وانما اراد هو واحمد وغيرهما من الائمّة النهى عن الخوض فى مسائل الكلام وكلام البخارى عندنا محمول على ذكر ذلك عند الاحتياج اليه فالكلام فى الكلام عند الاحتياج واجب والسكوت عند [عند dittography] عدم الاحتياج سنّة فافهم ذلك ودع خرافات المورخين واضرب صفحا عن تمويهات الضالّين الذين يظنون انهم محدثون وانهم عند السنة واقفون

(† 242 A. H.). This man was an earnest opponent of the Jahmî and Murjî [1]) sects, of the former because they professed that

وهم عنها مبعدون وكيف يظن بالبخارى انه يذهب الى شىء من
اقوال المعتزلة وقد صحّ عنه فيما رواه الفربرى وغيره انه قال انى
لاستجهل من لا يكفّر الجهمية ولا يرتاب المصنف فى ان محمد بن يحيى
لحقته آفة الحسد التى لم يسلم منها الا اهل العصْم وقد سال بعضهم
البخارى عما بينه وبين محمد بن يحيى فقال البخارى كم يعترى
محمد بن يحيى الحسد فى العلْم والعلم رزق الله يعطيه من يشاء
ولقد ظرف البخارى وابان عن عظيم حكاية حيث قال وقد قال له
ابو عمرو الخفاف ان الناس قد خاضوا فى قولك لفظى بالقران مخلوق
يابا عمرو احفظ ما اقول لك من زعم من اهلِ نيسابور وقومس [والرقى
dittography] والرى وهمذان وبغداد والكوفة والبصرة ومكة والمدينة انى
قلت لفظى بالقران مخلوق فهو كذاب فانى لم اقله الا انى قلت افعال
العباد مخلوقة قلت تامل كلامه ما اذكاه ومعناه والعلم عندَ الله انى
لم اقل لفظى بالقران مخلوق لان الكلام فى هذا خوض فى مسائل
الكلام وصفات الله لا ينبغى الخوض فيها الا لضرورة ولكنى قلت افعال
العباد مخلوقة وهو قاعدة مُغنية عن تخصيصِ هذه المسألة بالذكر
فان كل عاقل يّعلم ان لفظنا من جملة افعالنا وافعالنا مخلوقة فالفاظنا
مخلوقة ولقد افصح بهذا المعنى فى رواية اخرى صحيحة عنه رواه حاتم
ابن احمد الكندى فقال سمعتُ مسلم بن الحجاج فذكر الحكاية وفيها
ان رجلا قام الى البخارى فساله عن اللفظ بالقران فقال افعالنا مخلوقة
والفاظنا من افعالنا وفى الحكاية انه وَقع بين القوم انذاك اختلاف على
البخارى فقال بعضهم قال [قال dittography] لفظى بالقران مخلوق وقال
اخرون لم يقل قلت فلم يكن الانكار الخ

1) For the doctrines of Jahm ibn Ṣafwân, the founder of the Jahmîa sect, v.

the Ḳorân was created, of the latter because they held that faith was mere profession without the inward trust and experience of the heart. The argument which he adopted toward the Jahmîa was that of the Ḳorân verses in which God speaks in his own person to Moḥammed announcing his Mission, and to Moses declaring himself to be his Lord and the Lord of the worlds. In the former case it is implied that if the *word* of the speaker be not that of God, Moḥammed's Mission is called in question. If it be the word of God, then it is eternally potential in him and inseparable from any true conception of him, and, therefore, it must be uncreated. In the case of Moses, if the speaker to him be a creature, then Moses himself and the worlds also, have a second lord, — for one Lord is admitted without question, — and the professors of such a doctrine are at once convicted of Shirk (شرك); but, supposing God to have really spoken, then we have again the proceeding forth of a word which we must not regard as created with its utterance, but rather as an inseparable adjunct of the Divine Knowledge, for how otherwise could the Divine Knowledge become efficient or communicative? The sin of the Jahmîa is their Shirk; this is the result of the reasoning, and without reasoning, from the standpoint of the orthodox apologist, they are guilty, as well, of forging a lie against God (افتراء) by declaring that God did not speak to Moses though the Ḳorân says he did.

Against the Karramîya Murji'a Ibn Aslam maintained the

Shahrastânî Haarbrücker's transl'n I, 89; Houtsma, De Strijd over het Dogma &c. pp. 102, 123 f. On the Murji'a v. Houtsma, De Strijd &c. pp. 34 ff., 40; Shahrastânî, Haarbrücker's transl'n I, 156 ff. The Murjite belief as presented in Houtsma, p. 36, differs from that set forth by Moḥammed ibn Aslam, but agrees with the second class of the Karramite sects (Houtsma, p. 39) and with the Ṣifatîya Karramîya (Shahrastâni, Haarbr. transl'n I, 119 ff., especially p. 127). Aḥmed ibn Ḥanbal, it will be remembered, composed two works bearing the titles, respectively, كتاب الرّد على الجهمية and كتاب الايمان, vid. p. 19.

doctrine that faith is a gift of God to the heart, a gift of illumination and of spiritual adornment, by means of which it is disposed to believe in God, his angels, his books, his messengers, the resurrection, the day of judgment, the final account, in foreordination to good and evil, in paradise and in hell-fire. This faith is given only to those upon whom God is pleased to bestow it, and is not complete without both the testimony of the lips as, at once, its expression and its confirmation, and the acts of the bodily members as the evidence that the confession of the lips and the antecedent faith of the heart are genuine. The testimony of the lips has for its subjects the things believed on by the heart. These it declares to be true; and, more specifically, it gives the formal confession that there is no God but Allah and that Moḥammed is his Prophet and his Messenger. The acts of the members lie in the performance of such things as God prescribes and in the abstention from such things as he forbids. These points are supported by arguments from the Ḳorân and Tradition; but by this man, as by others of the strict orthodox party, there is stress laid, as well, on arguments outside of either of these sources. For example, it is said by Moḥammed ibn Aslam that, should the Murjite view be proved correct, then the Prophet and the first Khalifs, who had not spent their whole lives in the confession of Islâm, but who had had true faith, notwithstanding, might be held inferior to any mere babbler of the sacred formulas who had been occupied long enough with his task. Those (also called Murji'a [1]) who held that works were the measure and substance of faith are opposed, too, and the argument of disparagement to the early worthies is applied here, likewise.

Moḥammed ibn Aslam was a believer in the eternal existence of the Divine attributes, but we have no record

---

1) Called especially الكرّامية v. De Goeje, Gloss. Bibl. Geog.

of his method of proving his position in this respect, nor have we any exposition of what it involved [1]).

1) Abû Nuʿaim, 162*a* ff, قال الشيخ واما كلامه فى النقض على المخالفين من الجهمية والمُرجئة فشائعٌ ذائعٌ وقد كان رحمه الله من المثبتة لصفات الله انها ازلية غير محدثة فى كتابه المترجم بالرد على الجهمية ذكرت منه فصلا وجيزا من فصوله . . . .
محمد بن اسلم رحمه الله يقول زعمت الجَهْمية انّ القرآن خلق وقد اشْركوا فى ذلك وهم لا يعلمون لان الله قد بين ان له كلاما فقال انى اصطفيتك على الناس برسالاتى وكلامى وقال فى اية اخرى وكلّم الله موسى تكليما فاخْبَر ان له كلاما وانّه كلم موسى عليه السلام فقال فى تكليمه ايّاه يا موسى انى انا ربك فمن زعم ان قولَه يا موسى انى انا ربك خلق وانه ليس بكلامه فقد اشرك بالله لانه زعم ان خلقا قال لموسى انى انا ربك فقد جعل هذا الزاعم ربا لموسى دون الله وقول الله تعالى ايضا لموسى فى تكليمه فاستمع لما يوحى انى انا الله لا اله الا انا فاعبدنى فقد جعل هذا الزاعم الهًا لموسى غير الله وقال فى اية اخرى لموسى فى تكليمه اياه يا موسى انى انا الله رب العالمين فمن لم يشهد انّ هذا كلام الله وقولُه تكلم به واللّهَ قاله وزعم انه خَلق فقد عَظُم شِركُه وافتراؤه على الله لانه زعم انّ خلقا قال لموسى يا موسى انى انا الله رب العالمين فقد جعل هذا الزاعم للعالمين ربا غير الله فاىّ شرك اعظم من هذا فتبقى الجَهْمية فى هذه القصة بين كُفْرين اثنين إنْ زعموا ان الله لم يكلم موسى فقد ردُّوا كتاب الله وكفروا وان زعموا ان هذا الكلام يا موسى انى انا الله رب العالمين من خلق فقد اشركوا بالله ففى هولآء الايات بيان انّ القرآنَ كلام الله وفيها بيان شرك مَن زعم ان كلامَ الله خَلق او قول الله خلق

Mystics and Ascetics. Al-Ḥârith al-Muḥâsibî. Aḥmed ibn Ḥanbal had a predilection in favor of mystics and ascetics, but toward one of these, al-Ḥârith ibn Asad al-Muḥâsibî, he conceived a strong antipathy because this man was said to use reasoning in theological matters. The reconciliation between

او ما اوحى الله الى انبيائه خلق واما نقضه رحمه الله على المرجئة
الكرامية التى زعمت ان الايمان هو القول باللسان من دون عقد القلب
الذى هو التصديق فقد صنّف فى الايمان وفى الاعمال الدالّة على
تصديق القلب و اماراته كتابا جامعا كبيرا . . . .
. . . . فقال رسول الله صلعم
الايمانُ ان تُؤمن بالله وملائكته وكتبه ورسله واليوم الاخر وبالقدر
كله خيره وشرّه الحديث وهذا اوّل حديث ذكره واستفتح به كتابه
وبنى عليه كلامه قال محمد بن اسلم فبدْءُ الايمان من قبل الله
قُرْبانا ورحمة ومنّا يمنّ به على من يشاء من عباده فيقذف فى قلبه
الايمانَ و يُحبّبه اليه فاذا نوّر قلبه وزيّن فيه الايمان وحببه اليه
آمن قلبُه بالله وملائكته وكتبه ورسله واليوم الاخر وبالقدر كله
خيره وشرّه [وهذا الحديث اول حديث ذكره واستفتح به كتابه وبنى
عليه كلامه قال محمدُ بن اسلم فبدأ الايمان من قبل الله قربانا ورحمة
ومنّا يمنّ به على من يشاء من عباده فيقذف فى قلبه نورا a repetition
يُنوّر به قلبه ويَشرح به صدره ويوثر فى قلبه الايمان [of preceding matter
ويحببه (ويصحبه Codex) اليه آمن قلبه بالله وملائكته وكتبه ورسله
واليوم الاخر وبالقدر كله خيره وشرّه وآمن بالبعث والحساب والجنة والنار
حتى كانه ينظر الى ذلك و ذلك من النُور الذى قذفه الله فى قلبه فاذا
آمن قلبه نطق لسانه مصدقا لما آمن به القلب واقرّ بذلك وشهد ان

them does not seem to have ever been openly effected; but there is a story to the effect that Aḥmed took the opportunity of secretly hearing al-Ḥârith, when the latter with

---

لا اله الا الله وانّ محمدًا رسول الله صلعم وانّ هذه الاشياء التى آمن بها القلب حقّ فاذا آمن القلب وشهد اللسان عَملت الجوارح فاطاعت امرَ الله وعَملَت بعَمَل الايمان وادّت حق الله عليها فى فرائضه وانتهت عن محارم الله ايمانا وتصديقا بما فى القلب ونطق به اللسان فاذا فعل ذلك كان مُومنا وقد بيّن الله تعالى ذلك فى كتابه انّ بدْء الايمان من قلبه فقال ولكنّ الله حبّبَ اليكم الايمان وزيّنه فى قلوبكم وقال افمن شرح الله صدره للاسلام فهو على نور من ربه وقال الذين اوتوا العلم والايمان وقال كتب فى قلوبهم الايمان وقال رسول الله صلعم للحارث بن مالك عبدٌ نوّر الله الايمان فى قلبه وقال نور يقذف فى القلب فينشرح وينفتح ثم بيّن الرسول انه تبين على المومن ايمانه بالعمل حين قيل له هل له علامة يُعرَف بها قال نعم الانابة الى دار الخلود والتجافى عن دار الغرور والاستعدادُ للموت قبل نزوله الا ترَوْن انه قد بَيّن أن ايمانه يعرف بالعمل لا بالقول وقد بين ان الايمان الذى فى القلب يَنفَعه اذا عَمِل بعمل الايمان فاذا عَمِل بعَملِ الايمان تبيّن علامةُ ايمانه انهُ مومن فهذا كلامه الذى عليه البناء والكتاب وانّه جعل الاعمال علامة الايمان قال الايمان هو تصديق القلب وانّ اللسان شاهدٌ يشهد ومُعبّرٌ يعبّر عما فى القلب لا انّ الشاهد المعبر نفس الايمان من دون تصديق القلب على ما زعمت الكرّامية وضمن هذا الكتاب من الاثار المسندة وقول الصحابة والتابعين احاديث كثيرة قال محمد بن اسلم قال المرجىّ الايمان واحد ويتفاضل الناس بالاعمال يُقال للمرجىّ قولك يتفاضل الناس بالاعمال

his companions had been invited to a feast, and that he was then convinced that his earlier impressions of the man, however just when formed, did al-Ḥârith some injustice at

---

خطأً لانّه زعم انّ من كان اكثر عملا فهو افضل من الذى كان اقل عملا فعلى زعمه انّ من كان بعد رسول الله كان افضلَ من رسول الله صلعم لانهم عَملوا بعدَه اعمالا كثيرة مِنَ الحجّ والعمرة والغزو وَالصلاة وَالصيام والصدقة والاعمال الجسمية ورسول الله صلعم افضل منهم ثم من كان بعد ابى بكر قد عملوا اعمالا كثيرة لم يبلغها ابو بكر وابو بكر افضل منهم ثم من كان بعد عمر قد عملوا الاعمال الكثيرة التى لم يعملها عمر ولم يبلغها وعمر افضل منهم ثم من بعد اصحاب رسول الله صلعم من التابعين قد عملوا اعمالا كثيرة اكثر مما عملته الصحابة والصحابة افضل منهم واى خطأً اعظم من خطأ هذا المرجئ الذى زعم ان الناس يتفاضلون بالاعمال انّما الفضل بيد الله يوتيه من يشاء يُفضل من يشاء من عباده على من يشآء عدلا منه ورحمة فكلّ مَن فضّله الله فهو اعظم ايمانا من الذى دونه لانّ الايمان قسم من الله قسمه بين عباده كيف شاء كما قسم الارزاق فاعطَى منها كل عبد ما شاء الا ترى الى قول عبد الله بن مسعود اذا احبّ اللهُ عبدا اعطاه الايمان فالايمانُ عَطيةٌ من الله يُعطيه من يشآء ويفضل من يشآء على من يشآء وهو قولُه ولكن الله حبب اليكم الايمان وزينه فى قلوبكم وقال اَفمن شرح الله صدره للاسلام فهو على نور من ربه افلا تَرون ان هذا التزيين وهذا النور من عَطيّة الله ورزقه يعطى من يشاء كما يشاء الا ترون ان الناس يَمُرون يوم القيامة على الصراط على قَدر نورهم فواحِد نُورُه مثل الجبل واخر نوره مثل بيت فكم بين الجبل والبيت من الزيادة والنقصان فاذا كان نور من خارج

that time. The change in Aḥmed's opinion does not seem to have been complete or to have saved al-Muḥâsibî from loss of credit in Baghdâd, for, at his death in 243 A. H., only four people attended his funeral. It is possible that this may, however, be explained as the consequence of some pious wish which he had expressed [1]).

مثل الجبل واخر مثل البيت فكذلك نورهما من داخل القلب على قدر ذلك فالمرجئةُ والجهمية قياسُهما قياس واحد فانّ التجهميّة زعمت انّ الايمان المعرفةُ فحَسب بلا اقرار ولا عمل والمُرجئة زعمت انه قول بلا تصديق قلب ولا عَمل وكلاهما من شيعة ابليس وعلى زعمهم ابليس مُوْمن لانه عرف ربه ووَحّده حينَ قال فبعزتك لاغوينّهم اجمعين وحين قال انى اخاف الله رب العالمين وحين قال رب بما اغويتنى فاىّ قوم ابْيَنُ ضلالة واظهَر جهلا واعظم بدعة من قوم يزعمون انّ ابليس مؤمن فضلُّوا من جهة قياسهم يقيسون على الله دينه ولا يقاس دينه فما عبَدت الاوثان والاصنام الا بالقياس فاحذروا يا امة محمد القياس على الله فى دينه واتبعوا ولا تبتدعوا فانّ دين الله استبان اقتداء واتباع لا قياس وابتداع

1) v. Shahrastânî Haarbrücker's transl'n I, 97, II, 389. A different view is given of Aḥmed's quarrel with this man in von Kremer, Herrsch. Ideen des Islâms, 68, note 1. For his biography v. Ibn Chall. N°. 151. Al-Subkî, p. 230, l. 9. فاعلم ان الامام احمد رضى الله عنه كان يشدد النكير على مَن يتكلم فى علم الكلام خوفا ان يجرّ ذلك الى ما لا ينبغى ولا شكّ ان السكوت عنه ما لم تدع اليه الحاجة اولى والكلام فيه عند فقد الحاجة بدعة وكان الحارث قد تكلم فى شىء من مسائل الكلام قال ابو القاسم النصراباذى بلغنى ان احمد بن حنبل هجره بهذا السبب قلت والظن بالحارث انه ربما تكلم حيث دعت الحاجة ولكل مقصد والله اعلم يرحمهما الله وذكر الحاكم ابو عبد الله ان ابا بكر احمد بن

With Bishr al-Hâfî († 226) and with al-Sarî al-Saḳ Aḥmed stood on terms of intimate friendship. He counted it his high privilege, indeed, to have seen some of the most holy men of his time in possession of little else than their piety and poverty. Those whose names are recorded beside the

اسحاق اخبره قال سمعت اسماعيل بن اسحاق السرّاج يقول قال لى احمد بن حنبل يبلغنى ان الحارث هذا يكثر الكون عندك فلو احضرته منزلك واجلستنى من حيث ان لا يرانى فاسمع كلامه فقصدت الحارث وسالته ان يحضرنا تلك الليلة وان يحضر اصحابه فقال فيهم كثرة فلا تزدهم على الكسب والتمر فاتيت ابا عبد الله فاعلمته فحضر الى غرفة وٱجتهد فى وِرده وحضر الحارث واصحابه فاكلوا ثم صلّوا القيٰمة ولم يصلّوا بَعدها وقعدوا بين يدى الحارث لا ينطقون الى قريب نصف الليل ثم ابتدا رجل منهم فسال عن مسالة فاخذ الحارث فى الكلام واصحابُهُ يستمعُون كأنّ على رؤوسهم الطير فمنهم مَن يبكى ومنهم من يحنّ ومنهم من يزعق وهو فى كلامه فصعد[ت] فى الغرفة لِأتعرّف حال ابى عبد الله فوجدته قد بكى حتى غشى عليه فانصرفت اليهم ولم يزل تلك حالهم حتى اصبحوا وذهبوا فصعدت الى ابى عبد الله فقال ما اعلم انى رايت مثل هؤلاء القوم ولا سمعت فى علم الحقائق مِثل كلام هذا الرجل ومع هذا فلا ارى لك صحبتهم ثم قام وخرج وفى رواية ان احمد قال لا انكر من هذا شيئا قلت تامل هذه الحكاية بعين البصيرة واعلم ان احمد بن حنبل انما لم يرِ لهذا الرجل صحبتهم لقصوره عن مقامهم فانهم فى مقام ضيق لا يسلكه كل احد فيخاف على سالكه والا فاحمد قد بكى وشكر الحارث هذا الشكر ولكل رأى واجبها وحشرنا اللهُ معهم اجمعين فى زمرة سيد المرسَلين صلعم

... mentioned are Abdallah ibn Idrîs († 192) Abû Dâûd al-Ḥafarî and Ayûb al-Najjâr [1]).

Dâûd ibn ʿAlî. Dâûd ibn ʿAlî, the founder of the Zahirite school, († 270) was one of Aḥmed's pupils. There was made to Aḥmed a very unlikely report against him to the effect that he had been teaching in Khorasân that the Ḳorân was created (by fashioning that which already existed محدث), and that his Lafẓ al-Ḳorân was created (by being made from nothing مخلوق). This influenced Aḥmed so that he refused to receive him, and we have no knowledge that he afterwards changed his decision; but the Zahirites are known to have been even more strict than Aḥmed on the uncreated nature of the Ḳorân, and it may be assumed that Dâûd did not long continue to be suspected by him. It is to be remarked that the informant of Aḥmed was Moḥammed ibn Yaḥya al-Dhuhlî, the same man who in jealousy accused al-Bokhârî of heretical views on the Lafẓ al-Ḳorân. Further, it should be noted that the incident is said to have occurred during the lifetime of Isḥâḳ ibn Râhawaih († 238 A. H.) when Dâûd must have been a comparatively young man. If the account be true his views must have undergone

1) al-Maḳrîzî, p. 1, ولقى خلقا كثيرا من الصالحين الزهاد وقال الامام ابو بكر المروزى سمعت احمد بن حنبل يقول ما أُعدل بالفقر شيئا رايت قوما صالحين لقد رايت عبد الله بن ادريس وعليه جبة من لبود وقد اتى عليه السنون والدهور ورايت ابا داود الحفرى وعليه جبة مخرقة قد خرج القطن منها يصلى بين المغرب والعشآء وهو يترجح من الجوع ورايت ايوب بن النجار بمكة قد خرج مما كان فيه ومعه رشاء [Cod. رشا] يستقى به بمكة وقد خرج من كل ما كان يملكه وكان من العابدين وكان فى دنيا فتركها فى يدى يحيى القطان فى أنلس أُخر ذكرهم

change during the remaining years of his life. He was born in 202 A. H. and died in 270 A. H. [1]).

Ibrâhîm ibn Ismâ'îl al-Mu'talizî. In the year 218 A. H. there died in Egypt Ibrâhîm ibn Ismâ'îl Abû Isḥâḳ al-Baṣrî al-Asadî al-Mu'talizî, known as Ibn 'Ulayya. He was a professor of the doctrine that the Ḳorân was created and had discussions about Fiḳh with al-Shâfi'î in Egypt, and with Aḥmed ibn Ḥanbal in Baghdâd about the Ḳorân. Aḥmed regarded him as a dangerous heretic [2]). The Ibn 'Ulayya al-Akbar whose name figures in the history of the Miḥna under al-Ma'mûn, appears to have been a different person, who was of orthodox reputation hitherto. Taken together with the similarity of the names, the seeming readiness with which Ibn 'Ulayya al-Akbar complied with the test as to the Ḳorân's creation might suggest, however, that he was in some way related to the party here mentioned. But this is only hypothetical.

II.

MIḤNA. *Historical Development.* In the beginning of the second century of Islâm al-Ja'd ibn Dirham, teacher of the Khalif Marwân II, held the doctrine that the Ḳorân was created, and, at that time, imaginative adversaries of the belief declared themselves to be able to trace the steps of Tradition by which the heresy was to be carried back from Ja'd to Lebîd, a Jew, whom the Prophet had declared to have bewitched him and thereby produced in him a sickness [3]). However the doctrine came to him, Ja'd was put to death by Khâlid ibn Abdallah, Governor of 'Irâḳ, at the command of the Khalif Hishâm. After this we hear no more of the doctrine until the time of the Abbaside Hârûn al-Rashîd [4]). The account of the

1) Goldziher, Zahiriten, p. 134. The incident is also found in al-Subkî, p. 232.
2) Abu'l-Maḥâsin I, 647.
3) Weil, Moḥammed, 94, note 121.
4) Houtsma, De Strijd over het Dogma, 101 f.

historical development (of the doctrine of the creation of the Ḳorân)[1]) which led up to the inquisition under al-Maʾmûn and his successors is given by Abuʾl-Faraj ibn al-Jauzî, († 598 A. H.) as follows: Men did not cease to follow the good rule of the fathers of Islâm and their confession that the Ḳorân was the uncreated Word of God, until the Muᶜtazilites (freethinkers)[2]) appeared, professing the creation of the Ḳorân. This they did secretly until the time of al-Rashîd. Then, they ventured to teach their view more openly, until al-Rashîd said one day, 'I have heard that Bishr al-Marîsî[3]) says that the Ḳorân is created; now, verily, if God give him into my hand, I will kill him in such a way as I have never yet killed anyone'. On learning this Bishr remained hidden for about twenty years during the days of al-Rashîd. (This would carry back his public profession of the doctrine in question to about 173 A. H.) When al-Rashîd died, the matter remained in the same position during the time of his son al-Amîn; but when al-Maʾmûn succeeded, some of the Muᶜtazilites led him astray and made the doctrine of the creation of the Ḳorân to appear plausible to him[4]).

1) On this subject cf. Weil, Chalifen II, 262, note 1; von Kremer, Herrsch. Ideen des Islâms, 233 ff. and chronological note 20, p. 127, in the same work.

2) On the name Mu'tazila and the rise of the sect, vid. Steiner, Die Muᶜtaziliten, 25 f.; Houtsma, De Strijd over het Dogma, 51. On the history of the sect, Steiner, 48 ff.; Dozy, Het Islamisme, 183, 184. On their doctrines, Maçoudi VI, 20 ff.; Steiner, 3 ff.; Houtsma, 55, 80, 89, 121 f.; Haarbrücker's transl'n of Shahrastânî I, 40. On their doctrine of the Ḳorân, Steiner, 75 ff.; Houtsma, 104 f.

3) Von Hammer, Lit. Geschichte III, 205; Abuʾl-Maḥ. I, 647 and note 9; Ibn Chall. N°. 114; Steiner, Die Muᶜtaziliten, 78. He is called by Houtsma, De Strijd over het Dogma, 79 (cf. note 1), one of the leading Murjites of his time. By Shahrastânî, Haarbr. I, 94, he is called, as the result of false pointing of the letters, Bishr ibn Attâb, instead of Bishr ibn Ghiyâth al-Marîsî. For his views vid. Shahrastânî, Haarbr. I, 161, 162, cf. I, 243.

4) al-Maḳrîzî, p. 3, فصل فى محنة الامام رضى الله عنه وما وقع فيها
على سبيل الاختصار قال الحافظ ابو الفرج بن الجوزى لم يزل الناس
على قانون السلف وقولهم انّ القران كلام الله غير مخلوق حتى نبغت

A Prediction by al-Shâfiʿî. It is reported that the Imâm al-Shâfiʿî, before his death in 204, had a dream, in which he was forewarned by the Prophet of the trial, in years to come, of Aḥmed ibn Ḥanbal for the sake of the Ḳorân. He is alleged to have sent word to Aḥmed informing him of the communication he had received, and report says that Aḥmed, on reading the letter, exclaimed, 'I hope that God will verify that which al-Shâfiʿî says' [1]). We may, probably, infer from

المعتزلة فقالوا بخلق القران وكانوا ويتستّرون بذلك الى زمن الرشيد حتى ان الرشيد قال يوما بلغنى ان بِشْر المَريسى يقول القران مخلوق والله علىّ ان اظفرنى الله به لاقْتلنه قِتلة ما قتلتها احدا فكان بِشر مُتواريا ايام الرشيد نحوًا من عشرين سنة فلما توفى الرشيد كان الامر كذلك فى زمنِ ولده الامين فلما وَلِىَ المامون خالَطه قوم من المعتزلة فحسّنوا له القول بخلق القران

1) al-Makrîzî, p. 3, فصل فى بشارة النبى صلعم له بالمحنة قبل وقوعها بسنين على لسان الامام محمد بن ادريس الشافعى رضى الله عنه كان الامام الشافعى رضى الله عنه لما دخل مصر راى النبىّ صلعم فى المنام واخبرَه ان الامام احمد سيُمتحن قال الربيع بن سليمان فكتَب الشافعى على يَدى كتابا الى ابى عبد الله احمد بن حنبل ثم قال لى يابا سليمن انْحَدِر بكتابى هذا الى العراق ولا تقراه فاخذتُ الكتاب وخرجت من مصر حتى قدمتُ العراق فوافيتُ مسجدَ احمد ابن حنبل فصادفته يصلى الفجرَ فصلّيت معه وكنتُ لم اركع السُّنة فقمت أركَع عقيب الصلاة فجعل ينظر الىَّ مَليًا حتى عرفنى فلما سلمت من صلاتى سلمت عليه واوصلت الكتاب اليه وقلت له هذا كتاب اخيك الشافعى من مصر فجعل يسالنى عن الشافعى طويلا قبل ان ينظر فى الكتاب ثم قال لى نظرتَ فيه قلت لا ففكّ ختمه

this incident that the doctrine of the creation of the Ḳorân had already begun to make some stir when al-Shâfiʿî was in Baghdâd, and that Aḥmed was at this early stage a vigorous opponent of the tenet.

Al-Maʾmûn. The interest of al-Maʾmûn in theology is emphasized by all the historians [1]). He had been thoroughly trained in the knowledge of Tradition, of the Ḳorân sciences, and of the Ḳorân itself from early childhood, and had had among his teachers Mâlik ibn Anas, Hushaim ibn Bashîr and his own father [2]). His ability as a pupil soon brought him

---

وقراه حتى اذا بلغ مَوضعا منه بكى وقال ارجو الله تعالى ان يحقق ما قاله الشافعى قلت يابا عبد الله اى شىء قد كتبَ اليك قال ذكرَ فى كتابه انه راى النبى صلعم فى نومه وهو يقول له يابنَ ادريس بَشِّر هذا الفتى ابا عبد الله احمد بن حنبل انه سيُمتحن فى دين الله ويُدْعى ان يقول القران مخلوق فلا يَفعل فانه سيُضرب بالسياط وان الله عز وجل ينشر له بذلك عَلَمًا لا يُطوى الى يوم القيامة فقلت بشارة فاى شىء جائزتى عليها وكان عليه ثوبان فنزع احدهما فدفعَه الىّ وكان مما يلى جلده واعطانى جواب الكتاب فخرجت حتى قدمت على الشافعى فاخبرته بما جرى قال فاين الثوب قلت هُوذا فقال ليس نفجعُك به ويُروى ان الشافعى رضى الله عنه قال للربيع لا نبتاعه منك ولا نستهديه ولكن اغسله وجئنا بمائه قال فغسلته وحملت ماءه اليه فجعله فى قِنّينة وكنت اراه فى كل يوم ياخذ منه فيمسح على وجهه تبركا باحمد بن حنبل

1) Cf. Abu'l-Maḥâsin I, 644; Hammer-Purgstall, Lit. Gesch. III, 26; al-Suyûtî, Taríkh al-Kholafâ, Calcutta, 1857, p. 310; Dozy, Het Islamisme, 1880, p. 152. The notices of al-Maʾmûn's character found in al-Subkî, p. 144, and al-Maḳrîzî, p. 3, are in accordance with the accounts found in the works just mentioned.

2) Houtsma, De Strijd over het Dogma, 13, says that al-Maʾmûn first

to a foremost place as a theologian, but a mind li.h ibl is, eager for much wider ranging than was afforded within the narrow bounds of the orthodoxy of Islâm, soon shewed its sympathy with the revived philosophy which had begun to be popular under the dominion of the Khalifs, and with the different branches of Arabic letters and sciences. Following his bent of mind [1]), he gathered to his court from different parts of his empire, philosophers and men of more liberal tendency of thought than had been found among the companions of his predecessors [2]). Al-Ma'mûn, however, is not looked upon as a man naturally impious nor was his interest in sacred subjects one merely controversial in its character. It is related of him that he used to complete 33 recitations of the Ḳorân in the month of Ramaḍân [3]). He also gave special gifts of money to relieve the needs of the teachers of Tradition, and all accepted of his beneficence except Aḥmed ibn Ḥanbal [4]). The letters written by al-Ma'mûn in connection with the Miḥna, however, do not give us a favorable impression of his character. The orthodox historians say that his companions at Court were wholly responsible for al-Ma'mûn's

---

attended the lectures of the Mutakallims and later took an interest in orthodoxy. He does not cite his authority for the remark, and it does not harmonise with what I have been able to gather from the authorities I have consulted. They invert the order, and I have followed them in my narrative.

1) Steiner (Die Mu'taziliten, p. 16) expresses the opinion that the tendency toward liberal theological views, which was so strongly advanced by the influence of the Greek Philosophy, had already set in before the Arabs became acquainted with Greek philosophical thought.

2) For the patronage of letters and philosophy by the Abbaside sovereigns with its direct effect in the rise of the men of the Kalâm, and its indirect or reactionary effect in increasing the zeal in study of the men of the Tradition, vid. Houtsma, De Strijd over het Dogma, 86 f.

3) Goldziher, Moh. Studien II, 58, 59; Von Kremer, Herrsch. Ideen d. Isl. 301, note 15; Steiner, Die Mu'taziliten, 6, note 5; Al-Subkî, p. 144, قيل ختم فى رمضان ثلاثا وثلاثين ختمة.

4) Abû Nu'aim, 143 b, دفع المامون مالا فقال اقسمه على اصحاب الحديث فانّ فيهم ضعفآء فما بقى احد الا اخذ الا احمد بن حنبل

hau a.
Bagh'
he op. oxy in theology, and for the consequent persecution of the stricter theologians on which he entered. It would appear to be more in accordance with the facts, to say that al-Ma'mûn himself found the atmosphere of orthodoxy oppressive and sought relief by surrounding himself with men whose minds were of his own liberal cast [1]). That these men should then put forth this or that doctrine is not so much to be considered as that the Khalif himself found heterodoxy a more congenial environment than orthodoxy. That Aḥmed ibn Abî Dowâd, the Chief-Ḳâḍî, was responsible for the inquisition known as the Miḥna may be said [2]); but it should not be forgotten that before Ibn Abî Dowâd obtained his ascendency over the mind of al-Ma'mûn, the latter would himself have set on foot the Miḥna for the creation of the Ḳorân had he not been afraid to do so. The Khalif's public adoption of the doctrine of the Ḳorân's creation dates from Rabîᶜ I, 212 A. H. (827 A. D.) [3]).

The following incident shews clearly the state of al-Ma'mûn's mind previous to this date. Yazîd ibn Hârûn, who is mentioned in connection with the incident, died in 206 A. H., six years before al-Ma'mûn publicly professed the doctrine that the Ḳorân was created, and twelve years before the beginning of the Miḥna. Yaḥya ibn Aktham related; "Al-Ma'mûn said to us, 'If it were not for Yazîd ibn Hârûn I would assuredly make public declaration of the doctrine that the Ḳorân is created'. On this one of his courtiers said, 'Nay! but who is Yazîd ibn Hârûn that the Commander of the Faithful

1) Cf. Houtsma, De Strijd over het Dogma, 108.

2) Cf. Abu'l-Maḥ. I, 733; De Goeje, Fragm. Hist. Arab., 547; Al-Subkî, p. 136, وكان معظما عند المامون امير المومنين يقبل شفاعاته ويصغى الى كلامه واخباره فى هذا كثيرة فدسّ ابن ابى دواد له القول بخلق القران وحسّنه عنده وصيّره يعتقده حقا مبينا الى ان اجمع رايه فى سنة ثمان عشرة ومائتين على الدعاء اليه

3) Ṭab. III, ١٠٩٩.

should fear him?' His reply was, 'I am afraid, [illegible] it publicly, that he will retort upon me, and me[illegible]ke h[illegible] at discord in their opinions, and thus there will come trouble, to which I am averse'. One of those who were present then said to al-Ma'mûn, 'I will make trial of the matter with Yazîd ibn Hârûn'. So this man went down to Wâsiṭ and, coming upon Yazîd in the Mosque, said to him, 'O Abû Khâlid, the Commander of the Faithful greets thee and would inform thee that he wishes to make public declaration that the Ḳorân is created'. Yazîd answered, 'You lie against the Commander of the Faithful! If you speak the truth, wait here until the people come together to me'. So next day when the people came to him, the Khalif's messenger repeated what he had said the day before, and asked, 'What have you to say about the matter?' Yazîd retorted, 'You have lied against the Commander of the Faithful. The Commander of the Faithful will not force men to profess that which they have not hitherto known, and which none of them has ever professed'. After this passage the man returned to the Commander of the Faithful, told him of the result, and acknowledged that al-Ma'mûn had been more accurate in his forecast than he himself had been. Al-Ma'mûn replied, 'He has made jest of you'' [1]).

1) al-Maḳrîzî, p. 3, [قال البيهقي († 458)] قال يحيى بن اكثم قال لنا المأمون لولا مكانُ يزيد بن هرون لأُظهِرَنّ القول بخلق القران فقال له بعض جلسائه ومَن يزيد بن هرون حتى يُتّقيَه امير المومنين فقال انى اخاف ان اظهرته يَرُدّ علىّ فيختلف الناس وتكون فتنة وانا اكره الفتنة فقال الرجل للمامون انا أُخبِرُ ذلك من يزيد بن هرون فخرج الى واسط فجاء الى يزيد فدخل عليه المسجد فقال يابا خالد ان امير المومنين يقرئك السلام ويقول لك انى اريدُ ان اظهرَ القول فى ان القران مخلوق فقال له كذبت على امير المومنين فان

The public adoption of the doctrine that the Ḳorân was created was conjoined with the public declaration of the superiority of ᶜAlî over Abû Bekr and ᶜOmar. Al-Maʾmûn was a pro-ᶜAlyite Khalif [1]), even as al-Mutawakkil, who revoked the royal edict announcing the Ḳorân's creation, was an anti-ᶜAlyite Khalif. The Shyites were, in fact, Muᶜtazilites in theological opinion, and it is not surprising that the ruler who gave out their tenet touching the Ḳorân should, at the same time, prefer their great leader before the orthodox Abû Bekr and his successor, even as it is not surprising that the ruler who revoked their tenet should restore to the orthodox Khalifs their primacy. Political capital was made out of both events by partisans, but in both cases it seems to us that the intention of the Khalifs was primarily to effect a religious reform [2]).

For six years al-Maʾmûn was undecided as to whether or not he should make the tenet that the Ḳorân was created obligatory upon his subjects; finally, when he had deposed Yaḥya ibn

كنت صادقا فاصبر الى ان يجتمع علىّ الناسُ قال فلما كان الغدُ
واجتمع عليه الناس قلت يا ابا خالد انّ امير المومنين يقرئك
السلام ويقول لك انى أُريدُ ان أُظهر القول بخلق القران فما عندك
فى ذلك قال كذبت على امير المومنين اميرُ المومنين لا يَحمل الناس
على ما لا يعرفونه وما لم يَقل به احد قال الرجل فلما رجعت الى
امير المومنين قلت له يا امير المومنين انك كنت اعلمَ بالامر منا
كان من القصة كيت وكيت فقال امير المومنين انه تلعّب بك

cf. von Hammer, Lit. Gesch. III, p. 159, Yazîd ibn Hârûn.

1) Houtsma, De Strijd etc. 97. Al-Maʾmûn, who had hoped to effect something by political alliance with the ᶜAlyites, found in time that there was nothing to be gained and much to be lost by such an alliance and gave it up, though still friendly to the ᶜAlyite party and favorable to many of its views. Houtsma, 99.

2) Houtsma, De Strijd etc. 99 f. On this subject cf. Weil, Chalifen II, 258 ff.; von Kremer, Herrsch. Ideen, 333 ff.

Aktham, in the year 217 A. H., from the Chief-Ḳâḍî's office [1]) and appointed Aḥmed ibn Abî Dowâd as his successor, he was encouraged to take the step by his new favorite until, in the last year of his life 218 A. H., he ordered the application of the Miḥna, or test [2]).

Ibn Abî Dowâd. Aḥmed ibn Abî Dowâd, who held a position of great power under the three Khalifs, al-Ma'mûn, al-Muʿtaṣim and al-Wâthiḳ, and was the most vigorous advocate of the Miḥna during their reigns [3]), is pictured in the accounts given by the orthodox biographers of Aḥmed ibn Hanbal in much too unfavorable a light. He was a learned man, gifted in the Kalâm, — he studied the Kalâm with Hayyâj ibn al-ʿAlâ al-Sulamî, a pupil of Wâçil ibn ʿAṭâ [4]), and was the first who publicly employed it in speaking before the Khalifs, though he refrained from employing it in the presence of Ibn al-Zayyât the Vizier. The Khalif al-Muʿtaṣim was completely under the power of Ibn Abî Dowâd.

1) De Goeje, Fragm. Hist. Arab. 376.

2) p. 52, note 2.

3) Steiner, Die Muʿtaziliten, 78.

4) for Wâçil ibn ʿAṭâ cf. Dozy, Het Islamisme, 133 f.; Steiner, Die Muʿtaziliten, pp. 25, 50. Houtsma (De Strijd etc. 103) says that Wâçil ibn ʿAṭâ does not appear to have taught the creation of the Ḳorân.

al-Subkî, p. 136, كان القاضى احمد بن ابى دواد ممن نشا فى العلم وتضلع
بعلم الكلام وصحب فيه هياج بن العلاء السلمى صاحب واصل بن عطآء
احد رووس المعتزلة وكان ابن ابى دواد رجلا فصيحا قل ابو العَيناء
[Cod. no points; cf. Abu'l-Maḥâsin, I 475, 733] ما رايت رئيسًا قط افصح
ولا انطق منه وكان كريمًا ممدحا وفيه يقول بعضهم "لقد أنْسَتْ
مساوِىَ كل دهرٍ، محاسنُ احمد بن ابى دُوَادِ، وما طُوِّفتُ فى الافاقِ
الّا، ومن جدواك راحلتى وزادِى، يقيم الظن عندك والامانى،
وإنْ قلقت [Cod. وأن قلب Abu'l-Feda Ann. II, 678, corrects as in text]
ركابى فى البلاد،

He entered the service of al-Ma'mûn in the year 204 A. H., on the recommendation of Yaḥya ibn Aktham, and at this Khalif's death was warmly recommended by him to his successor, al-Muʿtaṣim. In the very beginning of al-Mutawakkil's reign Aḥmed was paralyzed, and his son Moḥammed was made Chief-Ḳâḍî in his place, but was deposed in the same year, 232 A. H. Ibn Abî Dowâd was an eloquent man and a poet whose praises were loudly celebrated by poets and others. He was, also, a man of large generosity, and a lover of good living and entertainment [1]. In contrast to this estimate of the man is the representation of him as an impetuous, ignorant and narrow bigot, which we find in most of the orthodox accounts. In 236 or 237 A. H. Ibn Abî Dowâd came into disfavor at the Court, and was imprisoned and his property confiscated; later, he was sent to reside in Baghdâd, where he lived till his death. Both father and son died in disgrace in the year 240 A. H., the son twenty days before his father [2].

First Letter of al-Ma'mûn to Baghdâd.

The first step taken by al-Ma'mûn to secure conformity to the view which he had adopted was to send a letter to his lieutenant at Baghdâd, Isḥâḳ ibn Ibrâhîm, cousin of Ṭâhir ibn al-Ḥasan, ordering him to cite before him the ḳâḍîs and traditionists, and to demand of them an answer to the test as to the

1) On the luxurious life of the chief Muʿtazila cf. Houtsma, De Strijd etc. 81 f.; Steiner, Die Muʿtaziliten, 10 infra.

2) Weil, Chalifen II, 334; Goldziher, Moḥ. Stud. II, 58; Maçoudî VI, 214; Ibn Chall. N°. 31; Abu'l-Maḥ. I, 733; De Goeje, Fragm. Hist. Arab. 547; cf. Abû Nuʿaim, 152a, وجَعل يَعقوب وعتاب يصيران اليه فيقولان له يقول لك امير المومنين ما تقول فى ابن ابى دواد فى ماله فلا يجيب فى ذلك بشىء وجَعل يعقوب وعتاب يخبرانه بما يحدث فى امر ابن ابى دواد فى كل يوم ثم احدر ابن ابى دواد الى بغداد بعدما اشهد عليه ببيع ضياعه

creation of the Ḳorân. This letter ran as follows [1]: That which God has laid upon the imâms of the Muslims, their Khalifs, is to be zealous in the maintenance of the religion of God, which he has asked them to conserve; in the heritage of prophecy, which he has granted them to inherit; in the tradition of knowledge, which he has asked them to hold in charge; in the government of their subjects according to right and justice, and in being diligent to observe obedience to God in their conduct toward them. Now, the Commander of the Faithful asks God to assist him to persevere in the right way and to be energetic in it, to act justly, also, in those interests of his subjects over which God by his grace and bounty has appointed him to have rule. The Commander of the Faithful knows that the great multitude, the mass of the insignificant folk, and the vulgar public, who, in all regions and countries, are without insight and deep reflection, and have not a method of reasoning by means of such proof as God approves under the guidance which he gives, and no enlightenment by the light of knowledge and its evidences, are a people ignorant of God and too blind to see him, too much in error to know the reality of his religion, the confession of his unity and the belief in him; perverted, also, so as not to recognize his clear tokens, and the obligation of his service; unable to grasp the real

---

1) The text on which I have based all the translations of the Khalif al-Ma'mûn's letters in relation to the Miḥna is that found in the Leiden edition of Ṭabarî's Annales III (2nd vol.), ١١١٢—١١٣٣. It has the appearance of being a verbal copy of the letters, while the text in Abu'l-Maḥâsin I, ٦٣٧—٦٤١, De Goeje, Fragm. Hist. Arab. II, ٤٦٥, Abu'l-Feda Annales II, 154 f., and in al-Subkî, 136 ff. represents the letters in greatly abridged form. The later writers appear to have used Ṭabarî for their text, for all shew much the same variations from the extended form of the letters found in his work; that is, where they furnish the same portions of the letters (for some of the authorities mentioned have abridged more than others, and in some there is but one or, it may be, two letters found). The above mentioned authorities, beyond the help already gathered from the collation with Abu'l-Maḥâsin, do not afford any assistance to improve the text found in Ṭabarî.

measure of God, to know him as he really is, and to distinguish between him and his creation, because of the weakness of their views, the deficiency of their understandings, and their turning aside from reflection and recollection; for they put on an equality God and the Ḳorân which he has revealed. They are all agreed and stand unequivocally in accord with one another that it is eternal and primitive, and that God did not create it, produce it, or give it being; while God himself says in his well-ordered Book, which he appointed as a healing for what is within the breasts and as a mercy and right guidance for the believers, 'We have made it a Ḳorân in the Arabic tongue' [1]), and everything which God has made he has created. He says, also, 'Praise be to God who *created* the heavens and the earth and *made* the darkness and the light' [2]). He speaks also thus, 'We will tell thee tidings of that which went before' [3]); he says here that it is an account of things *after* whose happening he *produced* it, and with it he followed up their lead. Then he says, آلر, 'A book whose verses were well-ordered, and, then, were divided by order of a Wise and Knowing One' [4]). Now, for everything that is ordered and divided there is one who orders and divides; and God is the one who orders well his Book and the one who divides it, therefore, he is its creator and producer. They, also, are those who dispute with false arguments, and call men to adopt their view. Further, they claim to be followers of the Sunna, while in every chapter of God's Book is an account, which may be read therein, that gives the lie to their position, declares their invitation [to adopt their opinions] to be false, and thrusts back upon them their view and their religious pretentions. But they give out, in spite of that, that they are the people of the truth and the [real] religion and the communion of believers, all others being the people of falsehood, unbelief and schism; and they boast themselves of

1) Ḳorân, 43. 2.
2) Ḳorân, 6. 1.
3) Ḳorân, 20. 99.
4) Ḳorân, 11. 1.

that over their fellows, so deceiving the ignorant, until persons of the false way, who are devoted to the worship of another God than Allah, and who mortify themselves for another cause than that of the true religion, incline toward agreement with them and accordance with their evil opinions, by that means getting to themselves honour with them, and procuring to themselves a leadership and a reputation among them for honorable dealing. Thus they give up the truth for their falsehood, and find apart from God [1]) a supporter for their error. And, so, their testimony is received, because they [sc. the ignorant or people of the false way] declare them [sc. those who *pretend* to be the people of the truth] to be veracious witnesses; and the ordinances of the Ḳorân are executed by them [sc. those who pretend to be the people of the truth] notwithstanding the unsoundness of their religion, the corruption of their honour, and the depravation of their purposes and belief. That is the goal unto which they are urging others, and which they seek in their own practice and in [their] lying against their Lord, though the solemn covenant of the Book is upon them that they should not speak against God except that which is true, and though they have learned what the condition is of 'those whom God has made deaf and whose eyes he has blinded. Do they not reflect upon the Ḳorân? or are there locks upon their hearts?' [2]) The Commander of the Faithful considers, therefore, that those men are the worst and the chief in error, being deficient in the belief in God's unity, and having an incomplete share in the faith — vessels of ignorance, banners of falsehood, the tongue of Iblîs, who speaks through his friends and is terrible to his enemies who are of God's religion; the ones of all others to be mistrusted as to their truthfulness, whose testimony should be rejected, and in whose word and deed one can put no confidence. For one can only do good works after assured persuasion, and there [really] is assured persuasion

1) cf. Ḳorân, 9. 16.

2) Ḳorân, 47. 25—26.

only after fully obtaining a real possession of Islâm, and a sincere profession of the faith in God's unity. He, therefore, who is too blind to perceive his right course and his share in the belief in God and in his unity, is, in other respects, as to his conduct and the justness of his testimony, still more blind and erring. By the life of the Commander of the Faithful, the most likely of men to lie in speech and to fabricate a false testimony is the man who lies against God and his revelation, and who does not know God as he really is; and the most deserving of them all to be rejected when he testifies about what God ordains and about his religion is he who rejects God's testimony to his Book and slanders the truth of God by his lying. Now, gather together the ķâḍis under thy jurisdiction, read unto them this letter of the Commander of the Faithful to thee, and begin to test them to see what they will say, and to discover what they believe concerning the creation of the Ķorân by God and its production by God. Tell them, also, that the Commander of the Faithful will not ask assistance in his government of one whose religion, whose sincerity of faith in God's unity, and whose [religious] persuasion are not to be trusted; nor will he put confidence in such a man in respect to what God has laid upon him and in the matter of those interests of his subjects which he has given into his charge. And when they have confessed that [sc. that the Ķorân is created] and accorded with the Commander of the Faithful, and are in the way of right guidance and of salvation, then, bid them to cite the legal witnesses under their jurisdiction, to ask them in reference to the Ķorân, and to leave off accepting as valid the testimony of him who will not confess that it is created and produced, and refuse thou to let them [the ķâḍîs] countersign it. Write, also, to the Commander of the Faithful the reports that come to thee from the ķâḍîs of thy province as to the result of their inquisition and their ordering that these things be done. Get acquainted with them and search out their evidences, so that the sentences of God may not be carried out, except on the testimony of such as have insight into real religion and are sincere in the belief in God's unity, and then, write unto the Commander of the Faithful of what comes of it all.

This letter was writen in the month of Rabî' I, 218 A. H., before al-Ma'mûn set out on his last expedition to the frontiers, and about four months before his death. It must be confessed that the spirit of the document is that of the bigot, rather than that of a broad and liberal mind. Nor can we suppose that a man of al-Ma'mûn's character would let a document of this kind be composed in any spirit but his own. Its indications all point to arrogant intellectual self-sufficiency coupled with a contempt of opinions different from those held by himself. The contemptuous Khalif would appear to have been convinced by those about him that he could now safely terrorize the orthodox, securing assent to his own views from such as were weak enough to be frightened by his threats or tortures, and blotting out the obstinate ones from the face of the earth, when they were found incorrigible.

The Beginning of the Mihna elsewere. Egypt.

This letter was sent to all the provinces. The copy of that which was addressed to Kaidar, governor of Egypt, is practically the same as that whose translation has been given, but it did not reach Egypt until the month of Jumâdâ II. The Ḳâḍî in Egypt at this time was Hârûn ibn Abdallah al-Zuhrî. He gave in his assent on the test as to the Ḳorân being applied to him, as did also the constituted witnesses except some whose testimony was by their refusal rendered invalid. Kaidar had made a beginning with the examination of the faḳîhs and 'ulamâ, but had evidently adopted no harsh measures, when the news of al-Ma'mûn's death came to him in the month after the receipt of the order for the Miḥna. On the receipt of this news the inquisition was suspended [1]).

There is mention of some trials for the sake of the Ḳorân at Damascus, but there, as well as in other provinces, little appears to have been done, for the notices are

---

1) Abu'l-Maḥ. I, 636, 637.

very slight; and, from the way in which Abu'l-Maḥâsin's record reads, one might infer that the order for the Miḥna to places outside of ʿIrâḳ and Egypt came later than to these places. If this inference be just the time of the inquisition in these other parts must have been short, at least, in the Khalifate of al-Ma'mûn. It is to be concluded, too, that the success of the persecution at Baghdâd led al-Ma'mûn to order a general introduction of the Miḥna throughout his empire.

Damascus. In the year 218 A. H., al-Ma'mûn went in person to Damascus, probably on his last expedition to Asia Minor, and personally conducted the testing of the doctors there concerning the freedom of the will (عَدْل) and the divine unity, the second of which in his view involved a test as to the creation of the Ḳorân [1]). The governor of Damascus under al-Ma'mûn, as well as under his successors, al-Muʿtaṣim and

---

1) al-Jaʿqûbî II, 571, The Muʿtazila called themselves the Ahlu't-Tauhîd wa'l-ʿAdl, the men of the Divine Unity and Righteousness, chiefly for the reason that they, on the one hand, rejected the orthodox view of the Divine attributes and of the Ḳorân as out of harmony with the unitarian faith of Islâm; and held, instead, that the so-called attributes were only empty names, or were not real and distinct existences, but particular presentations of the Divine essence itself: that is, God as wise, God as powerful etc. They, on the other hand, rejected the orthodox doctrine of the Divine foreordination of the actions and destinies of men as inconsistent with the absolute righteousness of God, and held that the human will was free, and man thus the determiner of his own destiny. Hence it is that in polemic literature Ahlu't-Tauhîd wa'l-ʿAdl has a much more special meaning than that indicated in the beginning of this note, generally standing for those who believe, 1) in the non-existence of the attributes of God or their identity with his essence, and in the creation of the Ḳorân (اهل التوحيد). 2) in the freedom of the will (اهل العدل); cf. Houtsma, De Strijd etc. 55, 92, 133 Steiner, Die Muʿtaziliten, 30, 50 and note 3); Shahrastânî, Haarbrücker's transl'n I, 39, 42.

If Jaʿqûbî be correct, Houtsma's statement (p. 108) "dat hij [al-Ma'mûn] niet den vrijen wil ook meteen [with the creation of the Ḳorân] als staats dogma vaststelde" must be modified. The probabilities are in favour of the Khalif's having done what Jaʿqûbî says, though we, in general, do not find Jaʿqûbî a very satisfactory authority as far as the Miḥna is concerned. His usual accuracy in recording events is seemingly wanting at this point.

al-Wâthiḳ, was Isḥâḳ ibn Yaḥya. During the Khalifate of al-Muʿtaṣim, that Khalif wrote him a letter ordering him to urge the Miḥna on the people under his authority. He, however, dealt leniently with them in regard to the order he had received. In 235 A. H., this man was appointed governor of Egypt by al-Mutawakkil [1]).

Kûfa. When the order came to Kûfa there was a great assembly of the sheikhs in the general mosque of the city, and, on the Khalif's (the name of the Khalif is not given) letter being read to them, the feeling was against yielding to the order it contained. Abû Nuʿaim al-Faḍl ibn Dukain, a Kûfite, who died in 219 A. H., said that he had met over 870 teachers, from the aged al-Aʿmash to those who were young in years, who did not believe the Ḳorân to be created, and that such teachers as were inclined to the heterodox view were charged by their fellows with being Zindîḳs (atheists) [2]). Abû Nuʿaim ibn Dukain was present at the opening of the Miḥna in Kûfa. This fact shews us the approximate date of the event there, for this man, as we have said, died in the year 219 [3]).

Citation of the Seven Leaders. The result of the letter of al-Maʾmûn to Baghdâd was to produce, as we may justly conjecture, a feeling of resistance, the most zealous inciter of

---

1) Abu'l-Maḥ. I. 711 f.

2) On the origin of the name and its use among the orthodox v. Houtsma, De Strijd etc. 75.

3) al-Maḳrîzî, p. 13, واما الحافظ ابو نعيم الفضل بن دكين فروى الحافظ ابو الفرج بسنده الى محمد بن احمد بن عمرو بن عيسى قال سمعت ابى يقول ما رايت مجلسا انبل من مجلس اجتمع فيه المشايخ بجامع الكوفة فى وقت الامتحان فقرئ عليهم الكتاب الذى فيه المحنة فقال ابو نعيم ادركت ثمانى مائة شيخ ونيفا وسبعين شيخا منهم الاعمش فمن دونه فما رايت احدا يقول بهذه المقالة يعنى بخلق القران ولا تكلم احد بها الا رمى بالزندقة

which would be Aḥmed ibn Ḥanbal [1]). Still, al-Ma'mûn did not yet venture to apprehend the latter. His next step was one which was calculated to shew him just how far he was safe in going in his enforcement of conformity to his views.

Second Letter of al-Ma'mûn. He wrote a second letter to Isḥâḳ ibn Ibrâhîm, the governor of ʿIrâḳ, ordering him to send seven of the leading traditionists of Baghdâd that he might test them himself. For his purpose, this was a sagacious move. Away from the moral support of their fellow-traditionists, and face to face with the state of the Court and the terrors which the Khalif brought to bear upon their minds, resistance was much more difficult than it would have been at Baghdâd. And the compliance of these leaders being secured, smaller men needed not to be feared. The name of Aḥmed ibn Ḥanbal was, at first, upon the list bearing the names of the seven referred to, but was erased at the instance of Ibn Abî Dowâd, — at least, so the latter claimed [2]).

Those now summoned [3]) to the Court were Moḥammed ibn Saʿd the secretary of al-Wâḳidî, Abû Muslim the amanuensis of Yazîd ibn Hârûn, Yaḥya ibn Maʿîn, Zuhair ibn Ḥarb Abû Khaithama, Ismâʿîl ibn Dâûd, Ismâʿîl ibn Abî Masʿûd and Aḥmed ibn Ibrâhîm al-Dauraḳî. These seven men all yielded assent under the pressure which al-Ma'mûn used with them. Having obtained his desire, the Khalif sent the men back to Baghdâd, where Isḥâḳ ibn Ibrâhîm, acting under al-Ma'mûn's orders, had them repeat their confession before the faḳîhs and traditionists [4]).

Its Effect. The fall of these seven men from orthodoxy was a source of much grief to Aḥmed ibn Ḥanbal. His judgment

---

1) The Baghdâd people had in the year 215, and even earlier, protested against al-Ma'mûn's heterodoxy touching the Ḳorân, cf. Abu'l-Maḥ. I, 631.

2) Vid. p. 82.

3) Ṭabarî ١١١٦, text of letter not given.

4) Ṭabarî ١١١٦ f. A biographical notice of Moḥammed ibn Saʿd is found Ibn Chall. N°. 656; of Yaḥya ibn Maʿîn, al-Nawawî, Biog. Dict. p. 628; of Aḥmed ibn al-Dauraḳî, Dhahabî Ṭabaḳât 8, N°. 98; of Zuhair ibn Ḥarb, id. 8, N°. 23. I have not been able to find notices of the other three.

was that if they had stood their ground nothing more would have been heard of the Miḥna in Baghdâd. Al-Ma'mûn would have been afraid to deal harshly with them seeing they were the leading men of the city; but, when they gave way, he had little hesitation in dealing with others [1]). Their assent was by themselves excused on the ground of Taḳîa (exemp-
ι' from observance of religious duty when it involved risk
nc ie), but the real cause of their doing as they did was
fr of execution if they had not done so. Yaḥya ibn Ma'în
ιth weeping used to confess that this was the case [2]). It
as unfortunate that the seven leaders proved themselves
o weak, for it is not unlikely that their firmness might have deterred al-Ma'mûn from prosecuting further his effort for uniformity of belief; and after his death, the succeeding Khalifs were not such as would likely have revived an inquisition like this when it had once been given up.

Third Letter. A third letter from the Khalif was now sent to Baghdâd to Isḥâḳ ibn Ibrâhîm the governor. Its text was as follows [3]): That which God has a right to expect from his vicegerents (khalifs) on his earth [and] those entrusted by him with rule over his servants, upon whom he

---

1) al-Maḳrîzî, p. 4, [قال احمد بن حنبل] فاجابوا ولو كانوا صبروا وقاموا لله لكان انقطع الامر وحذّرهم الرجل يعنى المامون ولكن لمّا اجابوا وهم عين البلد اجترأ على غيرهم وكان ابو عبد الله اذا ذكرهم يغتمّ ويقول هم اول من ثلم هذه الثلمة

2) al-Subkî, p. 137, وسبب طلبهم انهم توقفوا اولا ثم اجابوه تقية وكتب الى اسحق بن ابراهيم بان يُحضر الفقهاء ومشايخ الحديث ويُخبرهم بما اجاب به هؤلاء السبعة ففعل ذلك فاجابه طائفة وامتنع آخرون فكان يحيى بن معين [al-Sujûtî, 314, adds وغيره] يقول اجبنا خوفا من السيف

3) Ṭabarî III, ١١١٧ ff.

has been pleased to lay the maintenance of his religion, the care of his creatures, the carrying out of his ordinance and his laws, and the imitation of his justice in his world, is that they should exert themselves earnestly for God, do him good service in respect to that which he asks them to guard and lays upon them, make him known by that excellency of learning which he has entrusted to them a~h the knowledge which he has placed within them, guianight him the one who has turned aside from him, bring tious him who has turned his back on his command, mark onn-for their subjects the way of their salvation, tell them aboue the limits of their faith and the way of their deliverance, and protection, and discover to them those things which are hidden from them, and the things which are doubtful to them [clear up] by means of that which will remove doubt from them and bring back enlightenment and clear knowledge unto them all. And [part of that which he claims of them is] that they should begin that by making them go in the right way, and by causing them to see [things] clearly, because this involves all their actions, and comprehends their portion of felicity in this world and the next. They [the Khalifs] ought to reflect how God is one who holds himself ready to question them about that for which they have been made responsible, and to reward them for that which they have done in advance and that which they have laid up in store with him. The help of the Commander of the Faithful is alone in God, and his sufficiency is God, who is enough for him. Of that which the Commander of the Faithful by his reflection has made plain, and has come to know by his thinking, and the great danger of which is clear, as well as the seriousness of the corruption and harm which will come to religion thereby, are the sayings which the Muslims are passing round among themselves as to the Ḳorân, which God made to be an imâm and a lasting monument for them from God's Messenger and elect Servant, Moḥammed, and [another thing is] the confusedness of the opinion of many of them about it [sc. the Ḳorân] until it has seemed good in their opinions and right in their minds that it has not been cre. and, thus, they expose themselves to the risk of deny. the creating by God of all things, by which [act] he is distinguished from his creation. He in his glory stands apart in the bringing into being of all things by his wisdom and the creation of them by his power, and in his priority in time over them by reason of his being Primitive Existence, whose beginning cannot be attained and whose duration cannot be reached. Everything apart from him is a creature from his creation, — a new thing which he has brought into existence. [This perverted opinion they hold] though the Ḳorân speaks clearly of God's creating all things, and proves it to the exclusion of all difference of opinion. They are, thus, like the Christians when they claim that ʿIsâ ibn Maryam was not created because he was the Word of God [1]). But God says, 'Verily we have made it a Ḳorân in the Arabic language' [2]); and the explanation of that is, 'Verily we have created it', just as the Ḳorân says, 'And he made from it his mate that he might dwell with her' [3]). Also, it says, 'We have made the night as a garment and the day as a means of gain' [4]). 'We have made every living thing from water' [5]). God thus puts on equal footing the Ḳorân and these creatures which he mentions with the indication of 'making'. And he tells that he alone is the One who made it, saying, 'Verily it is a glorious Ḳorân (something to be read) on a well-guarded table' [6]). Now, he says that on the supposition that the Ḳorân is limited by the table, and only that which is created can be limited (by surrounding bounds) [7]). He says, likewise, to his Prophet, 'Do not move in it thy tongue to make haste in it' [8]). Also, 'That which came to them was a newly created religion (ذكر) from their Lord' [9]).

---

1) cf. Sura 112; cf. Steiner, Die Muʿtaziliten, p. 90 and note.
2) Ḳorân, 43. 2.
3) Ḳorân, 7. 189.
4) Ḳorân, 78. 10.
5) Ḳorân, 21. 31.
6) cf. Ḳorân, 85. 21—22.
7) cf. Shahrastânî, Haarbrücker's transl'n I, 72, l. 20 ff.
8) Ḳorân, 75. 16.
9) Ḳorân, 21. 2.

has,' 'And who is a worse liar than the man who inventeth thie against God or charges his verses with being false'[1]. He tells, too, about men whom he blames because of their lying, in that they say, 'God has not sent down [by revelation] to men anything'[2]. Then, by the tongue of his Messenger he declares them liars, and says to his Messenger, 'Say, who sent down the book which Moses brought?'[3]. So God calls the Ḳorân something to be read, something to be kept in memory, a faith, a light, a right guidance, a blessed thing, a thing in the Arabic language, and a narration. For he says, 'We relate unto thee a most beautiful narration in that which we reveal unto thee, — this Ḳorân'[4]. Furthermore, he says, 'Say, surely, if men and jinns were gathered together to bring forth such as this Ḳorân, they could not bring forth one like it'[5]. Also, 'Say, bring ten suras fabricated like it'[6]. Also, 'Falsehood shall not come up to it either from before or after it'[7]. Thus, he puts [at least, by possibility] something before and after it, and so indicates that it is finite and created. But these ignorant people, by their teaching concerning the Ḳorân, have made large the breach in their religion and the defect in their trustworthiness; they have also levelled the way for the enemy of Islâm, and confess fickleness and heresy against their own hearts, [going on] even till they make known and describe God's creation and his action by that description which appertains to God alone, and they compare him with it, whilst only his creation may be the subject of comparison. The Commander of the Faithful does not consider that he who professes this view has any share in the real religion, or any part in the real faith and in well-grounded persuasion. Nor does he consider that he should set any one of them down as a trustworthy person in regard to his being admitted as

1) Ḳorân, 6. 21.
2) Ḳorân, 6. 91.
3) ibid.
4) Ḳorân, 12. 3.
5) Ḳorân, 17. 90.
6) Ḳorân, 11. 16.
7) Ḳorân, 41. 42.

امين — مَعْدَل or شاهد or as one to be relied upon in speech or report, or in the exercise of authority over his subjects. Now, if any of them seem to act with equity, and to be known by his straightforwardness, still, the branches are to be carried back to their roots, and the burden of praise or blame is to be according to these. Thus, whosoever is ignorant in the matter of his religion, concerning that which God has commanded him in reference to his unity, he, as regards other things, is still more ignorant, and is too blind and erring to see the right way in other matters. Now, read the letter of the Commander of the Faithful unto thee to Ja'far ibn 'Isâ and Abd al-Raḥmân ibn Isḥâḳ the ḳâḍî, and cite them both to answer for their knowledge respecting the Ḳorân, telling them that the Commander of the Faithful in the affairs of the Muslims will not ask the assistance of any but those in whose sincerity of faith and whose belief in God's unity he has confidence; and that he has no belief in God's unity who does not confess that the Ḳorân is created. And, if they profess the view of the Commander of the Faithful in this particular, then, order them to test those who are in their courts for the giving of evidence touching rights of claimants, and [order them] to cite them to answer for their profession in respect to the Ḳorân. He who does not profess it to be created, let them declare his testimony invalid and refrain from giving sentence on what he says, even if his integrity be established by the equity and straightforwardness of his conduct. Do this with all the ḳâḍis in thy province, and examine them with such an examination as God can cause to increase the rightmindedness of the rightminded, and prevent those who are in doubt from neglecting their religion. Then, write unto the Commander of the Faithful of what thou hast done in this matter.

Citation of the Doctors in Baghdâd. Following out the instructions of this letter, Isḥâḳ ibn Ibrâhîm summoned to his presence a number of the faḳîhs, doctors and traditionists [1]). Among

1) Ṭabarî III, ۱۱۲۱ ff. is followed throughout the passage.

those summoned were Aḥmed ibn Ḥanbal, Bishr ibn al-Walîd al-Kindî, Abû Ḥassân al-Ziyâdî, ʿAlî ibn Abî Muḳâtil, al-Faḍl ibn Ghânim, Obaidallah ibn ʿOmar al-Ḳawârîrî, ʿAlî ibn al-Jaʿd, al-Ḥasan ibn Ḥammâd al-Sajjâda [1]), al-Dhayyâl ibn al-Haitham, Ḳutaiba ibn Saʿîd, who seems to have been only temporarily in Baghdâd, Saʿdawaih, Saʿîd ibn Suleimân Abû ʿOthmân al-Wâsiṭî [2]), Isḥâḳ ibn Abî Isrâʾîl, Ibn al-Harsh, Ibn ʿUlayya al-Akbar, Moḥammed ibn Nûḥ al-Maḍrûb al-ʿIjlî [3]), Yaḥya ibn Abd al-Raḥmân al-ʿOmarî, Abû Naṣr al-Tammâr, Abû Maʿmar al-Ḳaṭîʿî, Moḥammed ibn Ḥâtim ibn Maimûn, a sheikh of the descendants of ʿOmar ibn al-Khaṭṭâb who was ḳâḍî of al-Raḳḳa, Ibn al-Farrukhân, al-Naḍr ibn Shumail, Abd al-Raḥmân ibn Isḥâḳ, Ibn Bakkâ al-Akbar, Aḥmed ibn Yazîd ibn al-ʿAwwâm Abu 'l-Awwâm al-Bazzâz, Ibn Shujâ and Moḥammed ibn al-Ḥasan ibn ʿAlî ibn ʿÂsim. Others are mentioned in the account of the investigation which follows.

Bishr ibn al-Walîd.

When these men were brought before Isḥâḳ ibn Ibrâhîm, he read to them twice al-Maʾmûn's letter until they grasped its meaning and, then, asked them for their assent to the doctrine which the Khalif propounded. At first, they tried subterfuges and would neither affirm nor deny that the Ḳorân was created. The first to whom Isḥâḳ ibn Ibrâhîm put the test was Bishr ibn al-Walîd. 'What dost thou say respecting the Ḳorân?' he asked; and Bishr replied, 'I have more than once made my view known to the Commander of the Faithful'. Isḥâḳ said, 'But this letter is a new thing from the Commander of the Faithful. What is your view?' Bishr answered, 'I say the Ḳorân is the Word of God'. Isḥâḳ. 'I did not ask thee for that. Is it created?' Bishr. 'God is the creator of everything'. Isḥâḳ. 'Is not the Ḳorân a thing?' Bishr. 'It is a thing'. Isḥâḳ. 'And, there-

1) Abu'l-Maḥ. I. 638 and al-Maḳrîzî, p. 4, supply the name of Sajjâda الحسن بن حماد المعروف بسجّادة.

2) Abu'l-Maḥ. I, 665, supplies the name of Saʿdawaih.

3) Abu'l-Maḥ. I, 648; al-Subkî, p. 138, adds المضروب.

fore, created?' Bishr. 'It is not a creator'. Isḥâḳ. 'I did not ask for this. Is it created?' Bishr then confessed that he had yielded as far as he could yield, and could give no further answer; he contended, moreover, that the Khalif had given him a dispensation from speaking his mind on the subject. The governor now took up a sheet of paper that lay before him and read and explained it to Bishr. Then, he said, 'Testify that there is no God but Allah, one and alone, before whom nothing was and after whom nothing shall be and like to whom is nothing of his creation, in any sense whatsoever or in any wise whatsoever' [1]). Bishr said, 'I testify that and scourge those who do not testify it'. Isḥâḳ then turned to the secretary and said, 'Write down what he has said'.

ᶜAlî ibn Abî Muḳâtil. Turning next to ᶜAlî ibn Abî Muḳâtil he asked for his confession. He replied, 'I have told my opinion about this to the Commander of the Faithful more than once, and have nothing different to say'. The written test was then read to ᶜAlî and he gave the confession it required. Then the governor said, 'Is the Ḳorân created?' ᶜAlî answered, 'The Ḳorân is God's Word'. Isḥâḳ, as in the case of Bishr, told him he had not asked for that, and ᶜAlî answered, 'It is the Word of God; if, however, the Commander of the Faithful command us to do a thing we will yield him obedience'. Again, the scribe was bidden to record what had been said.

The next was al-Dhayyâl whose replies were in the same strain as those of ᶜAlî.

Abû Ḥassân. In the reply of Abû Ḥassân there is something naïvely submissive. 'The Ḳorân is the Word of God', he said, 'and God is the creator of everything; all things apart from

---

1) Houtsma (De Strijd etc. 108 infra) seems to imply that this written 'credo', which was to be subscribed by those to whom it was put, contained a confession that the Ḳorân was created. As Ṭabarî presents the case the document demanded only a profession of faith in God's unity. Its purpose was evidently to support the separate oral test as to the Ḳorân. None seem to have had any scruples about giving assent to the written test, while all would have avoided the other, had it been possible.

him are created. But the Commander of the Faithful is our imâm, and through him we have heard the whole sum of learning. He has heard what we have not heard, and knows what we do not know. God also has laid upon him the rule over us. He maintains our Hajj and our prayers; we bring to him our Zakât; we fight with him in the Jihâd, and we recognize fully his imâmate. Therefore, if he command us we will perform his behest, if he forbid us we will refrain, and if he call upon us we will respond'. Isḥâḳ said, 'This is the view of the Commander of the Faithful'. Abû Ḥassân rejoined, 'True! but sometimes the view of the Commander of the Faithful is one concerning which he gives no command to people, and which he does not call upon them to adopt; if, however, you tell me that the Commander of the Faithful has commanded thee that I should say this, I will say what thou dost command me to say, for thou art a man to be trusted and one on whom reliance is to be placed in respect to anything you may tell me from him. If, then, you order me to do anything, I will do it'. The governor's reply was, 'He has not commanded me to tell thee anything'. Abû Ḥassân said, 'I mean only to obey; command me and I will perform it'. Isḥâḳ said, 'He has not commanded me to command thee, but only to test thee'. The examination of Abû Ḥassân ends here.

Aḥmed ibn Ḥanbal. In the case of Aḥmed ibn Ḥanbal, Ibn Bakkâ al-Asghar suggested to Isḥâḳ ibn Ibrâhîm that he should ask him about the expression of the Ḳorân, 'He is the Hearing and Seeing One', which Aḥmed had used in his confession. Aḥmed, in harmony with the principles of men of his class, answered only, 'He is even as he has described himself'. Being further pressed to explain the words, he said, 'I do not know; he is even as he has described himself'. He was firm in adhering to the confession that the Ḳorân was the Word of God, and would add nothing to it by way of compromise or admission. Those who were examined subsequently all followed Aḥmed's example, except Ḳutaiba, Obaidallah ibn Moḥammed ibn al-Ḥasan, Ibn

ʿUlayya al-Akbar, Ibn al-Bakkâ, Abd al-Munʿim ibn Idrîs ibn Bint Wahb ibn Munabbih, al-Muẓaffir ibn Murajjâ, another man not a faḳîh who happened to be present, Ibn al-Aḥmar and the ʿOmarî Ḳâḍî of al-Raḳḳa. The answers of these are not furnished us but the implication seems to be that they compromised themselves. On this occasion when Aḥmed perceived the assent of his companions as the test was applied he was intensely angry [1]).

Ibn al-Bakkâ.

Ibn al-Bakkâ al-Akbar also compromised himself, but not fully, and with better grace than some of his fellows, for he stood on the ground of the Ḳorân text in making the admissions which he made. These admissions were that the Ḳorân was, on the one hand, something 'made' (مَجْعُول) and, on the other hand, something 'newly produced' (مُحْدَثٌ). For the former position the text adduced was one cited by the Khalif in arguing that the Ḳorân was created (مَخْلُوقٌ), namely, Ḳor. 43 : 2, 'Verily we have made it a Ḳorân (reading) in the Arabic language'. For the latter position the text was, likewise, one cited by the Khalif in his argument, Ḳor. 21 : 2, 'What came to them from their Lord was a newly produced religion (ذِكْرٌ)'. Isḥâḳ asked Ibn al-Bakkâ if the term مَجْعُولٌ were not the same in meaning as مَخْلُوقٌ,

---

1) Abû Nuʿaim, 146 *b* حدثنا سليمان بن احمد ثنا عبد الله ابن احمد بن حنبل حدثنى ابو معمر القطيعى قال لما احضِرْنا فى دار السلطان * ايام المحنة وكان ابو عبد الله احمد ابن حنبل قد أُحضِر فلما رأى انناس يجيبون وكان ابو عبد الله رجلا لينا فلما رأى الناس يجِيبُون انتفخت اوداجه واحمرت عيناه وذهب ذلك اللين الذى كان فيه فقلتُ انه قد غضب لله قال ابو معمر فلما رايتُ ما به قلتُ يابا عبد الله أَبْشِرْ

and he answered that it was. 'Then the Ḳorân is created (مَخْلوق)?' said the governor. 'Nay, that I will not say. I say it is something made (مَجْعول)', was the answer.

After all the other cases had been disposed of Ibn al-Bakkâ al-Asghar remarked that 'the two ḳâḍîs', whom we assume to be Abd al-Raḥmân ibn Isḥâḳ and Jaᶜfar ibn ᶜIsâ, should be examined; but the governor said they held to the same profession as the Commander of the Faithful. Ibn al-Bakkâ suggested that if they were ordered to tell their opinion it could be reported to the Khalif for them. The governor, however, seems to have been determined to avoid the examination of the two ḳâḍîs, probably, to save one who may have been his own son from exposure and humiliation. He simply said to the provoking questioner, 'If thou wilt serve as witness [1]) before them thou shalt know their opinion'.

Fourth Letter. Isḥâḳ ibn Ibrâhîm then wrote to al-Maʾmûn a detailed account of the answers received, and after a delay of nine days again summoned the doctors to hear the Khalif's reply. The following is a version of the letter [2]); — The Commander of the Faithful has received your answer to his letter touching that which the ostentatious among the followers of the Ḳibla and those who seek among the people of religion a leadership for which they are not the right persons, believe about the doctrine of the Ḳorân, in which letter of his the Commander of the Faithful commanded thee to test them, and discover their positions and put them in their right places. Thou dost mention thy summoning of Jaᶜfar ibn ᶜIsâ and Abd al-Raḥmân ibn Isḥâḳ on the arrival of the Commander of the Faithful's letter, together with those whom thou didst summon of those classed as faḳîhs and known as doctors of Tradition and who set themselves up to give legal

1) ان شهدت عندهما بشهادة.

2) Ṭabarî III, ١١٢٥ ff.

decisions in Baghdâd, and [thou dost speak of] thy reading unto them all the letter of the Commander of the Faithful. [Thou hast mentioned], too, thy asking of them as to their faith touching the Ḳorân and [thy] pointing out to them their real interest; also, their agreeing to put away anthropomorphic conceptions and their difference of view in the matter of the Ḳorân; further, thy ordering of those who did not confess it to be created to refrain from Tradition and from giving decisions in private or in public. [Thou hast mentioned], too, thy giving orders unto al-Sindî and Abbâs the client of the Commander of the Faithful, to the same effect as thou didst give orders concerning them unto the two ḳâḍîs, even the same which the Commander of the Faithful prescribed to thee, namely, the testing of the statutory witnesses who are in their courts. Again, [thou hast mentioned] the sending abroad of letters unto the ḳâḍîs in the several parts of thy province that they should come to thee, so that thou mightest proceed to test them according to that which the Commander of the Faithful has defined, whilst thou hast put down at the end of the letter the names of those who were present and their views. Now, the Commander of the Faithful understands what thou hast reported, and the Commander of the Faithful praises God much, even as he is the One to whom such belongs; and he asks him to bless his Servant and his Messenger, Moḥammed, and he prays God to help him to obey him, [sc. God] and to give him [sc. the Khalif], by his grace, effectual aid in his good purpose. The Commander of the Faithful has also thought over what thou hast written relating to the names of those whom thou hast asked about the Ḳorân, and what each of them answered thee touching it, and what thou hast explained as his view. As for what the deluded Bishr ibn al-Walîd says about putting away anthropomorphic conceptions, and that from which he keeps himself back in the matter of the Ḳorân's being created, while he lays claim to leave off speaking on that subject as having had an engagement [to that effect] with the Commander of the Faithful,

Bishr has lied about that, and has acted as an unbeliever, speaking that which is to be refused credit and false; for there has not passed a compact or exchange of opinion in respect to this or any other matter between the Commander of the Faithful and himself, more than that the Commander of the Faithful told him of his belief in the doctrine of the Ikhlâṣ [i. e. the belief in the unity of God] and in that of the creation of the Ḳorân. Call him before thee; tell him what the Commander of the Faithful has told thee in the matter; cite him to answer about the Ḳorân and ask him to recant; for the Commander of the Faithful thinks that thou shouldst ask to recant one who professes his view, seeing that such a view is unmixed infidelity and sheer idolatry in the mind of the Commander of the Faithful. Should he repent, then, publish it and let him alone; but, should he be obstinate in his idolatry and refuse in his infidelity and heterodoxy to confess that the Ḳorân is created, then behead him and send his head to the Commander of the Faithful. In the same way, also, deal with Ibrâhîm ibn al-Mahdî. Test him as thou hast tested Bishr, for he professes his view and reports about him have reached the Commander of the Faithful; and, if he say that the Ḳorân is created, then publish it and make it known; but, if not, behead him and send his head to the Commander of the Faithful [1]). As for ʿAlî ibn Abî Muḳâtil, say to him, "Art thou not the man who said to the Commander of the Faithful, 'Thou art the one to declare what is lawful and unlawful'? and who told him what thou didst tell him?" the recollection of which cannot yet have left him [sc. ʿAlî]. And as for al-Dhayyâl ibn al-Haitham, tell him that what should occupy his mind is the corn which he formerly stole in al-Anbâr, when he administered the government in the city of the Commander of the Faithful, Abu'l-Abbâs [2]); and that, if he were a follower in the footsteps of his forefathers, and went in their ways only, and

1) On death penalty for heresy cf. Goldziher, Moh. Stud. II, 216.

2) cf. Ṭabarî III, ٨٠, l. 18, seq.; De Goeje, Bibl. Geog. VII, ٣٢٧, 5 seq.

pushed on in their path, surely he would not go off into idolatry after having believed. As for Aḥmed ibn Yazîd, known as Abu'l-ʿAwwâm, and his saying that he cannot well answer about the Ḳorân, tell him that he is a child in his understanding, though not in his years, — an ignoramus; and that, if he do not see his way clear to answer he shall see his way clear to answer when he is disciplined, but should he not do it then, the sword will follow. As for Aḥmed ibn Ḥanbal and that which thou hast written about him, tell him that the Commander of the Faithful understands the import of that view and the manner of his conduct in it; and, from what he knows, he infers his ignorance and the weakness of his intellect. As for al-Faḍl ibn Ghânim, tell him that what he did in Egypt, and the riches which he acquired in less than a year are not hidden from the Commander of the Faithful, nor what passed in legal strife between him and al-Muṭṭalib ibn Abdallah about that; for a man who did as he did, and who has a greedy desire for dinârs and dirhems as he has, can be believed to barter his faith out of desire for money, and because he prefers his present advantage to everything else. [Remind him] that he, besides, is the one who said to ʿAlî ibn Hishâm what he did say, and opposed him in that in which he did oppose him. And what was it that caused his change of opinion and brought him over to another? And as for al-Ziyâdî, tell him that he is calling himself a client of the first false pretender in Islâm in whose case the ordinance of the Messenger of God was infringed. It is in harmony with his character that he should go in the way he goes. (But Abû Ḥassân denied that he was a client of Ziyâd or of anyone else, adding that he had the name of Ziyâd [ibn abîhi] for some other reason) [1]). As for Abû Naṣr al-Tammâr, the Commander of the Faithful compares the insignificance of his understanding with the insignificance of his business [date-merchant]. And as for al-Faḍl ibn al-

1) This parenthesis represents a gloss in Ṭabarî III, ١١٢٨, ll. 6—8, (line 7 read وذَكَّرَ for وذُكر).

Farrukhân, tell him that by the doctrine which he professes respecting the Ḳorân he is trying to keep the deposits which Abd al-Raḥmân ibn Isḥâḳ and others entrusted to him, lying in wait for such as will ask him to undertake trusts, and hoping to increase that which has come into his hand; for which there is no recovery from him, because of the long duration of the compact and the length of time of its existence. But say to Abd al-Raḥmân ibn Isḥâḳ, 'May God not reward thee with good for thy giving of power to the like of this man and thy putting of confidence in him, seeing that he is devoted to idolatry and disjoined from belief in God's unity!' And as for Moḥammed ibn Ḥâtim, and Ibn Nûḥ, and him who is known as Abû Maᶜmar, tell them that they are too much taken up with the devouring of usury to grasp properly the doctrine of the divine unity, and that, if the Commander of the Faithful had sought legal justification to attack them for the sake of God, and make a crusade against them on the sole ground of their practice of usury and that which the Ḳorân has revealed concerning such as they, he surely might have found it lawful; how will it be, then, now that they have joined idolatry to their practice of usury, and have become like the Christians? And as for Aḥmed ibn Shujâᶜ, tell him that not long ago thou wast with him, and thou didst extort from him that which he confiscated of the riches belonging to ᶜAlî ibn Hishâm; and [tell him] that his religion is found in dinârs and dirhems. And as for Saᶜdawaih al-Wâsiṭî, say to him, 'May God make abominable the man whose ostentatious preparing of himself for a 'colloquium doctum' on Tradition, while hoping to gain honour by that and desiring to be a leader in it, carries him so far that he wishes for the coming of the Miḥna, and thinks to ingratiate himself with me by it; let him be tried; [if he yield] he may still teach Tradition. And as for him who is known as Sajjâda and his denying that he heard from those traditionists and faḳîhs with whom he studied the doctrine that the Ḳorân is created, tell him that in his preparing of date-stones and his rubbing in order to improve his sajjâda [1]), and likewise in his care for the deposits which ʿAlî ibn Yaḥya and others left in trust with him lies that which occupies his attention so that he forgets the doctrine of the divine unity and that which makes him unmindful [of it]. Then ask him about what Yûsuf ibn Abî Yûsuf and Moḥammed ibn al-Ḥasan used to say, if he have seen them and studied with them. As for al-Ḳawârîrî, in what has been made known of his doings, in his receiving of gifts and bribes, lies that which sets in a clear light his real opinions, the evil of his conduct and the weakness of his understanding and his religion. It has also reached the Commander of the Faithful that he has taken upon himself the [settlement of] questions for Jaʿfar ibn ʿIsâ al-Ḥasanî; so, order Jaʿfar ibn ʿIsâ to give him up, and to abandon reliance upon him and acquiescence in what he says. And as for Yaḥya ibn Abd al-Raḥmân al-ʿOmarî, if he were of the descendants of ʿOmar ibn al-Khaṭṭâb, it is well known what he would answer. And as for Moḥammed ibn al-Ḥasan ibn ibn ʿÂsim, if he were an imitator of his ancestors, he would not profess that profession which has been related of him [2]). He is yet a child and needs to be taught. Now, the Commander of the Faithful is sending to thee also, him who is known as Abû Mushir [3]), after that the Commander of the Faithful has cited him to answer in his testing about the Ḳorân; but he mumbled about it and stammered over it, until the Commander of the Faithful ordered the sword to be brought for him, when he confessed in the manner of one worthy to be blamed. Now, cite him to answer about his confession; and, if he stand fast in it, then, make it known and publish it. But those who will not give up their idolatry, and profess that the Ḳorân is created, of those whom thou hast named in thy letter to the Commander of the

1) Callous patch of skin on the forehead produced, when genuine, by oft-repeated religious prostrations; when an imposture, by rubbing the skin.

2) Ṭabarî, III, ١١٣٠. read حُكيت.

3) d. 218 A. H. Dhahabî Tabaḳât 7, N°. 62.

Faithful and whom the Commander of the Faithful has mentioned or refrained from mentioning to thee in this letter of his, except Bishr ibn al-Walîd and Ibrâhîm ibn al-Mahdî, send them all in bonds to the camp of the Commander of the Faithful in charge of a watch and guards for their journey, until they bring them to the camp of the Commander of the Faithful and deliver them up to those to whom the delivery has been ordered [1]) to be made, so that the Commander of the Faithful may cite them to answer; and, then, if they do not give up their view and recant, he will bring them all to the sword. The Commander of the Faithful sends this letter by extra post [courier's letterbag] instead of waiting till all the letters have been gathered for the post, seeking to advance in the favor of God by the decree he has issued and hoping to attain his purpose, and to gain the ample reward of God thereby. So, give effect to the order of the Commander of the Faithful that comes to thee, and hasten to answer by extra p·iat [v. above] about that which thou hast done, not waiting he the other letter-bags, so that thou mayest tell the Comma now of the Faithful of what they will do.

Recantation of the Doctors. On this letter being read all of those mentioned in it recanted, with the exception of Aḥmed ibn Ḥanbal, Sajjâda, al-Ḳawârîrî and Moḥammed ibn Nûḥ al-Maḍrûb. These four were then cast into prison in chains and next day were again brought before the governor and given a chance to recant. Of this chance Sajjâda availed himself and was set free [2]). The following day, also, they were brought from the prison and given another opportunity to yield, which Obaidallah ibn ʿOmar al-Ḳawârîrî embraced and received his liberty. *Aḥmed and Moḥammed ibn Nûḥ Refuse to Recant.* Thus Aḥmed and Moḥammed ibn Nûḥ alone of those cited to appear remained firm in their faith; the others Aḥmed always excused on the ground of the Taḳîa

1) Variant يؤمرون adopted in the translation.

2) Abu'l-Maḥ. I, 738, says Sajjâda 'stood firm in the Sunna'.

as supported by Ḳorân, 16. 108, 'Except him who is forced, though he have no pleasure in it, while his heart rests in the faith [1]).

and are Cited to Tarsus. Isḥâḳ the governor now wrote a letter giving the results of his examination of the doctors [2]). Shortly after this, al-Ma'mûn ordered Isḥâḳ ibn Ibrahîm to send Aḥmed ibn Ḥanbal and Moḥammed ibn Nûḥ in chains to him to Tarsus. On their journey when they were in the neighbourhood of al-Anbâr Abû Ja'far al-Anbârî crossed the Euphrates to see Aḥmed in the khân where he was lodged, and reminded him of his responsibility as the leader to whom all men looked for an example. If he answered favorably, they, too, would assent to the doctrine; but should he refuse to assent, a great many, if not all, would be held back from recantation. He told him, besides, to remember that death would come to him in the natural course of things, and exhorted him, in view of what he had said, to maintain the integrity of his faith [3]).

---

1) Houtsma, De Strijd etc. 69 and note; al-Maḳrîzî, p. 4, وكان ابو عبد الله رحمه الله يُقيم عُذرهما ويقول اليس قد حُبسا وقُيِّدا قال الله تعالى الا مَن اكرِه وقلبُه مطمئن بالايمان [Kor. 16. 108] ثم قال ابو عبد الله رحمه الله القيد كُرْه والحبس كُرْه والضرب كُرْه فأما اذا لم ينَل بمكروه فلا عُذر له

2) Ṭabarî, III, ١١٣١.

3) al-Maḳrîzî, p. 4, ثم ورَد كتاب المامون الى اسحاق بن ابرهيم بحمل ابى عبد الله ومحمد بن نوح اليه ببلاد الروم فحُملا . . . . . وذكر ابن الجوزى بسنده الى ابى جعفر الانبارى [al-Subkî, p. 136, الابيارى] انه قال لما حُمِل احمد الى المامون أُخبِرتُ فعبرت الفرات فاذا هو جالس فسلمت عليه فقال ياابا جعفر تعَنّيت فقلت ليس فى هذا عَناء وقلت له انت اليوم راس والناس يقتدون بك فوالله لئن اجبت

In pursuance of the Khalif's order the two unyielding theologians were borne on camels from Baghdâd, Aḥmed's companion in the maḥmal being a man called Aḥmed ibn Ghassân. As they were on the way Aḥmed told his companion that he had a firm conviction that the messenger of al-Maʾmûn, Rajâ al-Ḥiḍârî, would meet them that night; and, in fact, Rajâ al-Ḥiḍârî did meet them and the prisoners were transferred to his care, but he was not allowed to proceed far with his charge before the news of the Khalif's death relieved him of the obligation to bring the men to Tarsus. When he had conducted them as far as Adhana, and was just setting out with them at night, a man met them in the gate of the town with news that al-Maʾmûn had just died at the river Bodhandhûn [Ποδενδουν] in Asia Minor, after leaving as a last charge to his successor to prosecute vigorously the Miḥna [1]).

الى خلق القران ليُجيبين باجابتك خلق من خلق الله وان انت لم تجب ليمتنعن خلق من الناس كثير ومع هذا فان الرجل يعنى المامون ان لم يقتلك تموت ولا بُد من الموت فثق بالله ولا تجبهم الى شىء قال فجعل ابو عبد الله يبكى ويقول ما شاء الله ما شاء الله

1) Abû Nuʿaim, 147 *a*, 147 *b*, (al-Subkî, p. 139, cf. al-Makrîzî, p. 4 infra, a fuller account), قال احمد بن غسّان حُملتُ انا واحمدُ بن حنبل فى محمل على جَمل يُرادُ بنا المامون فلما صرنا قُربَ عانةَ قال لى احمد قلبى يُحسّ ان رجآء الحضارى ياتى فى هذه الليلة فانْ اتى وانا نآئم فايقظنى وانْ اتى وانت نائم ايقظتك . . . . فلم يكن باسرع ان خرج علينا رجآء الحضارى فقال اين هؤلاء الاشقياء فقال احمد يا عدوّ الله انت تقول القرانُ مخلوق ونكونُ نحن الاشقياء قال [احمد بن غسّان] فانزلنا من المحامل وصيّرنا فى خيمة . . . . قال والله ما مضى الثلث الاول من الليل الا ونحن

Al-Ma'mûn Rejects the Plea of Taḳîa Offered by the Doctors.

In the meantime, al-Ma'mûn had received word that those who had recanted had done so claiming the Taḳîa as a justification, in accordance with the dispensation granted in the Ḳorân to such as are forced to confess a *false* faith, while their hearts continue to hold fast to the true [1]). This, of course, meant that what the Khalif believed and had propounded to them was false, a conclusion with which he was by no means satisfied, and, therefore, wrote again to Isḥâḳ

بصَيحة وضَجّة واذا رجــاء الحِصَارى قد اقبل علينا فقال صــدقت يــابــا عــبــد الله القران كــلام الله غير مخلوق قــد مات والله اميرُ المــومــنــيــن، [Aḥmed had previously prayed for a Divine interposition to demonstrate that he was in the right way].

فلما صِرْنا الى اَذَنَة ورحلنا منها وذلك فى جوف الليل فُتِح لنا [147*b*] بابُها فلقينا رجل ونحن خارجون من الباب وهو داخل فقال البُشرى قد مات الرجل قال ابى وكنتُ ادعو الله ان لا اراه قال ابو الفضل صالح فصار ابى ومحمد بن نوح الى طرسوس وجآء نَعى المامون من البذندُون فردّا فى اقــيــادهــمــا الى الرَّقــة واخــرجا من الرَّقة فى سفينة مع قوم مُحبَّسين فلما صارا بعانــات تــوُفّى محمّد بن نوح رحمه الله وتقدّم ابى فصَلّى عليه ثم صــار ابى الى بغداد وهــو مقيَّد فمكث بالياســريّــة ايامًا ثم صُيّر الى الحبس فى دار اكتُريت عند دار عُمارة ثم نقل بعد ذلــك الى حَبْس العامــة فى دربِ المَوصلية فمكث فى الحبس مــنــذ اخــذ وحُمل الى ان ضُـرب وخِلى عنه ثمانية وعشرين شهرا قال ابى فكنت اصلى بهم وانــا مُقيد وكنت ارى بُــوران يَحــمــل له فى زورَق مآءً باردا فيُذهب به اليه الى السجن،

1) Ṭabarî III, ١١٣١ f.; De Goeje, Fragm. Hist. Arab. II, 465 f.; Abu 'l-Feda Annales II, 155.

ibn Ibrâhîm to tell Bishr ibn al-Walid and the others who had pleaded that their case was similar to that of ʿAmmâr ibn Yâsir contemplated in the Korân's dispensation to recusants, that there was no similarity between the cases. He had openly professed a false religion, while at heart a Muslim; they had openly professed the truth while in their hearts believing what was false. To settle matters they must all be sent to Tarsus, there to await such time as the Khalif should leave Asia Minor. The following men were therefore sent after Aḥmed and his company: Bishr ibn al-Walîd, al-Faḍl ibn Ghânim, ʿAlî ibn Abî Muḳâtil, al-Dhayyâl ibn al-Haitham, Yaḥya ibn Abd al-Raḥmân al-ʿOmarî, ʿAlî ibn al-Jaʿd, Abu'l-ʿAwwâm, Sajjâda, al-Ḳawârîrî, Ibn al-Ḥasan ibn ʿAlî ibn ʿÂṣim, Isḥâḳ ibn Abî Isrâ'îl, al-Naḍr ibn Shumail, Abû Naṣr al-Tammâr, Saʿdawaih al-Wâsiṭî, Moḥammed ibn Ḥâtim ibn Maimûn, Abû Maʿmar, Ibn al-Harsh, Ibn al-Farrukhân, Aḥmed ibn Shujâ and Abû Hârûn ibn al-Bakkâ. They received the news of the Khalif's death when they arrived at al-Raḳḳa, and, on the order of ʿAnbasa ibn Isḥâḳ, the Wâlî of the place, were detained there until they were sent back to Baghdâd in charge of the same messenger as had brought them thence. On arriving at Baghdâd, the governor Isḥâḳ ordered them to keep to their dwellings [1]), but afterwards relaxed his severity toward them and allowed them to go abroad. Some of those who had been sent, however, had the temerity to leave al-Raḳḳa and come to Baghdâd without having obtained permission. As might have been expected, they suffered for their boldness when they reached the latter place, for Isḥâḳ punished them. Those who thus procured trouble to themselves were Bishr ibn al-Walîd, al-Dhayyâl, Abu'l-ʿAwwâm and ʿAlî ibn Abî Muḳâtil.

and Orders Them to be Sent to Him.

Death of al-Ma'mûn and its Consequences.

---

1) On 'keeping to their dwellings' cf. Goldziher, Moh. Stud. II, 94.

Aḥmed and Ibn Nûḥ Ordered back to Baghdâd. To return to Aḥmed and his companion Moḥammed ibn Nûḥ. These two were now sent back to al-Raḳḳa where they, also, remained in prison until the oath of allegiance was taken to the Khalif al-Muʿtaṣim. After this event, they were taken in a boat *Death of Ibn Nûḥ.* from al-Raḳḳa to ʿÂnât, at which place Moḥammed ibn Nûḥ died, and Aḥmed, after performing the offices of the dead over his friend, was brought back in bonds to Baghdâd [1]). At first, he was imprisoned, as it appears, in the street al-Yâsirîya for some days. From there he was transferred to the Dâr al-Sharshîr near to the Dâr ʿUmâra and lodged in a stable belonging to Moḥammed ibn Ibrâhîm (brother of Isḥâḳ) which had been rented as a place of detention. It was very small and his stay there was short. He took sick in Ramaḍân, and was then transferred to the common prison in the Darb al-Mausilîya [2]).

Among those who stood faithful in the inquisition during

---

1) See preceding note, p. 82, 1. Houtsma (De Strijd etc. 106) says that Moḥammed ibn Nûḥ, as well as Aḥmed ibn Ḥanbal, was scourged by al-Muʿtaṣim, but he, in fact, never appeared before that Khalif.

2) al-Subkî, p. 139, قال صالح صار ابى الى بغداد مقيدا فمكث باليامرية ايامًا ثم حبس بدار الشرشير عند دار عمارة ثم نقل بعد ذلك الى حبس العامة فى درب الموصلية [marg: Copy المفضلى] . . . . واما حنبل بن اسحق فقال حبس ابو عبد الله فى دار عمارة ببغداد فى اصطبل لمحمد بن ابراهيم اخى اسحق بن ابراهيم وكان فى حبس ضيق ومرض فى رمضانَ فحبس فى ذلك الحبس قليلا ثم حول الى سجن العامة فمكث فى السجن نحوًا من ثلاثين شهرا فكنا ناتيه وقرا علىّ كتاب الارجاء وغيره فى الحبس فرايته يصلى باهل الحبس وعليه القيد وكان يخرج رجله من حلقة القيد وقت الصلاة والنوم

Others who did not Recant. ʿAffân ibn Muslim.

the Khalifate of al-Maʾmûn, but whose name has not yet appeared, was ʿAffân ibn Muslim Abû ʿOthmân, whom the Khalif and Isḥâḳ ibn Ibrâhîm his lieutenant in ʿIrâḳ, in penalty for his refusal to obey the order to recant, deprived of the stipend which each of them granted to him. When asked what he had to say in reply to the demand made on him, he answered by reciting Sura 112, and enquiring whether that were created. His people were very angry with him for leaving them without means of support, for he had about 40 persons dependent on him. But the very day his stipend was cut off, a stranger brought to him a purse of 1000 dirhems (his stipend from al-Maʾmûn had been 500 per month), and promised him that he should receive the same amount each month from the same source. He died in Baghdâd in 220 A. H. During his life he was one of the leading men in Baghdâd and a friend of Aḥmed's who had much influence with him [1]). Another to whom the Miḥna was applied in

---

1) al-Maḳrîzî, p. 13, واما عفان بن مسلم فقال حنبل بن اساحاق كنت حاضرا عند عفان بعدَ ان امتُحن فساله يحيى بن معين بحضور ابى عبد الله احمد بن حنبل ونحن معه فقال يابا عثمن أَخبرنا بما قال لك اسحق بن ابراهيم فى المحنة وما رددت عليه فقال عفانُ لابن معين يابا زكريا لم اسوّد وجهك ولا وجوه اصحابك يعنى انه لم يجب الى القول بخلق القران فقال له فكيفَ كان فقال دعانى اسحق ابن ابراهيم فلما دخلت عليه قرا الكتاب الذى كتبه المامون من ارض الجزيرة الى الرَّقّة [Cod. الرِقة] فاذا فيه امتحن عفان وادّعه الى ان يقول القرانُ كذا وكذا فان قال ذلك فأقِره على امره وان لم يجبك فاقطع عنه الذى يجرى عليه وكان المامون يُجرى عليه فى كل شهر خمس مائة درهم قال عفان فلما قرأ علىّ الكتاب قال لى ما تقول فقرات عليه قُلْ هُوَ ٱللّٰهُ أَحَدٌ [Kor. 112] الى اخرها وقلت امخلوق هذا

Abû Nuʿaim al-Faḍl ibn Dukain.

this Khalifate, and who did not yield was the Kûfite, Abû Nuʿaim al-Faḍl ibn Dukain. When al-Maʾmûn's letter came to Kûfa he was told of its purport and exclaimed, 'It means only beating with whips'; and, then, taking hold of a button of his coat, he said, 'to me my head is of less consequence than that'. Of his trial we have no particulars, but he, at all events, does not appear to have died a violent death. He died in 219 A. H. [1]).

ʿAlî ibn al-Madînî.

ʿAlî ibn al-Madînî is classed with those who surrendered their faith at the time of the Miḥna, apparently about the beginning of its course. He bitterly regretted his weakness, however, and was firmly reestablished in the orthodox faith before his death in 234 A. H. [2]).

فقال لى اسحق ان امير المومنين امر ان لم تجبه بقطع عنك ما يجرى عليك وانْ قطع عنك امير المومنين قطعنا عنك نحن ايضا فقلت له قال الله تعالى وَفِى ٱلسَّمَآءِ رِزْقُكُمْ وَمَا تُوعَدُونَ [Kor. 51. 22] فسكت عنى اسحق وانصرفت فسُرَّ ابو عبد الله ويحيى ومَن كان حاضرا فلما رجع الى داره عَذله اهل بيته وكان اربعين نفسا فبعد قليل دَقّ عليه البابَ انسان فدخل ومعه كيس فيه الف درهم فقال يابا عثمن ثبتك الله كما ثبّتّ الدين وهذا لك فى كل شهر

1) al-Makrîzî, p. 13, وقال الامام ابو بكر بن ابى شيبة لما جاءت المحنة الى الكوفة قال لى احمد بن يونس الق ابا نعيم فقل له فلقيته فقلت له فقال انما هو ضرب الاسياط [so Cod.] ثم اخذ زِرّ ثوبه وقال راسى اهونُ علىّ من هذا Abû Nuʿaim al-Faḍl ibn Dukain was a Shyite according to Shahrastânî, Haarbrücker's transl'n I, 218.

2) al-Subkî, p. 185, وكان على المدينى ممن اجاب الى القول بخلق القران فى المحنة فنُقم ذلك عليه وزيد عليه فى القول والصحيح عندنا انه انما [Cod. انها] اجاب خشية السيف الخ . . . .

Aḥmed in Prison. In the common prison Aḥmed ibn Ḥanbal was confined for a considerable time, the whole period, from the time of his arrest until he was set free after being scourged by al-Muʿtaṣim, being twenty-eight months. While in the prison he used to lead the prayers with the inmates, and engaged in the study of books which were provided for him by his friends. His good friend Bûrân did him the kindness to send him daily cold water, by means of a boat.

During the first part of his imprisonment, his uncle Isḥâḳ ibn Ḥanbal spoke to the officials and attachés of the governor seeking to secure a release of his nephew from prison; but, failing to obtain any satisfaction, he appealed to Isḥâḳ ibn Ibrâhîm in person. With a view to securing from Aḥmed a modification of his position, Isḥâḳ then sent his chamberlain to the prison with Aḥmed's uncle, ordering him to report whatever might pass between them. When they came to the prison, Isḥâḳ ibn Ḥanbal urged his nephew to yield an assent to the doctrine which was being pressed upon him. He reminded him that his companions, with much less reason, had recanted and that he had justified them in doing so on the ground of the Taḳîa. Why then should he not recant? After much fruitless disputation, they made up their minds to leave him in prison; and he went on to say that imprisonment was a matter of very little concern to him — a prison or his own house it was all the same. To be slain with the sword, too, was not a matter which caused him great anxiety; the one thing that he feared was to be scourged. If that should befall him, he could not answer for his holding out against it. One of the prisoners then reminded him that in the case of scourging he need have no fear, for after two strokes of the whip, he would never know where

---

وقال محمد بن عثمان بن ابى شيبة سمعت على المدينى يقول قبل موته بشهرين القران كلام الله غير مخلوق ومن قال مخلوق فهو كافر

any that might follow would strike him. With this assurance the remaining anxiety of Aḥmed was completely dispelled [1]).

Another Citation before Isḥâḳ ibn Ibrâhîm. On the 17th of Ramaḍân, 219 A. H., that is, fourteen months from the time that he was stopped when on his way to al-Ma'mûn, he was brought from the common prison to the house of Isḥâḳ ibn Ibrâhîm, being bound with a single chain on his feet. While he was confined in the house of Isḥâḳ ibn Ibrâhîm, the latter sent

---

1) al-Maḳrîzî, p. 5, قال اسحاق ابن حنبل عمّ الامام احمد كنت اتكلم مع اصحاب السلطان والقُوّاد فى خلاص ابى عبد الله فلم يَتم لى امر فاستاذنت على اسحاق بن ابراهيم فدخلت اليه وكلمته فقال لحاجبه اذهب معه الى ابن اخيه ولا يُكلمِ ابنَ اخيه بشىء الا اخبرتنى به قال اسحاق فدخلت على ابى عبد الله ومعِى حاجبُه فقلت يا ابا عبد الله قد اجاب اصحابك وقد اعذرت فيما بينك وبين الله وبقيت انت فى الحبس والضيق فقال ابو عبد الله يا عم اذا اجاب العالم تَقِية والجاهل بجهل متى يتبين الحق قال فامسكت عنه قال فذكر ابو عبد الله ما رُوى فى التَّقية من الاحاديث فقال كيف تصنعون بحديث خباب انّ من كان قبلكم يُنشر احدهم بالمِنشار ثم لا يصُده ذلك عن دينه قال فيَئِسْنا منه ثم قال لستُ أبالى بالحبس ما هو ومنزلى الا واحد ولا قتلاً بالسيف انما اخاف فتنة بالسوط واخاف ان لا اصبر فسمعه بعض اهل الحبس وهو يقول ذلك فقال لا عليك يابا عبد الله ما هُو الا سوطان ثم لا تدرى اين يقع الباقى فلما سمع ذلك سُرّى عنه، قال ثم حُوّل ابو عبد الله الى دار اسحاق بن ابراهيم فى شهر رمضان

Abû Nuʿaim, 147b, adds [لليلة سبع عشرة خلت منه] سنة تسع عشرة ومائتين

to him every day two men to reason with him; their names were, respectively, Aḥmed ibn Rabâḥ and Abû Shuaib al-Hajjâm. These two men used to argue with him, and, finding him immovable, as they turned to go away each day they called for an extra chain to be placed upon his feet, until, finally, there were four chains upon them. One of the discussions which Aḥmed had was about the Knowledge of God. He asked one of the two inquisitors for his opinion on the subject, and the man said that the Knowledge of God was created. On hearing this Aḥmed called him an infidel, and, though reminded that he was casting insult upon the messenger of the Khalif, he refused to withdraw the charge. Aḥmed's reasoning was that the names of God as symbols of his attributes were in the Ḳorân; that the Ḳorân was part of the Knowledge of God, which is one of his attributes; that, therefore, he who pretended that the Ḳorân was created had denied God, and, also, that he who pretended that the names of God were created had denied God. Here the argument seems to be: The names of God are not created; but the names of God form some part of the Ḳorân; therefore, it follows that some part of the Ḳorân, at least, is not created.

Aḥmed Ordered to al-Muʿtaṣim. On the fourth night after he had been removed to the house of Isḥâḳ ibn Ibrâhîm, the messenger of the Khalif al-Muʿtaṣim, Bughâ al-Kabîr, arrived after the last prayer, bringing the command of the Khalif to Isḥâḳ to send Aḥmed to him. When Aḥmed was brought in to Isḥâḳ before going to al-Muʿtaṣim, the governor addressed him, reminding him that it was his life which was at stake, and that the Khalif had sworn that he would not kill him with the sword, but would scourge him stroke after stroke, and would throw him into a place where no light would ever reach him. Then, the governor proceeded to argue with him regarding the Ḳorân, quoting the text, 'Verily, we have made it a Ḳorân (reading) in the Arabic tongue', and he asked him, if there could be anything made unless it were created. Aḥmed answered with another text. 'He made them like grass to be eaten', and asked the governor, if he would conclude from such a text anything about their being created. In this case the argument turns upon the fact that the word جَعَلَ does not, necessarily, include the meaning of خَلَقَ.

Preparations were then made for bringing Aḥmed to al-Muʿtaṣim. The interest of Bughâ, the messenger of the Khalif, in his prisoner and his cause was no very intelligent interest. He inquired of Isḥâḳ ibn Ibrâhîm's messenger what Aḥmed was wanted for, and, on learning, he declared that he knew nothing about such things; that the limits of his faith as a Muslim did not extend beyond the declaration that 'there is no God but Allah, that Moḥammed is the Apostle of God, and that the Commander of the Faithful is of the relationship of the Prophet of God'. At the gate of the royal park they disembarked after a short trip on the Tigris. Aḥmed was taken out of the boat and put upon a beast, from which he was in danger of falling off, owing to his helplessness because of the weight of his chains. He was brought under these circumstances into the palace precincts [1]) and made to alight at a house in a room of which he was confined, without any lamp to enable him to see at night [2]). During the night

---

1) al-Muʿtaṣim's palace was in the eastern part of Baghdâd (vid. Jaʿqûbî, Bibl. Geogr. VII, ٢٥٥, 17). The general prison, if in the Darb al-Mufaḍḍal (but v. p. 85, note 2), was in the same quarter and Isḥâḳ the governor's residence may not have been at any great distance from this general prison. In any case it is clear that the trial and scourging took place in Baghdâd, where Aḥmed was well-known and had many admirers. Hence the popular demonstration against the Khalif when Aḥmed was flogged.

2) Abû Nuʿaim, 147b f. حدثنا محمد بن جعفر وعلى بن احمد والحسين بن محمد قالوا ثنا محمد بن اسماعيل ثنا ابو الفضل صالح ابن احمد بن حنبل قال قال ابى رحمه الله لما كان فى شهر رمضان لليلة سبع عشرة خلت منه حُوِلت من السجن الى دار اسحاق

he is said to have had a vision of ʿAlî ibn ʿÂsim, and in-

ابن ابرهيم وانا مقيد بقيد واحد يُوَجَّه الىّ فى كل يوم رجلان سماهما ابى قال ابو الفضل وهما احمد بن رَبَاح وابو شُعَيب الحجاج [الحجام .Cod. al-Makrîzî ,الحجاج] يكلمانى ويناظرانى فاذا ارادا الانصراف نُحى بقيد فقُيدت به فمكثت على هذه الحالة ثلاثة ايام وصار فى رجلى اربعةُ اقياد فقال لى [فقالى .Cod] احدهما فى بعض الايام فى كلام دارٌ وسَالتُه عن علم الله فقال علم الله مخلوق فقلت له يا كافر كفرتَ فقال لى الرسول الذى كان يَحضُر معهم من قِبلِ ابى اسحاق هذا رسول امير المومنين قال فقلت له ان هذا قد كفر وكان صاحبُه الذى يجى معه خارجا فلما دخل قلت له ان هذا زعم ان علم الله مخلوق فنظرِ اليه كالمُنْكر عليه ما قال ثم انْصَرفا قال ابى واسمآء الله فى القران والقران من علم الله فمن زعم ان القران مخلوق فهو كافر ومن زعم ان اسمآء الله مخلوقة فقد كفر قال ابى رحمه الله فلما كانت الليلة [ليلة .Cod] الرابعة * بعد العشآء الاخرة وجه المعتصم ببُغا الى اسحاق بن ابرهيم يأمُره بحملى فأُدخلت على اسحاق فقال لى يا احمد انّها والله نفسُك انه قد حلف ان لا يقتُلك بالسيف وان يَضْرِبك ضَربا بعد ضرب وان يُلْقِيَك فى موضع لا ترى فيه الشّمس اليس قد قال الله تعالى انّا جَعَلْنَاهُ قُرْاٰنًا عَرَبِيًّا [Kor. 43. 2] افيكُونُ مجعولٌ الا وهُوَ مخلوق قال ابى فقلت له قد قال الله فَجَعَلَهُمْ كَعَصْفٍ مَأْكُولٍ [Kor. 105. 5] افخلقهم فقال اذهبوا به قال ابى رحمه الله فانزلت الى شاطىٔ دجلة وأُحدرتُ الى الموضع المعروف بباب البستان ومعى بُغا الكبير ورسول من قبل اسحاق قال فقال بُغا لمحمد المحاربى بالفارسية ما تُريدون من هذا الرجل قال

terpreted it as being of good omen, assuring him of exaltation (علو) and protection from God (عصمة) [1]).

Trial before al-Muʿtaṣim. First Day. The next morning he was led to the palace in his chains and brought before the Khalif [2]). On this occasion, there were present with the Khalif Aḥmed ibn Abî Dowâd and his companions. It is said that

---

يُريدون منه ان يقول القرانُ مخلوق فقال ما اعرف شيئا من هذا الا
قول لا الٰه الا الله وانّ محمدا رسول الله وقرابةَ امير المومنين من رسول
الله قال ابى فلما صرنا الى الشط أُخرجت من الزورق فجُعلت
على دابّة والاقياد علىّ وما معى احد يُمسكنى فجعلت اكادُ اخِرّ
على وجهى حتى انتهى بى الى الدار فأُدخلت ثم عُرج بى الى
حجرة فصُيِّرتُ فى بيت منها وغلق على الباب واقعد عليه رجل
وذلك فى جوف الليل وليس فى البيت سراج فاحتجت الى الوَضوء
فمددْتُ يدى اطلب شيئا فاذا انا بإناء فيه ماء وطَسْت [Cod. وطَسْتة]
فتهيّأتُ للصلاة وقمتُ اصلى

1) al-Maḳrîzî, p. 4, قال حنبل بن اسحاق بن حنبل ابن عم الامام احمد سمعت ابا عبد الله يقول لما دعيت الى المحنة رايت فى المنام على بن عاصم فاوّلتها علوا وعصمة من الله عز وجل والحمد لله على ذلك

2) Abû Nuʿaim, 148 *a* ff. With a few exceptions which are indicated, the narrative is now drawn from this source until we reach p. 111; cf. Abu'l-Feda Annales II, 168. There is a short and mutilated account of the proceedings before al-Muʿtaṣim in al-Jaʿqûbî II. 576, 577. فلما اصبحت جاءنى الرسول فاخذ بيدى فادخلنى الدار واذا هو جالس وابنُ ابى دواد حاضر وقد جمع اصحابه والدّارُ غاصّة باهلها فلما دَنَوتُ منه سلمت فقال لى ادْنُهْ ادْنُهْ فلم يزل يُدنينى حتى قرُبتُ منه ثم قال لى اجلس فجلستُ وقد اثقلتنى الاقياد فلما مكثت هُنَيهة قلت تأذن فى الكلام فقال

when al-Muʿtaṣim first saw Aḥmed, he said to those about

تكلم قلت الى ما دعا اليه رسول الله صلى الله عليه وسلم فقال الى شهادة ان لا اله الا الله قال فقلت انا اشهد ان لا اله الا الله ثم قلت له انّ جَدَّك ابنَ عباس يَحكِى انّ وَفْدَ عبد القَيْس لما قَدِموا على رسول الله صلى الله عليه وسلم امرهم بالايمان بالله فقال اتدرون ما الايمانُ بالله قالوا الله ورسوله اعلم قال شهادةُ ان لا اله الا الله وانّ محمدا رسول الله واقامُ الصلاة وايتاء الزكاة وصَوْمُ رمضان وان تعطوا الخُمس من المغنم قال ابو الفضل حدّثناه ابى ثنا يحيى بن سعيد عن شعبة قال حدثنى ابو جمرة قال سمعت ابن عباس قال انّ وَفْدَ عَبدِ القيس لما قَدموا على رسول الله صلى الله عليه وسلم امرهم بالايمان بالله فذكر الحديث قال ابو الفضل قال ابى فقال لى عند ذلك لولا انى وجدتك فى يد من كان قبلى ما تَعَرّضت لك ثم التفت الى عبد الرحمن بن اسحاق فقال له يا عبد الرحمن الم آمُرك ان ترفع المحنة قال ابى فقلت فى نفسى الله اكبر انّ فى هذا نفرجًا للمسلمين قال ثم قال ناظروه وكَلِّموه ثم قال يا عبدَ الرحمن كَلمه فقال لى عبد الرحمن ما تقول فى القران قال قلتُ له ما تقول فى علم الله فسكت قال ابى فجعل يُكلمنى هذا وهذا فاردُّ على هذا واكلم هذا ثم اقول يا امير المومنين اَعْطُونى شيئا من كتاب الله او سنة رسول الله صلى الله عليه وسلم اقول به ما [Cod. omits] أراه قال فيقول ابن ابى دواد انت لا تقول الا ما فى كتاب الله او سنة رسول الله صلى الله عليه وسلم قال فقلت له تأوَّلتَ تاويلا فانتَ اعلم وما تَاولتَ ما يُحبَس عليه ويُقَيَّد عليه قال فقال ابن ابى دواد هو والله يا امير المومنين ضَالّ مُضل مبتدع * وهولاء قُضاتك والفقهاء فَسَلْهم فيقول لهم ما تقولون

him reproachfully, 'Did you not pretend that this was a

فيقولون يا امير المومنين هو ضال مضل مبتدع قال ولا يزالون يكلمونى قال وجعل صوتى يعلو على اصواتهم وقال لى انسان منهم قال الله مَا يَأْتِيهِمْ مِنْ ذِكْرٍ مِن رَبِّهِمْ مُحْدَثٍ [Korân 21. 2] افيكون محدث الا مخلوق قال فقلت له قال الله تعالى صٓ وَٱلْقُرْآنِ ذِى ٱلذِّكْرِ [Korân 38. 1] فالذكر هو القرآن وتلك ليس فيها الف ولا لام قال فجعل ابن سَماعة لا يَفهم ما اقول قال فجعل يقول لهم ما يقول قال فقالوا له انّه يقولُ كذا وكذا قال فقال لى انسان منهم حديث خبّاب يا هناه تقرب الى الله بما استطعت فانك لن تتقرب اليه بشىء هو احبُ اليه من كلامه قال ابى فقلتُ له نعم هكذا هو قال فجعل ابنُ ابى دواد يَنظر اليه ويَلحظ متغيظا عليه قال ابى وقال بعضهم اليس قال الله خالق كل شىء قال قلت قد قال تُدَمِّرُ كُلَّ شَىْءٍ [Korân 46. 24] فدَمَّرَتْ الا ما اراد الله قال فقال بعضهم فما تقول وذكر حديث عمران بن حصين انّ الله تعالى كتب الذكر فقال انّ الله خلق الذكر فقلت هذا خطأ حدثناه غير واحد .ان الله كتبَ الذكر قال ابى فكان اذا انقطع الرجل منهم اعترض ابنُ ابى دواد فتكلم فلما قاربَ الزوال قال لهم قُوموا ثم احتبس عبدَ الرحمن بن اسحاق فخَلا بى وبعبد الرحمن فجعل يقول لى اما تعرف صالحا الرشيدى كان مُودبى وكان فى هذا الموضع جالسا واشار الى ناحية من الدار قال فتكلم وذكر القران فخالفنى فامرتُ به فسُحبَ ووُطى ثم جعل يقول ما اعرفك الم تكن تاتينا فقال له عبد الرحمن يا امير المومنين اعرفه منذ ثلاثين سنة يرى طاعتك و الحج و الجهاد معك وهو ملازم لمنزله قال فجعل يقول والله انه لفقيه وانه لعالم وما يَسُرّنى ان يكون مثله معى

يرد على اهل الملل ولئن اجابني الى شيء له فيه ادنى فرج لاطلقن عنه بيدى ولاطان عقبه ولاركبن اليه بجندى قال ثم يلتفت الىّ فيقول ويحك يا احمد ما تقول قال فاقول يا امير المومنين أعطونى شيئا من كتاب الله او سنة رسول الله صلى الله عليه وسلم فلما طال بنا المجلس ضجر فقام فرددت الى الموضع الذى كنت فيه ثم وجه الىّ برجلين سماهما وهما صاحب الشافعى وغسّان من اصحاب ابن ابى دواد يناظرانى فيقيمان معى حتى اذا حضر الافطار وجه الينا بمآئدة عليها طعام فجعلا ياكلان وجعلت اتعلّل حتى ترفع المآئدة و اقاما الى غد فى خلال ذلك يجىء ابن ابى دواد فيقول لى يا احمد يقول لك امير المومنين ما تقول فاقول له اعطونى شيئا من كتاب الله او سنة رسول الله صلى الله عليه وسلم حتى اقول به فقال لى ابن ابى دواد والله لقد كتب اسمك فى السبعة فمحوته ولقد سآءنى اخذهم اياك وانه والله ليس السيف انه ضرب بعد ضرب ثم يقول لى ما تقول فارد عليه نحوا مما رددت عليه ثم يأتينى رسوله فيقول اين احمد بن عمار اجب للرجل [Cod. الرجل] الذى انزلت** فى حجرته فيذهب ثم يعود فيقول لى يقول لك امير المومنين ما تقول فارد عليه نحوا مما رددت على ابن ابى دواد فلا تزال رسله تاتى احمد بن عمار وهو يختلف فيما بينى وبينه ويقول يقول لك امير المومنين اجبنى حتى اجى فاطلق عنك بيدى قال فلما كان فى اليوم الثانى ادخلت عليه فقال ناظروه وكلموه قال فجعلوا يتكلمون هذا من هاهنا* وهذا من هاهنا فارد على هذا وهذا فاذا جاءوا بشىء من الكلام مما ليس فى كتاب الله ولا سنة رسول الله صلى الله عليه وسلم ولا فيه خبر ولا اثر قلت ما ادرى ما هذا قال

**) Cod. انزلتَ, but if we read للرجل the correction is obviously necessary; i. e. 'pointing to the man in whose dwelling I had been lodged'.

فيقولون يا امير المومنين اذا توجّهتْ له الحجة علينا وثب واذا كلمناه بشيء يقول لا أدرى ما هذا قال فيقول ناظروه ثم يقول يا احمد انى عليك شفيق فقال رجل منهم اراك تذكر الحديث وتنتحله [Cod. تنحله] قال فقلت له فما تقول فى قول الله تعالى يُوصِيكُمُ ٱللَّهُ فِى أَوْلَادِكُمْ لِلذَّكَرِ مِثْلُ حَظِّ ٱلْأُنْثَيَيْنِ [Kor. 4. 12] فقال خص الله بها المومنين قال فقلتُ له ما تقول ان كان قاتلا او عبدا او يهوديا او نصرانيًّا فسكت. قال انى فانما احتججْت عليهم بهذا لانهم كانوا يحتجون علىّ بظاهر القران ولقوله اراك تَنتَحِل الحديث وكان اذا انقطع الرجل اعترض ابن ابى دواد فيقول والله يا امير المومنين لئن اجابك لَهو احب الىّ من مائة الف دينار ومائة الف دينار فيَعُدّ ما شآء الله اليه من ذلك ثم امرهم بعد ذلك بانقيام وخَلا بى وبعّبد الرحمن فيدور بيننا [Cod. فينا] كلام كثير وفى خلال ذلك يقول تدعوا احمد بن ابى دواد فاقول ذلك اليك فيُوَجه فيجى فيتكلم فلما طال بنا المجلس قام ورُدِدتُ الى الموضع الذى كنت فيه وجآءنى الرجلان اللذان كانا عندى بالأمس فجعلا يتكلمان فدار بيننا كلام كثير فلما كان وقت الافطار جِىء بطعام على نَحوِ مما اتى به فى اول الليلة فافطروا وتعلّلْتُ وجعَلتْ رُسُله تاتى احمد بن عمار فيمضى اليه فيأتينى [Cod. بيأتينى] برسالة على نحوِ مما كان فى اوّل ليلة فجاء ابن ابى دواد فقال له انه قد حلف ان يَضربك ضربا بعد ضرب وان يَحبسك فى موضع لا ترى فيها الشمس فقلت له فما اصنَع حتى اذا كِدتُ ان اصبح قلت لخليقٌ ان يحدُث فى هذا اليوم من امرى شىء وقد كنتُ اخرجت تكّتى من سَراويلى فشدّدتُ به الاقياد احملها بها اذا توجهت اليه فقلت لبعض من كان مع

الموكّل بى أُريد لى خَيطا فجآءنى بخيط فشَدَدْتُ بها الاقياد واعدت التكة فى سراويلى ولبستها كراهِيَة ان يَحدث شىء من امرى فاتَعرى فلما كان فى اليوم الثالث أُدخلتُ عليه والقومُ حضور فجعلتُ أُدخَلُ من دار الى دار وقوم معهم السيوف وقومٌ معهم السياط وغير ذلك من الزِى والسلاح وقد حُشِيَت الدار بالجُند ولم يكن فى اليومين الماضيين كَبير احد من هولآء حتى اذا صِرت اليه قال ناظِروه وكلموه فعادوا بمثل مناظرتهم فدار بيننا وبينهم كلامٌ كثير حتى اذا كان فى الوقت الذى كان يخلو بى فيه نحّانى ثم اجتمعوا وشاورهم ثم نَحّاهم ودعانى فخلا بى وبعبد الرحمن فقال لى ويحك يَا احمد انا والله عليك شفيق وانى لأُشفِق عليك مثلَ شفقتِى على هرون ابْنى فاجبْنى فقلت يا امير المومنين اعطُونى شيئا من كتاب الله او سُنّةِ رسول الله صلى الله عليه وسلم فلما ضَجِر وطال المجلس قال عليك لَعنة الله لقد كنت طمِعتُ فيك خُذوه خَلِّعوه ثيابه اسحَبُوه قال فاخذت فَسُحِبتُ ثم خلعت ثم قال العُقابين [قال لى انعقاربين .Cod] والسَّياط فجىء بعُقابين [read بالعُقابين ?] والسياط فقال ابى وقد كان صار الىّ شعرتان من شَعر النبى صلى الله عليه وسلم فصَررتهما فى كم قميصى فنظر اسحاق بن ابرهيمَ الى الصُرّة فى كم قميصى فوجّه الىّ ما هذا مصرور فى كم قميصك [كمك Margin, variant] فقلت شعر من شعر النبى صلى الله عليه وسلم وسَعَى بعض القوم الى القميص ليُخرقه فى وقت ما اقمت بين العُقابين فقال لهم لا تخرقوه انزِعوه عنه قال ابى ظننت انه * درى عن القميص الخرق لسبب الشعر الذى كان فيه ,صيرت بين العُقابين وشدّت يدى وجِىء بكرسى فَوُضع له وابن ,ب دواد قائم على راسه والناس اجمعون قيام مِمّن حضر فقال لى

انسان مِمَّن شدّنى خُـذ نابَي الخَشَبَتيْن بيدكَ وشُدَّ عليهما فلم افهم ما قال قال فتخلّعتْ يـدى لما شُـددتُ ولم امسك الخشبتين قال ابـو الفضل ولم يـزل ابـى رحمه الله يتوجّـع منهما من الرُسغ الى ان توفى ثم قال للجلّادين تـقـدموا فنظر الى السياط فـقـال ائتوا بغيرها ثم قال تقدمـوا فقال لاحدهم ادنه اوْجع قطَع الله يدك فتقدم فضرَب سـوطين ثم تنحّى ثم قال ادنُـه شـد قطع الله يدَك فتقدم فضرَبنى سوطين ثم تنحى فلم يزلْ يدعو واحدًا بعد واحد فيضربنى سَوطين ثم يتنحى ثم قام حتى جاءنى وهم مُحدقون به فقال ويحك يا احمد تقتُل نفسَـك وَيْحك اجبْنى اطـلـق عنك بـيـدى قال فجعل بعضهم يقول لى وَيحك امـامُـك على راسك قآئم قال وجعل عُجَيفٌ ينخُسنى بقآئم سَيْفه ويقولُ تُريـد ان تغلب هولآء كلهم قال وجعَل اسحاق بن ابـرهيم يَقولُ وَيْلك الخليفة على راسـك قائـم ثم يقول بعضهم يـا اميرَ المومنين دَمُه فى عُنقى قال ثم رجع فجلس على الكرسى ثم قال للجلّاد ادْنُـه شـد قطعَ الله يدَك ثم لم يزَلْ يدعو جلّادا [Cod. جلّاد] بعد جلاد فيضربنى سوطين ويتَنَحّى وهو يقولُ له شُدَّ قطع الله يدك ثم قام الىَّ الثانية فجعل يقولُ يـا احمد اجِبْنى فجعل عبد الرحمن بن اسحاق يقول لى مَن صنَع بنفسه من اصحابك فى هذا الامر ما صنَعت هـذا يحيى بـن معين وهـذا ابـو خيثمة وابنُ ابى اسرائيل وجعل يُعددُ علىَّ من اجـاب وجَعل هو يقول ويحك اجِبنى قال فجعلت اقول نحوا مما كنت اقوله لهم قال فرجع فجلس ثم جعل يقول للجلّاد شُدَّ قطع الله يـدك قال ابى فـذهـب عقلى وما عَقَلتُ الا وانـا فى حُجْرٍ مطلق عـن الاقياد فقال انسان ممّن حَـضَـر انا كبّبناك على وجهك وطـرَحْنَا على ظهرك بـاريـة ودُسنَـاك قال ابى فقُلت ما شعرتُ بذلـ

قال فجاءونى بسويق فقالوا لى اشرَب وتقيَّأ فقلت لا افطر ثم جىء بى الى دار اسحاق بن ابرهيم قال ابى فنُودِى بصلاة الظهر فصلّينا الظهر فقال ابن سَماعةَ صليت والدمُ يَسيلُ من ضربك فقلت قد صلّى عُمر رضى الله عنه وجُرحه يَثعَبُ دما فسكت ثم خلى عنه فصار الى المنزل [قال ?Cod. omits] ووُجِّه الىّ برجل من السجن ممن يُبصِر الضرب والجراحات ويُعالِج منها فنَظر اليه فقال أنا والله لقد رايتُ من ضُرب الف سوط ما رايت ضربا اشد من هذا لقَدْ جُرّ عليه من خلفه ومن قدامه ثم أدخل ميلا فى بعض تلك الجراحات وقال لم يُنقب فجعل يانيه ويُعالجه وقد كان اصحاتّ [cf. Tâj al-ʿArûs] وجهه غير ضربة ثم يمكث يعالجه ما شآء الله ثم قال له ان هاهنا شيئا أُريدُ انْ اقطعه فجآء بحديدة فجعل يُعلق اللحم بها ويقطعُه بسكين معه وهو صابر بذلك يحمد الله فى ذلك فبرأ منه ولم يزل يتوجع من مواضع منه وكان اثر الضرب بينًا فى ظهره الى ان توفى رحمه الله، قال ابو الفضل سمعت ابى يقول والله لقد اعطيت المجهودَ من نَفسى ولوددتُ انى انجو من هذا الامر كفافا لا على ولا لى قال ابو الفضل واخبرنى احد الرجلين اللذين كانا معه وقد كان هذا الرجل يعنى صاحب الشافعى صاحب حديث قد سمع ونظر ثم جآءنى بعد فقال يابن اخى رحمةُ الله على ابى عبد الله ما رايت احدا بِعَيْنى يشبهُه لقد جعلت اقول له فى الوقت ما يوجه الينا بالطعام يابا عبد الله انتَ صائم وانت فى موضع تقيّة* ولقد عطِش فقال لصاحب الشراب نَاولنى نناوله قَدحًا فيه مآء وثلج فاخذه فنظر اليه هنيهة ثم ردّه عليه قال جعلت اعاجب اليه من صَبْره على الجوع والعطش وما هو فيه من بهول قال ابو الفضْل وكنت التمس واحتال ان اوصِل اليه طعاما او

young man, but this man is not young' [his age was 54] [1]). The Khalif, on his entering, commanded him to draw near and bade him sit down. Then Aḥmed asked permission to speak, and, having received it, put the question, 'To what did the Messenger of God give invitation?' The Khalif said, "To the testimony 'that there is no God but Allah'." Aḥmed replied, 'I testify that there is no God but Allah'; and, after he had professed his adherence to the five cardinal points of Islâm, the Khalif told him that if he had not been apprehended by his predecessor in the Khalifate he would not have taken any action against him. Then, turning to Abd al-Raḥmân ibn Isḥâḳ, al-Muʿtasim asked him if he had not given him command to abolish the Miḥna. On hearing this, Aḥmed was overjoyed, supposing that it was really the Khalif's intention to deliver his subjects from the objectionable test. Following this, there was disputation, in which the Khalif ordered Abd al-Raḥmân ibn Isḥâḳ to take a part. This man then put the question to Aḥmed, 'What dost thou say about the Ḳorân?' Aḥmed returned him no direct answer, but, in turn, asked him 'what he had to say about the Knowledge of God'. To this Abd al-Raḥmân made no reply. During the Miḥna this question was, with Aḥmed, a favorite device in argument and one by means of which he generally put his opponents in embarrassment. The force of the argument lies in the fact that the Ḳorân is declared to be knowledge from God, and Aḥmed and such as he regarded this as equivalent to its being inseparable from the Knowledge of

---

رغيفا او رغيفين فى هذه الايام فلم اقدر على ذلك واخبرنى رجل حضره قال تفقّدته فى هذه الايام وهم يناظرونه ويُكلمونه فما لحن فى كلمة وما ظننت ان احدًا يكونُ مثل شجاعته وشدة قلبه قدس الله روحه

1) al-Makrîzî, p. 5: فلما نظر اليّ المعتصم سمعته يقول لهم كالمنكر عليهم اليس قد زعمتم انه حدث السن هذا شيخ مكتهل

God. 'If this Knowledge', say they, 'be uncreated then the Ḳorân must be uncreated'. Another point which Abd al-Raḥmân urged was that 'God existed when a Ḳorân did not exist ; to this Aḥmed replied with the same argument, 'Did God exist and not his Knowledge?' [1]).

During the passage between Abd al-Raḥmân ibn Isḥâḳ and Aḥmed, the latter asked Abd al-Raḥmân what his master al-Shâfiʿî had taught him about the ritual washing of the feet, and Ibn Abî Dowâd, in great astonishment, exclaimed, 'Behold a man who is face to face with death indulging in questions over Fiḳh!' [2]).

One of those in the room recited a tradition of ʿImrân ibn Ḥuṣain that God created الذكر and الذكر is the Ḳorân; to this Aḥmed answered that he had the tradition from more than one authority in the form, 'God wrote الذكر'. The bearing of this tradition as corrected by Aḥmed is to the effect that the substance and words of the Ḳorân were not created but that the earthly record was. Another tradition which was adduced was that of Ibn Masʿûd, 'God did not create in paradise, hell, heaven and earth anything greater than the Throne verse' (Ḳorân 2. 256). Aḥmed's rejoinder was that the creation applied only to paradise, heaven, hell and earth, but

---

1) al-Maḳrîzî, p. 6, فقال لى عبد الرحمن كان الله ولا قران فقلت له اكان الله ولا علم فأمسك ولو زعم ان الله كان ولا علم كفر

2) Abû Nuʿaim, 144*b*, الحسن يقول أدخل احمد بن حنبل على الخليفة وعنده ابن ابى دواد وابو عبد الرحمن الشافعى فاجلس بين يدى الخليفة وكانو هوّلوا عليه وقد كانوا ضربوا عنق رجلين فنظر احمد الى ابى عبد الرحمن الشافعى فقال اى شىء تحفظ عن الشافعى فى المسح فقال ابن ابى دواد انظروا رجلا هوذا يقدم لضرب العنق يناظر فى الفقه،

did not apply to the Ḳorân — a construction which is admissible [1]).

Someone introduced the verse, 'What came to them of ذكر from their Lord was a thing newly produced', and asked, 'Can anything be newly produced unless it be created?' Aḥmed said the Ḳorân, Sura 38, declares, 'By the Ḳorân, the possessor of الذكر'; so الذكر is the Ḳorân but there is in that other (ذكر) no article. Here the argument is to shew that الذكر and the Ḳorân are identical in meaning, but ذكر without the article is not identical with the Ḳorân. Consequently, no argument can be based upon the declaration that ذكر was newly produced.

The words were cited, 'He is the creator of everything'. Against this Aḥmed quoted, 'Thou dost destroy everything'; and he added, 'Dost thou destroy except what God wills?' The argument is that the term 'everything' must be understood in harmony with declarations as to the unoriginate character of the Ḳorân found elsewhere within the Book itself.

It is said that, in the course of the discussion, Ibn Abî Dowâd lost his patience because Aḥmed insisted on keeping to the Ḳorân and the Tradition. Aḥmed's defence was to the effect that his course was justifiable, for Ibn Abî Dowâd was putting a construction upon the Ḳorân with which sincere minds could not agree, and, failing to agree, the men were being cast into prison and loaded with chains. With this Ibn Abî Dowâd called upon the Khalif to ask his ḳâḍîs and faḳîhs if Aḥmed were not a man misled, misleading

---

1) al-Maḳrîzî, p. 6, واحتجوا عليّ بحديث ابن مسعود وما خلق الله من جنة ولا نار ولا سماء ولا ارض اعظم من اية الكرسى [Ḳor. 2. 256] قال ابو عبد الله فقلت انما وقع الخلق على الجنة والنار والسماء والارض ولم يقع على القران

and heretical. On his enquiring of them they declared he was such. On this occasion Aḥmed repeatedly protested to the Khalif that his opponents were not adhering to the authorities which alone could settle such disputes [1]. Indeed, Aḥmed seems to have been the most vehement of all the disputants. Ibn Abî Dowâd shewed his zealot spirit, likewise, by frequently interjecting his opinion. On the first occasion of his interference, Aḥmed did not answer him, and, when al-Muʿtaṣim rebuked him for it, he replied that he was not aware that Ibn Abî Dowâd was a man of learning [2].

When it came to the time of closing the Khalif bade all present arise; and after the session was ended, the Khalif and Abd al-Raḥmân ibn Isḥâḳ had a private conference with Aḥmed, in which al-Muʿtaṣim mentioned to him the punishment he had visited upon his own private tutor Ṣâliḥ al-Rashîdî for opposing him in regard to the Ḳorân. He complained, too, that Aḥmed had not given him any chance to learn his views or their vindication. Abd al-Raḥmân, however, explained that he had known Aḥmed for thirty years as a pious Muslim who observed the Hajj and the Jihâd and was a loyal subject of the Khalif. In view of what Abd al-Raḥmân said, and of what he himself had heard of Aḥmed's answers, al-Muʿtaṣim then exclaimed, 'Surely, this man is a faḳîh! surely, he is a man of learning [ʿâlim]! and I would that I had men such as he with me to take part in managing my affairs, and to effectually answer the advocates of other religions'. He, further, professed himself ready to suspend at once all action against Aḥmed, and to support him with all his power, if he would but give him the very slightest

1) cf. Dozy, Het Islamisme, 152.

2) al-Maḳrîzî, p. 6, قال ابو عبد الله كان القوم اذا انقطعوا عن الحجة عرّض ابن ابى دُواد فتكلم وكلمنى مرة فلم التفت اليه فقال لى المعتصم الا تكلمه فقلت لست اعرفه من اهل العلم فاكلمه قال ابو عبد الله وكان ابن ابى دواد من اجهل بالعلم والكلام

mission as a ground for doing so. To this Aḥmed made answer in harmony with what he had said before, asking for some justifying passage from the Ḳorân or from the Tradition of the Prophet.

This closed the first day's proceedings, and Aḥmed was sent back to his place of confinement, where two men, one a follower of al-Shâfiʿî and a certain Ghassân, of the following of Ibn Abî Dowâd, visited him and engaged in conversation and disputation with him until the next morning. In the meanwhile, the evening meal was brought in and the two visitors partook; but Aḥmed, though strongly pressed and though suffering from hunger, would not touch anything. Before the audience of the next day Ibn Abî Dowâd himself brought a message from the Khalif enquiring as to whether Aḥmed had changed his mind or not. Ibn Abî Dowâd, also, expressed his personal sorrow at his arrest, especially in view of the Khalif's resolution not to execute him with the sword, in case he should refuse to recant, but to scourge him stroke after stroke until he should be brought to a change of mind or should die under the lash. He assured Aḥmed that the Khalif al-Ma'mûn had written his name among the first seven who were summoned, but that he had been instrumental in securing its erasure [1]). To all these persuasions Aḥmed replied with the same plea for some satisfactory ground from either the Ḳorân or the Tradition on which to base a change of faith. The man in whose house he was detained, Aḥmed ibn ʿAmmâr, was, also, sent to him repeatedly with messages from the Khalif, but all in vain.

Second Day. On the second day, the proceedings were much the same as those of the previous audience. Whenever they used the Ḳorân or a tradition of recognized authority Aḥmed shewed himself ready to meet them, and appears to have been fully able to hold his own. When, however, they adopted any other method of argument, he refused absolutely to recognize the validity of their proofs, and maintained a

1) cf. p. 64.

stubborn silence. He carried this practice out so thoroughl that his opponents complained to the Khalif that, when ever the argument was in his favor he had his answer ready, but, on the contrary, whenever it went in their favor he simply challenged the testimonies which they adduced. It seems to have troubled him that they should have insisted, as they sometimes did, on the letter of the Ḳorân; and, to shew them that they ought not to be too slavish in their adherence to the Ḳorân, he asked one of the disputants what he had to say about the text, 'God commanded you concerning your children, the male's portion shall be the portion of two females'. The man replied that the text related specially to the believers. Aḥmed then asked him, what would be the rule if the man were a murderer, a slave, a Jew, or a Christian. To this his opponent made no answer. This argument Aḥmed apologized for using on the ground of their annoying manner of argument with him; and it would appear from this case that he was prepared to follow the text of the Ḳorân as closely as practical necessity would allow, but admitted the need, in special cases, of modification or expansion by means of additional light from some other source. This additional light he apparently would have borrowed only from well-established Tradition.

On this day, as on the previous one, Aḥmed Ibn Abî Dowâd, whenever opportunity offered, took an active part in the discussion. In one of Aḥmed ibn Ḥanbal's three examinations in this trial, probably in the first or second, when he had declared his faith in the Ḳorân as uncreated, it was retorted upon him that he was setting up a similar being to God (dualistic view) [1]). His reply was, 'He is one God, eternal; none is like him and none is equal. He is even as he has described himself' [2]). At the close of this session a private conference between the Khalif, Abd

---

1) Steiner, 77, cf. 90 f.

2) al-Maḳrîzî, p. 4, وكان ابو عبد الله اذا دُعى الى القول بخلق

al-Raḥmân and Aḥmed again occurred, to which Aḥmed ibn Abî Dowâd was afterwards called in. At its close, Aḥmed was returned to the place of detention, and the history of the first night was repeated. Messengers came and went, and the two men who had been with him before came back and stayed with him through the night. Before the next day came, Aḥmed had a premonition that an issue would surely be reached at the coming session, and prepared himself for it.

Third Day. When the messenger came the next day Aḥmed was brought to the palace of the Khalif, and his fear began to be confirmed as he saw the great display of pomp and of armed men, apparently prepared for some special occasion. First, there was an audience, in which the learned men disputed with him, and then followed another private conference in which the Khalif, as before, besought Aḥmed to yield, in however slight a degree, so that he might grant him his freedom. The Khalif assured him of his having as much compassion for him as he would have for his own son Hârûn in such a case. Aḥmed's reply was the invariable one, asking for some ground for a change of faith adduced from the only sources which he recognized as authoritative. Finally the Khalif lost all patience when he saw that his hopes of a ground for leniency toward his prisoner were to be disappointed, and he ordered him to be taken away and flogged. The flogging then ensued. Before it occurred, a little knot was noticed in the sleeve of Aḥmed's ḳamîṣ, and he was asked what might be the explanation of it. He said that it held two hairs of the Prophet [1]). On learning this Isḥâḳ ibn Ibrâhîm saved

Aḥmed Scourged.

القران وضرب بالسياط يقول القران كلام الله غير مخلوق فاذا قيل له القول بذلك يؤدى الى التشبيه يقول احد صمد لا شبيه له ولا عدل وهو كما وصف به نفسه

1) On hairs of the Prophet as charms cf. Goldziher, Moh. Stud. II, 358.

the ḳamîṣ from being destroyed. Before and during the course of the flogging, the Khalif sought to secure from Aḥmed a recantation, and seems to have been moved by compassion for him, though equally moved by a determination to drive him to repent of his obstinate refusal. Ibn Abî Dowâd and the leaders who were with him did their best, however, to move the Khalif to put Aḥmed to death. When bound, Aḥmed complained to the Khalif that the punishment he was inflicting upon him was unlawful according to the declaration of the Prophet, who had said that the blood and possessions of any man who confessed that there was no God but Allah, and that he was God's Messenger, were inviolable. Aḥmed Ibn Abî Dowâd, thinking his master inclined to weaken out of admiration for Aḥmed's spirit and courage and from the conviction wrought by his arguments, reminded al-Muᶜtaṣim that, if he yielded, he would certainly be said to oppose the doctrines of the former Khalif al-Maʾmûn, and men would regard Aḥmed as having obtained a victory over two sovereigns, a result which would stimulate him to assume a leadership fraught with evil consequences to the dominion of the Khalifs [1]). As he was bound to the whipping-posts the lictors, one hundred and fifty in

---

1) al-Maḳrîzî, p. 7, قل ابو عبد الله وجُعلت بين العُقابين فقلت يا امير المومنين ان رسول الله صلعم قل لا يحل دم امرء مسلم يشهد ان لا اله الا الله وانى رسول الله الا باحدى ثلاث الحديث وقل رسول الله صلعم امرت ان اقاتل الناس حتى يقولوا لا اله الا الله فاذا قالوها عصموا منى دماءهم واموالهم فيمَ تستحل دمى ولم آتِ شيئا من هذا يا امير المومنين اذكر وقوفك بين يدى الله عز وجل كوقوفى بين يديك يا امير المومنين راقب الله فلما راى المعتصم ثبوت ابى عبد الله وتصميمه لَانَ لابى عبد الله فخشى ابن ابى دواد من رافته

number it is said, advanced in turn and each struck him two strokes and then went aside [1]). At first, with each stroke Aḥmed uttered a pious ejaculation, concerning the exact tenor of which the accounts vary [2]). There is an apocryphal story to the effect that, after he had been struck twenty-

---

عليه فقال يا امير المومنين ان تركته قيل انك تركت مذهب المامون وسخطت قوله وانه غلب خليفتين فهاجه ذلك وطلب كرسيا جلس عليه وقام ابن ابى دواد واصحابه على راسه ثم قال للجلادين الخ

1) al-Subkī, p. 136, حدثنا ابو بكر السهروردى بمكة قال رايت ابا دن [Cod. در] بسهرورد . . . . وكان ممن ضرب احمد [بن حنبل] بين يدى المعتصم قال دعينا فى تلك الليلة ونحن خمسون ومائة جلاد ان امرنا بضربه كنا نعدوا على ضربه ونَمُرّ ثم يجى الاخر على اثره ثم يضرب [cf. Abū Nuʿaim, 150*b*, ثم دعا بجلّاد له يقال له ابو الدَّنِ فقال فى كم تقتله قال فى خمسة او عشرة او خمسة عشر او عشرين فقال اقتله]

2) al-Maḳrīzī, p. 8, فلما ضُرب سوطا قال بسم الله فلما ضرب الثانى قال لا حول ولا قوة الا بالله فلما ضُرب الثالث قال القران كلام الله غير مخلوق فلما ضرب الرابع قال قل لن يصيبنا الا ما كتب الله لنا فضربه تسعة وعشرين سوطا وكانت تكة سراويله حاشية ثوب فانقطعت فنزل السراويل الى عانته [?read عورته] فقلت الساعة ينهتك فرمى ابو عبد الله طرْفه نحو السماء وحرك شفتيه فما كان باسرع من ان بقى السراويل لم ينزل قال ميمون فدخلت الى ابى عبد الله بعد سبعة ايام فقلت يابا عبد الله رايتك يوم ضربوك قد انحلّ سراويلك فرفعت طرفك نحو السماء ورايتك تحرك شفتيك فاىّ شىء قلتَ قال قلتُ اللهم انى اسالك باسمك الذى ملات به العرش ان كنت تعلم

nine strokes, Aḥmed's nether garment threatened to fall to the ground, but that it was miraculously restored to its place and fastened securely, in answer to a prayer which

---

انی علی الصواب فلا تهتك لی سترا وروی انه قال یا من لا یعلم العرش منه این هو الا هُو ان کنتُ علی الحق فلا تُبْدِ عَوْرتی انتهی وذکر البیهقی انه فی اول سوط قال بسم الله وفی الثانی قال توکلت علی الله وهذا فی رضی الله وفی الثالث قال ما شآء الله کان وکل شیء عنده بمقدار وفی الرابع قال لا حول ولا قوة الا بالله وفی الخامس قال یا امیر المومنین انك موقوف ومُسائَلٌ عنی بین یدی رب لا یَظلم ویاخذ للمظلوم من الظالم وفی السادس قال یا امیر المومنین سالتك بالله والدار الاخرة قال وهو لا یرفع راسه الیه وفی السابع قال یا امیر المومنین اذکر الوقوف بین یدی الله کوقوفی بین یدیك لا تستطیع مَنعا ولا عن نفسك دفعا فلما ضربه الثامن اضطرب المئزر فی وسطه قال المروزی وعباس بن مسکویه الهمذانی لقد راینا احمد رفع راسه الی السماء وحرك شفتیه فما استتم الدعا حتی راینا کفا مِن ذهب قد خرج من تحت مئزره فرَدّ المئزر الی موضعه بقدرة الله تعالی فضجت العامة وهمّوا بالهجوم علی دار السلطان فامَر بحَلّه قال المروزی وابن مسکویه فدخلنا علی ابی عبد الله فقلنا ای شیء کان تحریك شفتیك عند اضطراب المئزر قال رفعت بصری الی السماء ونادیت یا غیاث المستغیثین ویا رب العالمین ان کنت تعلمُ انی قائم بحق فلا تهتك عورتی فاستجاب الله تعالی قال فکان اسحق بن ابراهیم یقول انا والله رایت یوم ضُرب احمد وقد ارتفع السراویل من بعد انخفاضه وانعقد من بعد انحلاله وما رایت یوما کان اعظم علی المعتصم من ذلك الیوم والله لو لم یرفع عنه الضرب لم یبرح من مکانه الا میتا

he uttered. Some of the accounts go even so far as to say that a hand of gold was seen to go out from under his upper garment and adjust what was deranged [1]). As the flogging progressed Aḥmed lost consciousness under the blows, and was removed in an unconscious state into a room near by. Meanwhile, the crowd outside the Palace court became moved with anger at the Khalif's treatment of Aḥmed, perhaps, too, the report of his collapse had reached them; in any case, they were preparing to attack the Palace, when the Khalif ordered the suspension of the punishment. This order was due, it is likely, more to the fear of the multitude on the part of al-Muᶜtaṣim than to any other cause. One account relates that, even after Aḥmed was brought in unconsciousness to the room, his torturers continued their abuse by trampling upon him with their feet. When consciousness came back he was offered sawîḳ for the purpose of producing vomiting, but he refused to take it. Subsequent to this, he was removed to the house of Isḥâḳ ibn Ibrâhîm, where, after a short detention, he was set free, and went to his own dwelling. The date when all this occurred was within the last ten days of Ramaḍân 219 A. H., though the particular day is not known [2]). Aḥmed does not seem to have harbored blame against the Khalif for having done what he did, and, afterwards, declared that he had no ill-will against any of those who had taken part in his persecution.

Sequel to the Scourging. In his own dwelling he was visited by the prison physician and treated until he was cured of his wounds. The scars, however, remained on him to the day of his death; and he never ceased to suffer from the dislocation of his wrists, which was brought about by neglect to take hold, as he was advised to do, of the upper parts [lit. teeth] of the whipping posts. When he failed to do this the principal weight of his body was suspended from the wrists. After the scourging, al-Muᶜtaṣim brought

---

1) vid. foregoing note. 2) Ibn Chall. N°. 19.

out Isḥâḳ ibn Ḥanbal (Aḥmed's uncle) to the people, and asked them to witness that he would testify that he [the Khalif] gave over to them their Imâm without hurt or damage to his body. It is said that if the Khalif had not caused this deception to be practised, the people would have risen in insurrection. As it was however, they were calmed and evil consequences were averted. It was the wish of Ibn Abî Dowâd that Aḥmed should now be imprisoned; but al-Muʿtaṣim was angry at the suggestion, and commanded his lieutenant Isḥâḳ to set Aḥmed free. It is probable, that in this instance, likewise, fear of a popular uprising deterred the Khalif from continuing to use severe measures against his prisoner. As matters stood al-Muʿtaṣim gave him the gala dress, and as already related had him sent to his dwelling; and, as long as he was confined to his house, had his lieutenant Isḥâḳ enquire every day about his condition. The gala clothes, however, Aḥmed sold and distributed the price in alms [1]).

---

1) al-Maḳrîzî, p. 8, فصل فيما وقع له رضى الله عنه بعد انقضاء المحنة قال ابن ابى حاتم سمعت ابا زرعة يقول دعا المعتصم باسحق عمّ احمد بن حنبل ثم قال للناس تعرفونه قالوا نعم قال فانظروا اليه اليس هو صحيح البدن [i. e. 'Look ye at him. Thou, Isḥâḳ ibn Ḥanbal, Is he, Aḥmed ibn Ḥanbal, not sound in body?' Isḥâḳ, thereupon, nodded assent. Supply after اليه, ثم قال لاسحق and after البدن, فقال براسه نعم]. ولو لا انه فعل ذلك لوقع شر لا يقدر على دفعه فلما قال قد سلمته اليكم صحيح البدن هَدَأَ الناس وسكتوا وكان ابن ابى دواد يحاول الخليفة على حبس ابى عبد الله وعدم إطلاقه ويقول يا امير المؤمنين احبسه فانه فتنة فغضب المعتصم وقال لنائبه يا اسحقُ اطلقه قال ابو عبد الله فلا يجد بُدا من ان يخلى عنى ولو لا ذلك لكان قد حبّسنى وقال المعتصم لهم ليس هذا كما وصفتم قال البيهقى وذلك انهم وضعوا من قدره وقللوه وصغروه عنده فلما شاهده وراى ما عنده

It is related that he remained only sixteen days at the Camp, and during this period used altogether as food a rub[c] of sawîḳ (i. e. four handfuls of parched barley ground to meal). He took every night a dram of water and every third night a handful of sawîḳ. So much wasted was he by these experiences that it was a full six months after his return home before he seemed like himself again [1]).

Miḥna in Egypt in the Reign of al-Muᶜtaṣim. During the short governorship of al-Muzaffar ibn Kaidar, who succeeded his father in Egypt, there came to him a letter from the Khalif al-Muᶜtaṣim ordering a renewal of the Miḥna. Al-Muzaffar tested the doctors in pursuance of the order he had

---

عرف له فضله وقال ميمون بن الاصبع أُخرج احمد بعد ان اجتمع الناس وضجوا حتى خاف السلطان فخرج قال البيهقى قال حنبل وخلع عليه المعتصم مُبَطَّنة وقميصا وطيلسانا وخُفّا وقلنسوة وأُخرج على دابة عند غروب الشمس فصار الى منزله ومعه الناس فدخل منزله ورَمَى بنفسه على وجهه وخلع ما كان خلّع عليه فامر به فبيع واخّذ ثمنه فتصدق به وبلغنا ان ابا اسحق يعنى المعتصم ندم وأُسقط فى يده وامرّ اسحق نائبه ان لا يقطع عنه خبره قال فكان اسحق ياتينا كل يوم يتعرف خبره حتى صح وبَرَا بعد العلاج وخرج للصلاة والحمد لله

1) Abû Nuᶜaim, 142*b* f. حدثنا ابى والحسين بن محمد قالا ثنا احمد ابن محمد بن عمر قال سمعت عبد الله بن احمد بن حنبل يقول * مكث ابى بالعسكر عند الخليفة ستة عشر يوما ما ذاق شيئا الا مقدار رُبْع سويقا كل ليلة كان يَشرب شربة ماء وفى كل ثلاث ليال يستَفّ حفنة من السويق فرجع الى البيت ولم ترجع اليه نفسُه الا بعد ستة اشهر ورايت مُوْقَيْه دخلا فى حدقتيه

received, but it brought him only an increase of the troubles of his short term of authority, and of the success of the test we know nothing [1]). After him we have no specific record of trials for the Ḳorân in Egypt, but it is sure that al-Buwaiṭî underwent an examination in Egypt in the reign of al-Wâthiḳ. A little later on his case will be again noticed. In the year 231 A. H. al-Wâthiḳ sent a letter to his governors commanding the revival of the inquisition [2]). It must have been in the examinations which followed this command that al-Buwaiṭî was cited to answer for his faith [3]).

Al-Muʿtaṣim and the Miḥna. Al-Subkî is, probably, right when he asserts that al-Muʿtaṣim had not the learning which qualified him to decide whether the doctrine of the Ḳorân's creation was right or wrong, and that the prosecution of the Miḥna by him was due, in great part, to the charge which was left him in the testament of al-Maʾmûn, and to the moving spirit among those by whom he was surrounded [4]). We do not hear of any further action against Aḥmed on the part of this Khalif. He died in the year 227 A. H.

Al-Wâthiḳ and Aḥmed. After the death of al-Muʿtaṣim and the accession of his son Hârûn al-Wâthiḳ, Aḥmed became a very popular teacher, and was much resorted to. Al-Ḥasan ibn ʿAlî the Ḳâḍî of Baghdâd noticing this wrote to Ibn Abî Dowâd of the circumstance. Aḥmed ibn Ḥanbal, however, heard of what had been done, and of his own will refrained from teaching, before any action was taken against him. Ibn Abî Dowâd once again tried to persuade al-Wâthiḳ to per-

1) Abu'l-Maḥ. I, 649.

2) Abu'l-Maḥ. I, 683; al-Sujûṭî, Ṭarîkh al-Kholafâ, ٣٤٦.

3) Abu'l-Maḥ. I, 686.

4) al-Subkî, p. 145, قال المورخون ومع كونه كان لا يدرى شيئا من العلم حمل الناس على القول بخلق القران قلت لان اخاه المامون اوصى اليه بذلك وانضم الى ذلك القاضى احمد بن ابى دواد وامثاله من فقهاء السوء cf. Weil, Chalifen II, p. 334.

secute Aḥmed, but was unsuccessful. The Khalif let Aḥmed alone; whether he was moved at all by admiration for him, or by a superstitious fear that something might happen to him should he lay violent hands on so holy a man, does not clearly appear [1]). It is reported of al-Wâthiḳ in relation to the Miḥna that he did not personally wish it, but that the stimulus applied by his minister did not leave him much opportunity to escape from the work in which the latter was so zealous. The greater probability, as far as Aḥmed ibn Ḥanbal enters into consideration, is that al-Wâthiḳ, like his predecessor, feared a popular outbreak should anything further be visited upon the Imâm. And, for the reason that he wished to please all parties, he took the course of asking Aḥmed to leave Baghdâd, and dwell at a distance from him. Aḥmed, however, did not go away; he simply withdrew into a comparative seclusion, which he maintained for the greater part of his remaining life.

Al-Wâthiḳ Prosecutes the Miḥna. Al-Wâthiḳ did, nevertheless, carry on the policy of his predecessors. His command to all the governors of the provinces to apply again the Miḥna for the Ḳorân has been already mentioned [2]). It was issued

---

1) al-Maḳrîzî, p. 8 f. فلمّا مات المعتصم وولّى ابنه هرون الواثق اكثر الناس من الاخذ عن الامام* احمد فشق ذلك على اهل البدَع فكتب لحسن بن على التجْعد قاضى بغداد الى ابن ابى دُواد ان احمد قد انبسط فى الحديث فلما بلغ ابا عبد الله امسك عن الحديث من نفسه من غير ان يُمنع واستمر ابن ابى دُواد يُحسّن للواثق امتحان الناس بخلق القران ففعل ذلك لكنه لم يتعرض للامام احمد قال الحافظ ابو الفرج اما لما عَلم من صبره او لانه خاف على نفسه ان يعرض له شىء ببركته يعنى كما عرض لابيه الا انه ارسل يقول له لا تُساكننى بارضى فاختفى الى ان مات الواثق vid. Weil, Chalifen II, 340; Abu'l-Maḥâsin I, 691.

2) vid. p. 114.

in 231 A. H. It is said that he gave this order, notwithstanding the fact that he had withheld his father al-Muʿtaṣim from the application of the Miḥna [1]). We have no record of those who were subjected to this examination, beyond the names and accounts of one or two who would not confess the doctrine of the Ḳorân's creation and suffered for their faith.

Aḥmed ibn Naṣr al-Khuzâʿî.

The best known of those who suffered under this Khalif was Aḥmed ibn Naṣr ibn Mâlik al-Khuzâʿî [2]) from the city of Merv, who was of one of

1) Abu'l-Maḥ. I, 683; al-Sujûtî, Tarîkh al-Khol. 346.

2) v. Kremer, Herrsch. Ideen des Isl. 243; Weil, Chal. II, 341 f.; Dozy, Het Islamisme, 156; al-Sujûtî, Tarîkh al-Kholafâ, 346; al-Jaʿqûbî, II, 589; Ṭabarî, III, ١٣٤٣ ff.; De Goeje, Fragm. Hist. Arab., I, 529 f.; al-Maḳrîzî, 10 f. فامّا احمد بن نصر فكان من اهل الدين والصلاح والامارين بالمعروف سمع الحديث من مالك بن انس وغيره وروى عنه يحيى بن معين وغيره دعاه الواثق الى القول بخلق القران فابى فامَر بضرب عنقه فضُرب وحمل راسه الى بغداد فنُصب فى الجانب الشرقى اياما وفى الجانب الغربى اياما وأَما جسده فصُلب بِسُرَّ مَن راى وروى الحافظ ابو الفرج بسنده الى ابراهيم بن اسمعيل قال كان احمد بن نصر خُتّلى فلما قتل فى المحنة وصُلب راسُه أُخبرتُ ان الراس يقرا القران فمضيت فبِتُّ بقرب من الراس وكان قد وُكل به مَن يحفظه فلما هدأت العيون سمعت الراس يقرا القران الٓمٓ أَحَسِبَ النَّاسُ أَنْ يُتْرَكُوا أَنْ يَقُولُوا آمَنَّا وَهُمْ لَا يُفْتَنُونَ [Ḳor. 29. 1] فاقشعر جلدى ثم رايته بعد ذلك فى المنام وعليه السندس والاستبرق وعلى راسه تاج فقلت ما فعل الله بك قال غفر لى وادخلنى الجنة قال المروزى* سمعت ابا عبد الله احمد بن حنبل وذكَر احمد بن نصر فقال رحمه الله ما كان اسخاه لقد جاد بنفسه

the leading families of his tribe. One of his teachers was Mâlik ibn Anas and of his pupils one was Yaḥya ibn Maᶜin. Ibn Naṣr was, at first, left unmolested, but afterwards was apprehended for a cause that will be presently shewn. He was, according to Aḥmed ibn Ḥanbal, a man of noble spirit, and we know from other sources that he was of distinguished ancestry, both his father and grandfather having held high places under the Abbâside khalifs. At the same time, he had a great name among the orthodox traditionists and was himself a man of staunch orthodox belief. For this reason, he had a deep hatred toward the Khalif and Ibn Abî Dowâd, and openly defied both by his bold profession that the Ḳorân was the uncreated Word of God. When the people of the quarter of Baghdâd known as ᶜAmr ibn ᶜAṭâ saw his temper and considered his rank, they induced him to lend his moral and, it may be, also his material support to a conspiracy against the Khalifate. It was all arranged that the city of Baghdâd was to be taken on a certain night, when the drunkenness of some of the conspirators on the night previous to that which had been appointed led them to give the signal for the attack on that night, with the result that the mass of the confederates did not respond, and the leaders of the conspiracy were at once arrested by order of the acting-governor, Moḥammed ibn Ibrâhîm, their arrest being due to the turning State's-evidence of one of the subordinate plotters. Strangely enough, when brought before al-Wâthiḳ, the latter asked Ibn Naṣr nothing about his part in the incipient insurrection, but began, instead, to question him about the Ḳorân and the actual seeing of God on the day of Resurrection [1]); perhaps, because the case against him on this count was much stronger than it would have been on that of sedition. When al-Wâthiḳ questioned him about his belief relative to the Ḳorân, he, however, in reply, would give nothing but that he believed it to be the Word of God.

1) al-Wâthiḳ had forbidden his subjects to profess either of these beliefs, Houtsma, De Strijd over het Dogma, 109.

One rather inflated tradition represents that Ibn Abî Dowâd urged the Khalif to give his prisoner a delay, as he was an old man temporarily out of his senses and would come to a better mind if allowed time. Al-Wâthiḳ in the tradition appears as rejecting this view, and as declaring that Ibn Naṣr's unbelief had disciplined him to the view he had expressed. Whatever may be the truth of this story, the trial had not proceeded far when the Khalif called for the execution carpet and the sword Samsama; and, desiring to be allowed to personally strike off the obstinate infidel's head, as he expected to be rewarded by Heaven for disposing of him, he was allowed to try to despatch the martyr. He could not accomplish it, however, and Sîma al-Dimashkî had to come to his aid and dispose of the man. The head was then ordered to be sent to Baghdâd; where for some days it was exposed to view in the eastern part of the city, and then for some days in the western part, after which it was fixed up permanently in the eastern portion. The execution occurred on the second last day of Shaʿbân, 231 A. H., and the trunk and head remained exposed to public view for six years, until the Khalif al-Mutawakkil ordered them to be taken down, and handed over for burial to Aḥmed ibn Naṣr's relations [1]).

A fabulous story, to the effect that the head, after being exposed, recited the Ḳorân until it was buried, is equalled by another which relates that, long years afterwards, a hunting party found the body and head of Aḥmed ibn Naṣr buried in the desert sand, and that there was not the slightest indication of decay upon them [2]).

---

1) Abu'l-Maḥ. I, 719.

2) al-Subkî, p. 142 f. قلت وبلغنى وما اراه الا فى تاريخ للحاكم ان بعض الامراء خرج يتصيد فالقاه السير على ارض نزل بها فعبث بعض غلمانه فى التراب فحصر [Read فحفر?] حتى راى ميتا فى قبره طريا وهو فى ناحية وراسه فى ناحية وفى اذنه رقعة عليها شىء مكتوب

Nuʿaim ibn Ḥammâd. Nuʿaim ibn Ḥammâd was another who held out. He was the fourth of a quartette who came from Merv and endured with steadfastness the Miḥna; the first was Aḥmed ibn Ḥanbal and the others, Moḥammed ibn Nûḥ al-Maḍrûb and Aḥmed ibn Naṣr. Nuʿaim ibn Ḥammâd studied Tradition a great deal in the Hijâz and ʿIrâḳ and went, afterwards, to Egypt. In the Khalifate of al-Wâthiḳ, he was brought from Egypt and examined; and, not satisfying the demand made upon him to confess the Ḳorân to be created, he was thrown into prison where he died [1]).

Abû Yaʿḳûb al-Buwaiṭî. Abû Yaʿḳûb, Yûsuf ibn Yaḥya al-Buwaiṭî, the pupil of al-Shâfiʿî to whom he entrusted his circle of scholars at his death, was imprisoned for his refusal to acknowledge that the Ḳorân was created, and died in prison 232 A. H. One of his fellow Shâfiʿites, al-Rabîʿ ibn Suleimân, relates that he saw al-Buwaiṭî in his chains, and heard him saying, 'God created the creation by 'Kun' [Be!], but, if 'Kun' be created, then it is as if a created thing created what was created [2]). By God! I will die in these thy chains, that

---

فاحضر من قراه فاذا هو بسم * الله الرحمن الرحيم هذا راس احمد بن نصر هذه الكلمات السابقة فعلموا انه راس احمد الخزاعى فدفن ورفع سنام قبره وكان هذا فى زمن الحاكم ابى عبد الله الحافظ وهو على طراوته وكيف لا وهو شهيد رحمه الله ورضى عنه

1) al-Maḳrîzî, p. 11, واما نعيم بن حماد فكان من اهل مرو طلب الكثير من الحديث بالحجاز والعراق ثم نزل مصر ثم اشخص منها فى خلافة الواثق وسئل عن القران فلم يوافقهم على ما ارادوه منه يعنى القول بخلقه فحبس حتى مات

2) 'Kun' is here employed as synonymous with a manifestation of the Heavenly Word of God (as explained later in the present work). Al-Buwaiṭî seems to have been in full agreement with his master al-Shâfiʿî, and the latter in turn with Aḥmed, as far at least as the Ḳorân was concerned (cf. p. 49 and Abu'l-Maḥ. I, 686). The discussion of 'Kun' in Houtsma, De Strijd etc., 129, seems to look toward other views than those held by the orthodox at the time of the Miḥna.

those coming after us may know that men have died in their bonds for this cause; and, if I go in to him [al-Wâthiḳ], I will declare the truth before him'. From prison he wrote to al-Rabîᶜ ibn Suleimân entrusting him with the care of his circle of pupils, and bidding him be faithful to them [1]).

The remaining history of the Miḥna in the reign of al-Wâthiḳ is shortly told. There is one incident which is in keeping with the fanatical bigotry shewn by Aḥmed ibn Abî Dowâd in his efforts to establish the doctrine that the Ḳorân was created. In the year 231 A. H., it was proposed to ransom 4600 prisoners from the Greeks, when Ibn Abî Dowâd suggested that they should ransom only such as admitted the creation of the Ḳorân, and that these should each receive two dinârs on their release. This was actually done, and a small number of prisoners, who could not bring their consciences up to the point of meeting the test, were left unredeemed in the hands of the Greeks [2]).

Ransom of Prisoners from the Greeks.

---

1) Hammer-Purgstall, Lit. Gesch. III, p. 200, N°. 1050; al-Sujûtî, Tarîkh al-Khol. 350; Abu'l-Feda Ann. II, 132; Fihrist I, 212; Abu'l-Maḥâsin, I, 686; al-Maḳrîzî, p. 11, واما ابو يعقوب يوسف بن يحيى البويطى فاريد منه القول بخلق القران فامتنع فحُبس الى ان مات سنة اثنتين وثلاثين ومائتين قال الربيع بن سليمن صاحب الشافعى رايت البُويطى على بغل فى عنقه غُل وفى رجليه قيد وبين الغل والقيد سلسلة حديد فيها طُوبة وزنها اربعون رطلا وهو يقول انما خلق الله الخلق بكُن [cf. Kor. 6, 72] فاذا كانت كُن مخلوقة فكأنّ مخلوقا خَلَق مخلوقا والله لاموتنّ فى حديدك هذا حتى ياتى مِنْ بعدى قوم يعلمون انه قد مات فى هذا الشان قوم فى حديدهم ولئن دخلتُ عليه يعنى الواثق لَأُصْدُقنّه

2) Ṭabarî III, ١٣٥١ ff.; De Goeje, Fragm. Hist. Arab. II, 531; Abu'l-Maḥ. I, 684; al-Subkî, p. 146.

Al-Wâthiḳ Surrenders the Doctrine of the Korân's Creation. Alleged Cause.

Al-Wâthiḳ is generally considered to have given up the doctrine of the Miḥna before his death, and an incident [1]) which we may accept as fundamentally true, accounts for its surrender. Ibn Abî Dowâd caused to be brought before the Khalif a sheikh of Adhana on the charge of heresy. The Khalif bade him discuss the question of the creation of the Ḳorân with Ibn Abî Dowâd, but the old man objected on the ground that Aḥmed ibn Abî Dowâd was a Sabaean and was too unsound in his views to spend words upon. At this al-Wâthiḳ began to be very angry, but the sheikh promised to prove his points, if the Khalif would but give close attention to the discussion which was to take place between them.

To begin with, the sheikh asked Ibn Abî Dowâd if his view were to be looked upon as an essential of the believer's creed. The latter answered that it was to be so regarded. Then the sheikh pointed out that God, having sent Moḥammed with a revelation to his people, the Messenger of God did not leave unpublished any part of the Divine Message. Ibn Abî Dowâd allowed that Moḥammed had fully delivered the Message. His opponent then asked, if (on the basis of the revelation made through him) the Prophet had called upon men to accept the doctrine of the Ḳoran's created existence. Ibn Abî Dowâd gave to this no answer, and the sheikh claimed from al-Wâthiḳ one point established in proof of his charges. The Khalif allowed the point.

The second step was the quotation of Ḳorân 5 . 5, 'This day have I completed for you your religion and perfected my grace upon you'; and the sheikh asked how any new doctrine could be justifiable in view of such a passage. Ibn Abî Dowâd did not attempt a defence of his position against this assault upon it, and the sheikh claimed his second point, which al-Wâthiḳ conceded him.

---

1) v. Kremer, Herrsch. Ideen, 243 ff.; al-Sujûtî, Tarîkh al-Kholafâ, 347 f.; Abu'l-Maḥ. I, 691 f.; al-Maḳrîzî, p. 9 f.; al-Subkî, p. 143.

In the third place, the old man asked if the Prophet had known the doctrine now propounded, and if he had ever invited men to accept it. Ibn Abî Dowâd claimed that Moḥammed knew the doctrine, but he would not answer the question as to whether the Prophet had made its profession obligatory upon the believer or not. Here the sheikh claimed his third and final point. But he did not stop here. He argued that, allowing Moḥammed to have known the doctrine in point and the early Khalifs to have known it; seeing that both he and they had been satisfied to refrain from obliging men to confess the tenet of the Ḳorân's creation, was it the part of a modern zealot to do what they had not done? Supposing they did believe as he did, was it not his part to keep his belief a mere private opinion as they had done, instead of forcing people to think as himself? A companion of the Khalif al-Muhtadî who tells this story says that al-Muhtadî, who was present on the occasion, gave up the doctrine of the creation of the Ḳorân from this time, and that al-Wâthiḳ ordered the sheikh to be at once set free, and, apparently, himself believed no longer as he had believed relative to the Ḳorân. Other accounts say that al-Wâthiḳ changed his view before he died, and, in the connection where it occurs in the Arabic record, the testimony of al-Muhtadî is cited to shew that the incident above given occurred toward the end of al-Wâthiḳ's Khalifate [1]).

Al-Mutawakkil Abrogates the Miḥna. Al-Mutawakkil began to reign in 232, and the Miḥna continued to exist for two years in his reign, being brought to a close in the year 234. The whole term of its duration was, thus, from the last year of al-Ma'mûn, 218 A. H., to the second or third year of al-Mutawakkil, 234 A. H. In the latter year, al-Mutawakkil stopped the application of the test, and by public proclamation throughout the Empire forbade men on

1) Steiner, 78, says al-Wâthiḳ brought the Miḥna to a close. But the truth is that he went no further than to change his view in relation to the Ḳorân and to purpose abrogating the test. His death prevented him from actually carrying his purpose into effect.

pain of death [1]) to profess the creation of the Ḳorân. At this there was great rejoicing everywhere. Men praised the virtues of the Khalif, and forgot his vices; prayers for blessing upon him were heard on all sides and his name was mentioned with those of the good Khalifs Abû Bekr and ʿOmar ibn Abd al-Azîz. Two things alone were remembered against him by his Muslim subjects, both of which occurred in the year 236 A. H. The one was the permission granted for the sack of Damascus to the Turkish soldiery (the event however did not happen); and the other, the destruction of the tomb of al-Ḥosain together with the buildings round about it, and the conversion of the land into fields [2]).

1) On death penalty for heresy cf. Goldziher, Moh. Stud. II, 216.

2) cf. v. Kremer, Herrsch. Ideen d. Isl. 245 ff.; cf. Dozy, Het Islam. 163; cf. Ibn Chall. N°. 133; Abu'l-Maḥ. I, 691, 695, 702; al-Sujûtî, Tar. al-Khol. 352; al-Jaʿqûbî II, 592; al-Subkî, p. 143, وقد حنبل امر هذه الفتنة وطال شرّها واستمر من هذه السنة التى هى سنة ثمان عشرة ومائتين الى سنة اربع وثلاثين ومائتين فرفعها المتوكل فى مجلسه ونهى عن القول بخلق القران وكتب بذلك الى الافاق وتوفّر دعآء الخلق له وبالغوا فى الثناء عليه والتعظيم له حتى قال قائلهم الخلفاء ثلاثة ابو بكر الصديق يوم الردة وعمر بن عبد العزيز فى رده المظالم والمتوكل فى احيآء السنّة وسكت الناس عن ذنوب المتوكل وقد كانت العامة تنقم عليه شيئين احدهما [Abu'l-Maḥ. I, 714] انه ندب لدمشق افريدون التركى احد مماليكه وصيره واليًا عليها وكان ظالمًا فاتكا فقدم فى سبعة الاف فارس واباح لهم المتوكل القتل والنّهب على ما نقل الينا ثلاث ساعات فنزل ببيت لهيا واراد ان يصبح البلد فلما اصبح نظر الى البلد وقال يا يوم يصبحك منى فقدمت له بغلة فضربته بالزوج فقتلته وقبره ببيت لهيا ورد الجيش الذى معه خائبين وبلغ المتوكل فصلحت نيته لاهل دمشق والثانى [Abu'l-Maḥ. I, 712; Fragm. Hist. Arab. II, 546.]

General Survey of the Miḥna. Taking a general survey of the inquisition [1]) inaugurated by al-Ma'mûn, and carried on by the two succeeding Khalifs, we can say that as an attempt to stamp out by force moral convictions it was a failure from the start; for, in the Muslim world as everywhere else, there was an admiration and a moral support accorded by the great body of the people to those who suffered persecution, such as might have led men far less sincere than Aḥmed ibn Ḥanbal to stand out against a tyrannous crusade of repression [2]). That the principles of the strictest orthodox

---

انه امر بهدم قبر الحسين وهدم ما حوله من الدور وان يعمل مزارع ومنع الناس من زيارته وحُرث وبقى صحْراء فتألم المسلمون لذلك وكتب اهل بغداد شتمه على الحيطان والمساجد

al-Makrîzî, p. 10, وقال الحافظ ابو الفرج وَلِىَ المتوكل على الله سنة اثنتين وثلاثين ومائتين فاظهر الله به السُّنة وكشف تلك الغمة فشكره الناس على ما فعل ثم ذكر بسنده الى محمد بن خلف قال كان ابراهيم بن محمد التيْمىّ قاضى البصرة يقول الخُلفاء ثلاثة ابو بكر قاتل اهل الرِدّة حتى استجابوا له وعمر بن عبد العزيز رَدّ مظالم بنى امية والمتوكل مَحى البدَع واظهر السّنة

1) A short account of the Miḥna and its issues is to be found, Dozy, Het Islamisme, 154 ff.

2) Houtsma (De Strijd etc. 106 f.) appears to make the motive for the resistance of the orthodox theologians to their rationalistic opponents one of religious policy. If they surrendered the doctrine of the uncreated nature of the Ḳorân, the hope of the universal spread of Islâm would have to be given up. I have not found this motive alleged in any of my sources, but can well believe that it may have been a secondary, though not a primary one. The primary motive was altogether personal. Aḥmed and those who stood with him had a simple belief, incapable of analysis, in the eternity and unoriginateness of the Ḳorân; they hoped, too, for a reward if they maintained their faith at all costs, and feared grave spiritual consequences should the doctrine be given up. The honor of God, the Divine Legation of the Prophet, the unique and ineffable dignity of the Ḳorân, and, finally, the everlasting well-

as bla of which Aḥmed was the leading representative, wou not win their way in the following generations of Islâm as not because they had been killed out by persecution, ut because a more liberal and enlightened sentiment had been introduced into the Muslim commonwealth; because the yoke this Puritanism would have imposed was one which people could not bear amid the practical concerns of every-day life; and because the system rested upon casuistries, which, though deductively perfect, were false in their premises and could never have satisfied the untrammeled common sense of men. The inquisition only retarded the development of freer and purer conceptions among the adherents of the religion of the Prophet. But the retardation was not an unmixed evil. It checked, for a time, a philosophical movement, to give it a theological and religious concern, without which the Muslim people would have had for their teachers men indifferent to practical questions of religious life and observance, and unsympathetic in their attitude toward popular theological conceptions.

Of the men, persecuting and persecuted, connected with the Miḥna, Aḥmed ibn Ḥanbal comes out with the greatest credit to himself. Bishr ibn al-Ḥârith al-Hâfî had a saying that God had cast Aḥmed ibn Ḥanbal into the crucible and he had come out pure gold. Aḥmed's method of argument was no more unsound than that of his opponents [1]).

---

being of their own souls and the souls of those who looked to them for an example — these are expressed motives for the orthodox apologetic, which in some cases became a defence of conviction even unto death. The faith in the Divine and uncreated nature of the Ḳorân lay at the root of all their arguments and actions in this defence. In the historical instances of such a resistance as this the personal element of conviction, rather than any considerations of religious policy, has been the moving principle of the defence which has been put forward.

1) The statement of Houtsma (De Strijd etc. 106) would give the impression that the orthodox when in disputation with their opponents had no arguments worth mentioning to offer, and were quite incapable of dealing with those who stood against them. Judging from a modern point of view neither side had very strong points; but, judged from a Muslim standpoint, the

They had, on philosophical grounds, declared the [illegible] in- as well as the attributes of God, to be created; but, [illegible] they opposed him, they sought to convict him of error on his own ground, and by his own method of proof, and he seems to have had the better of them in most of their word passages. The arguments used were childish enough, but not more so for him than for them. The fact that he had earnest convictions to defend, and that many of those who stood against him had been either frightened or bribed into taking their present stand, stood him in good stead, and must command our respect as we, to-day, review the whole historical scene in which he is a figure.

As to al-Maʾmûn, he evidently disliked the slavishness of orthodoxy, and was impatient at its many absurdities; but he shewed at the same time how easy it is for a learned man to display a disdainful and narrow spirit toward the unlearned, for a philosopher to become a dogmatist, and for an advocate of liberal views to become a tyrant toward those of stricter beliefs.

Aḥmed ibn Abî Dowâd was a man whom one finds it difficult to credit with earnest convictions. His first master, al-Maʾmûn, may be credited with acting in the belief that he was right and in the consequent wish to secure the general adoption of his opinions; but his minister will not be misjudged if we look upon him as actuated by contempt and violent hatred toward men of strict life and toward zealous advocates of religious duties, whose puritanism appeared in his eyes to be but pharisaic hypocrisy. He is not

---

disputations which are recorded in these pages shew that the orthodox had the great arguments of the Word of God and the Tradition, and could wield these as well or better than their opponents. Isḥâḳ ibn Ibrâhîm the governor, Abd-al-Raḥmân ibn Isḥâḳ, and al-Muʿtaṣim are all said to have been impressed by the force of what Aḥmed ibn Ḥanbal said and the way in which he said it. Steiner (Die Muʿtaziliten, 8) says that the Muʿtazila used the [illegible] interpreting it allegorically and giving their reasonings a philosophical cast. Houtsma, (De Strijd etc. 80) speaks of the Muʿtazila as being, in general, men lacking in earnestness and given to dialectic trifling in disputation.

as black a character as the partisans of Aḥmed ibn Ḥanbal would represent him to be, but I have met no record of his connection with the Miḥna which shews him as other than arbitrary and unfeeling, except the isolated reference in the trial of Aḥmed ibn Naṣr the conspirator whom al-Wâthiḳ put to death. There, as we have already seen, Ibn Abî Dowâd suggests, when al-Wâthiḳ grows angry with Ibn Naṣr for persisting in his belief, that the prisoner is an old man whose mind is deranged, but who will see differently when he has had time to come to himself. This account, be it remarked, occurs in al-Subkî's Ṭabaḳât (life of Aḥmed ibn Ḥanbal), where Ibn Abî Dowâd finds from the author an apology for his acts in more than one instance, but in each case the apology is a personal opinion of the author of the book, rather than well supported historical tradition. In earlier accounts, and in later as well, Ibn Abî Dowâd is put before us as an able man, with eminent social qualities, but with a persecuting spirit in administration; and, though we have said that al-Maʾmûn wished to enforce the Miḥna before he really did so, we must remember that he actually did not do so of his own motion, but that it was Ibn Abî Dowâd alone who turned the scale which brought about the long tyranny of sixteen years ending shortly after al-Mutawakkil's accession. We can believe too, that had it not been for him the Miḥna would have lapsed for want of interest or from positive distaste on the part of al-Muʿtaṣim or al-Wâthiḳ.

For al-Muʿtaṣim's part in this movement we have not much to say. He found no pleasure in the wretched business of persecuting men's convictions, and clearly shewed in Aḥmed's case that, had it not been for obligations which he held to be inviolable, he would have had nothing to do with the enforcement of the test as to the Ḳorân.

Al-Wâthiḳ, as to his part in the Miḥna, is in somewhat greater degree a return to al-Maʾmûn. Like his predecessors he, too, was dominated by Ibn Abî Dowâd. The recorded cases, very few in number, of those whom he tried for the Ḳorân evince cruelty as a feature of this Khalif's character, and that of Aḥmed ibn Naṣr, in particular, is positively brutal [1]).

Not much can be said in favor of those who yielded in the Miḥna. The assent of the first seven who were summoned to the Khalif's presence was the fatal factor which led to the following up of the persecution. Still, it was not the less weakness in those who recanted afterwards that they should have been terrified into submission. The doctrine of the Taḳîa was generously applied to them by their friends and companions, and, no doubt, saved them a great deal in the estimation of the public; but their course was not felt by themselves to have been creditable, and bitter was the regret of men like Yaḥya ibn Maʿîn that the sword should have frightened them into surrender of a doctrine which was felt to be the truth. It is the fault of an age of controversy that theological opinions are based too much on the logic of words, and not upon verities from which the moral and intellectual judgment cannot separate itself. This was the case with the doctrine of the unoriginate nature of the Ḳorân. Its evidences were simply words, and it was only an exceptional character like Aḥmed ibn Ḥanbal, who had seen the purely speculative question of the Ḳorân's origin in relations, the maintenance of which seemed to him to involve the very existence of his religious life and faith, to whom a surrender of his opinion became of transcendent moment. Others had not the same great conception of the question that he had, they knew it only as one of the controverted points in the polemic which was going on about them. The surrender of it might be a victory for an opponent, but it was worth making for the sake of one's [illegible]ld. Those who yielded took, at a later date, a more serious view of what they had done, but, at the time when they

1) In the account of Aḥmed ibn Naṣr's execution, p. 118, we have suppressed the more harrowing features.

committed the act of denying their own confession, it appeared as simply a question of yielding an unessential point and acknowledging themselves beaten. Even their plea of the Taḳîa cannot be taken as rendering this explanation nugatory; though it might seem to suggest that they looked upon their act as one involving the cardinal sin of apostasy, to which sin the Taḳîa stood specially related. This plea was but an excuse used for effect upon the people, and was not, of course, an explanation of how they came to do what they had done. Aḥmed ibn Ḥanbal excused them on this ground, but his excuse contemplates the act after its commission and finds grounds of pardon for it. It does not offer any exposition of its inward cause and significance. The Taḳîa itself might render impossible the proving of an act to be apostasy, for it could often be urged that a man's apostasy was but in word, while in heart he was sound in the faith.

Notwithstanding the testimony of historians to al-Mutawakkil's cruelty, it cannot be said that he ever shewed any unkindness or impatience with Aḥmed ibn Ḥanbal. He might have been provoked to acts of harshness by Aḥmed's peevishness had he allowed himself to yield to the provocation, but he was, instead, constantly kind and thoughtful of the old man's comfort and welfare. He does not appear to have been as intolerant in matters of religion as his predecessors, unless his hostility to ʿAlyite movements be counted as of a religious character [1]). We are justified, in my judgment, in assuming that the interest in religion and theology which he shewed was not that of a persecuting partisan of a political faction, but of a sincere though fanatical religious bigot [2]). His connection with orthodoxy was, because free from any immediate and violent display of persecuting spirit [3]), hardly from a political motive. Counter persecution

---

1) On this hostility cf. pp. 140, 152; Abu'l-Maḥ. I, 712.

2) For a different view cf. Goldziher, Moh. Stud. II, 57, 66; Dozy, Het Islamisme, 163.

3) Houtsma, De Strijd etc. 113 infra.

would surely have followed the persecution already past, had al-Mutawakkil desired to make capital out of his connection with orthodoxy. It is more likely that his relation to theology and religion is to be explained by temperament and revulsion of feeling from the course of his predecessors. The latter, indeed, had already shewn strong signs that, personally, they were weary of the inquisition. They, however, still accorded in their theological views with the persecuting party and were subject to their influence. Al-Mutawakkil was, apparently, a Shâfiʿite [1]). None will deny that his theological position made him friends as a result, but, however black his record may be, and whatever there may be to blame in his narrow bigotry, we think that his intention was only to reform abuses in religion as he saw them [2]).

III.

Al-Mutawakkil and Aḥmed ibn Ḥanbal.

In the early years of al-Mutawakkil's reign there were those who sought to injure Aḥmed with the Khalif [3]). One report, in particular, was

---

1) al-Sujûtî, Tarîkh al-Khol. 359.

2) Nearly all European writers impute political motives to this Khalif, as well as to al-Ma'mûn when he inaugurated the persecution. It may be admitted that al-Mutawakkil recognized the futility of persecution as long as the great mass of his subjects were of orthodox sympathies (Houtsma, 112); but the fact, which appears to be well established, that al-Mutawakkil was personally orthodox in his theological convictions, as well as the other facts which have been noticed in the text, would seem to fully account for what he did. It is nowhere stated in the original sources which I have consulted that he had any other motive than that of personal religious preference. Out of this personal ground sprang his intention to bring about a restoration of orthodoxy. His antagonism to ʿAlyites, too, was more that of a fanatical representative of certain *views* than that of a man who hoped to make himself more popular with the majority by the step he took. The public feeling when he destroyed the tomb of al-Ḥusain shews this.

3) Abû Nuʿaim, 150 *b* ff. (This source is now followed with a few exceptions which are noted). ذكر ورود كتاب المتوكل بمحنته اولا ثم

that he had charged with Atheism the predecessors of

بجائزة له واشخاصه الى العسكر ثانيا رحمه الله حدثنا محمد بن جعفر والحسين بن محمد وعلى بن احمد قالوا ثنا محمد بن اسمعيل بن احمد ثنا ابو الفضل صالح بن احمد بن حنبل قال لما توفى اسحاق بن ابرهيم ومحمد ابنه وولى عبدُ الله بن اسحاق كتب المتوكل اليه ان وَجِّهْ الى احمد بن حنبل ان عندَك طَلِبة امير المومنين فوجه بحاجبه مظفر وحضر معه صاحب البريد. وكان يعرف بابن الكلبى وكتب له ايضا فقال له مظفر يقول لك الامير قد كتبَ الىَّ امير المومنين انَّ عنْدك [Cod. عَبْدك] طلبتَه [Cod. طَلْبته] وقال له ابن الكلبى مثلَ ذلك وكان قد نام الناس فدقع الباب وكان عَلى ابى رحمه الله ازار [Cod. ازارًا] ففتح لهم الباب وقعدوا على بارِيَة ومعهم نسآء فلما قرئ عليه الكتاب* قال لهم انى ما اعرف هذا وانى لأَرى طاعته فى العُسر واليُسر والمَنشط والمكره والاثرة وانى اتاسّف عن تخلّفى عن الصلاة وعن حضير الجماعة ودَعوة المسلمين وقد كان اسحاق بن ابرهيم وجّه الى انى ان الزم بيتك ولا تخرج الى جمعة ولا جماعة والا نزل بك ما نزل فى ايام ابى اسحاق ثم قال ابن الكلبى قد امرنى امير المومنين ان أُحلّفك ما عندك طلبتُه فتحلف فقال ان استحلفتنى حلفتُ فأحْلَفه [Cod. فأُحَلفه] بالله وبالطلاق ما عندَك [?ما عنـدهُ Read] طلبةُ [Cod. طلبته] امير المومنين فكانهم اوموا الى ان عنْده [Cod. عبْده] علويًّا ثم قال اريد ان أُفتّش مَنزلك قال ابو الفضل وكنت حاضرا فقال ومنزل ابنك فقام مظفر وابن الكَلبى وامرأتان معهما فدخلا ففتّشا البيت ثم فَتشت الامرأتان النساء والصبيان قال ابو الفضل ثم دخلوا مَنزِلى ففتّشوه ودلّوا شمعة فى البئر فنظروا ووَجّهوا بالنسوة ففتشوا الحرم وخرجوا فلما كان بعد

the Khalif — a report which the latter did not appear to con-

---

يومين ورد كتاب على بن الجهم انّ امير المومنين قد صحّ عنده
برآءتك مما قرفت به وقد كان اهل البدع قدّموا اعناقهم فالحمد لله
الذى لم يشمتهم بك وقد وجّه اليك امير المومنين يعقوبَ [Cod. يعقوبُ]
المعروف بقوصرّة ومعه جائزة ويامرك بالخروج فالله اللهَ ان تستعفى او
تردّ الجائزة، قال ابو الفضل ثم ورد من الغد يعقوب فدخل الى ابى
فقال له يابا عبد الله اميرُ المومنين يقرأ عليك السلام ويقول قد صحّ
نقآء ساحتك وقد احببتُ ان آنس بقربك واتبرك بدعآئك وقد
وجهت اليك عشرة آلاف درهم معونة على سفرك واخرج بدرة فيها صرة
نحو من مائتى دينار والباقى دراهم صحاح فلم ينظر اليها ثم شدّها
يعقوب وقال له اعودُ غدًا حتى انظر على ما تعزم عليه وقال له يابا
عبد الله الحمد لله الذى لم يُشمّت بك اهل البدع وانصرف فجئتُ
باجّانة [Cod. باجّانة] خضرآء كببتُها على البدرة فلما كان عِند المغرب
قال يا صالح خذ هذه صيّرها عندك فصيّرتها عند راسى فوق البيت
فلمّا كان سَحَر اذ هو ينادى يا صالح فقمت وصَعدتُ اليه فقال يا صالح
ما نمتُ ليلتى هذه فقلت له لِمَه فجعل يبكى وهو يقول سلمت مِن
هولآء حتّى اذا كان فى آخر عمرى بُليتُ بهم قد عَزمت على انْ افرّق
هذا الشىء اذا اصبحتُ فقلتُ ذاك اليك فلمّا اصبح جاءه الحسن
ابن البزّار والمشايخ فقال جئنى يا صالح بالميزان فقال وجّهوا الى ابنآء
المهاجرين والانصار ثم قال وَجّه الى فلان حتى يفرّق فى ناحيته والى
فلان فلم يزل حتى فرّقها كُلّها ونفض الكيس ونحن فى حالة الله بها
عليمٌ فجآء بُنى لى فقال يا ابه اعطنى درهما فنظر الى فاخرجتُ قِطعة
اعطيتُه وكتب صاحب البريد انّه تصدق بالدراهم من يومه حتى

sider very seriously, for he is said to have ordered the man

تَصَدَّق بالكيس قال على بنُ انجَهْم فقلتُ يا امير المومنين قد تَصدَّق بها وعلم النامُ انه قد قبل منك ما يصنعُ احمد بالمال وانما قوته رَغِيف قال فقال لى صدقت يا على' قال ابو الفضل ثم أُخرج ابى ليْلا ومعنا حُرّاسْ معهم النفاطات فلمّا اضآء الفجر قال يا صالح معك دَراهِم قلت نعم قال اعْطهم فاعطيتُهم درهمًا درهمًا.........قال ابو الفضل وقصّر ابى* فى خروجه الى العسكر وقال تُقصّر الصلاة فى اربعة برد وهى ستّة عشر فرسخا وصليتُ به يوما العصر فقال لى طوّلتَ بنا العصر تقرأ فى الركعة مقدار خمس عشرة آية وكنتُ اصلى به فى العسكر فلما صِرْنا بين الحائطين قال لنا يعقوب اقيموا ثم وجّه الى المتوكل بما عَمل فدخلنا العسكر وابى مُنكّسُ الراس وراسه مغطّى فقال له يَعقوب اكْشِفْ راسَك يابا عبد الله فكشَف ثم جاء وصِيفٌ يُريد الدار فلما نظر الى الناس وجَمعهم قال ما هولآء قالوا احمد بن حنبل فوجّه اليه بعد ما جاز بيحيى بن هَرثَمة فقال يقرئك السلام ويقول الحمد لله الذى لم يُشَمّت بك اهل البدع قد علمتَ ما كان حالُ ابن ابى دواد فينبغى ان نتَكلّم بما يجب لله ومضى بيحيى قال ابو الفضل انزل ابى دار ايتاخ فجآء على بن الجهم فقال قد امر لكم امير المومنين بعشرة آلاف مكانَ التى فرّقها [scil. ابوكم] وامركم ان لا يُعلَم بذلك فيَغتم ثم جاءه محمد بن معاوية فقال ان امير المومنين يُكثِر ذكرَك ويقول تقيم هاهنا تُحدِّثُ فقال انا ضعيف ثم وضَع اصبعه على بعض اسنانه فقال انّ بعضَ اسنانى يتَحرك وما أَخبَرتُ بذلك ولَدى ثم وجه اليه ما تقول فى بهيمتين انتطحتَا فعقرت احداهما الاخرى فسقطت فذُبح فقال انْ كان اطرَف بعَينه ومصع بذنبه وسال دَمُه يُوكل

who made it to be flogged for trying to injure a good subject.

قال ابو الفضل ثم صار اليه يحيى بن خاقان فقال يابا عبد الله قد امرنى اميرُ المومنين ان أُصير اليك لتركبَ الى ابى عبد الله [i. e. المعتزّ] ثم قال لى قد امرنى ان اقطع له سوادًا وطَيْلسانا وقَلنسوة فاى قلنسوة يلبس فقلت له ما رايته لبس قلنسوة قط فقال له انّ امير المومنين قد امرنى ان تَصير لك مرتبة فى اعلا المَرَاتب [Cod. omits] ويَصير ابو عبد الله فى حجرك ثم قال لى انّ امير المومنين قد امر ان يُجْرَى عليكم وعلى قراباته اربعةُ الاف درهم ففرقها عليهم ثم عاد يحيى من الغد فقال يابا عبد الله تركَب فقال ذاك اليكم فقال استخير الله فلبس ازاره وخُفّيه وقد كان خُفّه قد اتى له عنده نحو من خمسة عشر سنة مرقوع برقاع عدة فاشار يحيى الىّ يلبَس [Cod. تلبَس] قلنْسُوة فقلت له ما له قلنسوة قال كيف يدخل عليه حاسرا ويحيى قائم فطلبْنا له دابة يركبها فقال يحيى تُصَلّى [Cod. نُصَلّى] فجلس على التراب وقال مِنْهَا خَلَقْنَاكُمْ وَفِيهَا نُعِيدُكُمْ [Kor. 20. 57] ثم ركب بَغْل بعضٍ [Cod. بعضَ] التجار نَصَبينا معه حتى ادخِل دار المُعْتزّ فاجلس فى بيت الدهليز ثم جآء يحيى فاخذ بيده حتى ادخله ورفع الستر ونحن ننظر وكان المعتز قاعدا على دُكان فى الدار وقد كان يحيى تقدّم اليه فقال لا تمدّ يدك اليه فلما صَعِد الدُّكّان جلس فقال له يحيى يابا عبد الله ان امير المومنين جآء بك ليُسَرّ بقُربك ويَصير ابو عبد الله فى حجرك . . . .

وقد كانوا حدّثوا انه يخلع عليه سوادًا ثم انصرف فلما صار الى الدار نزع الثياب عنه ثم جعل يبكى ثم قال قد سَلمتُ من هولآء منذ

ستين سنة حتّى اذا كان فى آخر عمرى بُليتُ بهم ما احْسبنى
سلمت من دخولى على هذا الغلام فكيف بمن يجب علىّ نُصْحه
من وقت تقع عينى عليه الى انْ اخرُج من عنده ثم قال يا صالح
وَجّه بهذه الثياب الى بغداد تُباع ويتصدق بثمنها ولا يشترى احد
منكم شيئا قال ابو الفضل فوجّهْت بها الى يعقوب بن البختُمان فباعها
وفرق ثمنها وبقيت عندى القلنسوة ثم اخبرناه ان الدار التى هو
فيها كانت لايتاخ فقال اكتُب رُقعةً الى محمد بن الجراح ليَستعفى
لى من هذه الدار فكتبنا رقعة فامر المتوكل ان يُعفا منها ووجّه الى
قوم ليخرجوا من منازلهم فسال ان يُعفا من ذلك فاكتُريت له دار
بمائتَى درهم فصار اليها وأُجرى لنا مآئدة وثلج وضرب الخيش وفرش
الطبرى فلما رأى الخيْش والطّبرى نحى نفسه عن ذلك الموضع
والقى نفسه على مضرّبة له . . . .
. . . . وجعل يُواصل يُفطر كل ثلاث على ثُمن سَويق
فمكث خمس عشرة يُفطر فى كل ثلاث ثم جعل بعد ذلك يُفطر
ليلة ليلة لا يفطر الا على رغيف فكان اذا جيء بالمآئدة تُوضع فى
الدهليز لكى لا يراها فياكل من حضر فكان اذا جهده الحر تُبلّ له
خِرقة فيضعها على صَدره وفى كل يوم يُوجه اليه بابن
ماسُويهْ فينظر اليه ويقول يابا عبد الله انما اميل اليك
والى اصحابك وما بك علة الا الضّعْف وقلة الرزّ فقال له
ابن مَاسُويهْ انا ربّما امرنا عُبادنا باكل دُهن الحل [Cod. الخل] فانه يلين
وجعل يجيئه بالشيء ليشربه فيَصبه وقطع له يحيى دراعة وطيلسانا
سوادا . . . .
. . . . وكان ربّما صار اليه يحيى وهو يصلى فيجلس فى الدهليز

حتى يفرُغ ويجيء على بن الجهم فينزع سيفه وقلنسُوته ويدخل عليه وامر المتوكل ان تُشترَى [Cod. يُشترى] لنا دارٌ فقال يا صالح قلت لبّيك قال لئن اقْررْتَ لهم بشرَى ذلك لتكونن القطيعةُ بينى وبينكم انما يريدون ان يُصَيّروا هذا البلد لى ماوى ومَسْكنا فلم يزل يدفع شرى الدار حتى اندفع وصار الىّ صاحبُ المنزل فقال اعطيك كل شهر ثلاثة الاف مكان المآئدة فقلت لا افعل وجعلَتْ رُسُل المتوكل تاتيه يسئلونه عن خبره فينصرفون [Cod. فيصيرون] اليه ويقولون هو ضعيف وفى خلال ذلك يقولون يابا عبد الله لا بد له من ان يراك فسكت فاذا خرجوا قال الا تعجب من قولهم لا بد له من ان يراك وما علمُهم انه لا بد له من ان يرانى وكان فى هذه دار حجرةٌ صغيرة [Cod. الصغيرة] فيها بيتان فقال لى ادخلونى تلك الحجرة ولا تُسرجوا لى سراجا فادخلناه اليها فجآءه يعقوب فقال يابا عبد الله امير المومنين مشتاق اليك ويقول * انظر اليوم الذى تصير الى فيه اى يوم هو حتى اعرفه فقال ذاك اليكم فقال يوم الاربعاء يومٌ خال وخرج يعقوب فلما كان من الغد جآء فقال البشرى يابا عبد الله امير المومنين يقرأ عليك السلام ويقول قد اعفيتك عن لُبْس السواد والركوب الىّ والى ولاة العهود والى الدار فانْ شئت فالبس القطن وانْ شئت فالبس الصوف فجعل يحمد الله على ذلك . . . .

. . . . قال انى أُعطى اللهَ عهدا انّ ٱلْعَهْدَ كَانَ مَسْؤُلًا [Kor. 17. 36] وقد قال الله تعالى يَـٰٓأَيُّهَا ٱلَّذِينَ آمَنُوٓا أَوْفُوا بِٱلْعُقُودِ [Kor. 5. 1] انى لا أُحدّث حديثا تماما ابدا حتّى القى الله ولا أُستثنى منكم احدا فخرجنا وجآء على بن الجهم فقلنا له قال انّا للّه وانا اليه راجعون واخبر المتوكل بذلك وقال انما يُريدون

ان أُحدِّث فيكون هذا البلد حَبْسى وانما كان سبَبُ الذين اقاموا بهذا البلد لَمَا أُعطوا وأُمِروا فتحدَّثوا وكانوا يدخلون عليه فيتكلمون وهو مُغمَّض العينِ يتعلَّل وضَعُف ضَعفا شديدا فقلوا يخبرونه فيتوجَّع لذلك وجعل يقول والله لقد تمنيت الموت فى الامر الذى كان وانى لاتمنى الموت فى هذا وذاك انّ هذا فتنة الدنيا وكان ذاك فتنة الدين ثم جعل يَضم اصابع يده ويقول لو كانت نفسى فى يدى لارْسلتها ثم يفتح اصابعه وكان المتوكل يُوجه اليه فى كل وقت يَسئله عن حاله وكان فى خلال ذلك يومَر لنا بالمال فيقول يُوصَل اليهم ولا يَعلَمُ شيخهم فيغتَم ما يُريد منهم انْ كان هولآء يريدون [Cod. يريد] الدنيا فما يمنعهم وقالوا للمتوكل انه كان لا ياكل من طعامك ولا يجلس على فراشك ويُحرم الذى تشرب فقال لهم لو نُشر المعتصم لم اقبَلْ منه قال ابو الفضل ثم انى انحدرت الى بغداد وخلَّفتُ عبد الله عنده فاذا عبدُ الله قد قدم وجآء بثيابى التى كانت عنده فقلت ما جاء بك قال قال لى انحدر وقل لصالح لا تخرج [Cod. يخرج] فانتم كنتمُ آفتِى واللهِ لو استقبلْت من امرى ما استدبرتُ ما اخرجت واحدا منكم معى لولا مكانكم لِمَن كان توضع هذه المآئدة ولمن كان يُفرش هذا الفرش ويجرى الاجراء قال ابو الفضل فكتبتُ اليه اعلمه ما قال لى عبد الله فكتب الىّ بخطه بسم الله الرحمن الرحيم احسن الله عاقبتك ودفع عنك كلّ مَكروه ومَحذور الذى حملنى على الكتاب اليك والذى [Cod. للذى] قلت لعبد الله لا يأتينى احد منكم رجآء ان ينقطعَ ذكرى ويخمل فانكم اذا كُنتُم هاهنا فشا ذكرى وكان يجتمع اليك قوم ينقلون اخبارنا ولم يَكُن الا خيرا واعْلَم يابنى انّك ان اقمتَ [Cod. اقمتُ] فلا تاتينى انت ولا اخوك فهو رضآءى فلا

تجعل فى نفسك الا خيرا والسّلام عليك ورحمة الله وبركاته، قال ابو الفضل ثم ورد الى كتابٌ اخر بخطه يذكر فيه بسم الله الرحمن الرحيم احسن الله عاقبتك [Cod. عافيتك] ودفع عنك السوء برحمته كتابى اليك وانا فى نعم الله متظاهرة واسئله اتمامها والعونَ على أداء شكرها قد انفكّت عنّا عقد انما كان حُبس مَن هاهنا لما أُعطوا فقبِلوا وأُجرى عليهم فصاروا فى الحدّ الذى صاروا اليه وحدثوا ودخلوا عليهم فهذه كانت قيودهم فنسئل الله ان يُعيذنا من شرّهم ويخلصنا فقد كان ينبغى لكم لو قد فديتمونى باموالكم واهاليكم لهان ذلك عليكم للذى انا فيه فلا يكبرُ عليكم ما اكتب به اليكم فالزموا بيوتكم فلعل الله ان يخلصنى والسلام عليكم ورحمة الله ثم ورد غيرُ كتاب الىّ بخطه بنحو من هذا فلما خرجْنا من العسْكر رفعت المائدة والفرش وكل ما اقيم لنا قال ابو الفضل واوصى وصية بسم الله الرحمن الرحيم* هذا ما اوصى به احمد بن حنبل اوصَى انه يشهد ان لا اله الا الله وحده لا شريك له وانّ محمدا عبده ورسوله أرسله بِٱلْهُدَى وَدِينِ ٱلْحَقِّ لِيُظْهِرَهُ عَلَى ٱلدِّينِ كُلِّهِ وَلَوْ كَرِهَ ٱلْمُشْرِكُونَ [Kor. 9. 33; 61. 9] وأَوْصَى مَن اطاعه مِن اهله وقَرابته ان يَعبُدوا الله فى العَابدين ويَحمدوه فى الحامدين وان ينصحوا لجماعة المسلمين واوصَى أنّى قد رضيت بالله ربا وبالاسلام دينا وبمحمد صلى الله عليه وسلم نبيًّا واوصى انّ لعبدِ الله بن محمد المعروف ببُوران علىّ نحوا من خمسين دينارا وَهو مصدق فيما قال فيُقْضَى ما له علىّ من غلة الدار ان شآء الله فاذا استوفى أُعطى ولدُ صالح وعبدِ الله ابنىْ [Cod. ابن] احمد بن حنبل كل

First Invitation to Visit al-Mutawakkil

An invitation from the Khalif to Aḥmed to visit him was brought to him before the end of the year 235 A. H. by Isḥâķ ibn Ibrâhîm [1]), who on this occasion asked Aḥmed's forgiveness for the part which he had taken in the scourging under al-Muʿtaṣim. Aḥmed, in reply, assured him that he had fully forgiven all who had sought his hurt, or participated, in any way, on that occasion. Isḥâķ then proceeded to ask Aḥmed for his own private satisfaction about the Ķorân, and the latter expressed himself, as he uniformly did, to the effect that it was the uncreated Word of God. Isḥâķ then asked for the proofs of the statement, and Aḥmed, in answer, cited Ķorân 7. 52, 'Are not the Creation and the Command his?' and pointed out that in the passage a distinction was made between the Creation and the Command. The 'Command' الامر, in controversies of this kind refers to the eternal and heavenly Word of God, just as does 'Kun', on page 119. Isḥâķ said, 'The Command is created'. 'What!' exclaimed Aḥmed, 'the Command created! Nay, it creates that which is created'. Isḥâķ then asked, 'Who has handed down in Tradition the view that it is not created'? Aḥmed answered, "Jaʿfar ibn Moḥammed, who said, 'It is neither a creator nor a created thing" [2]). Then, this conversation being ended and Isḥâķ having secured Aḥmed's agreement to go to the camp, it was not long before he was on the way thither; but, for some unexplained cause, orders came while the

and Conversation with Isḥâķ ibn Ibrâhîm on the Subject of the Ķorân.

ذكر وانثى عشرة دَرَاهِمْ بعد وفاة مـل ابى محمد شهد ابو يوسف

وصالح وعبد الله ابنا احمد بن محمد بن حنبل،

1) Isḥâķ ibn Ibrâhîm, the governor of ʿIrâķ, as well as Isḥâķ ibn Ibrâhîm al-Mausilî, the favorite of the Khalifs, died in 235 A. H. The one referred to in the text is, of course, the former.

2) This appears to be not only an authentic tradition, but, as well, the clearest and most direct which was offered by the orthodox in support of their view.

journey was in progress for him to be returned to his home. It is altogether likely that a suspicion of ᶜAlyite leanings in Aḥmed ibn Ḥanbal afford an explanation of this fact. As will presently appear, Aḥmed was two or three times accused ot such leanings to this Khalif.

Aḥmed Accused of ᶜAlyite Intrigues. In the year 237 A. H., information was given to the Khalif charging Aḥmed with having sent one of his companions to meet an ᶜAlyite who was coming to him from Khorasân. On hearing this, the Khalif wrote a letter to Abdallah ibn Isḥâḳ, governor of Baghdâd, (who had succeeded his brother Moḥammed and his father Isḥâḳ ibn Ibrâhîm in the office) asking him to inquire of Aḥmed as to the truth of the charge laid against him, and, also, to search his premises and make sure in the matter. In pursuance of these directions, Abdallah sent his chamberlain Muẓaffar and the postmaster Ibn al-Kalbî [1]), together with women who were to examine the women's apartments, to carry out the orders which had come to hand. When they were come and had read to Aḥmed the Khalif's letter, he protested that the report was without foundation, and that he was in all respects a loyal subject [2]). The searching of the premises, too, revealed nothing to substantiate the charge against him.

The result was reported to the Khalif, and a day or two later, there came a letter from ᶜAlî ibn al-Jahm [3]) to Aḥmed saying that the Khalif was fully satisfied of the groundlessness of the report, and that it had been fabricated by heretics with the design of injuring him. The letter of ᶜAlî intimated, likewise, the Khalif's wish that Aḥmed should

1) For employment of postmasters in this sort of detective service vid. Houtsma, 71.

2) Aḥmed had been keeping to his house up to this time, following the orders of Isḥâḳ the former governor. On theologians keeping to their houses cf. Goldziher, Moh. Stud. II, 94. On the similar practice by the so-called Ḳaᶜada (still-sitters) cf. Houtsma, De Strijd etc., 26 f.

3) ᶜAlî ibn al-Jahm banished to Khorasân and killed there by al-Mutawakkil's directions, 239 A. H., vid. Ibn Chall. N°. 473; Abu'l-Maḥ. I, 730; Abu 'l-Feda Ann. II, 190.

Second Invitation from al-Mutawakkil. visit him, and advised that a messenger was on the way with a gift of money from the Khalif. The day following the arrival of the letter the messenger, Yaᶜḳûb Ḳausarra, arrived bringing, in official form, the invitation already alluded to, and handing over the sum of 10,000 dirhems as the royal gift (جائزة). Yaᶜḳûb then went away, telling Aḥmed that he would return next morning for an answer to his message. That night was a sleepless one for Aḥmed. The gift of al-Mutawakkil, which he had given into the charge of Ṣâliḥ his son, troubled him greatly. Finally, he made up his mind to be rid of the money altogether, and, rising betimes in the morning, he summoned persons whom he ordered to take portions to the descendants of the Muhajirûn and Anṣâr and to the general poor, until the whole sum received had been paid out. It was a great grief to him that now at the end of his life, after he had successfully resisted anything of the kind for so long a time, he was to be forced to be a compromised pensioner on the bounty of the Khalif, a relationship which he with all his might sought to avoid, and from which after this he succeeded in keeping himself almost entirely free to the very end of his days. When word came to the Khalif of Aḥmed's action, ᶜAlî ibn al-Jahm prevented his master's displeasure by the explanation that such a man as Aḥmed had no need of money, for his living consisted but of a crust of bread.

In a short time, Aḥmed was on his way to the Khalif. Of the journey nothing of special interest is recorded, save that he availed himself of the legal provision that the prayers might be shortened while travelling, and that he, interpreting the provision as positive and not merely permissive, on one occasion complained that Ṣâliḥ his son had made the prayers too long. Arrived at the camp, he was first lodged in the house of Îtâkh [1]), and word was sent to his sons from the Court that an allowance of 10,000 dirhems had been appointed

---

1) v. p. 144, note 2.

to be given them, in place of the money which had been given away by their father. It was, at the same time, specially ordered that their father should not be told of the matter. Al-Mutawakkil now sent his greeting to Aḥmed, and congratulated him on his escape from the attempts of his enemies to involve him in suspicions. If we may believe the record, and we probably may, al-Mutawakkil also expressed his pleasure at Aḥmed's presence, as he wished to consult him in the matter of Ibn Abî Dowâd, who had just fallen into disgrace [1]). Very soon a wish of the Khalif was made known to Aḥmed that he should remain with him to teach Tradition and give up the idea of returning to Baghdâd. Especially did the Khalif desire him to undertake the teaching of al-Muʿtazz, his favorite son [2]). From all this Aḥmed tried to excuse himself on the ground of physical infirmity, pointing to his loose teeth and other evidences of age and weakness. He declared his belief to be that the invitation and entertainment were, together, parts of a conspiracy to keep him in restraint — to make him a prisoner while yet the guest of his Sovereign. And he vowed a vow that he would never as long as he lived tell another complete tradition. Some say that this vow extended over the last eight years of his life; but if he came to the Khalif in 237 A. H., and took upon him the vow in order to escape detention where he was, the duration of its binding force was a little over four years. It may be that the vow was taken when al-Wâthiḳ requested him to leave Baghdâd, for we know that he ceased to teach during the latter months of that Khalif's reign; still, as a matter of fact, we have in this case more than eight years, and, on the whole, it seems desirable to date his final cessation of teaching from the time of this visit to al-Mutawakkil, when he was 73 years of age and, as we really know, a man much weakened in his physical constitution.

Aḥmed Objects to Remain at the Camp

and Virtually Gives up Teaching.

1) vid. note 2, p. 56.

2) al-Sujûtî, Taríkh al-Khol. 357.

The Interest of al-Mutawakkil in Aḥmed. It appears to have been some time before Aḥmed was summoned to the Palace; but, in the meantime, the Khalif shewed a friendly interest in him and evinced a respect for his learning by submitting to him questions for his judgment upon them. One of these was the following: Supposing two animals to be fighting with their horns, and the one mortally wound the other; may the wounded animal if slaughtered be used for food? Aḥmed's answer was that, if the animal shewed signs of life by moving its eyelids and by switching its tail, and if its blood was still flowing and not congealed, it might be slaughtered and eaten.

His Visit to the Palace. At last, he was ordered to appear in the presence of the Khalif's son al-Muᶜtazz. It was a sore affliction to Aḥmed when Yaḥya ibn Khaḳân came to fit on him the Court costume, but he was induced to allow it to be put upon him, though put it on himself he would not. On this occasion, Yaḥya ibn Khaḳân told the sons of Aḥmed that a stipend of 4000 dirhems per month had been ordered to be paid to them, but that their father was not to know of it. On arriving at the Palace, Aḥmed was well received, though there is but a very scant notice of the audience. After his return to his lodgings from this first visit to his new protégé, he felt badly over the sin he thought he had committed in wearing the fine clothes he had been obliged to put on; and, at once removing them, he ordered his son Ṣâliḥ to send them to Baghdâd, where they were to be sold and their price given to the poor. His own family he forbade to reserve any of the garments for their personal use; but, notwithstanding, Ṣâliḥ kept the bonnet. Aḥmed's peace of mind was much disturbed at this time, also, over his prospective visits to the Sovereign himself, and the charge he should have as tutor to the Khalif's son; for it seems that al-Mutawakkil did not, at first, take into consideration the vow which Aḥmed had taken not to tell Tradition perfectly.

It is not likely that he really appeared before al-Mutawakkil at all; at least, we have nothing to shew that he did, nor have we any evidence that he actually had the charge of the Khalif's son. Al-Muᶜtazz, at the time of Aḥmed's arrival at Surramanra, was not more than six years of age, if as old as that [1]).

Asks a Change of Residence

Aḥmed's next grievance arose when he learned that the house in which he was lodged had belonged to Îtâkh [2]). On hearing this, he had a letter written to Moḥammed ibn al-Jarrâḥ, seeking that al-Mutawakkil would release him from the obligation to remain there. The Khalif granted this request, and then sought to engage another home for him, by asking some people to move out of the house which they were occupying. This Aḥmed did not wish and it was given up. Finally, a suitable place was hired for him at a rent of 200 dirhems.

and is Offended at the Luxurious Provision Made for Him.

Here he was grieved at the luxury with which the house was furnished, and, leaving the finely furnished apartments, contented himself with a humble mattress which he had brought with him. The bountiful table which was placed at his disposal was, likewise, a great offence to him; a fact which we can readily believe, when we are informed that the landlord of the house offered Ṣâliḥ ibn Aḥmed a sum of 3000 dirhems a month for it, and was refused. Those of his family who were desirous of retaining the table were obliged to have it set down in the vestibule of the house, where he might not see it.

Fasting and Sickness.

He himself fasted most of the time, partaking only of a little sawîḳ and bread, until, at last, he was taken sick and the well-known physician Ibn Masûyah had to be sent to prescribe for him. He examined Aḥmed, assured him that his trouble was not really a disease, but simply weakness and wasting of the body from lack of nourishment, and prescribed for him sesame oil, which he declared that he, as a Christian, was accustomed to give to the ascetics of his own faith when they had brought

---

1) He was born 232 A. H., Abu'l-Maḥ. II, 24.

2) Îtâkh the Turk killed 234 A. H., Abu'l-Maḥ. I, 702.

themselves to a similar condition. Aḥmed at this time seems to have received every attention at the hands of al-Mutawakkil and those about him; though, it does not surprise us to find him sometimes refusing kindnesses which were proffered.

Consulted about Ibn Abî Dowâd. At different times, attempts were made to draw from Aḥmed an expression of opinion regarding Aḥmed ibn Abî Dowâd his former persecutor, who had now fallen from favor. But neither about the man, nor about his estates and their disposition would he express himself at all. Nor was he any more willing to hear reports of the public gossip about his old adversary and the course of action which had been adopted towards him [1]).

Proposal to Buy a House for Him. After a time al-Mutawakkil proposed that he should buy a house for Aḥmed, but the latter obstinately refused his consent to the proposal, and ordered his son Ṣâliḥ to be no party to such a project. In the end the idea was given up.

Aḥmed again Urged to Attend on the Khalif The Khalif now began to urge that Aḥmed should attend continuously on him, as had been his intention in bringing him from Baghdâd. The day that he should begin had actually been agreed upon. Aḥmed, however, never concealed from anyone how extremely distasteful to him the obligation was. His uncle Isḥâḳ ibn Ḥanbal also urged him to go in to the Khalif and offer him direction and cited the example of Isḥâḳ ibn Râhawaih, who had done this with Ibn Ṭâhir (with advantage to himself). Aḥmed replied that he did not approve of Ibn Râhawaih or his course, and that in his conviction to be near persons in authority or to keep company with them was to imperil faith and violate conscience. Even as it was, he did not feel himself safe from guilt. After *but is Released.* all this a message came from the Khalif releasing him from all obligation to appear before either himself or his successors, and from the wearing of the black

1) vid. note 2, p. 56; Abu'l-Maḥ. I, 719.

Court costume. He might wear cotton or wool just as pleased him. It appears, in fact, to have been a general dispensation from fulfilling any requests from persons in authority which might be distasteful to him [1]). Now, at last, he was released from his fear that they were going to make of him an attaché of the Court, and on this point had ease of mind. For his fellow-traditionists who remained at Court his feeling appears to have been one of censuring contempt. They were afraid to do that which would deprive them of their stipends from the Khalif, and, possibly, bring upon them much worse consequences. Aḥmed had accomplished his end in securing his exemption from attendance at Court; not, however, by a direct refusal of the Khalif's mandate, but by persistent excuses; by shewing a dislike to what he was expected to do; and by his discontent with the general arrangements which were made for him by al-Mutawakkil's orders. He obstructed as far as possible the royal wishes, but did not deny them.

Correspondence with his Sons. His two sons, Ṣâliḥ and Abdallah, now returned to Baghdâd, and, after they had gone away, the fine furnishings of the house were removed, and the Khalif's daily provision ceased to be provided. By Abdallah, who left him later than his brother, he sent word to Ṣâliḥ, telling him that both he and his brother were not desired to attend on him any further, for he regarded most of the

---

1) al-Makrîzî, p. 10, قال المروزى سمعت اسحق بن حنبل عم احمد ونحن بالعسكر يناشده ويساله الدخول على الخليفة ليامره وينهاه وقال انه يقبل كلامك هذا اسحق بن راهويه يدخل على ابن طاهر فيامره وينهاه فقال له ابو عبد الله تحتجّ علىّ باسحق وأنا غير راضٍ بفعله ما له فى رؤيتى خير ولا لى فى رؤيته خير يجب علىّ اذا رايته ان آمره وانهاه الدنوّ منهم فتنة والجلوس معهم فتنة نحن متباعدون منهم ما أرانا نسلم فكيف لو قرّبنا منهم

unpleasant experiences through which he had passed as due to their not supporting him in the stand he had taken and their want of active sympathy with his principles. Their acceptance of the Khalif's fine provision, if they came back, would bring him only into ill-favor with the public; and their acceptance of the Khalif's stipend, against his known wish and sense of duty, he considered a grave breach of filial piety. They both might go where they would with his prayers following them, but he desired that they should not cumber him further by their presence. Such was the tenor of his first two letters to his son Ṣâliḥ. In a third he reproaches his sons for not taking steps to secure his release from his unwilling detention. But he advises them to keep to their dwellings [1]), and expresses the hope that God, by some means will open up his way.

Aḥmed's Testament. While at the camp, Aḥmed made his testament, which was as follows: In the name of God, the Merciful, the Gracious. This is the testament of Aḥmed ibn Ḥanbal. He testifies that there is no God but Allah, alone and without fellow, and that Moḥammed is his Servant and his Messenger whom He sent with the right guidance and the true religion, that he might make it known as the perfect religion, though the idolaters be displeased. He, further, testifies that those who obey his family and his relatives worship God among those who worship, praise him among those who offer praise and do good service to the Community of the Muslims. I, also, testify that I am satisfied with Allah as Lord, with Islâm as a religion, and with Moḥammed as Prophet. I, further, testify that Abdallah ibn Moḥammed, known as Bûrân, has a claim against me for about fifty dinârs, and that he is to be credited in whatever he may say. Let what is due to him be paid from the rent of the house, if God will, and after he has been paid, the children of Ṣâliḥ and Abdallah, sons of Aḥmed ibn Ḥanbal, are to receive, each male and female, ten dirhems,

1) p. 140, note 2.

after the payment of the money to Abû Moḥammed. Witnessed by Abû Yûsuf and Ṣâliḥ and Abdallah the two sons of Aḥmed ibn Moḥammed ibn Ḥanbal.

Permission Granted to Return to Baghdâd. It was not a great while before Aḥmed again requested a change of residence [1]), and the Khalif, with great kindness, acceded to his request and, not only allowed him to engage another dwelling, but sent to him one thousand dinârs that he might

---

1) Abû Nuʿaim, 153*a*, (The narrative now follows this source for a time.) قال ابو الفضل ثم سال ابى رحمه الله ان يحوّل من الدار التى اكتريَت له فاكرى هو دارا وتحوّل اليها فسال المتوكل عنه فقيل انه عليل فقال كنتُ احب ان يكون فى قربى فقد اذنت له يا عبيدَ الله احمل اليه الف دينار يَقسِمُها وقال لسعيد تُهيّء له حَرّاقة ينحدر فيها فجآءه على بن الجهم فى جوف الليل فاخبره ثم جآء عُبَيد الله ومعه الف دينار فقال ان امير المومنين قد اذن لك وقد امر لك بهذه الالف دينار فقال قد اعْفَانى امير المومنين مما اكره فردّها وقال انا رقيق على البَردِ [so Cod.] والظهرُ ارْفق بى فكُتب له جواز فكتب الى محمد بن عبد الله فى بره وتعاهده فقدم علينا فيما بين الظهر والعصر فلما انحدر الى بَغداد ومكث قليلا قال لى يا صَالح قلت لبيك قال احب ان تَدَعَ [Cod. تَدَعْ] هذا الرزق فلا تاخذه ولا تُوكِل فيه احدا فقد علمت انكم انما تاخذونه بسببى فسكتُّ فقال ما لَك فقلتُ أكره انْ اعطيَك شيعا بلسانى واخالف الى غيره فاكونَ قد كذبتك ونافقتك ولَيس فى القَوم اكثرُ عِيالا مِنى ولا أَعذَرُ وقد كُنتُ اشكو اليك فتقول امرُك منُعقَد بامرى ولعل الله ان تُحلّ عنى عن [del.?] هذه العقدة ثم قُلتُ له وقد كنتَ تَدْعو لى فارجو ان يكونَ الله استجاب لك قال ولا تفعل قلتُ لا فقال قم فعل الله بك وفعل

distribute it in alms. At the same time, he gave him leave to return home and ordered a pleasure barge to be

---

فامر بسَدِّ الباب بينى وبينه فتلقانى عبدُ الله فسَألنى فاخبرته فقال ما
اقولُ انا قلت ذاك اليك فقال له مثل ما قالِ لى فقال لا افعل فكان منه
اليه نحوُ ما كان منه الىَّ فلقينا عَمُه فقال لو اردتم ان تقولوا له
ما علمه اذا اخذتم شيعا فدخَل عليه فقال ياابا عبد الله لستُ اخذ
شيعا من هذا فقال الحمد لله وهَجَرنا وسَدَّ الابواب بيَنَنا وبينه ومحامى
منزلنا ان يَدخل منها الى منزِله شىء . . . .
قال ابو الفضل فلما مَضى نحوٌ من شهرين كُتِبَ لنا بشىء فجىء
به الينا فاوُلُ من جآء عَمه فاخذ فاخبر فجآء الى الباب الذى كان
سَدَّه بينى وبينَه وقد فتح الصبيان كوة فقال ادعو لى صالِحا فجآء
الرسول وقلتُ له قل له لستُ اجىء فوجَّه الىَّ لِمَ قال [؟قلتَ] لا
تجىء فقلت قُل له هذا الرزق تَرتَزِقه جماعة كثيرة وانما انا واحد
منهم وليس فيهم اعذر منى واذا كان توبيخ خُصِصتُ به انا فلما نادَى
عمه بالاذان خرَج فلما خَرج قيل لى انه قد خرج الى المسجد
فجئتُ حتى صِرتُ فى موضع اسْمع فيه كلامه فلما فرغ
التفت الى عمه ثم قال له نافقْتَنى وكذبتنى وكان غيرك اعـ
زعمت انك لا تاخذ من هذا شيعا ثم اخذته وانت تستغل سى
درهم وعمدت الى طَريق المسلمين تَستغله انما اشفق عليك ان تُطوَّق*
يوم القيامة سبع ارضين اخذت هذا الشىء بغير حقه فقال قد
تصدقتُ فقال تصدقتَ بنصف درهم ثم هجره وترك الصلاة فى المسجد
وخرج الى مسجد خارج يصلى فيه. The account of his difficulties with the members of his family over the Khalif's allowances is in the Ms. considerably extended, but the rest of it has no special interest, and varies but slightly from the extract here given.

made ready to take him to Baghdâd; this last favor however, Aḥmed declined, preferring to travel by land on account of risk to his health from the coldness of the river journey. When he left for home, al-Mutawakkil had a letter written to Moḥammed ibn Abdallah, the governor of Baghdâd, ordering him to deal kindly with Aḥmed and take good care of him.

Objects to his Family Receiving Stipends. From the time of his return to Baghdâd, the story of Aḥmed's life is little more than a record of his differences with his family — in particular, with his sons Ṣâliḥ and Abdallah, and his paternal uncle Isḥâḳ ibn Ḥanbal, — about the receiving of the Khalif's stipends and gifts which came to them from time to time. He would block up the doorways between his sons' houses and his own, when they expressed determination to accept the moneys, which they needed for the support of their families, and vigorously dissented from his view that their position was the same as his own, and that what was good for him was, likewise, good for them. For as long as two or three months together he would have nothing to do with his sons; and it was, apparently, only as their children in playing made their way into their grandfather's house and touched a more sympathetic chord of his nature, or as the offices of his good friend Bûrân (Abdallah ibn Moḥammed) were called in that reconciliation was brought about. His uncle Isḥâḳ certainly played worthy part toward him. He pretended great friendship and complete deference to his wishes as to the receiving of money, and at the same time accepted it with the rest. When Aḥmed discovered the dissimulation, he was very angry; and it was all to no purpose that Isḥâḳ tried to excuse himself on the ground that he had used the money in giving alms, for he knew, and Aḥmed knew, that he had not done so. Aḥmed then ceased to worship in the mosque where his sons and uncle worshipped, and for the necessary prayers went to a mosque outside the city quarter in which he lived.

Harassed as they were by him, the members of Aḥmed's

family agreed once or twice to receive no more money; but, after a period of abstinence, the urgent needs of their families forced them to give up the self-denial and again claim their stipends. At last, Aḥmed went so far as to write to Yaḥya ibn Khaḳân, telling him that he had made up his mind to request the withdrawal of the regular aid which was granted to his family. Ṣâliḥ anticipated his father, however, by informing the officer who was over that part of Baghdâd in which they resided, and he succeeded in preventing Aḥmed's letter from accomplishing its object. The aid was continued and, not only that, but all that was due to the family, 40,000 dirhems, being the undrawn stipend for ten months, was paid over to his sons. And, though the Khalif had ordered his officers not to inform Aḥmed of the payment, Ṣâliḥ himself sent word of it to his father. The old man, when he heard the message, exclaimed after a meditative silence, 'What can I do when I desire one thing and God orders another!' [1])

---

1) Abû Nuʿaim, 153*b*, قال ابو الفضل ثم كتب ابى رحمه الله الى يحيى ابن خاقان يسعله ويَعزم عليه ان لا يعيننا على شىء من ارزاقنا ولا يتكلم فيها فبلغنى فوجهت الى القيم لنا وهو ابو غالب بن بنت معاويَة بن عَمرو وقد كنت قلت له يا ابه انه يكبُر عليك وقد عزمتُ اذا حدث امر اخبرتك به فلما وصل رسوله بالكتاب الى يحيى اخذه صاحب الخبَر فاخذ نسختته ووصلت الى المتوكل فقال لعبيد الله كم من شهر لولد احمد بن حنبل فقال عشرة اشهر قال يُحمَل اليهم الساعة اربعون الف درهم من بيت المال صحاح ولا يُعلم هو بها قال فقال يحيى للقيم انا اكتب الى صالح واعلمه فورَدَ علىّ كتابُه فوجهت الى ابى أُعلمه فقال الذى اخبرَه انه سكت قليلا وضرب بذَقْنه [Cod. بذقْنه] ساعة ثم رفع راسه فقال ما حِيلتى اذا اردتُ امرًا

Again Suspected of ᶜAlyite Intrigues.

After Aḥmed's return to Baghdâd (the date of which we do not know) some talebearer reported to al-Mutawakkil the old slander that Aḥmed was harboring an ᶜAlyite. The Khalif sent word to Aḥmed of the report, and told him that he had imprisoned the man who made it until he should advise him as to what truth there was in the report, and direct him what to do to the man. Aḥmed answered asserting his ignorance of the whole matter, but advised that the man should be set free, as to visit him with death might bring affliction to many others who were no sharers in his crime.

A man whose name is given as Abû Jaᶜfar ibn Dharîḥ al-ᶜUkbarî relates that, in the year 236, (which appears to be a mistake, for the circumstances point to the time of the second accusation of harboring an ᶜAlyite, and this was after Aḥmed's return to Baghdâd from his visit to the camp in 237 A. H.) he sought Aḥmed to ask him some doctrinal question, but was told at his house that he had gone outside that quarter of the city to prayers. So Abû Jaᶜfar sat down at the gate of the street to wait for his return. Presently, an old man, tall, with dyed hair and beard, and of a dark brown complexion, came up and entered the street, the visitor entering with him. At the end of the street, Aḥmed, for such it was, opened a gate and entered it, closing it after him and at the same time bidding his companion go his way. Just then, the latter noticed at the gate a mosque, in which an old man, also with dyed hair, was leading the prayers. When he had finished, Abû Jaᶜfar asked a man who was at the prayers about Aḥmed ibn Ḥanbal and why he had refused to answer him. The man re-

---

واراد الله امرا، قال ابو الفضل وجآء رسول المتوكل الى ابى يقول لو سَلِم احدٌ من الناس سلمتَ رفع رجُل الىّ فى وقت كذا انّ عَلويا قدم من خراسان وانك وجهت اليه بمن يلقاه وقد حَبَستُ الرجل واردتُ ضربَه وكرِهتُ ان تغتم فمُر فيه فقال هذا باطل ويُخلى سبيله

plied that Aḥmed had been suspected of harboring an ʿAlyite; that, on this account, the prefect of police had surrounded his dwelling with a cordon of police and then had proceeded to search it. For this reason he avoided speaking to people. The police had, however, found nothing to give substance to the suspicion which had been raised. Abû Jaʿfar, then, enquired who it was whom he had seen leading the prayers, and, on learning that it was Aḥmed's uncle Isḥâḳ, he asked why Aḥmed ibn Ḥanbal did not pray behind his uncle in this mosque which was near his own door. The man answered that he did not worship with his uncle, nor even his own sons, nor speak with any of them, because they had accepted the stipends and gifts of the Khalif [1].

---

1) Abû Nuʿaim, 142 a, حدثنا ابو بكر احمد بن جعفر بن مالك ثنا ابو جعفر بن ذريح العُكبرى قال طلبت احمد بن حنبل فى سنة ست وثلاثين لاسئله عن مسئلة فسألتُ عنه فقالوا خرج يصلى خارجا فجلَسْتُ له على باب الدرب [so marg.; text الدار] حتى جآء فقمت فسلمت عليه فردَّ علىّ السلام وكان شيخًا مخْضُوبًا طوالا اسْمَر شَديدَ السُمرة فدخل الزقاق وانا معه اماشِيه خطوةً بخَطوة فلما بلغْنا آخرَ الدرب اذا باب يفرج دفعه وصار خلفه وقال اذهَبْ عافاك الله فثنيتُ عليه فقال اذْهَبْ عافاك الله قال فالتفتُّ فاذا مسجد على الباب وشَيخ مخضوب قائم يصلى بالناس فجلسْت حتى سَلم الامام فخرج رجل فسألته عن احمد بن حنبل وعن تَخلفه عن كلامى فقال أُدّعِى عليه عند السلطان انّ عنده عَلويا فجاء محمد ابن نصر فاحاط بالمَحلة ففُتِشَتْ فلم يوجد فيها شيء مما ذكر فاعْتجَم عن كلام العامة فقلت هذا الشيخ من هو قال عَمّه اسحاق قلت فما له لا يُصَلى خلفه قال ليس يُكلم ذا ولا بنيه لانّهم اخذوا جآئزة السلطان،

Al-Mutawakkil never ceased to shew his interest in Aḥmed's welfare, and to make frequent inquiries about him. This was, for some reason which is hard to divine, most disagreeable to Aḥmed; and he professed himself as preferring to die rather than have to live through such incessant attentions [1]). Among the evidences of the Khalif's interest was a letter written by ʿObaidallah ibn Yaḥya on his account, asking Aḥmed to write him his views on the Ḳorân, not by way of assurance of his accordance with the opinion of the Sovereign, but merely for the information of the Commander of the Faithful. In reply Aḥmed dictated to his son a letter to ʿObaidallah, in which he said [2]): —

The Khalif Asks for Aḥmed's View as to the Ḳorân.

---

1) Abû Nuʿaim, 153 *b*, قال وكان رسولُ المتوكل ياتى الى يُبلغه السلام ويسئله عن حاله فنُسَرُّ نحن بذاك فياخذه نغضة [Cod. نَعضه] حتى تُدَثّره [Cod. no points] يقول والله لو ان نفسى فى يدى لارسلتُها ويضُم اصابعه ثم يفتحها

2) Abû Nuʿaim, 153 *b* ff. حدثنا سليمان بن احمد ثنا عبد الله ابن احمد بن حنبل ح وحدثنا محمد وعلى والحسين قالوا ثنا محمد ابن اسمعيل ثنا صالح بن احمد بن حنبل قال كتبَ عُبَيد الله بن يحيى الى ابى رحمه الله يُخبره ان امير المومنين امرَنى ان اكتبَ اليك اسالك عن امر القران لا مسئلة امتحان ولكن مسئلة معرفة وبَصيرة فاملَى علىّ ابى رحمه الله الى عُبَيد الله بن يحيى وحدى ما معى احد بسم الله الرحمن الرحيم احسن الله عاقبتك ابا الحسن فى الامور كلها ودفع عنك مكاره الدنيا والاخرة برحمته قد كتبت اليك رضى الله عنك بالذى سال عنه امير المومنين بامر القران بما حضرنى وانى اسئل الله تعالى ان يديم توفيق امير المومنين فقد كان الناس فى خوض من الباطل * واختلاف شديد يغتمسون فيه حتى افضت الخلافة الى

Aḥmed's Letter in Reply. I ask God to continue his aid to the Commander of the Faithful, for men were in the depth of falsehood and immersed in violent differences of opinion until the Khalifate came to the Commander of the Faithful, and God banished by means of the Commander

---

امير المومنين فنفى الله بامير المومنين كلّ بدعة وانجلى عن الناس ما كانوا فيه من الذل وضيق المحابس [Cod. المجالس] فصرَف الله ذلك كله وذهب به بامير المومنين وَقع ذلك من المسلمين موقعا عظيما ودعوا الله لامير المومنين فاسئل الله ان يستجيب فى امير المومنين صالحَ الدعآء وان يُتمّ ذلك لامير المومنين وان يزيد فى نيته ويُعينه على ما هو عليه فقد ذكر عن عبد الله بن عباس رضى الله عنه انه قال لا تضرِبوا كِتاب الله بعضَه ببعض فانّ ذلك يُوقِع الشك فى قلوبكم وذُكِر عن عَبد الله بن عمر [Cod. عمرو] رَضى الله عنه ان نفرًا كانوا جلوسا بباب النبى صلى الله عليه وسلم فقال بعضُهم الم يقُل الله كذا وقال بعضهم الم يقل الله كذا قال فسَمِع ذلك رسول الله صلى الله عليه وسلم فخرج كانما فُقِئَ فى وجهه حَبُّ الرمّان فقال افبهذا أُمِرتم ان تضربوا كتاب الله بعضَه ببعض انما ضلّت الامم قبلكم فى مثل هذا انّكم لستم مما هاهنا فى شىء انظروا الذى أُمِرتم به فاعملوا به وانظروا الذى نُهيتم عنه فانتهوا عنه، وروى عن ابى هريرة رضى الله عَنْهُ [Cod omits] عن النبى صلى الله عليه وسلم انه قال مرآء فى القران كفر وروى عن ابى جهيم رجلٍ من اصحاب النبى صلى الله عليه وسلم عن النبى صلعم قال لا تمارُوا فى القران فانّ مرآء فيه كفر، وقال عبد الله بن عباس رضى الله عنه قدم على عمر بن الخطاب رضى الله عنه رَجُل فجعل عمر يسئله عن الناس فقال يا امير المومنين قد قرأ القرانَ منهم كذا وكذا فقال ابنُ عباس فقلت والله

of the Faithful every heresy, and took away from men the straitness and humiliation of the prisons. God has, thus, changed all that, and removed it through the Commander of the Faithful, [all of] which has made a great impression upon the Muslims; hence, they pray God to bless the Commander of the Faithful, and I ask God to hearken to all

---

ما أُحِب ان يتسارعوا يومهم هذا فى القران هذه المسارعة قال فزبرنى عمر وقال مَه فانطلقتُ الى منزلى مُكتئبا حزينا فبينا انا كذلك اذ [اذا .Cod] اتانى رجل فقال اجبْ امير المومنين فخرجْتُ فاذا هو بالباب ينتظرنى فاخذ بيدى فخلا بى وقال ما الذى كرهتَ مما قال الرجلُ آنفا فقلت يا امير المومنين متى يتسارعوا هذه المسارعة يحتقوا ومتى ما يحتقوا يَختصموا ومتى ما [لا .Cod] يَختصموا يختلفوا ومتى ما يختلفوا يقتتلوا قال لِلّه ابوك والله انْ كنت لاكتمها الناس حتى جئتَ بها، وروى عن جابر بن عبد الله رضى الله عنه قال كان النبى صلعم يَعرِضُ نفسَه على الناس بالموقف فيقول هل من رجل يحملنى الى قَومه فانّ قريشا قد منعونى ان ابلغ كلام ربّى، وروى عن جُبَيْر بن نُفَيْر قال قال رسول الله صلعم انكم لن تَرجعوا الى الله بشىء افضلَ مما خرج منه يعنى القرآن، وروى عن عبد الله بن مسعود رضى الله عنه انه قال جَرّدوا القران ولا تكتُبوا فيه شيئا الا كلام الله، وروى عن عمر بن الخطاب رضى الله عنه [Cod. omits] انه قال هذا القرانُ كلامُ الله فضَعُوه مواضِعَه، قال رجل للحسن البصرى يابا سعيد انى اذا قرأتُ كتابَ الله وتدبرته كدتُ ان آيَس وينقطع رجآءى قال فقال الحسن انّ القران كلام الله اعمال بنى آدم الى الضعف والتقصير فاعمل وابشر، وقال فروة بن نوفل الاشجعى كنت جار الخبّاب وهو من اصحاب النبى صلى الله عليه

good petitions for the Commander of the Faithful and to perfect [all] that for the Commander of the Faithful, that he may go on in his design; [I ask God] to help him, also, in that in which he is engaged. Now, it is related from Ibn ʿAbbâs

---

وسلم فخرجت معه يوما من المسجد وهو آخذ بيدى فقال يا هناه تَقَرَّب الى الله بما استطعت فانك لن تُقرَّب الله بشىء احبَّ اليه من كلامه، وقال رجل للحكم بن عيينة ما حمل اهلَ [اهلُ .Cod] الاهوآء على هذا قال الخصومات، وقال معاوية بن قُرّة* وكان ابوه ممن اتى النبى صلعم اياكم وهذه الخصومات فانها تحبط الاعمال، وقال ابو قِلابَة وكان قد ادرك غير واحد من اصحاب رسول الله صلعم لا تجالسوا اصحاب الاهوآء او قال اصحاب الخصومات فانى لا آمن ان يَغمسوكم فى ضلالتهم ويلبسوا عليكم بعض ما تعرفون، ودخل رجلان من اصحاب الاهوآء على محمد بن سِيرِين فقالا يابا بكر نُحدثك بحديث فقال لا فقالا فنقرأ عليك آية من كتاب الله قال لا لتقومان عنى او لأقومَنّه قال فقام الرجلان فخرجا فقال بعض القوم يابا بكر وما عليك ان تُقرأ عليك آية من كتاب الله فقال له ابن سيرين انى خشيت ان يقرأا [يقرءا .Cod] علىّ اية فيُحرفانها فيقر ذلك قلبى، وقال محمدٌ لو أعلم انى اكون مِثلِى الساعة لتركتهما، وقال رجل من اهل البدع لايوب السختيانى يابا بكر اسألك عن كلمة فى فولّى وهو يقول بيده ولا نصف كلمة، وقال طاووس بن طاوس لابن له وتكلم رجل من اهل البدع يابنى أدخل اصبعيك فى اذنيك حتى لا تسمع ما يقول ثم قال اشْدُد اشدد، وقال عمر بن عبد العزيز من جعل دينه غرضا للخصومات اكثر التنقّل، قال ابو الفضل وجدت فى كتاب ابى بخطه ثنا اسمعيل عن يونس قال نبئت

that he said, 'Do not smite God's Book one part of it with another part, for that casts doubt into your hearts'. And it is told from Abdallah ibn ʿOmar that he said, 'Some persons were sitting at the Prophet's door, and some of them

---

عمر بن عبد العزيز قال من جعل دينه غرضا للخصومات اكثر التنقّل، وقال ابرهيم النَخَعِىُّ ان القوم لم يُدَّخر عنهم شىء [Cod. شيا] حتى لكم لفضل عندكم، وكان الحسن يقول شرُّ دآء خالط قلبا يعنى الاهوآء، وقال حُذَيْفَة بن اليمان رضى الله عنه وكان من اصحاب رسول الله صلعم اتّقوا الله مَعشر القرّآء وَخُذوا طريق من كان قبلكم والله ـن اسْتَبَقْتُم لقد سُبقتم سبقا بعيدا ولئن تركتموه يمينا وشمالا نقد ضللتم ضلالا بعيدا او قال مُبينا قال ابى وانما تركتُ ذكر الاسانيد لما تقدم من اليمين التى حلفتُ بها مما قد عَلمه اميرُ المومنين لو لا ذاك ذكرتُها باسانيدها وقد قال الله تعالى وإنْ أَحَدٌ مِنَ ٱلْمُشْرِكِينَ ٱسْتَجَارَكَ فَأَجِرْهُ حَتَّى يَسْمَعَ كَلَامَ ٱللّٰهِ [Ḳor. 9. 6] وقال أَلَا لَهُ الخَلْقُ وَٱلْأَمْرُ [Ḳor. 7. 52] فَاخْبَرَ بالخلق ثم قال والامر فَاخْبَرَ ان الامر غيرُ الخلق وقال تعالى الرَّحْمٰن عَلَّمَ القُرْآنَ خَلَقَ ٱلْإِنْسَانَ عَلَّمَهُ البَيَانَ [Ḳor. 55. 1, 2, 3] فاخبر تعالى ان القُران من علمه وقال وَلَنْ تَرْضَى عَنْكَ اليَهُودُ وَلَا النَّصَارَى حَتَّى تَتَّبِعَ مِلَّتَهُمْ نلْ انَّ هُدَى ٱللّٰهِ هُوَ ٱلْهُدَى ولَئِنْ ٱتَّبَعْتَ أَهْوَآءَهُمْ بَعْدَ ٱلَّذِى جَآءَكَ ـنَ ٱلْعِلْمِ مَا لَكَ مِنَ ٱللّٰهِ مِنْ وَلِيٍّ وَلَا نَصِيرٍ [Ḳor. 2. 114] وقال لَئِنْ أَتَيْتَ ٱلَّذِينَ أُوتُوا ٱلْكِتَابَ بِكُلِّ آيَةٍ مَا تَبِعُوا قِبْلَتَكَ وَمَا أَنْتَ نَابِعٍ قِبْلَتَهُمْ وَمَا بَعْضُهُمْ بِتَابِعٍ قِبْلَةَ بَعْضٍ ولَئِنِ ٱتَّبَعْتَ أَهْوَآءَهُمْ مِنْ ند مَا جَآءَكَ مِنَ ٱلْعِلْمِ انَّكَ اذًا لَمِنَ ٱلظَّالِمِينَ [Ḳor. 2. 140] وقال نَذٰلِكَ أَنْزَلْنَاهُ حُكْمًا عَرَبِيًّا ولَئِنِ ٱتَّبَعْتَ أَهْوَآءَهُمْ بَعْدَ مَا جَآءَكَ مِنَ

were saying, Does not God say so and so? while others were saying, Nay! does not God say so and so? and the Messenger of God heard that, and went out — and it was as if pomegranates [1]) had been burst over his face — and he said, 'Was it this ye were commanded to observe, to smite God's Book one part of it with another? The peoples who were before you erred thus, but ye have nothing to do with this. Observe what ye are ordered to do and do it; and observe what ye are forbidden to do and abstain from it'. It is related from Abû Huraira from the Prophet that he said, 'Disputation about the Ḳorân is unbelief.' It is related from Abû Juhaim, one of the Companions of the Prophet, from the Prophet that he said, 'Do not dispute over the Ḳorân, for disputation over it is unbelief.' Abdallah ibn ʿAbbâs said, 'A man came to ʿOmâr ibn al-Khaṭṭâb, and ʿOmâr began to ask him about the people, and he said, 'O Commander of the Faithful, so and so many of them recite the Ḳorân (or, supply مَرَّةً: 'Some of them have read the Ḳorân so and so many times'?).' And Ibn ʿAbbâs said, 'So I said, By God, I do not like them to vie with each other in rapid reading of the Ḳorân, but ʿOmâr

---

ٱلْعِلْمِ مَا لَكَ مِنَ ٱللّٰهِ مِنْ وَلِيٍّ وَلَا وَاقٍ [Kor. 13. 37] فالقرآن من علم الله وفى هذه الايات دليل على انّ الذى جاءه صلعم هو القرآن لقوله ولئن اتبعت اهوآءهم بعد الذى جاءك من العلم، وقد رُوِى عن غير واحد ممن مضى مِن سلفنا انهم كانوا يقولون القرآن كلام الله غير مخلوق وهو الذى اذهب اليه لَسْتُ بصاحب كلام ولا ارى الكلام فى شىء من هذا الامر الا ما كان فى كتاب الله او فى حديث عن النبى صلعم اوْ عن اصحابه او عن التابعين فلمّا غير ذلك فانّ الكلام فيه غير محمود،

1) حبّ الرمان "the seeds of the pomegranate", but often "the pomegranate" itself.

blamed me for saying this, and said, 'Stop! Hush!' I went down, then, to my dwelling afflicted and grieving [because he seemed to oppose my zeal for the Ḳorân]. And, while I was in this state of mind, a man came to me and said, 'Answer the summons of the Commander of the Faithful'. So I went out, and lo! he was at the door waiting for me, and he took me by the hand, went aside with me, and said, 'What was that with which you were displeased in what the man said a little while ago?' I said, 'O Commander of the Faithful, when they indulge in this rivalry to see who can read fastest, they read with mumbling voice; and if they read with mumbling voice, they dispute with one another; and if they dispute with one another, they fall into discord; and if they fall into discord they fight with one another. He said, 'Very good! Verily, by God, I was concealing it [the same opinion] from anyone until you said it'. It is related from Jâbir ibn Abdallah that he said, 'The Prophet was presenting himself to the men in the Mauḳif [at Arafât] and he said, Is there any man who will take me to his people? for the Ḳoreish have refused me the right to make known the Word of my Lord'. It is related from Jubair ibn Nufair that he said, 'The Messenger of God said, You cannot return unto God by means of anything more excellent than that which went out from him. He meant the Ḳorân'. It is related from Abdallah ibn Masᶜûd that he said, 'Write the bare Ḳorân, but do not write in it anything except the Word of God'. It is related from ᶜOmar ibn al-Khaṭṭâb that he said, 'This Ḳorân is the Word of God; give it, then, its proper place'. A man said to al-Ḥasan al-Baṣrî, 'O Abû Saᶜîd, when I read the Word of God, and think over it, I almost despair and give up hope'. And al-Ḥasan said, 'The Ḳorân is the Word of God; the works of the children of Adam incline toward weakness and insufficiency, but work and be of good cheer!' Farwa ibn Naufal al-Ashjaᶜî said, 'I was a neighbour of al-Khabbâb, who was one of the Companions of the Prophet, and I went out with him one day from the mosque, he holding me by the hand, and he said, O you! draw near to God by means of that which you are able to use as means, but you cannot draw near to God by means of anything dearer unto him than his Word'. A man said to al-Ḥakam ibn ʿUyaina, 'What leads the sceptics [1]) unto this [state of theirs]?' He said, 'Disputation'. Muʿâwia ibn Ḳurra, whose father was one of those who came to the Prophet said, 'Beware of these disputations, for they spoil good works'. Abû Ḳilâba said (and he had met more than one of the Companions of the Messenger of God), 'Do not keep company with sceptics, (or he said, 'With disputatious people') for I do not feel secure that they will not plunge you in their error, and make obscure unto you a part of what ye know'. There entered two sceptics unto Moḥammed ibn Sîrîn, and they said, 'O Abû Bekr, let us tell thee a tradition'. He said, 'Nay'. Then they said, 'Then let us recite unto thee a verse from the Ḳorân'. He said, 'Nay; ye surely shall go away from me, or else I shall go away'. So the two men arose and went out, and one of those present said, 'O Abû Bekr, what was the matter, that a verse from the Ḳorân might not be recited unto thee?' and Ibn Sîrîn said to him, 'I was afraid that they would recite a verse unto me and would pervert it and that that should become fixed in my heart'. Moḥammed however, added, 'Had I known that I should be as I am now, I would certainly have allowed them'. A sceptic once asked Ayûb al-Sakhtiyânî, 'O Abû Bekr, I would ask thee just a word'; but he turned his back, and motioned with his hand, 'Nay; not half a word'. Ṭâûs ibn Ṭâûs said to a son of his, when a sceptic was speaking, 'O my son, put your fingers in your ears so that you shall

1) This word does not quite represent the idea of the original اهل الأهواء. These were a class of men who were not prepared to accept the religious systems of other persons, except as their own reasoning confirmed their positions. They were thus in the first instance sceptical and then eclectic, taking from different systems such views as they approved or 'desired' to take. The name Ahluʾl-ʾAhwâ 'men of desires', is thus appropriate. v. Shahrastânî, Haarbrücker's transl'n I, p. 1 and note; Steiner, Die Muʿtaziliten, 6.

not hear what he says'. Then he said, 'Run! Run!' ᶜOmar ibn Abd al-ᶜAzîz said, 'He who makes his religion a butt for disputations is the most unsettled of men'. (*Abu'l Faḍl* said, 'I found it in a book of my father's in his own handwriting, 'Ismaᶜîl told us from Yûnus saying, I was told that ᶜOmar ibn Abd al-ᶜAzîz said, 'He who makes his religion a butt for disputations is the most unsettled of men'). Ibrâhîm al-Nakha'î said, 'These people shall have nothing laid up in store for them until there is with you an excellent provision'. Al-Ḥasan used to say, 'The worst diseased person is the man diseased at heart'; he meant the desires [i. e. men of desires — sceptics]. Hudhaifa ibn al-Yamân said, 'Fear God, O ye Reciters of the Ḳorân, and go in the way of those who were before you; for, if ye strive for precedence, ye have yet been preceded by a great distance, and if ye leave this way to the right or left ye have clearly committed error'. The letter went on to say: 'I have omitted the mention of the Isnâds because of the oath that I previously swore, of which the Commander of the Faithful is cognizant. If it were not for that, I should have mentioned them [the traditions] with their Isnâds. The Ḳorân, too, has said, 'And, if one of the idolaters seek protection of thee, grant him protection that he may hear the Word of God (Ḳorân 9.6). 'Do not the Creation and the Command belong to him?' (Ḳorân 7.52). So he tells about 'the Creation', and then he says, 'and the Command', thus he tells us that the 'Command' is something else than 'the Creation' [1]). Also, 'The Merciful taught (علّم) the Ḳorân, he created man, he taught him the explanation' (Ḳorân 55.1, 2, 3). Thus God tells that the Ḳorân is from his Knowledge (علْم). He, also, says, 'And the Jews will not be content with thee, nor the Christians, until thou dost follow their religion. Say, 'Verily the direction of God is the right direction; but, surely, if thou dost follow their passions and their desires, after that which has come to thee

1) cf. p. 119 and, also, p. 139.

of knowledge (علم) there is for thee from God neither friend nor helper' (Ḳorân 2 . 114). He says also, 'Even if thou dost give to those to whom the Book has been given every sign, they will not follow thy ḳibla, and thou wilt not follow their ḳibla, and one part of them will not follow the ḳibla of the other part. And, surely, if thou dost follow their passions, after what has come to thee of knowledge (علم), in that case, thou art, verily, one of those who do evil' (Ḳorân 2 . 140). And also, 'And, thus, we have sent it down as a decision in the Arabic language; and, surely, if thou dost follow their passions, after what has come to thee of knowledge (علم), there shall be for thee from God neither friend nor helper' (Ḳorân 13 . 37). Now, the Ḳorân is from the Knowledge of God; and in these verses is a proof that that which came to him [the Messenger of God] is the Ḳorân, according to his [God's] saying, 'And, surely, if thou dost follow their passions, after what has come to thee of knowledge (علم)'.1)

It has been related, moreover, from more than one of those who went before us that they used to say, 'the Ḳorân is the Word of God uncreated', and that is what I believe. I am no dialectical theologian; I approve of argument in a matter of this kind only by means of what is in God's Book or a tradition from the Prophet, or from his Companions, or from those who followed them (Tâbiʿiûn), but, as for anything else, argument by means of it is not to be commended.

On one occasion, when al-Mutawakkil came to al-Shamasîya on his way to al-Madâ'in, it was expected that Aḥmed and his family would come, or send, to pay their respects to him, but Aḥmed would neither go himself nor would he

1) "Passions" in these passages represents the word 'ʾAhwâ' found in the name Ahlu'l-ʾAhwâ, so that the passages must be taken as condemning rationalism in theological matters.

Visit of Yaḥya ibn Khaḳân to Aḥmed.

allow Ṣâliḥ to go, for fear he should call attention to himself. The result of this was that the next day Yaḥya ibn Khaḳân came with a great retinue to visit Aḥmed, bringing him greeting and many friendly enquiries from the Khalif, who, at the same time, besought the prayers of the Imâm. These last Aḥmed assured Yaḥya were offered up every day for his master. Yaḥya then offered him a thousand dinârs for distribution among the poor. These, however, Aḥmed would not accept, pleading exemption, as he did on other occasions, on the ground that the Khalif had agreed to excuse him from obligation to do anything that might be distasteful to him. The money was finally given to Aḥmed's sons.

Invitation from Moḥammed ibn Abdallah ibn Ṭâhir.

On another occasion, Moḥammed ibn Abdallah ibn Ṭâhir besought Aḥmed to pay him a visit and strongly urged his request. This invitation, however, Aḥmed also declined, offering as an excuse the Khalif's dispensation. After these incidents he took upon himself a rigid fast, abstaining from all fat and, apparently, from meat, for the record states that *before* this time he had been provided with a dirhem's worth of meat, from which he ate for a month! [1])

---

1) Abû Nuʿaim, 155*a*, قال ابو الفضل وقدم المتوكل فنزل الشماسيّة يريد المدآئن فقال لى ابى يا صالح احِبُّ ان لا تذهب اليهم ولا تُنَبِّه [Cod. without points] علىّ فلما كان بعد يوم وانا قاعد خارجا وكان يومُ مَطرٍ اذا يحيى بن خاقان قد جآء والمَطر [Cod. المطر] عليه فى موكب عظيم فقال سُبحان الله لم تصير الينا حتى تُبلِغ امير المومنين السلام عن شيخك حتّى وجّه بى ثم نزل خارج الزقاق فجهدت به ان يدخل على الدابة فلم يفعل فجعل يخوض المطر فلما صار الى الباب نزع جُرموقه وكان على خفه ودخل وابى فى الزاوية* قاعد عليه كسآء مربع وعمامة والستر الذى على الباب خيش فسلم

Aḥmed's Sickness and Death. In the course of events we have been brought now to the year 241 A. H. On the first day of Rabî' I of this year [1]), Aḥmed was taken with a

---

عليه وقبّل جبهته وسائله عن حاله وقال امير المومنين يقرئك السلام ويقول كيف انت فى نفسك وكيف حالك وقد آنست بقربك ويسألك ان تدعو له فقال ما يأتى علىّ يوم الا وانا ادعو له ثم قال قد وجه معى الف دينار لك تفرقها على اهل الحاجة فقال له يابا زكريّاء انا فى البيت منقطع عن الناس وقد اعفانى من كل ما اكرَه وهذا مما اكره فقال يابا عبد الله الخلفاء لا يحتملون هذا فقال يابا زكرياء تلطّف فى ذلك فدعا له ثم قام فلما صار الى الدّار رجع وقال هكذا لو وجّه اليك بعض اخوانك كنتَ تفعل قال نعم فلما صرْنا الى الدهليز قال قد امرنى امير المومنين ان ادفعها اليك وتفرقها فقلت تكونُ عندك الى ان تمضى هذه الايام، قال ابو الفضل وقد كان وجه محمد بن عبد الله بن طاهر الى ابى فى وقت قدومه مع العسكر احب ان تصير [Cod. تصيّر] الىّ وتعلمنى اليوم الذى تعزم عليه حتى لا يكونَ عندى احد فوجّه اليه انا رجل لم اخالط السلطان وقد اعفانى امير المومنين مما أكره وهذا مما اكرَه فجهد ان يصير اليه فابى وكان قد ادمن الصوم لما قدم وجعل لا ياكل الدّسم وكان قبلَ ذلك يُشترى له لحم بدرهم وياكل منه شهرا فترك اكل الشحم وادامَ الصوم والعمل فتوهّمت انه كان قد جعل على نفسه ان سَلِم ان يفعل ذلك وكان حُمل الى المتوكل سنة سبع وثلاثين ومائتين ثم مَكث الى سنة احدى واربعين وكان قلّ يوم يمضى الا ورسول المتوكل ياتيه Moḥammed ibn Abdallah ibn Ṭâhir came from Khorasân, and was appointed over 'Irâḳ in 237 A. H. Abu'l-Maḥ. I, 719.

1) The sources now used are the following extracts; al-Maḳrîzî, p. 15, فصل فى ذكر مرضه ووفاته قال صالح لما كان فى اول يوم من شهر ربيع

fever attended with difficulty in breathing, and became so weak that his limbs would not support him. A physician came to see him, and prescribed for his sickness roast

---

الاول سنة احدى واربعين ومائتين حُمَّ ابى فدخلت عليه وهو محموم فتنفس نفسا شديدا فقلت على ما افطرت البارحة فقال على ماء باقلا ثم اراد القيام فقال خذ بيدى فاخذت بيده فلما صار الى الخلا ضعفت رجلاه حتى توكا علىّ وكان يختلف اليه غيرُ متطبب كلهم مسلمون فوصف له متطبب قرعة تشوى ويُسقى ماءها فقال يا صالح قلت لبيك قال لا تشوى فى منزلك ولا فى منزل عبد الله اخيك وأتى الفتح بن سهل وعلى بن الجَعْد فحجبتهما وكثر الناسُ قال فاىّ شىء ترى قلت تاذن لهم فيدعون لك فاذنّا لهم فجعلوا يدخلون عليه افواجا حتى تمتلئُ الدار وكثر الناس وامتلأ الشارع واغلقنا باب الزقاق وجاء رجل من جيراننا قد خَضَبَ فقال انى لارى الرجل يُحيى شيئا من السنّة فأفرح به فجعل الرجل يدعو له فيقول ابى ولجميع المسلمين ثم قال لى اقبض من السّكان دراهم واشتر تمرًا وكفِّر عنى كفارة يمين فاشتريت وكفّرت واخبرته فقال الحمد لله قلت وزاد الدينورى فى كتاب المجالسة ان الامام احمد قال فانى حنِثت فى دهرى فى يمين واحدة ثم قال لى أحضِر الوصية واقراها وكان كتبها قبل ذلك فقراتها فاقرّها على ما هى عليه . . . .

قال واشتدت به العلة يوم الخميس فلما كان يوم الجمعة اجتمع الناس حتى ملؤا السّكك والشوارع قال حنبل وكان عنده ثلاث شعرات من شعر النبى صلعم فاوصى عند موته ان يجعل على لسانه شعرة وعلى كل عين شعرة ففعل به ذلك عند موته قال ولده عبد الله قال لى ابى فى مرضه الذى توفى فيه اخرِج لى كتاب عبد الله بن ادريس فاخرجت الكتاب فقال لى اخرج احاديث ليث بن ابى سُليم

pumpkin, with the liquor of the pumpkin to be taken as a drink. Aḥmed asked particularly that this might not be prepared in the houses of either of his sons. As soon as it was learned that he was sick, people began to come in crowds to visit him, until it became necessary to close the door of the street; and the governor, hearing of the crowds,

---

فاخرجتها فقال لى اقرا علىّ حديث [Cod. repeats حديث] ليث قلت لطلحة ان طاوسًا كان يكره الانين فى المرض فما سُمع له انين حتى مات رحمه الله فقرات ذلك على ابى فما سمعته أنّ فى مرضه الى ان توفى . . . . وسُئل عبد الله هل عقل ابوك عند الموت المعاينة قال نعم كنا نوضئه [Cod. نوصيه] فجعل يشير بيده فقال لى صالح اىّ شىء يقول فقلت هو يقول خللوا اصابعى فخللنا اصابعه ثم ترك الاشارة فمات من ساعته تغمده الله برحمته وذلك لاثنتى عشرة ليلة خلت من ربيع الاول سنة احدى واربعين ومائتين وهو ابن سبع وسبعين سنة فصل فى غسله وتكفينه والصلاة عليه وعدد من اسلم يوم موته قال ولده صالح لما توفى ابى كان المتوكل غائبا فوجّه الامير ابن طاهر حاجبه ومعه غلامان معهما مناديل فيها ثياب وطيب وقالوا الامير * يقرئك السلام ويقول لك قد فعلتُ ما لو كان امير المومنين حاضرا لفعله فقلت له اقرئه منى السلام وقل له ان امير المومنين قد كان اعفاه فى حياته مما كان يكره ولا أُحب ان اتبعه بعد موته بما كان يكرهه فى حياته فعاد وقال يكون شعارَه ولا يكون دثاره فاعدت عليه مثل ذلك وردّدته عليه وكفّناه فى ثلاث لفائف قال المروزى لما اردت ان اغسله جاء بنو هاشم واجتمع فى الدار خلق كثير فادخلته البيت وغطيته بثوب وارخيت الستر حتى فرغت من امره فلما اردت تكفينه غلبنا عليه بنو هاشم واخذوا فى البكاء عليه

considerately placed guards before the street door, while the family also placed guards before the door of the house. Only his physicians and such as he himself desired to see were then admitted. Among those who were thus allowed to see him was a neighbor, an elderly man with dyed hair and beard, on seeing whom Aḥmed became greatly excited, and called the attention of those about him to this man as one 'who

---

وجعل اولادهم ينكبّون عليه ويقبلونه قال صالح وارسَل الىّ ابن طاهر يقول مَن يصلى على ابيك قلت انا فلما صِرْنا الى الصحراء وجدْنا ابن طاهر فخَطا الينا خطوات وعَزّانا فلما وُضع السرير تقدمت للصلاة فجاءنى ابن طالوت ومحمد بن نصر وقبضا على يدىّ وقالا الاميرُ فمانعْتهم فغلبوا علىَّ وصَلى ولم يعلم اكثر النلس بتقدمه فلما كان من الغد وعلموا بذلك صاروا ياتون القبر افواجا فيصلون عليه ومكثوا على ذلك ايلما قال ولده عبد الله وكُنا نحن والهاشميون صلينا عليه داخل الدار قال الخلال سمعت عبد الوهاب الورّاق يقول ما بلغنا انّ جمعا كان فى الجاهلية والاسلام مثله حتى ان المواضع التى وقف الناس فيها مُسحت وحُزرت فاذا هى نحو من الف الف وحزرنا على السور نحوًا من ستين الف امراة وقال ابو زرعة بلغنى ان المتوكل امَر ان يمسح الموضع الذى وقف الناسُ فيه للصلاة على احمد بن حنبل فبلغ مقام الفى الف وخمس مائة الف وفتح الناس ابواب المنازل فى الشوارع والبيوت والدروب وصاروا ينادُون من اراد الوضوء وقال احمد بن الحسن المقانعى كنت ببغداد وانا فى بستان لصديق لى فاذا بشيخ وشابّ وعليهما طمران فسلمت عليهما وقلت اراكما من غير هذا البلد قالا نعم نحن من جبل اللُكام [Cod. اللِكام] حضرنا جنازة احمد بن حنبل وما بقى احد من الاولياء

was keeping alive the good rule of the Prophet'. Daily reports of the sick man's condition were now sent from Baghdâd to the Khalif at the camp. These were never very encouraging, however, as Aḥmed sank gradually day by day until he died. He seems to have borne his sickness with great fortitude, in which he was supported by a tradition of Ṭâûs,

---

لا حضرها وقال عبد الوهاب الوراق اظهر الناس فى جنازة احمد بن حنبل السّنة والطعن على اهل البدع قال جعفر بن محمد النسوى شهدت الناس فى جنازة احمد بن حنبل يلعنون بشرا المريسى والكرابيسى باصوات عالية واقام الناس ايام يزدحمون على القبر حتى قال ابو الحسن التميمى مكثتُ اياما رَجاء ان اصل الى القبر فلم اصل اليه الا بعد اسبوع

Al-Subkî, p. 134 f. قال المروزى رضى الله عنه مرض ابو عبد الله ليلة الاربعاء لليلتين خلتا من ربيع الاول ومرض تسعة ايام وكان ربما اذن للناس فيدخلون عليه افواجا يسلمون عليه ويرد عليهم وتسامع الناس وكثروا وسمع السلطان بكثرة الناس فوكل ببابه وبباب الزقاق الرابطة واصحاب الاخبار ثم اغلق باب الزقاق فكان الناس فى الشوارع والمساجد حتى تعطل بعض الباعة وحيل بينهم وبين البيع والشراء وكان الرجل * اذا اراد ان يدخل اليه ربما تخلّل من بعض الدور وطور الحالة ربما تسلق وجآء اصحاب الاخبار فقعدوا على الابواب وجاء حاجب ابن طاهر فقال ان الاميرَ يقرئك السلام وهو يشتهى ان يراك فقال هذا مما اكره وامير المومنين اعفانى مما اكره واصحاب الخبر يكتُبون بخبره الى العسكر والبرد تختلف كل يوم وجآء بنو هاشم فدخلوا عليه وجعلوا يبكون عليه وجآء قوم من القضاة وغيرهم فلم يؤذن لهم ودخل عليه شيخ فقال اذكر وقوفك بين يدى

who is reported to have 'disliked groaning in sickness', on the ground that it was tantamount to complaining against God. Aḥmed, therefore, was never heard to groan, except on the day in which he died. Two or three days before his death, he enquired for his purse, and asked his son Ṣâliḥ to look what was in it. Ṣâliḥ did so and found a solitary

---

الله فشهق ابو عبد الله وسالت الدموع على خديه فلما كان قبل وفاته بيوم او يومين قال ادعوا لى الصبيان بلسانٍ ثقيل فجعلوا ينضمون اليه وجعل يشمهم ويمسح بيده على رؤسهم وعينه تدمَعُ وادخلت الطشت تحته فرايت بوله دمًا عبيطا ليس فيه بول فقلت للطبيب فقال هذا رجل قد فتت الحزن والغم جوفه . . . .

. . . . قال موسى بن هرون الحافظ يقالُ ان احمد لما مات مسحت الارض المبسوطة التى وقف الناس للصلاة عليها فحصر مقادير الناسِ بالمساحة ستمائةِ الف واكثر سوى ما كان فى الاطراف والاماكن المتفرقة قلت وقيل فى عددِ المصلين عليه كثير قيل كانوا الف الف وثلاثمائة الف سوى من كان فى السُّفُن فى الماء كذا رواه خشنار بن سعيد وقال ابن ابى حاتم سمعت ابا زرعة يقول بلغنى ان المتوكل امر ان يمسح الموضع الذى وقف عليه الناسُ حيث صُلِّيَ على احمدَ فبلغ المقام الفى الف وخمسمائة وعن الوركانى وهو رجل كان يسكن الى جوار الامام احمد قال اسلم يوم مات احمد من اليهود والنصارى والمجوس عشرون الفا وفى لفظ عشرة الاف قال شيخنا الذهبى وهى حكاية منكرة تفرد بها الوركانى والراوى عنه قال والعقل يحيل ان يقع مثل هذا الحادث فى بغدادَ ولا يرويه جماعة تتوفر دواعيهم على نقل ما هو دونه بكثير وكيف يقع مثل هذا الامر ولا يذكره المروزى ولا صالح بن احمد

dirhem. This his father directed him to use, together with some of the rent to be collected from the lodgers in his house, in buying dates to discharge an oath of almsgiving which he had taken upon himself. Ṣâliḥ carried out the order he had received, and returned to his father one-third of a dirhem, on receiving which Aḥmed rejoiced at the prospect of dying as poor as he had lived.

The duration of his sickness was not long. The physician declared that grief and the hard ascetic character of his life had ruptured the internal organs of his body and could give the family little hope of his recovery. A characteristic incident occurred when he was being washed preparatory to the performance of the last devotions in which he took part. He was unable to speak, but, strong in the ruling passion of scrupulousness in the law, he made a sign that his sons who were washing him should wash *between* his fingers as well as on the back and front of them. When this was done, it is said that he rested quietly until he passed away. His prayers he performed to the very last, his sons assisting him in the rakʿas. One of his last charges was that three hairs of the Prophet which he had in his possession should at his death be placed, one on each eye and one on his lips, and this was actually done [1]). So he died. The date of the

---

ولا عبد الله ولا حنبل الذين حكوا من اخبار ابى عبد الله جزئيّات كثيرة قال قالوا فوالله لو اسلم يوم موته عشرة انفس لكان عظيما ينبغى ان يرويه نحو من عشرة انفس

Abû Nuʿaim, 155 a, وكنتُ انلم بالليل الى جَنبه فاذا اراد حاجةً حرّكنى فاناولهُ وجعل يُحرك لسانه ولم يَئِنّ الا فى الليلة التى توفى فيها ولم يَزل يُصلى قائما أُمسكه فيركع ويَسجد وارفعه فى ركوعه واجتمعَتْ عليه اوجاعُ الحُصر وغير ذلك ولم يزل عقله ثابتا فلما كان يوم الجمعة لاثنتى عشرة ليلة خلت من شهر ربيع الاول لسَاعتَين من النهار توفى رحمة الله عليه ومغفرته ورضوانه،

1) cf. Goldziher. Moh. Stud. II, 358 and note 5.

event was Friday, the twelfth of Rabîᶜ I, 241 A. H., his age being a few days, or it may be hours, more or less than seventy-seven years.

His Funeral. There was the most wonderful scene of grief all over the city of Baghdâd, and even in distant places, when the news of his death became known. The scene at the funeral, on the afternoon of the day of his death, was one such as must have been seldom witnessed anywhere. The estimates of the number of those who attended are very discrepant. Some say 600,000 were present on the spot where the prayers were held over him; others say 2,500,000, and other figures fall between these two [1]). It is said that there were 10,000, and some say even 20,000, converts to Islâm from the other religions on the occasion of Aḥmed's death; but inasmuch as the family and others specially interested in him knew nothing of any such number, al-Subkî's teacher Dhahabî thought such figures to be absurd and that ten converts would be nearer the truth. The Emîr Ibn Ṭâhir wished to furnish the burial suit of Aḥmed but Ṣâliḥ refused to accept it, as he knew that his father when living would have been unwilling to accept any gift from the Emîr. The filial respect of Ṣâliḥ for his dead father's wishes in regard to receiving gifts or attentions from persons of state now took very decided form. It was only by main force that his friends withheld him from displacing Ibn Ṭâhir in the official conduct of the prayers at the funeral [2]). Indeed, it was not known by the people that Ibn Ṭâhir had prayed over Aḥmed, until the day after he was buried. When they knew they flocked in crowds to his grave in the cemetery of the Bâb-Ḥarb [3]); so much so, that one man who attended the funeral, declared that it was a week before he was able to come near the tomb. His own family and the Hâshimites also conducted prayers for him inside their own quarters on the evening of the day of his death [4]). In the time of Ibn Challikân the

1) cf. Ibn Chall. N°. 19.

2) Maçoudî VII, 229.

3) cf. Ibn Chall. N°. 19.

4) Ibn Chall. N°. 19.

tomb of Aḥmed in the cemetery of the Bâb-Ḥarb was known far and wide and was much visited [1]). At a later time, the raised work of the tomb was destroyed and the grave made level with the surface of the ground because of the undue reverence which was being shewn to it [2]).

His Biographers. Among those who are said to have written of the Manâḳib of Aḥmed are Abu'l-Ḥasan ibn al-Munâdî [3]), the Ḥâfiẓ al-Manda [4]), al-Baihaḳî [5]), Abû Ismâ'îl al-Anṣârî, the Faḳîh Abû 'Alî ibn al-Bannâ, commentator of al-Khurkî, the Ḥâfiẓ Ibn Nâṣir, the Ḥâfiẓ Abu'l-Faraj ibn al-Jauzî [6]), Abd al-Raḥmân ibn Abî Hâtim al-Râzî and al-Ḥasan ibn Moḥammed al-Khallâl [7]) [8]).

IV.

His Family. The immediate descendants of Aḥmed ibn Ḥanbal [9]), except his two sons Ṣâliḥ and Abdallah, both of whom

1) Ibn Chall. N°. 19; vid. also al-Nawawî, p. 146.

2) Goldziher, Moh. Stud. I, 257.

3) al-Fihrist I, 38 f.; Dhahabî Ṭabaḳât 11, N°. 55.

4) Dhahabî, Ṭabaḳât 13, N°. 29.

5) Ibn Chall. N°. 27; Dhahabî Ṭabaḳât 14, N°. 13.

6) In his book الجرح والتعديل, Chapter on the Manâḳib of Aḥmed ibn Ḥanbal. v. al-Nawawî Biog. Dict. 143; cf. on Ibn al-Jauzî, Goldziher, Moh. Stud. II, 186 and note 2.

7) Dhahabî, Ṭabaḳât 13, N°. 68. The others I have not been able to trace in the authorities at command.

8) al-Maḳrîzî, p. 18, وقد افرد جماعة من الائمة مناقبه بالتصنيف كالامام ابى حسن بن المنادى والحافظ ابن مندة والبيهقى وشيخ الاسلام الانصارى والفقيه ابى على بن البنّا شارح الخُرقى والحافظ ابن ناصر والحافظ ابى الفرج بن الجوزى وعبد الرحمن بن ابى حاتم الرازى والحسن بن محمد الخلال وغيرهم رضى الله عنهم اجمعين انتهى

9) al-Maḳrîzî, p. 2, واما اولاده فاكبرهم صالح وكنيته ابو الفضل وُلد

were men of eminence, were not remarkable in their time. His eldest son was Ṣâliḥ, surnamed Abu'l Faḍl, who was born in the year 203. He related Tradition from his father and from Abu'l Walîd al-Ṭayâlisî and ʿAlî ibn al-Madînî, and had as pupils his own son Zuhair, who died in 303, al-Baghawî and Moḥammed ibn Makhlad. Ṣâliḥ occupied the office of Ḳâḍî of Ispahân. His mother was ʿAbbâsa bint al-Faḍl. His death occurred in the year 265 [1]). The second son was Abdallah Abû Abd al-Raḥmân [2]). He studied a great deal with his father, and studied, also, with Abd al-Aʿlâ ibn Ḥammâd, Yaḥya ibn Maʿîn, Abû Bekr ibn Abî Shaiba, and many others. He was a man thoroughly conversant with

---

سنة ثلاث ومائتين وروى عن ابيه وابى الوليد الطيالسى وعلىّ بن المديني وروى عنه ابنه زُهير والبغوى ومحمد بن مخلد وولى قضاء اصبهان وهو من زوجته عبّاسة بنت الفضل توفى سنة خمس وستين ومائتين وعبد الله وكنيته ابو عبد الرحمن سمع من ابيه واكثر عنه ومن عبد الاعلى بن حماد ويحيى بن معين ومن ابى بكر بن ابى شيبة وخلق كثير قال الذهبى كان اماما خبيرا بالحديث وعلله مقدّما فيه ولما مرض قال ادفنونى بالقطيعة فقيل له الا تُدفن عند ابيك يعنى بمقبرة باب حرب فقال صَحّ عندى ان بالقطيعة نبيا مدفونا ولأن اكون فى جوار نبى احب الىّ من ان اكون فى جوار ابى وكانت وفاته فى سنة تسعين ومائتين وسِنّه سبع وسبعون سنة كأبيه وللامام احمد ولد اسمه سعيد من سُرّية يقال لها [Cod. له] حسْن وَلِىَ قضاء الكوفة ولهُ منها ولدٌ اسمُه محمد واخَرُ اسمه الحَسن ولهُ منها بنت اسمها زينب وله منها ولدان توءمان احدهما الحسن والاخرُ الحسين وماتا بالقرب من ولادتهما وله بنتٌ اسمها فاطمة والله اعلم

1) Ibn Chall. Nº. 19, says 'Ramaḍân 266 A. H.'

2) Abu 'l-Maḥ. II, 136. cf. his relation to the Musnad of his father, p. 24.

Tradition and the arguments for it. The special distinction which he enjoyed, however, was that of being the greatest authority on the traditions of his father. It is related of him that, when he was on his death-bed, he asked to be buried in the quarter called commonly al-Ḥarbîya [or القطيعة = the quarter of the city or the plot of ground in which his house stood?]. Those present asked him if he would not rather be buried with his father in the cemetery at the Bâb-Ḥarb, but he said he preferred to be under the protection of a prophet whom he knew by trustworthy reports to have been buried in al-Ḥarbîya to being under the protection of his father. He died at the age of 77 in the year 290 A. H. [1]) By a concubine named Ḥisn Aḥmed had a third son, who was named Saʿîd and who became in time Ḳâḍî of Kûfa. By the same mother he had, further, two sons Moḥammed and al-Ḥasan and a daughter Zainab, and, likewise, by the same mother, twin sons al-Ḥasan and al-Ḥusain, who died soon after their birth. Finally, he had another daughter whose name was Fâṭima. [2]) This is all that is known of his family.

Testimonies of Esteem. A few evidences of the esteem in which Aḥmed was held will assist us to place him in the position which he really occupied in the estimation of his own and of following generations. His pupil Abû Zurʿa said he had never met with any one in whom learning (عِلْم), selfdenial, knowledge of the law and general knowledge (معرفة) were so combined as in his master [3]). This is one opinion out of a host of similar ones, all of which are ex-

1) Ibn Chall. N°. 19 says, '8th day remaining of Jumâdâ I, some say Jumâdâ II'.

2) cf. Abû Nuʿaim, 153 *b*, قال ابو الفضل صالح ثم كُتب لنا بشيء الى بادوريا فبلغه فجاء الى الكوة التى فى الباب فقال يا صالح انظرِ ما كان للحسن وأُم على فاذهب به الخ The ʾUmm ʿAlî here referred to may be the Zainab or Fâṭima named above.

3) Abû Nuʿaim, 139 *a*, اخبرنا ابو بكر محمد بن احمد بن محمد

ceedingly fulsome in expression, but still afford us the substantial truth of his high worth in the view of the men among whom he moved. By many testimonies he is placed at the side of the greatest doctors of Islâm in the ages which had preceded him, — Sofyân al-Thaurî, Mâlik ibn Anas, Abd al-Raḥmân ibn Amr al-Auzâʿî, al-Laith ibn Saʿd and Ibn ʿAbbâs. The regard in which Aḥmed ibn Ḥanbal was held is also seen in the way in which he is cited as giving an opinion on the doctors of his time; as, for example, by al-Nawawî, biographies of ʿAlî ibn al-Madînî, Yazîd ibn Hârûn, Yaḥya ibn Saʿîd al-Kaṭṭân, Yaḥya ibn Maʿîn; also Ibn Challikân on Abû Thaur and Isḥâḳ ibn Râhawaih. Al-Dhahabî, too, in his Ṭabaḳât adduces Aḥmed's opinion in regard to the men of his time with great frequency and with evidence of much respect. It used to be held that, if Aḥmed discredited anybody, he could not fail to suffer for it in the eyes of people generally [1]). A noteworthy testimony is that of al-Ḥusain ibn ʿAlî ibn Yazîd al-Karâbîsî, a man with whose theological views Aḥmed had little sympathy. He said that those who spoke evil of Aḥmed were

---

ثنا عبد الله بن محمد بن عبد الكريم قال سمعت ابا زرعة يقول ما رأتْ عينى مثلَ احمد بن حنبل فقلت له فى العلم فقال فى العلم والزهد والفقه والمعرفة وكلّ خير ما رأتْ عينى مثله

1) Abû Nuʿaim, 140 a, قال (عمر بن الحسن القاضى) سمعت ابا يحيى الناقد يقول كنا عند ابراهيم بن عَرْعَرة فذكروا على بن عاصم فقال رجلٌ احمدُ بن حنبل يُضعّفه فقال رجل وما يضرّه من ذاك اذا كان ثقةً فقال ابراهيمُ بن عَرْعَرة والله لو تكلم احمدُ بن حنبل فى عَلقَمة والاسود لضَرّهما The force of the passage is clear. For ʿAlḳama and al-Aswad cf. Dhahabî علقمة بن قيس Ṭabaḳ. 2, 1; الاسود النخعى ib. 6; Abu'l-Maḥ. I, 280, l. 2.

like people who tried to kick over the mountain Abû Ḳubais with their feet [1]).

Aḥmed as a Faḳîh. As a faḳîh he bore a great reputation among his companions, as well as with others in his own generation and the generations following. The reputation of Aḥmed in Baghdâd at the time of Abû Jaʿfar Moḥammed ibn Jarîr al-Ṭabarî († 310 A. H.) is shewn by the anger of the Baghdâd people that al-Ṭabarî should have omitted reference to Aḥmed in his book upon 'the Faḳîhs and their distinctive doctrines'. His reason was that Aḥmed was no faḳîh but rather a traditionist [2]). The opinion was given out in his own day that he was a greater faḳîh than ʿAlî ibn al-Madînî [3]). One traditionist in speaking of Aḥmed's authority on the subject of Tradition said that when Aḥmed supported him in a tradition he was indifferent as to who might differ from him in relation to it [4]). He was credited with extraordinary power of discrimination in the judging of sound and unsound traditions [5]). The general impression that one gets from the biographical details which we have brought together in the present work, and from less important notices which could not with propriety be introduced into the narrative, is that Aḥmed's judgment on points of Fiḳh was seriously reached and often shrewd, but always shewed narrowness. His general reliance upon the Ḳorân and the Tradition cannot be
2) discredited from a Muslim standpoint, and was a safer course,
·ewed from that point of view, than any setting aside of such
3) ·idences in favor of individual judgment could have been [6]).
ıt his principle of slavish literalness and his incorrigible ar-
·rariness in the interpretation of his evidences was that

---

1) Abû Nuʿaim, 141 *a*, يقول (الكرابيسى) مثل الذين يذكر احمد بن حنبل مثل قوم يجيئون الى ابى قبيس يريدون ان يهد بنعالهم

4)

2) cf. Goldziher, Ẓahiriten, p. 4 (from Abu'l-Feda Ann. II, p. 344).

3) al-Nawawî, p. ١٤٢.

4) al-Nawawî, p. ١٤٢.

5) cf. p. 28.

6) cf. Houtsma, De Strijd etc. 95.

which vitiated his claim to direct men to sound and permanent positions in theology. Such was impossible with his method. Belief founded on the letter of any standard of faith will always be narrow, dogmatic and polemical. Life founded on the letter of any rule of conduct can be only hard and exclusive in character. Just but not genial; irreproachable, but unattractive — such is the life. Sincere and earnest and, with its own postulates, correct, but, still, wrong at its foundation and unsightly in its superstructure — such is the opinion.

Habits of Life.

We subjoin a few remarks about the traits of character and habits of life of Aḥmed ibn Ḥanbal, with a passing notice of his personal appearance. He was abstemious in the extreme, so much so, in fact, that his life might be termed a continuous fast. He is reported never to have bought a pomegranate, quince or any other kind of fruit, unless it might be a melon or grapes, which he ate with bread. In eating his bread he frequently dispensed with the use of vinegar. It was often the case that his sons bought things which they deemed permissible or even necessary, but which were luxuries in his eyes; and to escape in such a case his strictures they hid the things from him altogether [1]). It is said that when he appeared before Isḥâḳ ibn Ibrâhîm after his long imprisonment in 219 A. H., Isḥâḳ looked in the little basket which Aḥmed had with him and found his store of food to consist of two pieces of bread, a piece of cucumber and some salt [2]).

He had a profound dislike to the receiving of money assistance from others, and took very little pains to secure a

---

1) al-Nawawî, p. ١٤٥.

2) al-Maḳrîzî, p. 5, بعث اسحاق بن ابراهيم فاخذ الزنبيل الذى فيه افطار ابى عبد الله فنظر اليه فاذا فيه رغيفان وشىء من قثاء وملح فعجب اسحاق من ذلك

money for himself. His happiest moments were those when he was left without a coin in his purse [1]). His needs were few and his expenses next to nothing [2]). We have had in the course of the narrative abundant illustration of his selfdenial and his preference for poverty, and, were it desirable to do so, much more of the same kind of incident could be furnished.

Characteristics. His demeanor was that of a man abstracted from the common concerns of life, though in questions of learning he always shewed the liveliest interest [3]). He was a man of gentle nature, but capable of being roused to vehemence at the sight of injustice or wrong done to men or of impiety shewn toward God [4]). That he was looked upon as a scrupulously just man, even among those who were not Muslims, is shewn in many ways. One incident may be mentioned. It is related that two Magian women had a dispute about an inheritance before a Muslim Ḳâḍî, and when judgment had been rendered, the woman against whom the judge had decided said to him, 'If thou hast decided against me according to the decision of Aḥmed ibn Ḥanbal, I am content; if not, I will not acquiesce in it'. The narrator of the story thought it such a strong testimony to Aḥmed's character that he told it far and near to those whom he met [5]). Aḥmed's aversion toward lightness,

1) al-Nawawî, p. ١٤٥.

2) al-Nawawî, ١٤٤, cf. pp. 141, 164.

3) Abû Nuʿaim, 138 *b*, حدثنا سليمان بن احمد ثنا احمد بن محمد القاضى قال سمعت ابا داود السجستانى يقول لقيت مائتين من مشايخ العلم فما رايت مثل احمد بن حنبل لم يكن يخوض فى شىء مما يخوض فيه الناس من امر الدنيا فاذا ذُكِرَ العِلم تكلّم

4) cf. pp. 73, 150.

5) Abû Nuʿaim, 141 *a*, حدثنا ابى ثنا ابو الحسن ثنا عبد الله بن احمد بن حنبل حدثنى نوح بن حبيب القُومسى قال كان عندنا

particularly in men of learning, was pronounced. On a certain occasion Yazîd ibn Hârûn was indulging in pleasant badinage with his amanuensis, when some one in the room gave a slight cough. Yazîd enquired who it might be that had given the apparent sign of disapproval, and, on being told that it was Aḥmed, he smote his forehead, and, turning to those nearest to him, asked them reproachfully why they had not told him of Aḥmed's presence that he might have observed becoming gravity before him [1]).

People used to say that Aḥmed himself was a touchstone or Miḥna. A versifier, Ibn Aᶜyan, has the lines, 'Ibn Ḥanbal is a safe test (Miḥna): By the love borne to Aḥmed the pious man is known; But when one is seen who defames him, Then be sure that his true character will be disclosed' [2]).

يعنى بلدهم امرأتان مَجوسيّتان فاختصمتا [Cod. فاختصما] فى مواريث لهن الى رجل من المسلمين فقضى لواحدة منهنّ على الاخرى فقالت له ان كنتَ قضيتَ علىّ بقضآء احمد بن حنبل رضيتُ والّا فانى لا ارضى قال نوح فحدثت به اهلَ طرسُوس والشامات

1) Abû Nuᶜaim, 140 *a*, حدثنا سليمان بن احمد ثنا الحسن بن على المعمرى قال سمعت خلف بنَ سالم يقول قال كنّا فى مجلس يزيدَ ابن هرون فمَزَح يزيد مع مُستمليه فتنَحْنح احمد بن حنبل وكان فى المجلس فقال يزيد من المتنَحْنِح فقيل له احمد بن حنبل فضرب يزيدُ بيده على جَبِينه وقال الّا اعلمتونى انّ احمد هاهنا حتى لا امْزح

2) al-Subkî, p. 134, قال (ابو جعفر محمد بن دينار الموصلى) انشدنى ابن اعين فى الامام احمد بن حنبل رضى الله عنه

'اضحى ابن حنبل محنةً مأمونةً
وبحُبّ احمد يعرفُ المُتَنَسِّك'

Religious Character. An indication of Aḥmed's character from the religious point of view is found in the following verses, which are said to be of his composition and furnish the only discoverable trace of his poetic talent. 'Whenever thou art alone at any time, do not say I am alone, but say over me is a Watcher; And do not think that God is indifferent to what has passed by, and that what thou hidest from him is out of his sight. We give ourselves no care until sins follow upon the track of sins; But then! would that God would grant us repentance, and we would repent! [1])

It is said that he was wont to pray every day 300 rak'as, and that, even after he was scourged and his bodily weakness was extreme, he reached the number of 150 daily. He completed a recitation of the Ḳorân once in every seven days. It was his custom at night after the last prayer of the day, to sleep for a short time, and then to arise and pray formal or extemporized prayers until the morning [2]).

'واذا رايتَ لاحمد متنقصًا

'فاعلم بان ستوره سَتُهَتَّك

1) Abû Nu'aim, 155 *a*, حدثنا ابو على عيسى بن محمد الخريجى [Cod. الجرىحى] ثنا احمد بن يحيى ثَعْلَب النحوى قال كنت احب ان ارى احمد بن حنبل فدخلت عليه فقال لى فيم تنظر فقلت له فى النحو والعربية والشعر فانشدنى احمد بن حنبل

'اذاما خلوتَ الدهر يوما فلا تَقُل، خَلوتُ ولكن قُل علىّ رَقيبُ،

ولا تَحسبنّ الله يُغفل مَا مَضَى، وأَنّ الذى تُخفى عليه يغيبُ،

'لَهَونَا عن الايام حتى تَتابعَتْ، ذُنوب على اثارهن ذنوبُ،

'فيَا لَيتَ أَن الله يَغفِر مَا مضَى، ويأذَن لنا فى توبة فنتُوبُ،

2) Abû Nu'aim, 143 *a*., حدثنا سليمان بن احمد ثنا عبد الله ابن احمد بن حنبل قال كان ابى يصلى فى كل يوم وليلة ثلثمائة

When at home in Baghdâd he is said to have perseveringly kept to his house, so that none ever saw him, unless it were at public worship, at a funeral, or visiting the sick [1]). He was scrupulous in his adherence to Tradition and to the ritual observances. We have already cited the incident of the ritual ablutions performed on him by his sons just before his death, when, though unable to speak, he made signs that they should wash between, as well as upon the front and back of his fingers [2]).

Personal Appearance. In personal appearance, Aḥmed was of beautiful countenance and of medium height.· He used to dye his hair and beard with henna and katam, but not a

---

ركعة فلما مرِض من تِلك الاسواط اضْعَفَتْه* وكان يصلى فى كل يوم وليلة مائة وخمسين ركعة وقد كان قرب من الثمانين، حدثنا سليمان بن احمد ثنا عبد الله بن احمد بن حنبل قال كان ابى يَقرأ فى كل يوم سُبعا يختم فى كل سبعة ايام وكانت له خَتْمَة فى كل سبع ليال سِوَى صلاة النهار وكان ساعةَ يُصَلّى عشآء الاخرة ينام نومة خفيفة ثم يقوم الى الصباح يصلى ويدعو

1) Abû Nuʿaim, 143 *b*, قال عبد الله وكان ابى اصبر الناس على الوحدة لم يره احد الا فى مسجد او حضور جنازة او عيادة مريض وكان يكره المشى فى الاسواق، . . . . حدثنا ابى ثنا احمد ثنا عبد الله بن احمد بن حنبل قال خرج ابى الى طرسوس ماشيا وخرج الى اليمن ماشيا وحج خمس حجج ثلاثا منها ماشيا ولا يمكن لاحد ان يقول راى ابى* فى هذه النواحى يوما الا اذا خرج الى الجمعة وكان اصبر الناس على الوحدة وبِشْر رحمه الله فيما كان فيه لم يكن يصبر على الوحدة فكان يخرج الى ذا ساعة والى ذا ساعة

2) vid. p. 171.

deep red, for in his beard were seen black hairs. He began the practice of dyeing his hair and beard when in his sixty-third year, and then wholly out of regard for the practice of the Prophet [1]).

V.

His Views. Aḥmed ibn Ḥanbal was a man whose peculiar temperament disposed him not only to the kind of life which he lived — intense, ascetic, and fierce in its protest against liberalism, — but also to those views and beliefs which were, to a certain extent, the springs of such a life [2]). His beliefs were not entirely free from adjustment to the circumstances of his age, but the measure of accommodation was the least that could be made. In fact, look where we will in Aḥmed's life, and the elements of concession and compromise are never found to be present by his own wish, and, when found, their degree is the minimum possible.

Sources. We propose to generalize on the basis of the narrative already furnished and the few other sources of information accessible, in order to reach, if we can, a fair notion of the leading theological opinions or principles by which Aḥmed ibn Ḥanbal directed his life. His testament, which has been given in the foregoing pages [3]), is a very colorless document, and affords no view of his characteristic beliefs. The confession it contains comprises stock phrases, which might come from a Muslim of any kind or character. The letter to ʿObaidallah ibn Yaḥya, in an-

---

1) Ibn Chall. N°. 19; Abû Nuʿaim, 138 *b*, قال عبد الله وخضب ابى راسه ولحيته بالحنّاء والكتم وهو ابن ثلاث وستّين سنة

2) Abû Nuʿaim, 153 *b*, فدخلتُ اليه فاكببْتُ عليه وقلت له يا ابة تُدخِلُ على نفسك الغمّ فقال يابنى ياتينى ما لا املكه

3) p. 147.

swer to the Khalif's enquiry relative to the Ḳorân, has so much that is characteristic that we may credit it with representing accurately Aḥmed's belief [1]). The conversation on the Korân with Isḥâḳ ibn Ibrâhîm is fully in the spirit of Aḥmed's life, and lends us an interesting view of his faith as touching the Ḳorân [2]). The trials before Isḥâḳ ibn Ibrâhîm and al-Muʿtaṣim, with the conversations connected with them, furnish much light on Aḥmed's opinions and the individual element which they contain [3]).

The Ḳorân. First, Aḥmed ibn Ḥanbal's doctrine of the Ḳorân [4]). The Ḳorân he asserted to be the Word of God, by which he meant the expression of God's Knowledge, as such expression must be thought to be eternally present to God's Being. Or, if we must modify this at all, it would be to say, that, as long as there has been present to God that which is objective to Himself, so long has there been a Word of God as the expression of his Knowledge. Before the Objective came into existence, the Word of God was potential in Him and not actual. This gives us the Eternity of the Word of God. Then, as the Divine Knowledge cannot be conceived to be without the eternal adjunct of symbolic expression, and as speech is to be looked upon as a faculty expressing itself in energy and not a creation, the Word of God is not only eternal but uncreated as well. It may be objected that *a* Word of God is not the point in question, but the Ḳorân, *the* Word of God as known to men. Be it noted, however, that the distinction between the written or otherwise presented Ḳorân and the heavenly and essential Word of God is clearly drawn [5]). This, too, is

---

1) p. 155. 2) p. 139. 3) p. 93 ff.

4) p. 101. cf. Goldziher, Ẓahiriten, p. 138 ff. The Word of God was said by some of the orthodox to be an attribute of God, Houtsma, De Strijd etc. 103 f. cf. Shahrastânî. All the evidence at command, however, shews that Aḥmed ibn Ḥanbal's belief was as I have set it forth.

5) cf. von Kremer, Herrsch. Ideen d. Isl. 227; Steiner, Die Muʿtaziliten, 38 f. The accounts given of the orthodox view as to the Ḳorân differ from that which I have inferred Aḥmed ibn Ḥanbal to have held. Nor does he

not drawn for the purposes of mere controversy, but represents, as we take it, a belief in the difference of extent between the visible and invisible Word of God. All the words spoken to Moses are the Word of God [1]); certainly, not as belonging to the visible Ḳorân, but as belonging to the one eternal Word of God. All God's words to Moḥammed and to the prophets are the Word of God; all those which were spoken to ʿIsâ ibn Maryam are equally the Word of God. And, in controversy, the words spoken to these various persons are used to prove the uncreated and eternal nature of the *visible* Ḳorân, though they form no part of the Book. Why? Because they, with the substance of the Ḳorân, are the revelations of the Eternal Word, not revelations coextensive with it but partial revelations. This leads to the doctrine that the Word of God is one as well as eternal and uncreated [2]). It could not be one if the visible words were taken in evidence, but regarded as a faculty of expression, latent or energizing, belonging to a Being, we

---

seem to have been alone in his idea of the Ḳorân, but had both among the learned and unlearned a large number who sympathized with his opinions. Most of those who have expounded the orthodox view make the distinction between the visible and invisible *Ḳorân* and go no further, thus making the Book as known to men the equivalent of that preserved in Heaven. The great distinction to be drawn is between the visible *Ḳorân* and the invisible *Word of God*, the latter being not an equivalent but infinitely more extensive than the former. The connection with the doctrine of the Logos as held by Syrian Christians (Houtsma 101, note 1) confirms the presentation of the Ḳorân doctrine which is given in the text. The manifestation of the Logos in Jesus Christ is to be set over against the Heavenly and Uncreated Logos which is in the bosom of the Father. As for the 'Well-guarded Table' of the Ḳorân, Sura 85, 22, (cf. Steiner 39 and note 5, also in the preceding account in these pages, p. 67) this, it is true, was an archetype of the visible Ḳorân kept in Heaven, but, still, even this celestial archetype was not coextensive with the eternal and uncreated Word of God of which it was one manifestation. We thus think that the orthodox in Aḥmed's day held to three elements in their doctrine of the Ḳorân: 1st, the Visible Ḳorân; 2nd, the Heavenly Ḳorân; 3rd, the Eternal Word of God.

1) p. 38.

2) cf. Goldziher, Ẓahiriten, p. 138 ff.; Houtsma, De Strijd etc. 129.

may see how the Word of God came to be looked upon as a continuous unity; or, as we may better express a fact in relation to a Being not knowing any succession of time, as a unity in an eternal present. Such a Word of God, considered both as to its thoughts and words, is necessarily without fault and infallible [1]). The Word of God is, thus, Eternal, Uncreated, One and Infallible. This we conceive to have been the doctrine of the Ḳorân held by Aḥmed ibn Ḥanbal and the theologians of his type. We have used modern expression to voice his ideas; the ideas, however, are not ours but his.

The Ḳorân, in terrestrial relations [2]), is to be regarded as a manifestation of the One Word of God such as constitutes a revelation of the perfect religion, a means of salvation and a right guidance for men. In all the forms of its existence among men, written, recited or committed to memory, the substance and the unexpressed words in which the substance is embodied in God's thought are eternal, uncreated, infallible [3]). The human acts in relation to the substance and the words as found in connection with these human acts are temporal, created, fallible. This is the doctrine of the so-called Lafẓ al-Ḳorân.

This Ḳorân doctrine [4]) is strongly suggestive of Pantheism, for the Word of God as spoken to Moses, to Moḥammed and as found in the Ḳorân is the One Word — not parts of it — coming to manifestation; just as the moon at its quarter may be called a particular manifestation of the moon, but not a part of the moon. The Pantheistic suggestion is much the same as that found in the Christian doctrine of the Logos, from Eternity resident in God, inseparable from a true conception of Deity, and proceeding to manifestation at the coming into being of Objective Existence.

---

1) cf. Houtsma, De Strijd etc. 101.

2) Ẓahiriten, as in note 2, p. 185, especially p. 141, l. 18 ff.; cf. present work, pp. 32 ff.

3) cf. Houtsma, De Strijd etc. 117 f.

4) cf. von Kremer, Herrsch. Id. d. Isl., 41. On the whole much like the doctrine of al-Ash'arî, Houtsma, De Strijd etc. 118.

The Divine Unity. We are now prepared to consider the doctrine of the Divine Unity. Aḥmed ibn Ḥanbal was firm in his belief in the unity of God [1]), and, when we keep in view the doctrine of the Ḳorân which we believe him to have adopted, it is easy to understand with what vigor and conviction he would resist the charge of polytheistic heresy which his opponents sought to fasten upon him. We may, by the way, notice his belief in the eternity of the Divine attributes [2]). His view, except in the case of the Divine Sovereignty and Knowledge, the attributes formally connected with the origin of the Ḳorân, is stated but not elaborated in the sources to which I have had access. We have, however, in the case of the two attributes named sufficient data to enable us to arrive at his opinions. He stated, with all emphasis, that God could not exist without his Knowledge. And, though his adversaries declared that to make eternal and uncreated anything which was in thought separated from the bare idea of Deity was to make as many more deities as there were things so thought of [3]), Aḥmed, taking the concrete view of an unphilosophical mind, could not think of Absolute Being, except as involving all the fulness of a perfect, or yet to be perfected, finite creature, and a finite creature he could not think of except as having attributes. The Absolute was the infinite correspondent and correlate of the perfect finite.

The Anthropomorphic Attributes. The same conviction evidently lay at the basis of Aḥmed ibn Ḥanbal's faith in the anthropomorphic attributes given to Deity in the Ḳorân [4]).

---

1) p. 106 infra. For the Muᶜtazilite doctrine of the Divine Unity, vid. Steiner, Die Muᶜtaziliten, 50.

2) pp. 90, 101 f., 139; cf. a slightly different view, von Kremer, Herrsch. Id. d. Isl., 40 f.

3) For the Muᶜtazilite view of the attributes of God, vid. Steiner, Die Muᶜtaziliten 50, 52, 59; Houtsma, De Strijd etc. 103, 124; Shahrastânî, Haarbrücker's transl'n I, 71.

4) p. 72; cf. Goldziher, Moh. Stud. II, 186; von Kremer, Herrsch. Id. d. Isl. 41 f. (a more positive view).

Puzzled by philosophical arguments the untrained mind, though resting on the analogy of perfect human being, and holding fast to this as the undoubted ground and explanation of the Ḳorân's anthropomorphisms, asserted its impotence to answer philosophizing objections by saying, 'He is even as he has described himself, I will say no more than this' [1]). There was a much less arbitrary answer, which may not have been fully formulated in Aḥmed ibn Ḥanbal's mind any more than it was in that of Moḥammed himself, but which, had it been clear to the mind of either, would have seemed a blasphemy in its utterance, and would have involved inevitably a proof of the charge made by those who were arguing on the other side. This answer would have been to assert the literal truth of the Ḳorân's anthropomorphisms. Aḥmed's belief was anthropomorphic. That was the simple fact [2]). And the Prophet's was not the less so. The principle on which Aḥmed formed his notion of Deity was essentially right, 'the absolute is the perfection and infinitude of the perfect finite'; but his opponents properly objected to the giving of accidents of human nature, which may or may not be found when the human creature is in other environments, to the Being in connection with whom to speak of accidents and environments would be paradoxical and contradictory.

The fact of the matter in relation to these anthropomorphic attributes is that Aḥmed ibn Ḥanbal had to set himself up not only, as his own apologist, but, also, as the apologist of the Ḳorân and the Prophet, and he knew that — at least, so it

---

1) cf. Dozy, Het Islamisme, 136; an argument of the Ṣifatîya, Shahrastânî, Haarbrücker's transl'n, I, 95.

2) cf. Goldziher, Ẓahiriten, p. 133, l. 24 ff. The so-called negative position of Mâlik ibn Anas and Aḥmed ibn Ḥanbal in this connection is hard to understand (vid. Shahrastânî, Haarbrücker's transl'n, I, 97, 114 f.). Refusing to accept the figurative meaning of the anthropomorphic expressions, and yet insisting on the real force of these same expressions, as Aḥmed certainly did, how can passivity be conceived to exist in such minds? Insistence on the positive meaning, and yet not stating what the specific meaning was, though denying it to be figurative, leaves only anthropomorphism over.

seems to us. If Aḥmed had believed differently from the Ḳorân and Moḥammed, its human author, the case would have been a hard one for him; but anthropomorphism existed in higher quarters. Aḥmed had the Word of God to uphold, as well as his own theological character and he made the best defence that could be made under the circumstances. He asserted that God was describing himself, and who knew about himself more or better than he did? To such an argument there is no direct answer. One must follow the much more circuitous route of proving the apologist's conception of the Ḳorân revelation to be wrong, and once this is done the controversy on minor points would be time lost. The allegorical interpretation of the anthropomorphic expressions appears to be justly repudiated by any man who wishes to expound the Ḳorân according to the temper of the man who composed it, the temper of the men to whom it was first addressed, and the special intention actually present in the mind of Moḥammed, as far as this can be learned.

Ḳorân Interpretation. The step to the consideration of Aḥmed ibn Ḥanbal's principle in the interpretation of the Ḳorân is not a great one [1]). He believed that the Ḳorân was to be explained literally, except in cases where the Book itself indicated a limitation or modification of this method to be necessary, and in cases where a practical impossibility was involved. We say practical impossibility, for purely abstract necessity he was loth to admit as a regulating principle. There are so few ascertainable instances of allegorical interpretation on his part, that one can say that his general principle of hermeneutics governed him in dealing with the portions of the Ḳorân which might seem to some to be figurative. The indications of the Book itself and practical necessity would determine for him the application of the literal or some other method to such passages. In all cases

---

1) cf. his use of texts pp. 72, 90 f., 101 ff., 106, 139, 162 f. For the freer method of the Muʿtazila, v. Steiner, Die Muʿtaziliten, 79.

where the literal method had to he given up the interpretation handed down in Tradition ever found favor with Aḥmed.

Extra-Korân Sources of Doctrine. Closely allied with the interpretation of the Ḳorân is the question as to the authoritative source of doctrine and rules of conduct, where the Ḳorân fails to give sufficiently explicit directions. For Aḥmed ibn Ḥanbal this lay in the Tradition. What had the Prophet said? What had the Prophet done? What had the Companions of the Prophet reported from him? Or, their Followers? Or, the second generation of Followers? What was the consensus of opinion and practice in the Muslim Communion? The admission of the Ḳiyâs or of Ra'y was generally opposed, but admitted where there was no better help to be found [1]). His monumental work, the great collection of traditions called the Musnad, had for its declared purpose the furnishing, in all conceivable instances, of sound traditional arguments to those who might resort to it [2]). Its composition and the importance Aḥmed attached to it shew that Tradition next to the Word of God itself was the great rock on which he stood. Many testimonies go to prove that he was more tenacious of Tradition than any of the other doctors of his age [3]). We find that when he forgave his persecutors it was because of a traditional interpretation of a Ḳorân verse [4]).

1) Goldziher, Moh. Stud. II, 217, note 4; Sachau, Zur Aeltesten Gesch. d. Moh. Rechts, 17; Houtsma, De Strijd etc. 91 f.; cf. Goldziher, Ẓahiriten, 20, note 1. Houtsma's words p. 92, l. 16 ff. seem to be too favorable to the Muʿtazila. Their interpretation of the Ḳorân as far as the attributes of God, the anthropomorphic expressions regarding God, and the predestination passages are concerned was wholly figurative, and we know how large a part of the polemic which they waged was over these points. The name Rationalists, or Freethinkers, is justly applied to the Muʿtazila and implies that the Ḳorân with them was authoritative, not absolutely or as far as practical necessity would admit, but only as far as the rational demands of human life and comfort and the fair requirements of human thought allowed.

2) p. 19.

3) Ibn Khaldûn, Proleg. III, 6; Goldziher, Ẓahiriten, 23, l. 25; Sachau, Zur Aeltesten Gesch. d. Moh. Rechts 15; cf. present work p. 16 f.

4) Abû Nuʿaim, 150 *a*, قال ابو الفضل دخلت على ابى يوما فقلت

When the author of the Ḥilya relates that Aḥmed was angry [غضبه لله] with those who weakened under the test in the days of al-Ma'mûn, he follows up the incident with a tradition of some of the Prophet's Companions having been very angry when they were called upon to give up any part of their religion [1]). The author's purpose in introducing the tradition where it stands, is to point out the analogy between Aḥmed's case and that cited, and to justify Aḥmed in view of what the Prophet's Companions had done. He may wish to intimate, also, that Aḥmed acted knowing this precedent, and being stimulated by it to feel as he did.

The Interpretation of Tradition. His interpretation of Tradition also leaned to the most rigorous view. A provision for relief in exceptional cases he often made imperative in such

---

له بلغنى ان رجلا جاء الى فَضْل الانماطى فقال له اجعلنى فى حل انى لم اقم بنُصرتك فقال فضل لا جعلتُ احدا فى حل فتبسم ابى وسكت فلما كان بعد ايام قال لى مَرَرْتُ بهذه الآية فَمَنْ عَفَا وَأَصْلَحَ فَأَجْرُهُ عَلَى ٱللّٰهِ [Kor. 42. 38] فنَظرتُ فى تفسيرها فاذا هُوَ ما حدثنى به هاشم بن القلسم ثنا ابن المبارك حدثنى من سمع الحسن يقول اذا جثَتِ الامم بَيْن يدى رب العالمين يوم القيامة نودُوا ليَقُم من اجْرُه على الله فلا يقوم الا من عفا فى الدنيا قال ابى فجعلت المَيِّتَ فى حِل من ضَربه اياى ثم جعل يقول وما على رجل الا يعذب الله بسببه احدا

1) Abû Nu'aim, 147 *a*, حدثنا محمد بن فضيل بن غَزوان عن الوليد بن عبد الله بن جُمَيع عن ابى سلَمَة بن عبد الرحمن ابن عَوف قال كان مِن اصحاب النبى صلى الله عليه وسلم من اذا أُريد على شىء من امر دينه رايتَ حماليقَ عينيه فى راسه تَدورُ كانه مجنون

instances, even if the persons concerned had no wish to avail themselves of the dispensation or the cases were in detail not the same as that originally provided for in the tradition. Hence, what was meant to be a relief became, instead, a burden [1]).

The Reason for his Method and for the Manner of his Life.

The belief he held in the merit of good works [2]) was so strong that a rigid exegesis of the Korân and of Tradition was the most natural thing to be expected of him. The same belief explains his persistent application of himself to a life of ascetic rigor and fasting [3]). His love of the ascetic life, in its turn, throws light upon the mystic character of his piety and his faith in dreams [4]). Solitude, hunger, and the absence of distracting comforts made the subjective life seem more real than the objective, and led Aḥmed to feel an aversion to a life such as other men lived; for in such a life the reality of the interior world which he had created for himself was shattered, and mysticism with its revelry of religious imagination dissipated [5]).

---

1) For illustration of his rigorous interpretation, see Goldziher, Ẓahiriten, pp. 87, 88 f., 103 l. 20 ff.; cf. p. 141 infra; Goldziher, Moh. Stud. II, 250.

2) cf. p. 164 and note 1 infra. Houtsma, De Strijd etc. 85, says that the close adherence to the letter of the Ḳorân on the part of the orthodox revived a strict conception of life such as was found especially among the Ḥanbalites. But we would call attention to the fact that there was at this time a deep current of popular sentiment favoring a stricter religious life, and this great tendency of the life of individuals and of society at large expressed itself in high views of the Ḳorân and a rigid interpretation of its precepts. The stricter conception of the Ḳorân then reacted and gave definite form to the life tendency of the nation and its members. It was the conception of life that affected the conception of the Book which was the rule of life, rather than otherwise. Such is my reading of the circumstances, but Houtsma's explanation will also find many advocates.

3) cf. Abu'l-Maḥ. I, 364, obituary notice of Yazîd ibn Abî Yazîd al-Azdî, containing a reference to his ascetic life and imitation of Aḥmed ibn Ḥanbal.

4) al-Maḳrîzî, p. 18, ونقل من كثير من السلف انهم رأوا الله تعالى
فى المنام كالامام ابى حنيفة والامام احمد بن حنبل رضى الله عنهما
cf. pp. 92 f., 82.

5) Abû Nuʿaim, 142 *b*, قال [Cod. inserts لى] بوران ابو محمد لابى

Reverence for Relics. This ascetic-mystic aspect of his character comprises a reverence for relics, which has found expression once or twice in the course of the preceding narrative [1]).

Foreordination of Events. To one holding such views as those of which we have been speaking, the belief in a predestined order of life is the only explanation of human events. Aḥmed appears to have held that there was no contingency, either in the actions which men do, or in the events through which they are called to pass [2]).

The Doctrine of Faith. The doctrine of Faith expounded by his friend Moḥammed ibn Aslam was, apparently, held by Aḥmed ibn Ḥanbal, likewise. That is, that Faith is in the spirit, is expressed by the lips, and is confirmed by the acts. His declaration that discipline and trial would serve to increase his faith favors such a view [3]).

Aḥmed's Attitude toward Patronage. His attitude toward patronage and favors on the part of rulers was that of an extremist, but there can be no doubt that his high con-

---

عندى خفّ ابعثُ به اليك فسكت فلما عاد اليه ابو محمد قال يابا محمد لا تَبعَثْ بالخف فقد شغل قلبى علىّ

1) Abû Nuʿaim, 144 *a*, ورايت ابى ياخذ شعرة من شعر النبى صلى الله عليه وسلم فيَضَعها على فيه يقبلها واحسب انى رايته [يضعها على عينيه ويغمسها فى المآء ثم يشربه يستشفى بها .Marg ورايته] قد اخذ قصعة النبى صلى الله عليه وسلم فغسلها فى حُبّ الماء ثم شرب فيها ورايته غير مرة يشرب ماء زمزم يستشفى به ويمسح به يديه ووجهه cf. p. 107.

2) note 2, p. 109; p. 151.

3) al-Makrizi, p. 12, وكنت فى السجن اكل وذلك عندى زيادة فى ايمانى الخ The faith which was increased by his adversity appears to have been an inward exercise of the mind. cf. Moḥammed ibn Aslam's view p. 38 f.

ception of his vocation as a teacher led him to keep as clear of compromise as possible [1]. Surramanra would become his prison, he said, were he to stay there and teach while, at the same time, receiving the fixed salary of the Khalif [2]. Isḥâḳ ibn Râhawaih he said he would rebuke, if he ever saw him, for his truckling to the Emîr Abdallah ibn Ṭâhir [3]. The wilfulness of Aḥmed, doubtless, contributed to his opposition to a Court position; he was master of his own circle in his own way in Baghdâd, but at the Court such would have been impossible. And, then, his real hatred of easy and congenial conditions on the ground of religious principle presented a crowning obstacle [4].

Aversion to Systematic Theology and its Result. The character of Aḥmed as a traditionist, and his aversion to generalization and deduction, prevented him from leaving behind any system of opinions. We may formulate for him in these days, but he would not have been willing to do so. Hence, the uninfluential character of the Ḥanbalite school. Their master's teaching was unsystematic, and much ground was lost ere his spirit and teaching could be put before the world in such a form as to accomplish any powerful effect. His personality in his lifetime and after his death was a great force in the Muslim world; and the personality seems yet to be as powerful in its influence as the opinions which he enunciated, though his following has never been great in comparison with that of the other three orthodox Imâms.

---

1) p. 112 infra, p. 141; cf. attitude of Mâlik ibn Anas toward Hârûn al-Rashîd, von Hammer, Lit. Gesch. III, 101, 102.

2) p. 142. 3) p. 145.

4) On this whole subject, cf. Goldziher, Moh. Stud. II, 39.

INDEX.

ʿAbbâs, the client of al-Maʾmûn, 75.
ʿAbbâsa bint al-Faḍl, 174.
Abd al-Aʿlâ ibn Ḥammâd, 174.
Abdallah ibn ʿAbbâs, 157, 159, 176.
Abdallah ibn Aḥmed ibn Ḥanbal, 20 ff., 26, 28, 146 ff., 150, 173 f.
Abdallah ibn Idrîs, 46.
Abdallah ibn Isḥâḳ, 140.
Abdallah ibn Masʿûd, 102, 160.
Abdallah ibn Moḥammed, known as Bûrân, 88, 147, 148.
Abdallah ibn al-Mubârak, 11.
Abdallah ibn ʿOmar, 158.
Abdallah ibn Ṭâhir, 18, 194.
Abd al-Malik ibn Abd al-Ḥamîd al-Maimûn, 26.
Abd al-Munʿim ibn Idrîs ibn bint Wahb ibn Munabbih, 73.
Abd al-Raḥmân ibn ʿAmr al-Auzâʿî, 176.
Abd al-Raḥmân ibn Abî Hâtim al-Râzî, 173.
Abd al-Raḥmân ibn Isḥâḳ, 70, 74, 78, 101 ff.
Abd al-Razzâḳ, 12, 15 ff., 26.
ʿAffân ibn Muslim, 86.
Ahluʾl-ʾAhwâ, 161 n. [1]), 163 n. [1]).
Ahluʾt-Tauhîd waʾl-ʿAdl, 62 n. [1]).
Ibn al-Aḥmar, 73.
Aḥmed ibn ʿAmmâr, 105.
Aḥmed ibn Abî Dowâd, 3, 4, 52, 55 f., 64, 93, 102 ff., 120, 121, 126 f., 142.

Aḥmed ibn Ḥanbal, his greatness and influence, 2 ff.; his biographers etc., 5, 173; birth, family and early years, 10; teachers of, 11 ff.; performance of the Hajj, 14; at Mecca, 14; at Sanʿâ, 16; period of teaching, 18 f.; works, 19; Musnad, 19 ff.; his pupils, 26; method of teaching, 26; contemporaries, 27 ff.; friendship for mystics and ascetics, 41 ff.; his trial predicted, 49; regrets apostasy of his companions, 64 f.; cited before Isḥâḳ ibn Ibrâhîm, 70, 72; referred to in al-Maʾmun's letter, 77; refuses to recant, 80; ordered to Tarsus, 81; sent back to Baghdâd and his imprisonment there, 85; second citation, 89; discussion before Isḥâḳ, 90 f.; taken to al-Muʿtaṣim, 91; trial, 93 ff.; discussions before al-Muʿtaṣim, 101 ff.; ordered to be flogged, 107 ff.; set free, 111; relations with al-Wâthiḳ, 114 f.; invited to visit al-Mutawakkil, 139; conversation with Isḥâḳ ibn Ibrâhîm, 139; accused of ʿAlyite leanings, 140; second invitation of al-Mutawakkil, 140 f.; vow to renounce teaching, 142; royal gifts, 141, 143; fasting and sickness, 144 f.; consulted about Ibn Abî Dowâd, 142, 145; released by al-Mutawakkil, 145 f.; correspondence with his sons, 146 f.; his testament, 147 f.; returns to Baghdâd, 148 ff.; objects to his family receiving stipends, 150 f.; accused to the Khalif again, 152; al-Mutawakkil asks for his view as to the Ḳorân, 154; his letter in reply, 155 ff.; Yaḥya ibn Khaḳân visits him, 164; Moḥammed ibn Abdallah ibn Ṭâhir invites him, 164; fasting, 164; sickness and death, 165 ff.; his funeral, 172; his tomb, 172 f.; family, 173 f., testimonies of esteem, 175 f.; Aḥmed as a faḳîh, 177; habits of life, 178; characteristics, 179; religious character, 181; personal appearance, 182; *His Views*, 183 f.; on the Ḳorân, 184 ff.; on the Divine Unity, 187; on anthropomorphic attributes, 187 ff.; on interpretation of the Ḳorân, 189; on extra-Ḳorân sources of doctrine, 190 f.; on interpretation of Tradition, 191; the reason for his method and for the manner of his life, 192; reverence for relics, 193; foreordination of events, 193; the doctrine of Faith, 193; his attitude toward patronage,

193; aversion to systematic theology and its result, 194.
Aḥmed ibn Abi'l-Hawârî, 26.
Aḥmed ibn Ibrâhîm al-Daurakî, 64.
Aḥmed ibn Moḥammed ibn Hânî al-Ṭâ'î al-Athram, 26.
Aḥmed ibn Naṣr al-Khuzâ'î, 116 ff., 119, 127, 128.
Aḥmed ibn Rabâh, 90.
Aḥmed ibn Shujâ', 70, 78, 84.
Aḥmed ibn Yazîd ibn al-'Awwâm Abu'l-'Awwâm al-Bazzâz, 70, 77, 84.
'Alî (the Khalif), 54.
'Alî ibn 'Âsim, 92.
Abû 'Alî ibn al-Bannâ, the Fakîh, 173.
'Alî ibn Hishâm ibn al-Barîd, 12.
'Alî ibn al-Ja'd, 70, 84.
'Alî ibn al-Jahm, 140.
'Alî ibn al-Madînî, 12, 26, 31, 87, 174, 176, 177.
'Alî ibn Abî Mukâtil, 70, 71, 76, 84.
'Alî ibn Yaḥya, 79.
'Alkama, 176 n. [1]).
al-A'mash, 63.
'Ammâr ibn Yâsir, 84.
'Anbasa ibn Isḥâk, 84.
al-Aswad, 176 n. [1]).
Ibn A'yan, 180.
Ayûb ibn al-Najjâr, 46.
Ayûb al-Sakhtiyânî, 161.

al-Baghawî, 26, 174.
Bahr ibn Asad, 12 n. [3]).
al-Baihakî, 173.
Bakî ibn Makhlad al-Andalusî, 26.
Ibn Bakkâ al-Akbar Abû Hârûn, 70, 73, 84.
Ibn Bakkâ al-Asghar, 72, 74.
Abû Bekr, 54, 123.
Abû Bekr ibn Abî Shaiba, 174.
Bishr ibn Ghiyâth al-Marîsî, 48 and n. [3]).
Bishr ibn al-Ḥârith al-Hâfî, 45, 125.

Bishr ibn al-Mufaḍḍal, 12.
Bishr ibn al-Walîd al-Kindî, 70 f., 75 f., 80, 84.
al-Bokhârî, 26, 34.
Bughâ al-Kabîr, 90, 91.

Ibn Challikân, 176.

Abû Dâûd, 26.
Dâûd ibn ʿAlî al-Ẓâhirî, 46.
Abû Dâûd al-Ḥafarî, 46.
al-Dhahabî, 176.
al-Dhayyâl ibn al-Haitham, 70, 71, 76, 84.
al-Dhuhlî, see Moḥammed ibn Yaḥya.
Divine attributes, The doctrine of, 39 f., 90, 187.
Divine Unity, 187.
Duḥaim al-Shâmî, 26.
Ibn Abî Dunya, 26.

al-Faḍl ibn al-Farrukhân, 70, 77 f., 84.
al-Faḍl ibn Ghânim, 70, 77, 84.
Faith, Doctrine of, 39, 193.
Abu'l Faraj ibn al-Jauzî, 48, 173.
Farwa ibn Naufal al-Ashjaʿî, 160.
Fâṭima bint Aḥmed, 175.
Fiḳh, 13, 177.
Freedom of the will, 62.

Ghundar, 12.
Goldziher, I, 7.

Hairs of the Prophet as charms, 107 f.
al-Haitham ibn Jamîl, 29.
Hajjâj ibn al-Shâʿir, 26.
al-Ḥakam ibn ʿUyaina, 161.
Ḥammâd ibn Zaid, 11.
Ḥanbal ibn Isḥâḳ, 10, 26.

Ḥanbalite School, Origin of, 4 f., 194.
Abû Ḥanîfa, 30.
al-Ḥarbîya, 175.
al-Ḥârith ibn Asad al-Muḥâsibî, 41 ff.
Ibn al-Harsh, 70, 84.
Hârûn ibn Abdallah al-Zuhrî, 61.
Hârûn al-Rashîd, 47, 48, 50.
Abu'l Ḥasan ibn Abd al-Hâdî al-Sindî, 21.
al-Ḥasan ibn Aḥmed, 175.
al-Ḥasan ibn ʿAlî, 114.
al-Ḥasan al-Baṣrî, 160, 162.
al-Ḥasan ibn Ḥammâd al-Sajjâda, 70, 78, 80, 84.
al-Ḥasan ibn Moḥammed al-Khallâl, 173.
al-Ḥasan ibn Mûsâ al-Ashyab, 12.
Abû Ḥassân al-Ziyâdî, 70, 71, 77.
Abû Ḥâtim al-Râzî, 26.
Hayyâj ibn al-ʿAlâ al-Sulamî, 55.
Hishâm, 47.
Hisn, concubine of Aḥmed ibn Ḥanbal, 175.
Hudhaifa ibn al-Yamân, 162.
Abû Huraira, 159.
al-Ḥusain, Tomb of, 123.
al-Ḥusain ibn ʿAlî al-Karâbîsî, 32 f., 176.
Abu'l-Ḥusain ibn al-Munâdî, 173.
Hushaim ibn Bashîr, 11, 50.

Ibrâhîm al-Ḥarbî, 26.
Ibrâhîm ibn Ismâʿîl al-Muʿtazilî, known as Ibn ʿUlayya, 47.
Ibrâhîm ibn al-Mahdî, 12, 26, 76, 80.
Ibrâhîm al-Nakhaʿî, 162.
Ibrâhîm ibn Saʿd, 12.
Ikhlâs, Doctrine of, 76.
ʿImrân ibn Ḥuṣain, 102.
Isḥâḳ ibn Ḥanbal, 3, 10, 88, 112, 145, 150.
Isḥâḳ ibn Ibrâhîm al-Mausilî, 139 n. [1]).
Isḥâḳ ibn Ibrâhîm ibn Musʿab, 56, 64, 70 ff., 83, 84, 85, 88, 89, 90, 139 and n. [1]), 140, 178, 184.

Isḥâḳ ibn Abî Isrâʾîl, 70, 84.
Isḥâḳ ibn Râhawaih, 12, 14, 18, 46, 145, 176, 194.
Isḥâḳ ibn Yaḥya, 63.
Abû Ismâʿîl al-Anṣârî, 173.
Ismâʿîl ibn Dâûd, 64.
Ismâʿîl ibn Ibrâhîm ibn Bistam, 12 n. [3]).
Ismâʿîl ibn Abî Masʿûd, 64.
Ismâʿîl ibn Ulayya, 11.
Îtâkh, the Turk, 141, 144.

Jâbir ibn Abdallah, 160.
al-Jaʿd ibn Dirham, 47.
Jarîr ibn Abd al-Ḥamîd, 12.
Abû Jaʿfar al-Anbârî, 81.
Abû Jaʿfar ibn Dharîḥ al-ʿUkbarî, 152.
Jaʿfar ibn ʿIsâ al-Ḥasanî, 74, 79.
Jaʿfar ibn Moḥammed, 139.
Abû Jaʿfar Moḥammed ibn Jarîr al-Ṭabarî, 5, 9, 177.
Jahmîa, 37 ff.
Jahm ibn Ṣafwân, 37 n. [1]).
Jubair ibn Nufair, 160.
Abû Juhaim, 159.

Kaidar, Governor of Egypt, 61.
Kalâm, 32 and n. [2]), 41, 55.
Ibn al-Kalbî, the postmaster, 140.
Karrâmîya Murjiʾa, see Murjiʾa.
al-Khabâb, 160.
Khalaf ibn Hishâm al-Bazzâr, 12 n. [3]), 31.
Khâlid ibn Abdallah, 47.
Abû Ḳilâba, 161.
Ḳiyâs, 190.
Knowledge of God, 90, 101 f., 187.
Ḳorân, Orthodox doctrine of, 184 n. [5]).
von Kremer, A., 7.
Ḳubaisa ibn ʿOḳba, 12 n. [3]).
"Kun", its significance, 119 and n. [2]).

Kuṣṣâṣ, 24 n. [1]).
Kutaiba ibn Saʿîd ibn Jamîl, 12 n. [3]), 70, 72.

Lafẓ al-Korân, 32 and n. [3]), 34 f., 46, 186.
al-Laith ibn Saʿd, 176.

Abu'l-Maḥâsin, 5.
Ibn Mahdî, vid. Ibrâhîm ibn al-Mahdî.
al-Maḳrîzî, 8.
Mâlik ibn Anas, 11, 50, 117, 176, 188 n. [2]), 194 n. [1]).
Abû Maʿmar al-Ḳaṭîʿî, 70, 78, 84.
al-Ma'mûn, 3, 6 f., 19, 47, 48, 50 ff., 52 f., 54, 55, 82, 83, 84, 105, 122, 126, 130 n. [2]). His letters, 9, 56 ff., 63, 64, 65 ff., 74 ff., 83.
al-Manda, the Ḥâfiẓ, 173.
Marwân II, 47.
Ibn Masʿûd, see Abdallah ibn Masʿûd.
Miḥna, 1 n. [1]), 19, 47 ff.; in Egypt, 61, 113 f.; at Damascus, 61, 62; at Kûfa, 63; general survey, 124 ff.
Moḥammed ibn Abdallah al-Maḳdisî, 21.
Moḥammed ibn Abdallah ibn Ṭâhir, 164 and n. [1]), 167, 172.
Moḥammed ibn Abd al-Waḥîd, 21.
Moḥammed ibn Aḥmed, 175.
Moḥammed ibn Aḥmed ibn Abî Dowâd, 56.
Moḥammed ibn Aslam, 36 ff., 193.
Moḥammed ibn Ḥanbal, 10.
Moḥammed ibn al-Ḥasan, 29, 79.
Moḥammed ibn al-Ḥasan ibn ʿAlî ibn ʿÂsim, 70, 79, 84.
Moḥammed ibn Ḥâtim ibn Maimûn, 70, 78, 84.
Moḥammed ibn Ibrâhîm, 85.
Moḥammed ibn Isḥâḳ, 140.
Moḥammed ibn Isḥâḳ al-Ṣaghânî, 26.
Moḥammed ibn al-Jarrâḥ, 144.
Moḥammed ibn Makhlad, 174.
Moḥammed ibn Nûh al-Maḍrûb al-ʿIjlî, 70, 78, 80, 81, 85, 119.
Moḥammed ibn Saʿd, 64.

Moḥammed ibn Sîrîn, 161.
Moḥammed ibn Yaḥya al-Dhuhlî, 26, 46.
al-Mu'aiṭî, 31.
Mu'âwia ibn Ḳurra, 161.
al-Muhtadî, 122.
Murji'a, 37 ff.
Mûsâ ibn Hârûn, 26.
Abû Mushir, 79.
Abû Muslim, 64.
Muslim, 26.
Musnad, 5, 19 ff.
Mu'tamar ibn Suleimân, 12.
al-Mu'taṣim, 3, 6, 23 n. 2), 55, 62, 63, 85, 90, 93 ff., 114, 127.
al-Mutawakkil, 4, 6, 7, 19, 54, 63, 118, 122, 129, 130 ff., 163, 169.
Mu'tazila, 2, 6, 48 and n. 2), 62 n. 1), 187 n. 2), 189 n. 1), 190 n. 1).
al-Mu'tazz, 142, 143, 144.
al-Muṭṭalib ibn Abdallah, 77.
Muẓaffar, chamberlain of Abdallah ibn Isḥâḳ, 140.
Muẓaffar ibn Kaidar, 113.
al-Muẓaffar ibn Murrajjâ, 73.

al-Naḍr ibn Shumail, 70, 84.
Names of God, 90.
Ibn Nâsir, the Ḥâfiẓ, 173.
Abû Naṣr al-Tammâr, 70, 77, 84.
al-Nawawî, 176.
Abû Nu'aim, Aḥmed ibn Abdallah al-Ispahânî, 8.
Abû Nu'aim al-Faḍl ibn Dukain, 63, 87 and n. 1).
Nu'aim ibn Ḥammâd, 119.
Ibn Numair, 12.

'Obaidallah ibn Moḥammed ibn al-Ḥasan, 72.
'Obaidallah ibn Moḥammed Abu'l-Ḳâsim, 26.
'Obaidallah ibn 'Omar al-Ḳawârîrî, 70, 79, 80, 84.
'Obaidallah ibn Yaḥya, 154, 183 f.

ʿOmar ibn Abd al-Azîz, 123, 161 f.
ʿOmar ibn Aḥmed al-Shammâ al-Ḥalabî, 21.
ʿOmar ibn al-Khaṭṭâb, 54, 159 f.
ʿOthmân ibn Saʿîd al-Dârimî, 26.

al-Rabîʿ ibn Suleimân, 119 f.
Rajâ al-Ḥiḍârî, 82.
Rationalism, vid. Muʿtazila.
Raʾy, 190.

Saʿdawaih al-Wâsiṭî, vid. Saʿîd ibn Suleimân.
Saʿîd ibn Aḥmed, 175.
Saʿîd ibn Suleimân Abû ʿOthman al-Wâsiṭî, 70, 78, 84.
Ṣâliḥ ibn Aḥmed ibn Ḥanbal, 26, 141, 146 ff., 150, 151, 164, 170 f., 173 f.
Ṣâliḥ al-Rashîdî, 104.
Samsama, 118.
al-Sarî al-Saḳatî, 45.
al-Shâfiʿî, 2, 13, 27 ff., 49 f.
Abû Shuaib al-Hajjâm, 90.
Ibn Shujâʿ, see Aḥmed ibn Shujâʿ.
Shyites, 54 and n. 1).
Sîma al-Dimashḳî, 118.
al-Sindî, 75.
Sofyân al-Thaurî, 176.
Sofyân ibn ʿUyaina, 11, 12, 13.
Steiner, H., 7.
al-Subkî, 8, 127, 172.

Tâbʿiûn, 163.
Taḳîa, 65, 83, 88, 128, 129.
Tashbîh, 106.
Tauhîd, 62.
Ṭâûs ibn Ṭâûs, 161, 169 f.
Abû Thaur, 176.

Ibn ʿUlayya al-Akbar, 12, 47, 70, 73.

Wâçil ibn ʿAṭâ, 55 and n. 4).
Wakîʿ ibn al-Jarrâh, 12 and n. 3), 13.
al-Walîd ibn Muslim, 12.
Abu'l-Walîd al-Ṭayâlisî, 26, 174.
al-Wâthiḳ, 4, 6, 55, 63, 114, 115 ff., 121, 127 ff.

Yaḥya ibn Abd al-Raḥmân al-ʿOmarî, 70, 79, 84.
Yaḥya ibn Aktham, 52, 54 f., 56.
Yaḥya ibn Khâḳân, 143, 151, 164.
Yaḥya ibn Maʿîn, 12, 16, 31, 64, 117, 128, 174, 176.
Yaḥya ibn Saʿîd al-Kaṭṭân, 12, 176.
Yaḥya ibn Abî Zâ'ida, 12.
Yaʿkûb Ḳausarra, 141.
Yaʿkûb ibn Shaiba, 26.
Yazîd ibn Hârûn, 12 and n. 3), 26, 29 f., 52, 176, 180.
Abû Yûsuf, the Ḳâḍî, 12.
Yûsuf ibn Yaḥya al-Buwaiṭî, 114, 119.
Yûsuf ibn Abî Yûsuf, 79.

Zainab bint Aḥmed, 175.
Ibn al-Zayyât, the Vizier, 55.
Ziyâd al-Bakaʿî, 12.
Zuḥair ibn Ḥarb Abû Khaithama, 64.
Zuḥair ibn Sâliḥ, 174.
Abû Zurʿa al-Dimashkî, 26.
Abû Zurʿa al-Râzî, 26, 175.

INDEX OF NAMES OCCURRING IN ARABIC FOOTNOTES.

(Names occurring only in Isnâds or as names of Râwi's are omitted).

ابراهيم بن اسمعيل 116.
ابراهيم بن عرعرة 176.
ابراهيم النخعى 158.
احمد بن الحسن المقانعى 168.
احمد بن ابى دواد 52, 55, 56, 97 ff., 102, 104, 108 f., 112, 114, 115.
احمد بن عمار 97.
احمد بن غسان 82.
احمد بن نصر الخزاعى 116, 118 f.
احمد بن يحيى ثعلب النحوى 181.
احمد بن يونس 87.
اسحاق بن ابراهيم بن مصعب 65, 81, 86 f., 98 f., 110, 112, 131, 178.
اسحاق بن حنبل 89, 112, 146, 149, 153.
اسحاق بن راهويه 14, 18, 146.
ابن ابى اسرائيل 99.
اسمعيل بن علية 12.
الاسود النخعى 176.
الاعلى بن حماد 174.
الاعمش 63.
ابن اعين 181.
افريدون التركى 123.
الامين 49.
انس 30.
الانصارى 173.
ايتاخ التركى 133, 135.
ايوب السختيانى 157.
ايوب بن النجار 46.

(محمد بن اسمعيل البخارى) 33, 35 ff.
بشر بن الحارث 182.
بشر بن غياث المريسى 49, 169.

الحكم بن عيينة 157.
حماد بن زيد 12.
حميد 30.
حنبل بن اسحاق 171.
ابو حنيفة 30, 192.

خلف بن سالم 180.
الختلى 156.
ابو خيثمة 99.

ابو داود الحفرى 46.
ابو داود السجستانى 179.
دحيم الشامى 27.
ابو الدن 109.
الدينورى 166.

الذهبى 34, 170.

الربيع بن سليمان 49 f, 120.
رجاء الحضارى 82.

زهير بن صالح بن احمد 174.
زينب بنت احمد بن حنبل 174.

سعيد بن احمد بن حنبل 174.
سفيان بن عيينة 12, 15.
سلمة بن كهيل 13.
ابو سليمان الجوزجانى 30.

الشافعى 13, 14, 27ff, 33, 49, 102.

بغا الكبير 92 f.
البغوى 174.
ابو بكر بن سماعة 15.
ابو بكر بن ابى شيبة 174.
ابو بكر الصديق 43, 123, 124.
البيهقى 173.
ابو جعفر الانبارى 81.
ابو جعفر بن ذريح العكبرى 153.
جعفر بن محمد النسوى 169.
جهم بن صفوان 34.
الجهمية 40 f.

الحارث بن اسد المحاسبى 33, 44 f.
حارث بن مالك 42.
حذيفة بن اليمان 34, 158.
الحسن بن احمد بن حنبل 174, 175.
الحسن بن احمد بن حنبل (الثانى) 174.
الحسن البصرى 156.
ابو الحسن التميمى 169.
الحسن بن حماد السجادة 70.
حِسن سُرّية احمد بن حنبل 174.
الحسن بن على الجعد 115.
الحسن بن محمد الخلال 173.
ابو الحسن بن المنادى 173.
الحسين بن احمد بن حنبل 174.
الحسين بن على (الشهيد) 124.
الحسين بن على بن يزيد الكرابيسى 33 f., 169, 177.

صالح بن احمد بن حنبل 131 ff, 148 f, 151 f, 164, 166 ff, 170 f, 173 f. 183, 190 f.

ابن طالوت 168.
عبد الله بن طاهر v. ابن طاهر
طاووس بن طاوس 157, 167.
ابو طيبة الحجام 17.

عباس بن مسكويه الهمذانى 110.
عباسة بنت الفضل 174.
عبد بن حميد 17, 18.
عبد الله بن احمد بن حنبل 20, 28, 137, 149, 166 ff, 171, 174.
عبد الله بن ادريس 46, 166.
عبد الله بن اسحاق 131.
عبد الله بن طاهر 18, 146.
عبد الله بن عباس 155.
عبد الله بن المبارك 11.
عبد الله بن محمد (المعروف ببوران) 83, 138, 192 f.
عبد الله بن مسعود 43, 103, 156.
عبد الرحمن بن اسحاق 97, 98, 99, 102.
عبد الرحمن بن ابى حاتم الرازى 173.
عبد الرزاق 17 f.
عبد العزيز بن ابان 20.
عبيد الله بن يحيى 148, 154.
عتاب 56.
عجيف 99.
عفان بن مسلم 86.

علقمة بن قيس 176.
ابو على بن البنّاء 173.
على بن الجعد 166.
على بن الجهم 132, 133, 136.
على بن عاصم 176.
على بن المدينى 31, 87 f, 174.
عمر بن الخطاب 43, 155, 156.
عمر بن عبد العزيز 123, 124, 157.

ابو غالب بن معاوية بن عمرو 151.
الغزالى 28.

فاطمة بنت احمد بن حنبل 174.
الفتح بن سهل 166.
ابو الفرج بن الجوزى 173.
فروة بن نوفل 156.
فضل الانماطى 191.
الفضل بن دكين 63, 87.

ابو القاسم النصرباذى 44 f.
ابو قلابة 157.

الكرّامية 39, 41.
ابن الكلبى صاحب البريد 131.

ليث بن ابى سليم 166 f.

ابن ماسويه 135.
مالك بن انس 11, 116.
المامون 49, 51, 53 f, 65, 81, 82, 86, 109.

المتوكل 123, 124, 130 f, 148 f, 151 f, 154 f, 164, 167 f, 170.
محمد بن ابرهيم 85.
محمد بن احمد بن حنبل 174.
محمد بن اسحق بن ابرهيم 131.
محمد بن اسلم 40 ff.
محمد بن الجراح 135.
محمد بن الحسن 30.
محمد بن حنبل 10, 11.
محمد بن سيرين 157.
محمد بن عبد الله بن طاهر 148, 165, 167 ff.
محمد بن مخلد 174.
محمد بن معاوية 133.
محمد بن نصر صاحب الشرطة 153.
محمد بن نصر المروزى 33, 167 f, 170.
محمد بن نوح المضروب 81, 83.
محمد بن يحيى الذهلى 35.
المرجئة 40 ff.
المروزى vid. محمد بن نصر
المظفر حاجب عبد الله بن اسحاق 131.
معاوية بن قرة 157.
المعتز 134.
المعتزلة 49, 55.
المعتصم 92 ff, 101, 104, 108 ff, 112 f, 114, 115, 131.
معمر 18.
ابو معمر القطيعى 73.
ابن مندة 173.
موسى بن حزام 30.
ميمون بن الاصبغ 109, 113.
ابن ناصر الحافظ 173.
نعيم بن حماد 119.
هارون الرشيد 49.
هشيم 12, 29.
هياج بن العلاء السلمى 55.
الهيثم بن جميل 29.
الواثق 115, 116, 119, 120.
واصل بن عطاء 55.
الوركانى 170.
وصيف 133.
وكيع بن الجراح 13 f.
ابو الوليد الطيالسى 174.
يحيى بن اكثم 53.
يحيى بن خاقان 134, 135 f, 151, 164.
يحيى بن سعيد القطان 30.
يحيى بن معين 10, 17, 65, 86 f, 99, 116, 174.
ابو يحيى الناقد 176.
يحيى بن هرثمة 133.
يحيى بن يحيى 18.
يزيد بن هارون 30, 53, 180.
يعقوب بن البختمان 135.
يعقوب المعروف بقوصرة 132 f, 136.
يوسف بن يحيى البويطى 120.

CORRIGENDA.

Page 3, line 5, Read Abî for Abû.
" 4, " 3, " " " "
" 19, n. 1, Read cf. p. 114 and p. 142.
" 23, n. 2, last line, Read cf. Arabic, p. 97, l. 2 ff.
" 28, line 6, Read al-Shâfiʿî's for al-Shafiʿî's.
" 38, note, l. 4 infra, Read Shahrastânî for Shahrastâni.
" 46, line 2, Read Ayûb ibn al-Najjâr.
" 47, " 5, also Side-heading, Read al-Muʿtazilî for al-Muʿtalizî.
" 53, last line, Read: made a jest.
" 70, line 6, Dele comma after "Saʿdawaih".
" 73, " 2, Read Muẓaffar for Muẓaffir.
" 75, " 12 infra, Dele comma after "him".
" 83, " 11 " Read طرسوس.
" 96, " 10 " " يَعُود for يعُود.
" 102, " 4 " " وكانوا " وكانو.
" 109, " 5 " " باسرع " باسع.
" 172, " 17, Insert after "and": — confirmed their judgment.
" 200, " 10 infra, Read al-Khabbâb for al-Khabâb.

RESOURCES IN ARABIC AND ISLAMIC STUDIES

Number 4
Al-Maʾmūn, the Inquisition, and the Quest for Caliphal Authority
by John Abdallah Nawas
(2015)

Number 3
Hadith, Piety, and Law: Selected Studies
by Christopher Melchert
(2015)

Number 2
The Economy of Certainty: An Introduction to the Typology of Islamic Legal Theory
by Aron Zysow
(2013)

Number 1
A Reader of Classical Arabic Literature
by Seeger Bonebakker and Michael Fishbein
(2012)